The Emotionally
Focused Casebook

The Emotionally Focused Casebook

New Directions in Treating Couples

Edited by James L. Furrow,
Susan M. Johnson, and Brent A. Bradley

Routledge
Taylor & Francis Group
New York   London

Routledge
Taylor & Francis Group
270 Madison Avenue
New York, NY 10016

Routledge
Taylor & Francis Group
27 Church Road
Hove, East Sussex BN3 2FA

Library of Congress Cataloging-in-Publication Data

The emotionally focused casebook : new directions in treating couples / Edited
   by James L. Furrow, Susan M. Johnson, and Brent A. Bradley.
      p. ; cm.
   Includes bibliographical references and index.
   ISBN 978-0-415-99875-8 (pbk. : alk. paper)
      1. Couples therapy--Case studies. 2. Emotion-focused therapy--Case studies.
   I. Furrow, James L., editor. II. Johnson, Susan M., editor. III. Bradley, Brent A.,
   editor.
      [DNLM: 1. Couples Therapy--methods--Case Reports. 2. Marital
   Therapy--methods--Case Reports. WM 430.5.M3]

   RC488.5.E475 2011
   616.89'1562--dc22   2010049068

Visit the Taylor & Francis Web site at
http://www.taylorandfrancis.com

and the Routledge Web site at
http://www.routledgementalhealth.com

Contents

SECTION III   Specific Treatment Populations and Emotionally Focused Couple Therapy

Contributors

John Amodeo
Department of Psychology
Meridian University
Petaluma, California

Brent Bradley
MFT Program, Department of
    Psychology
University of Houston, Clear
    Lake
Houston, Texas

Adam D. Coffey
Private Practice
Dallas, Texas

Tracy L. Dalgleish
School of Psychology
University of Ottawa
Ottawa, Ontario, Canada

Wayne H. Denton
Department of Family and
    Child Sciences
Florida State University
Tallahassee, Florida

Lorie Ediger
Briercrest Seminary
Caronport, Saskatchewan,
    Canada

George Faller
New York City Fire
    Department Counseling
    Services
New York, New York

James L. Furrow
Department of Marriage and
    Family, Graduate School of
    Psychology
Fuller Theological Seminary
Pasadena, California

Gillian Gailey
Aphasia Centre of Ottawa
Ottawa, Ontario, Canada

Susan M. Johnson
Department of Psychology
University of Ottawa
Ottawa, Ontario, Canada
Department of Marital and
    Family Therapy
Alliant International
    University
San Diego, California

Leigh Karos
Centre for Interpersonal
    Relationships
Ottawa, Ontario, Canada

Martin Landau-North
Department of Marital and
    Family Therapy
Alliant International
    University
San Diego, California

Ting Liu
Department of Psychology
Kean University
Union, New Jersey

Judy A. Makinen
Royal Ottawa Mental Health
  Centre
Ottawa Couple and Family
  Institute
Ottawa, Ontario, Canada

Sandra Naaman
Faculty of Medicine
University of Ottawa
Ottawa, Ontario, Canada

Gail Palmer
Ottawa Couple and Family
  Institute
Ottawa, Ontario, Canada

Karam Radwan
Department of Psychiatry and
  Behavioral Neurosciences
University of Chicago
Chicago, Illinois

Kathryn Stiell
Ottawa Couple and Family
  Institute
Aphasia Centre of Ottawa
Ottawa, Ontario, Canada

Andrea Wittenborn
Department of Human
  Development
Virginia Polytechnic
  University
Falls Church, Virginia

Dino Zuccarini
Centre for Interpersonal
  Relationships
Ottawa, Ontario, Canada

Introduction

The development of emotionally focused therapy (EFT) for couples began with listening and learning from couples. Over 25 years later, EFT practitioners and researchers have developed a compelling model for effective and lasting change in couple therapy. EFT fosters new, secure bonding interactions and unleashes powerful new positive emotions as partners experience each other in new ways that promote support and growth. The process of EFT focuses on the creation of interactions that address deep, primary human needs and promote a felt sense of being safe, held, comforted, and loved. These bonding events can reverse the destructive effects of long-standing and destructive couple distress (Johnson, 1996, 2004; Lebow, Chambers, Christensen, & Johnson, in press).

EFT integrates experiential and systemic theories under the umbrella of attachment theory (Bowlby, 1988; Mikulincer & Shaver, 2007). It offers a unique combination of empirically supported change processes and techniques informed by an explicit theory of adult love. In just over 20 years, EFT has become one of only two empirically supported treatment approaches to couples therapy (Lebow et al., in press; Snyder, Castellani, & Whisman, 2006). It continues to grow in popularity because of its ever expanding research base, its application to new and diverse clinical populations, and its strength-based and unapologetic humanness that innately appeals to so many. We believe that EFT is the most scientifically and clinically compelling model of contemporary couples therapy.

Recent developments in couple therapy point to the importance of specializing treatment approaches to a variety of presenting conditions. Research studies continue to illustrate the important adjunctive role of couple therapy in the treatment of individually based disorders (e.g., substance abuse, trauma exposure, and depression) (Snyder & Whisman, 2003). A review of the EFT literature details its application with couples where issues of chronic illness, infidelity, trauma and posttraumatic stress disorder, and depression are prevailing treatment concerns (Dalton, Johnson, & Classen, in press; Denton, Wittenborn, & Golden, in press; Dessaulles, Johnson,

& Denton, 2003; Johnson, 2005; Johnson & Williams-Keeler, 1998; Knowal, Johnson, & Lee, 2003).

That this model has been used with so many different populations speaks to its relevance and generalizability. It is a model that addresses the great universals—affect and attachment—but it also values individual differences and varying emotional realities. Currently, no one source brings together the rich and diverse clinical applications of EFT into one summary volume. The time has come to capture and clearly illustrate the numerous and relevant ways that EFT is being applied in clinical practice.

This casebook creates a primary clinical resource for clinicians, supervisors, students, and scholars seeking an understanding of the practical application of EFT to a variety of populations and clinical problems. Following a hands-on case study approach, the chapters in this edited volume provide concrete guidance and illustrate the application of EFT to couples with specific treatment conditions. The book's format includes attention to the unique concerns endemic to treating specific presenting problems. Each chapter provides a distinctive conceptualization of the underlying attachment-related issues likely to be faced in using EFT treatment in a particular context. Throughout the various chapters, authors illustrate how attachment processes in a couple's relationship ultimately provide both a resource and a point of intervention that support a couple's resilience in the face of physical and psychological challenges.

The casebook contains three sections offering specific direction for conceptualizing EFT with couples facing a variety of conditions and/or differences in background. In Section I, "Foundations for Innovation," James Furrow and Brent Bradley provide an overview of EFT, including relevant empirical support and several common challenges faced by therapists in mastering the approach. Sue Johnson (Chapter 2), the principal proponent of EFT with couples, explains the critical role that attachment theory plays in the conceptualization of couple issues and its crucial relevance as a powerful theory of adult love. Brent Bradley's chapter offers new insights into the EFT change process by delineating key fundamentals utilized in effective EFT and moment-by-moment, in-session details on how to work powerfully and systemically with core affect states.

In Section II, "Application of Emotionally Focused Couple Therapy," a number of authors present unique applications of

EFT across a variety of treatment issues based on their first-hand experience. For example, chapters in this section illustrate the treatment of couples where their relationship has been impacted by a medical disorder or disability (e.g., breast cancer, aphasia). Additional chapters describe using EFT when a partner suffers with a mental disorder or psychological distress (e.g., depression, posttraumatic stress disorder, addictions, and sexual dysfunction). Authors illustrate their use and refinement of EFT by describing actual treatment application with specific case examples. Other chapters focus on unique challenges, including infidelity and remarriage. Chapters include transcript examples providing practical illustration of in-session work with a specific treatment situation. Each author's commentary provides an innovative perspective for the successful application of EFT to more complex presentations of couple distress.

The final section, "Specific Treatment Populations and Emotionally Focused Couple Therapy," comprises chapters describing the use of EFT with particular populations. These chapters explore applying EFT with culturally diverse couples, same-sex couples, and religious and spiritual couples. Authors review the competencies needed to work sensitively and effectively with unique perspectives and concerns found among couples from diverse backgrounds. This section highlights the importance of therapist awareness and ability in attending to the individual concerns of couples and cultural contexts that inherently shape their experience of more intimate relationships.

The book concludes with an overview and synthesis of EFT innovations. The various insights and practices highlighted throughout this book illustrate the creative pulse of therapists finding new ways to reach new couples with the power of EFT. In closing, we consider various future directions, recognizing the essential contribution that EFT has made to the broadening role of couples therapy.

Our hope is to provide a substantive reference for clinicians, students, professors, and supervisors who teach and train in the practice of EFT. We believe this resource serves as a much-needed and timely complement to the other major EFT training materials: *The Practice of Emotionally Focused Couple Therapy: Creating Connection,* 2nd edition (Johnson, 2004), and *Becoming an Emotionally Focused Couple Therapist: The Workbook* (Johnson et al., 2005). This casebook is a practical, hands-on resource for those searching for examples of specific ways to think about couple issues within an EFT frame and modify the application of this model to fit the specific needs of their clients. To date, there is no single resource that has compiled the many creative applications of EFT with the myriad of clinical populations being served by this model today.

Now there is.

REFERENCES

Bowlby, J. (1988). *A secure base.* New York, NY: Basic Books.

Dalton, J., Johnson, S. M., & Classen, C. (in press). Treating relationship distress and the effects of childhood abuse with emotion focused couple therapy: A randomized controlled trial. *Journal of Marital and Family Therapy.*

Denton, W. H., Wittenborn, A., & Golden, R. N. (2010). Augmenting antidepressant medication treatment of depressed women with emotionally focused therapy for couples: A randomized pilot study. Manuscript submitted for publication.

Dessaulles, A., Johnson, S. M., & Denton, W. H. (2003). Emotionally focused therapy for couples in the treatment of depression: A pilot study. *American Journal of Family Therapy, 31,* 345–353.

Johnson, S. M. (1996). *The practice of emotionally focused couple therapy: Creating connection.* New York, NY: Brunner/Mazel.

Johnson, S. M. (2004). *The practice of emotionally focused couple therapy: Creating connection* (2nd ed.). New York, NY: Routledge.

Johnson, S. M. (2005). Broken bonds: An emotionally focused approach to infidelity. *Journal of Couple and Family Relationship Therapy, 4,* 17–29.

Johnson, S. M., Bradley, B., Furrow, J. L., Lee, A., Palmer, G., Tilley, D., & Wooley, S. (2005). *Becoming an EFT therapist: The workbook.* New York, NY: Brunner/Routledge.

Johnson, S. M., & Williams-Keeler, L. (1998). Creating healing relationships for couples dealing with trauma: The use of emotionally focused marital therapy. *Journal of Marital and Family Therapy, 24,* 25–40.

Knowal, J., Johnson, S. M., & Lee, A. (2003). Chronic illness in couples: A case for emotionally focused therapy. *Journal of Marital and Family Therapy, 29,* 299–310.

Lebow, J. L., Chambers, A., Christensen, A., & Johnson, S. M. (in press). Marital distress. In D. Sprenkle & R. Chenail (Eds.), *Effectiveness research in marriage and family therapy*. Washington, DC: AAMFT.

Mikulincer, M., & Shaver, P. R. (2007). *Attachment in adulthood*. New York, NY: Guilford Press.

Snyder, D. K., & Whisman, M. A. (Eds.). (2003). *Treating difficult couples: Helping clients with coexisting mental and relationship disorders*. New York, NY: Guilford Press.

Snyder, D. K., Castellani, A. M., & Whisman, M. A. (2006). Current status and future directions in couple therapy. *Annual Review of Psychology, 57*, 317–344.

I

FOUNDATIONS
FOR INNOVATION

One

Emotionally Focused Couple Therapy
Making the Case for Effective Couple Therapy

JAMES L. FURROW AND BRENT BRADLEY

INTRODUCTION

Emotionally focused therapy (EFT) for couples is considered a leading approach in the treatment of relational distress. EFT is well established in terms of its efficacy and innovative application to the life challenges faced by partners in long-term relationships (Lebow, Chambers, Christensen, & Johnson, in press). It remains one of only two couple therapies recognized as empirically supported treatments (Chambless & Ollendick, 2001; Lebow et al., in press).

Among couple therapies, EFT is also distinguished by two other crucial features. First, it is the only couple intervention based on a broad, systematic, and extensively researched theory of adult love—namely, attachment theory (Johnson, 2003; Mikulincer & Shaver, 2007). Second, the practice of EFT is supported by a series of process research findings (Bradley & Furrow, 2004; Greenberg, Ford, Alden, & Johnson, 1993; Johnson & Greenberg, 1988; Makinen & Johnson, 2006). These studies inform EFT's theory of change and provide specific guidance to a therapist in the use of interventions aimed at creating key emotional and interactional shifts in a distressed relationship. This chapter briefly reviews the development of EFT, the EFT process of change, and the breadth and significance of EFT's scientific support; it concludes with an overview of the common challenges therapists face in learning this approach.

OVERVIEW

The introduction of EFT marked a significant shift in the nascent field of couple therapy. During the late 1970s and 1980s Neil Jacobson and colleagues established behavioral marital therapy (BMT) as the only research-validated couple treatment of relationship distress (Baucom, Shoham, Mueser, Daiuto, & Stickle, 1998). Therapists informed by this approach followed principles of behaviorism and the social exchange theory of relationships to promote relationship satisfaction. Primary therapeutic interventions were designed to increase positive interactions through behavior exchange, communication training, and problem solving (Jacobson & Margolin, 1979). This approach conceptualized a couple's relationship in quid pro quo terms, casting the therapist primarily as a coach or facilitator of communication skills.

As behaviorism's prominence grew in the emerging field of couple therapy, alternative theories of couple intervention were being proposed. Johnson (1986) questioned whether a couple's intimate relationship was best seen as a profit versus loss exchange of behaviors that couples negotiate. Instead, Johnson called for a paradigm shift, suggesting that relationships might be better understood as a relational emotional "bond" rather than a negotiated rational "bargain."

John Bowlby's (1969) attachment theory offered an alternative theoretical perspective on human behavior that seemed significantly relevant to the tasks of couple therapy. Bowlby's focus on "affectional ties" provided an "emotional rationale" for the rigid patterns and ineffective actions common to couples ensnared in relational distress (Johnson, 2003). From this perspective heightened periods of separation distress undermine a couple's felt sense of security and trigger fears of abandonment, rejection, and isolation. In response, individuals react to a growing insecurity through actions that follow increasingly predictable patterns of avoidance and anxious pursuit.

Over time, these responses become set in rigid reactive patterns of behavior. These stuck patterns, reinforced by a couple's ongoing experience of negative affect, foster greater insecurity and a growing despair about the future of the relationship. Attachment theory provides a map and an in-session compass for guiding couples in restructuring the emotional ties that hold sway in intimate relationships (Johnson & Best, 2002).

An Integrated Approach

The original formulation of EFT (Greenberg & Johnson, 1988) was based primarily on experiential and family systems approaches. EFT interventions were developed as a result of reviewing taped therapy sessions and noting consistent patterns of practice that led to desirable clinical outcomes (Johnson, 2009). This discovery-oriented approach allowed for the description of a nine-step change process and specific change events. Theoretically, EFT draws on a synthesis of humanistic/experiential and systemic assumptions (e.g., Minuchin & Fishman, 1981; Rogers, 1951); each is evident in the dynamic use of new emotional experience to engage partners in the enactment of more adaptive relational patterns. Shortly after Johnson and Greenberg's (1988) initial outcome study and the sudden growth of the literature on adult attachment (Hazan & Shaver, 1987), EFT began to reflect a growing integration of attachment concepts into its conceptualization of couple distress and therapist interventions. The approach became increasingly focused on strengthening a couple's bond through increased emotional accessibility and responsiveness.

The current treatment manual for EFT (Johnson, 2004) describes this brief systematic approach (8–20 sessions). EFT combines a shared focus on interpersonal interaction patterns and intrapsychic processes, which are understood in terms of adult attachment theory (Mikulincer & Shaver, 2007). The therapist serves as a process consultant keenly engaged in facilitating in-session shifts in attachment related interactions and associated inner emotional processes. She intently builds a safe and collaborative therapeutic alliance that enables partners to gently explore their emotional worlds. The EFT therapist helps to provide a felt sense of security as each partner takes steps to restructure his or her negative responses and address unmet needs for security. The approach assumes that couples have mutual goals and a workable commitment to changing their relationship. EFT is not meant for use with violent partners or with couples demonstrating explicit incompatible relationship goals (Johnson, 2004).

Stages of Change

EFT is conceptualized within three stages of change built on a progression of nine steps. These steps describe a shifting focus from processing patterns and positions, accessing underlying experiences, and building new patterns of interaction based on the mutual sharing of underlying needs and vulnerability. For a list of these stages and corresponding steps, see Table 1.1. As couples progress through each stage, the therapist works differently with the positions and patterns that define relationships.

In Stage 1, the therapist facilitates a shift in the couple's complaints about their presenting problem to a focus on a problematic pattern or cycle that is currently defining the nature of emotional engagement in their relationship. The therapist helps a couple recast their common fights over household chores, for example, and infrequent sex as a negative cycle of pursuit and withdrawal. This problematic pattern is most apparent in times of distress. The EFT therapist helps the couple move toward de-escalation of their reactive pattern by helping each partner acknowledge underlying primary attachment emotions, such as sadness about feeling alone, and reactive secondary emotional responses, such as numbing or anger that fuels their negative cycle.

Table 1.1   Nine Steps of Emotionally Focused Couple Therapy

Stage 1. Cycle de-escalation

1. Assessment: creating an alliance and explicating the core issues in the marital conflict by using an attachment perspective
2. Identifying the problem interactional cycles that maintain attachment insecurity and marital distress
3. Accessing the unacknowledged emotions underlying interactional positions
4. Reframing the problem in terms of the cycle, the underlying emotions, and attachment needs

Stage 2. Restructuring interactional patterns

5. Promoting identification with disowned needs and aspects of self and integrating these into relationship interactions
6. Promoting acceptance of the partner's new construction of the relationship and new interactional behavior
7. Facilitating the expression of specific needs and wants

Stage 3. Consolidation

8. Facilitating the emergence of new solutions to old relationship problems
9. Consolidating new positions and new cycles of attachment behavior

In Stage 2, the therapist's focus is on moving partners into more accessible and emotionally engaged positions. Here the therapist concentrates treatment on a deeper accessing, expanding, and processing of attachment-related experience associated with each person's position. As new experiences and new awareness are shared, the therapist promotes each partner's acceptance of the softer, emerging vulnerability of the other. This gradually facilitates partners taking new positions where they can coherently reach for and sensitively respond to each other, creating a more secure bond.

In Stage 3, the therapist works to consolidate partners taking new positions while ongoing processing of the challenges inherent in the effort to resist old patterns takes place. Partners are now more available to each other and can begin actively creating trust and attachment security in their relationship. The positive emotional experiences associated with these new patterns enable couples to "broaden and build" the resources that support a more resilient and flourishing relationship (Fredrickson & Losada, 2005; Mikulincer & Shaver, 2009). The following sections reviews each of these stages in further detail.

Stage 1. Cycle De-escalation

A couple's level of attachment insecurity and strategies for dealing with this insecurity color each partner's experience of their presenting problem. In the first stage of EFT the therapist creates a process for understanding, accepting, and de-escalating a couple's experience of distress. This is an experiential process involving tracking predictable patterns of behaviors and reflecting the underlying emotional realities that move partners into reactive and fixed positions. The enduring pain and distance of distress devitalizes a couple's sense of efficacy and hope for their shared future. The therapist provides a safe alliance for each partner and reframes their negative patterns as self-defeating struggles to minimize conflict and hopefully reconnect their negative pattern as a self-defeating struggle to minimize conflict and reconnect.

In the cycle de-escalation phase of EFT, the therapist aids partners in identifying and experiencing primary emotions that have gone unacknowledged. These powerful, more vulnerable emotions are usually immediately tucked safely out of harm's way while secondary reactive anger and contempt rush in to mask the real source of pain and fear. But as the EFT therapist tracks these negative cycles and accompanying secondary emotions, each partner slowly begins to become experientially aware of underlying attachment affect, or primary emotion, as well.

Cycle de-escalation describes the change event that culminates in the transition from Stage I to Stage II. Here the couple is able to make sense of the ways in which they become ensnared in a vicious cycle of defensive responses aimed at managing the distress that defines their relationship. Early in treatment, the pain in a couple's relationship is usually attributed to the traits of the other partner. "I don't like Steve's personality. He is not the person I thought he was," Carol states contemptuously. In cycle de-escalation, the criticism and contempt are lessened and the problem is seen in terms of the couple's pattern. Carol says, "We got caught again. I felt the tension rising and I was ready to set him straight. Then I thought to myself, 'Here we go again, it's our cycle. We both get hurt here.'"

Rather than educating partners about couple patterns from a top-down stance, the EFT therapist engages the lived experience of a couple's cycle in-session through tracking behavior patterns and reflecting emotional experience. As the therapist validates the typical positions that partners take in times of distress, the couple begins to recognize the powerful role that "their cycle" plays in keeping them from the connection they desperately seek. Cycle de-escalation results not only in a general decrease in each partner's reactive responses and an increase in felt security. As a result, partners are better able to own the ways that their individual ways of regulating emotion (e.g., withdraw, pursuit) have fueled the couple's perpetual cycle of distress and distance.

Stage 2. Restructuring Positions

The process of de-escalating conflict cycles makes way for a more intense focus on the vulnerabilities and attachment fears that underlie fixed and reactive ways of responding in times of distress. The therapist moves in a deliberate fashion to expand a withdrawing partner's underlying affect. Increasing a withdrawn partner's availability and responsiveness provides a first step toward replacing the anxious and critical responses of the other partner with expressions of vulnerability and need.

For example, as Steve shrinks away in the face of Carol's angry disapproval, he struggles to name what he feels. The therapist joins Steve in exploring and deepening his experience through focusing on his present felt experience, such as a tightness in Steve's chest, an image of a dark cloud descending, and an overwhelming sense of despair. The therapist aids Steve in staying with his present emotion and to move into actively feeling his sadness and fear. As Steve's emotional world becomes more vivid and new meanings rise into awareness, the therapist actively draws connections between his vulnerable state and his tendency to avoid or withdraw, typically hiding his feelings of insecurity from Carol. Specific attention is then given to helping Carol process her experience of this new "Steve" unfolding in session and promoting her acceptance and responsiveness to his emerging needs and longing. This prepares the way for supporting Steve in sharing his attachment fears and associated needs with Carol, which represents a clear shift into reengagement. A similar process is followed with Carol that enables her to move from her critical defending stance to a softer, more vulnerable position in their relationship.

In Stage 2, the therapist's focus is more explicitly on the underlying emotional processes of each partner as he or she informs the positions partners take in the couple's pattern of distress. The process of restructuring interactional patterns in Stage 2 entails accessing, expanding, deepening, and sharing attachment-related emotion (e.g., fears and longings). Bowlby (1988) argued that the experience of dysregulated fear distorts and blocks effective bids for responsiveness from attachment figures. Steve hides his insecurity from Carol for fear she would reject him if she were really to see his need for her support. His still silence, designed to calm her down, triggers her distress and proximity-seeking behaviors (Hazan & Shaver, 1987). Since neither partner's signals are successful in prompting support from the other, Carol becomes caught in escalating intensifying strategies to deal with her anxiety; while Steve turns to dismissing strategies and becomes more silent (Mikulincer & Shaver, 2005). In a distressed couple, these strategies become fixed ways of responding that then serve to reinforce the insecurity of the relationship and perpetuate negative interaction patterns.

The EFT therapist provides safety with an empathic emotional presence that enables partners to access and process these emotional responses. Bowlby (1988) concludes that changes in enduring attachment strategies, or what he termed "internal working models," requires the use of emotional communication. EFT has long focused on the role of heightened emotional experience as the basis for change—particularly change in interactional positions. Therefore, in Stage 2 the EFT therapist intensifies her focus on evocative interventions. Interventions are framed in attachment terms to prompt a couple's shared experience and to create a context for their mutual attempts to gain felt security.

In the preceding example, Steve's sadness and loneliness are framed in terms of his relationship to Carol: "So, Steve, you feel so empty and alone, wishing there was some way to connect with Carol?" Through his emotional experience, the therapist appeals to his most basic sense of seeking comfort in a relationship of attachment significance. The therapist uses empathic conjecture, heightening, and evocative responding to move Steve to a more profound experience of his fear of abandonment and rejection. Steve can then ask for the reassurance and acceptance he needs from Carol. When he asserts his needs in a congruent way, he trusts his experience, feels more competent, and becomes more present and engaged. He becomes, in effect, a viable secure attachment figure for his wife. A couple's ability to risk to reach for each other, and to actively respond to attachment longings and desires is the basis for a more secure bond. The resulting felt security acts as an antidote to the anxious responses that trigger their pattern of distress (Johnson, 2003).

Stage 3. Consolidation

In the final stage the therapist facilitates the consolidation of a couple's efforts to strengthen their bond and new opportunities for strengthening their bond are explored as issues of past conflict are revisited in new ways. Couples may now confront enduring disagreements related to everyday preferences and dispositions (e.g., finances, parenting, sexual practices) that provoked their previous problem pattern. In these final stages, a couple can reprocess past issues by sharing the underlying fears and hurts that often triggered these historic issues and cooperatively reach for support from one another. Problem solving is exponentially less difficult when both partners experience the relationship as a safe haven and a secure base.

Carol and Steve regained confidence in the trust and closeness they shared; yet, ongoing differences in parenting expectations left Steve ceding responsibility to Carol for disciplining their two children. Carol felt anxious and resentful as Steve remained disinterested, placating her wishes. The couple came to therapy after a "classic blowup," nervous that their new-found connection was eroding. The therapist guided them through this fight and the familiar pattern they soon recognized. Catching on, Steve offered his fears of disappointing Carol and his struggle with her expectations. The therapist helped Steve explore and share his fears and needs with Carol, who was responsive and hoped to better understand his concerns. Carol expressed her struggle, feeling alone in parenting, and expressed her need for his support. They each concluded that parenting was difficult enough without its coming between them and agreed on ways they could support each other.

As the couple succeeds and confidence is strengthened in their renewed bond, the EFT therapist fosters a new understanding of their relationship based on these new experiences of safety. Attachment rituals are encouraged that help couples find ways to symbolize their ongoing commitment and deepen their shared bond (Johnson et al., 2005). The therapist's work with emotion and attachment continues in helping couples celebrate their successes and reflect upon the new connections they have made.

RESEARCH SUPPORT

There is broad empirical support for the effectiveness of EFT. Conceptually, the core assumptions of EFT's model of relational distress are consonant with empirical research on the nature of marital distress (Gottman, 1998; Huston, Caughlin, Houts, Smith, & George, 2001). Rigorous clinical trials continue to find that EFT demonstrates significant effects when tested against wait list control groups and other interventions. The breadth of EFT research is evident in the various studies conducted by researchers other than the originators of the model (e.g., Denton, Burleson, Clark, Rodriguez, & Hobbs, 2000; James, 1991) and in the successful treatment of couples with other problems and comorbidities (Lebow et al., in press).

The effects of EFT are broad and have been found to have a positive impact not only on relationship adjustment and satisfaction, but also on intimacy, trust, forgiveness of injuries, depression, and anxiety. The effect sizes found in a meta-analysis of EFT studies have not been achieved by other models of couple therapy and, most importantly, the data on the stability of results and lack of relapse remain consistently strong. As an intervention, EFT appears to obtain relatively large effects with many different kinds of distressed couples and these effects seem to last. The following section examines a series of primary studies supporting the strong empirical base of EFT.

Clinical Trials and Couple Distress

Results from six randomized clinical trials demonstrate that EFT is a beneficial and efficacious treatment for couple distress (Dandeneau & Johnson, 1994; Denton et al., 2000; Goldman & Greenberg, 1992; James, 1991; Johnson & Greenberg, 1985a; Walker, Johnson, Manion, & Cloutier, 1996). These findings, based on treatment of over 200 couples, show that couples receiving EFT treatment consistently reported increased marital satisfaction as compared to wait-list and alternate treatment controls. Results from a meta-analysis based on four EFT clinical trials indicated an effect size of 1.3. In these studies 70–73% of treated couples moved out of the range for distress and 86% experienced significant improvement in levels of distress (Johnson, Hunsley, Greenberg, & Schindler, 1999). Denton and colleagues (2000) demonstrated that EFT treatment effects were robust even under demanding conditions (e.g., novice therapists, limited sessions). Additionally, three related studies—not including randomized control conditions (Johnson & Greenberg, 1985b; Johnson & Talitman, 1997; Makinen & Johnson, 2006)—also offer support for EFT as an efficacious treatment for couple distress.

EFT has shown superior treatment results when compared to alternate couple therapy interventions. Johnson and Greenberg (1985a) found that couples in EFT treatment reported higher levels of relationship satisfaction compared to couples in a cognitive behavioral treatment comparison group. These findings included evidence of posttreatment change. James (1991) examined the effects of EFT treatment and EFT with the addition of communication training. Study findings demonstrated that, as a whole, EFT couples reported lower rates of marital distress at posttreatment and at follow-up follow-up. The addition of a communication training component to the EFT treatment failed to improve the effects of EFT significantly. In a study comparing EFT and cognitive marital treatment (CMT) to enhance intimacy among a sample of nondistressed couples, Dandenau and Johnson (1994) found significantly higher scores for the EFT couples on observational measures of empathy and self-disclosure at posttest and self-reported intimacy at follow-up. These results also suggest greater durability of the enhancements made by EFT couples because their treatment gains did not recede at follow-up as was the case for the CMT couples.

Some reviewers have questioned the generalization of these EFT findings to populations of more severely distressed couples (e.g., Baucom et al., 1998). While further evaluation of this concern requires more definitive study (e.g., randomized clinical trials with severely distressed couples), existing research does offer support for the use of EFT with couples in severe relational distress. Every clinical study of EFT has in fact contained severely distressed couples who scored well below the treated group mean on marital adjustment; Johnson and Talitman (1997) found that a couple's level of distress played only a minor role (4% of the variance in treatment outcome) in predicting relationship adjustment at follow-up assessment.

Further, EFT has been found to demonstrate significant results among populations at high risk for relational distress and divorce (Walker et al., 1996) and with couples where relationship distress is accepted as particularly difficult to treat (MacIntosh & Johnson, 2008). The application of EFT to couples facing various physical and mental illnesses, as illustrated in the chapters of this book, provides new opportunities to study the treatment effects of EFT with couples facing significantly high levels of personal and relationship distress (e.g., aphasia, cancer, trauma exposure, and depression).

EFT and Couples With Related Psychological Problems

The empirical support for EFT includes a broadening array of studies evaluating its use with a variety of related clinical problems. These include inhibited sexual desire (MacPhee, Johnson, & Van Der Veer, 1995), depression (Dessaulles, Johnson, & Denton, 2003), trauma associated with childhood sexual abuse (Dalton, Johnson, & Classen, 2010), complex PTSD associated with childhood sexual abuse (MacIntosh & Johnson, 2008), attachment injuries requiring forgiveness (Makinen & Johnson, 2006), distress in relationships in parents coping with chronically ill children (Walker et al., 1996), and distress in couples coping with breast cancer (Naaman, Johnson, & Radwan, in press). Also, a small study with bulimic adolescents found positive results for the use of EFT as a family intervention (Johnson, Maddeaux, & Blouin, 1998). Findings from these studies provide further evidence of the systemic and robust effects of EFT on relationship and mental health outcomes associated with couples facing psychological issues that are comorbid with couple distress.

In terms of the EFT treatment studies that demonstrate positive treatment effects for couple distress and related psychological problems, perhaps the least positive result was found by MacPhee and colleagues (1995). Brief EFT treatment only somewhat benefited couples seeking help for inhibited sexual desire. Female participants in couples receiving EFT were more likely to report increased sexual desire on some measures and showed lower rates of depression compared to treatment controls, but these differences were not found among men in the sample.

Other research on the treatment effects of EFT and depression, a key factor associated wiht relational distress, found that use of EFT with couples where female partners were diagnosed with major affective disorder demonstrated promising results (Dessaulles et al., 2003). Women receiving EFT treatment showed significant decrease in depressive symptoms at posttreatment and 6-month follow-up. While similar treatment gains were evident among adults in a comparison group (medication) at posttreatment, this group did not show additional gains at posttreatment. Female participants in the EFT treatment condition also reported significant reduction in levels of marital conflict compared to the medication sample. In a related study, Denton, Wittenborn, and Gordon (2010) examined the ancillary effects of EFT treatment for couples where a female partner was being treated with antidepressant medication for a major affective disorder. Results from this random trial indicated significantly greater relationship improvement for couples in the EFT plus medication condition compared to those that received only medication. These findings add further support for the beneficial effects of EFT in promoting and sustaining recovery from depressive conditions through the reduction of relational distress.

Expanding the scope of intervention, a recent study has examined EFT treatment of couples where past emotional injuries have created relational distress and often obstruct the typical course of couple therapy. Makinen and Johnson (2006) found that almost two thirds (63%) of couples treated for a significant breech of trust in their relationship (e.g., infidelity) resolved relationship distress and were able to forgive these specific attachment injuries successfully. The effect of treatment and resolution of these events was found to be stable at a 3-year follow-up (Halchuk, Makinen, & Johnson, 2010). Nonresolving couples in this study made it clear that dealing with these injuries as well as general relationship distress required more than the relatively brief number of sessions offered to them.

In terms of the treatment of trauma, Dalton and colleagues (2010) examined the effects of EFT treatment with couples where a woman partner had a history of childhood abuse (CSA). Findings from the study indicated that 70% of couples recovered from relationship distress (i.e., scored in the nondistressed range) and wives reported reduction in trauma-related symptoms following 20 sessions of EFT treatment. Similarly, in a preliminary study of 10 couples where female partners reported CSA and showed complex PTSD symptoms, MacIntosh and Johnson (2008) reported clinically significant improvements in relationship satisfaction for half of the couples involved in the study. These same couples reported a reduction in the experience of trauma-related symptoms by the partner with a CSA history.

A series of studies have also examined use of EFT with couples whose lives have been impacted either directly or indirectly by physical illness. Walker and others (1996) examined the effects of EFT treatment for couple distress with couples raising chronically ill children. Findings of this study show that couples made significant gains in reducing couple distress compared to controls; perhaps more interestingly, these gains were sustained or actually increased at 2-year follow-up evaluations (Cloutier, Manion, Walker, & Johnson, 2002). Naaman and colleagues (in press) conducted a multiple baseline treatment study of relational distress among breast cancer survivors to examine the effects of EFT on a population at significant risk for psychological distress. At least half of the couples receiving EFT treatment demonstrated significant improvement on measures of relationship adjustment, quality of life, mood, and trauma-related symptoms. Follow-up assessment of these couples indicated continued improvement in marital adjustment and quality of life with no evidence of relapse.

Taken together, these studies provide substantive evidence that EFT offers a robust approach to a variety of conditions related to couple distress. Overall, the changes couples report as a result of EFT treatment have consistently demonstrated statistical and clinical significance (i.e., change from a distressed to nondistressed state; Jacobson, Follette, & Revenstrorf, 1984). For example, James (1991) found that almost all participants (90%) receiving EFT treatment reported significant improvement and that 75% of these couples were no longer in a distressed state at the conclusion of treatment. In terms of relapse, studies have consistently indicated sustained recovery and even continued improvement at follow-up for couples completing EFT treatment (Cloutier et al. 2002; Halchuck et al., 2010).

As previously mentioned, meta-analytic studies have established a comprehensive estimate of the effectiveness of EFT treatment for couples (e.g., 70–73% rate of recovery from distress). In a comparison with effect sizes drawn from other meta-analyses, Wood, Crane, Schaalje, and Law (2005) concluded that EFT was significantly more effective than specific BMT interventions for treatment of moderately distressed couples. Byrne, Carr, and Clark (2004) offered a similar conclusion in their review of BMT and EFT outcome studies, noting the superior short- and long-term treatment effects for EFT treatment with couples of moderate levels of relationship distress. Dunn and Schwebel (1995) concluded that insight-oriented marital therapies, including EFT, were significantly more effective than no treatment conditions and more effective than BMT and cognitive BMT in producing change in a couple's relationship quality. In sum, Shadish and Baldwin (2003) described EFT as a meta-analytically supported treatment signaling the model's convincing breadth of empirical support.

Process Research

The use of process research in the development and study of EFT remains a primary distinction of this approach. Process research provides a detailed examination of the therapist's actions and client's responses in session. These studies often provide an in-depth analysis of "best sessions" or "successful events" that mark significant changes in the treatment process. Four process research studies illustrate the significant role this research has played in the shaping and understanding of EFT and its practice.

In one of the first process studies, Johnson and Greenberg (1988) examined "best sessions" from cases where couples had completed successful EFT treatment. In these sessions the therapists focused significant attention on eliciting deeper experiences and expressions of emotion. As a result, partners were more likely to respond to these disclosures with care and support. These best sessions included examples of "softening events," where the more critical or blaming partner risked engaging in a more open and vulnerable way with his or her partner, constituting a breakthrough or watershed event for the couple. Similar findings were described in a series of smaller studies conducted by Greenberg and colleagues (1993).

Bradley and Furrow (2004) conducted a task analysis on successful softening events in light of their association to successful therapy outcome and the specific therapist interventions that promote completion of these events. Findings from this study informed a minitheory of blamer softening, including six thematic shifts common to successful performance in this critical change event. In analyzing these events, Bradley and Furrow found that a therapist's focus on processing a blaming partner's fears of reaching with vulnerability to be critical in a successful softening event. The therapist's ability to conceptualize and deepen fears within both a blaming partner's attachment "views of self" and "views of other" was found to be very important. The use of evocative interventions such as heightening, evocative responding, and empathic conjecture proved significant in promoting the blamer's reach of vulnerability, as well as in processing the impact of this action on the other partner.

Makinen and Johnson (2006) conducted a process research study to examine the successful resolution of a couple's attachment injury. Attachment injuries describe specific events when one partner's actions fail to fulfill the other's expectation to provide safety and comfort in a time of significant distress or danger. In this study Makinen and Johnson found that couples were more likely to resolve these injuries when their therapy included deeper levels of emotional experiencing. Correspondingly, this emotional experiencing was associated with increases in supportive responses from their partners. Couples who resolved their attachment injuries were more likely to disclose and express their needs in session and to show an understanding of these needs. Overall, fewer defensive responses, such as blaming and withdrawing, were found among couples in the resolved group. Softening events provided a deep personal and emotional connection. These couples experienced a clear shift toward a new pattern of relating that was distinct from the couple's previous attachment injury pattern.

The EFT steps that lead to forgiveness of attachment injuries were further validated in a study examining resolved and unresolved attachment injuries (Zuccarini, 2010). The process of successful attachment injury resolution paralleled the deepening of emotion and interactional shifts that are characteristic of general softening events in EFT. The study also confirmed that evocative interventions identified by Bradley and Furrow's (2004) study of blamer softening were also characteristic of sessions that led to attachment injury resolution.

In conclusion, the preceding review illustrates the contributions of process and outcome research in the ongoing development of EFT. These studies demonstrate the efficacy of the model as a treatment of couple distress and provide examples of EFT's use with couples facing various psychological issues and comorbid conditions. Process research studies offer further insight into the nature of successful practice in this model. Findings from these studies emphasize the importance of a therapist's ability to engage and deepen emotional experience and set up affiliative enactments between partners These studies and supporting evidence are invaluable in training therapists to practice and effectively adopt EFT treatment interventions.

BECOMING AN EFT THERAPIST: LEARNING THE APPROACH

When emotion is prized and utilized as the most potent element in creating lasting change, a therapist will work with emotions in many different ways. Theories of development, pathology, and intervention inform the assumptions and practices guiding EFT's work with emotion. Clinical training programs often relegate the use of humanistic and experiential practices to only introductory courses focused on developing a therapeutic alliance through warmth, genuineness, and unconditional positive regard. Consequently, many therapists are not prepared for the shift in perspective that is required in EFT—an approach that relies heavily on a process experiential approach to emotion (Greenberg, Rice, & Elliot, 1994). The core practices of EFT require therapists to engage emotional experience actively as the means for change. The final section of this chapter reviews common challenges facing therapists learning EFT, along with resources available for mastering its practice.

Palmer and Johnson (2002) argued that learning EFT challenges one's ability to "work with" and engage emotional experience actively rather than simply "working on" emotion from an interpretive or skills-based stance. The process of change in EFT is grounded in accessing adult attachment processes and facilitating a couple's movement toward a more secure connection. Accessing, processing, regulating, integrating, and coherently expressing emotions are at the heart of these changes. Modifying underlying attachment strategies that drive relational distress requires a type of emotional communication that is typically found in more secure relationships where emotion can be modulated and inform each partner's response to expressed attachment needs (Bowlby, 1988). Learning EFT requires seeing couple processes through an attachment lens, where dependence is adaptive, emotions are powerful agents of change, and adult love relationships are a primary source of safety and security.

Therapist as Process Consultant

EFT's guiding assumptions reflect the long-standing traditions of humanistic and experiential psychotherapies that honor the intrinsic value of personal experience and an individual's potential for growth. By implication, the EFT process emphasizes the therapist's ability to engage and expand each partner's felt experience as a means of promoting individual and relational change. The therapist offers an emotional presence that is attentive and responsive to a client's experience in session. The therapist provides a type of secure attachment environment that promotes a safe and thriving context for exploration. Overall, the felt security of the therapeutic alliance provides a secure base for exploring relationship issues that have become dangerously off limits.

As a "process consultant," the EFT therapist demonstrates expertise through collaborating with a couple on a shared understanding of their personal and mutual concerns (Palmer & Johnson, 2002). This stance enables the therapist to join with the couple around the problem and their emerging awareness of the destructive pattern now driving their relationship. As a process consultant, the EFT therapist attunes to the reactions each partner has to this pattern and adopts a nonpathologizing stance, validating the efforts of each partner to cope in response to mounting confusion, flooding, and relationship distress. For example, a therapist is likely to see Andre's cool and distant response to Sarah's demanding pleas for his attention as a possible sign that he is withdrawing to cope with his fear of her rejection and his hope not to worsen things between them. Andre pulls away rather than confront Sarah directly. The therapist understands his withdrawal in the context of his internal experience of fear, rather than as self-absorption or a negative feature of his personality.

Much of the work of the EFT therapist is in the moment. Habitual patterns of emotional responding command a therapist's attention in moments of conflict. At other times, the attunement to a client's subtle indication of affect demonstrates the EFT imperative of being focused on the present moment. An EFT therapist's attention to these entry points to underlying emotional experience opens new ways for couples and partners to begin to respond to one another. In session the EFT therapist engages in a process of discovery, recognizing that while there is often a predictable pattern or order in relational conflict, each individual's experience is unique to the person and the relationship (Johnson, 2004). Therefore, a key challenge faced by therapists learning EFT is to take a step away from the more didactic and expert role of the clinician to join couples more effectively in their experience of the moment, as one who is intrigued by and respectful of their unique experience.

Working With Emotion Experientially

Teaching therapists to be emotion focused begins with helping therapists "tune in" to affect. The language of feeling is commonplace in expressive and supportive therapy. Yet, the process of working with emotion through accessing, expanding, and delineating emotional experience is an adjustment for therapists learning this model. Many couple therapists have relied on communication training and behavioral techniques to help couples regulate their conflicts through managing or distancing from emotional content. In EFT, a therapist must be facile in tuning in to the emotional music happening between partners and also within each person's experience.

Carefully, the therapist reflects and validates each partner's experience, creating a space where a couple's polarized positions can be understood and reframed as a stuck pattern. In later stages of the model, the therapist's ability to deepen emotional experience through heightening and empathic conjecture becomes critical to accessing each partner's more adaptive attachment-related needs and longings. These shifts are accomplished through working with and through emotion. As in individual models of EFT, a therapist's ability to attend and reflect on a client's emotional experience promotes client progress and positive outcomes in treatment (Greenberg & Pascual-Leon, 2006).

A common challenge faced by therapists learning this model includes reviewing their personal beliefs about emotions. For example, a therapist may struggle to work with intensifying emotional experience because of his or her discomfort with and lack of trust in emotional intensity. Here a client may express fears of opening up further to an overwhelming sense of sadness; rather than engaging this fear, the therapist moves to cognitive reflections in an attempt to understand the fear rather than engage with the client's emerging experience.

The therapist's efforts to regulate his or her own fear of emotion map on the client's fear of accessing and moving into more deeply felt emotion. Similarly, a therapist whose training emphasized containing and processing experience more reflectively may question whether moving toward a deeper experience of emotion will prove disruptive and destabilizing. Still others find it challenging to slow the pace of the session and redirect attention to emotional cues because they are more accustomed to moving to insight as opposed to inviting a partner to move into his or her experience.

The process of unpacking emotion and ordering it into a coherent and relational whole is outlined in the literature (Johnson, 2004). The EFT therapist focuses on the elements that constitute an emotion—namely, an initial perception or trigger (typically, attachment related), bodily felt response, cognitive meaning making, and an action tendency that has impact on a partner and on the way the relationship is defined. Once emotion is accessed and ordered, it becomes tolerable and workable; it does not need to be down-regulated (dismissed or numbed), nor does it have to be up-regulated (i.e., exaggerated or endlessly engaged).

Maintaining an Attachment Frame

Learning EFT invites a therapist to see couple processes through an attachment lens. This begins with the therapist's alliance with a couple. EFT necessitates that a therapist establish, monitor, and, when needed, repair his treatment alliance with each partner. A therapist's active creation of this alliance provides an experiential base of felt safety for the couple's evolving process of discovery and change. A therapist's accessibility and responsiveness to each partner provide greater attunement to their emerging experience as the treatment unfolds (Palmer & Johnson, 2002). Empathic attunement and tentative language in interventions provide room for a more responsive engagement of a couple's experience and a secure base of sorts for exploring new areas of emotional experience. The process itself requires a therapist to "slow down" a couple's interaction and to focus on individual experiences. Similarly, a therapist's personal experience of attachment security provides an important experiential reference for assessing the quality of the alliance shared with a couple.

EFT assumes therapists will conceptualize a couple's pattern of distress in attachment terms. For example, a therapist uses attachment theory to conceptualize Sarah's disappointment and sadness in light of her hope for closeness with Andre. Her disappointment gives way to despair as she feels more distance in a relationship that has attachment significance. The therapist not only appeals to the sadness generally, but also places this sadness in the context of her underlying attachment need or longing for her partner (i.e., her search for closeness). The therapist might say: "Sarah, this is a sad place for you; you feel his distance and long for the closeness you once shared." The therapist frames her sadness as a response to Andre's absence but also to her longing for connection. This extra step frames her experience in attachment terms that mirror her experience and also underscore the relationship she seeks.

By the therapist's acknowledging her underlying experience and placing her sadness in the context of a search for security, both partners and the therapist begin to see and understand the couple's pattern in light of a struggle to connect. Attachment theory provides a lens for seeing couples' often unacknowledged and unsuccessful attempts to connect. (For more on this, please see Chapter 3 in this volume.) It also provides the EFT therapist with a much needed end point for therapy including an image and procedural model of what a successful loving relationship looks like.

Training Resources and Certification

Training in process experiential therapy approaches has long emphasized the importance of viewing taped examples of in-session work (Greenberg & Goldman, 1988). Effective training in an experiential therapy ideally requires conceptual instruction, experiential learning, skill training with modeling and role plays, video reviews of EFT therapy sessions, video reviews of one's own in-session work, and supervision from someone well versed in this approach. Several recent studies have begun to demonstrate the effectiveness of training resources and the challenges faced by therapists seeking to master EFT practice.

Research has demonstrated the lasting effect of an intensive 4-day EFT externship in promoting therapist knowledge and skill in EFT (Montagno, Svatovic, & Levenson, 2010). Therapist gains in EFT knowledge were sustained at follow-up and gains were evident in therapist's self-reported competence in use of EFT skills. Sandberg and Knestel (2010) explored the personal impact and challenges experienced by therapists' learning EFT. They found participants learning EFT reported positive effects on relationships in their personal lives, including further recovery from past difficult life events. This study also highlighted various challenges therapists reported in learning EFT. These included recognition of the personal dedication and a commitment necessary to become proficient in adopting EFT's more intense focus on attachment and emotion. Finally, Duplassie, Macknee, and Williams (2008) noted that EFT skill development was associated with supervision that included feedback on in-session processes.

New resources are available to assist therapists and supervisors in viewing recordings of their EFT sessions. Denton, Johnson, and Burleson (2009) published the emotion-focused therapy fidelity scale to provide a practical resource for supervision and self-evaluation of a therapist's practice of the model. Bradley and Furrow (2004) developed the emotionally focused therapy coding scale to identify EFT-specific interventions. Other resources include a practice workbook offering practical exercises and illustration of the steps and interventions used in the EFT approach (Johnson et al., 2005). This resource, along with numerous training tapes, provides multiple demonstrations of the model's use in everyday practice (see International Center for Excellence in Emotionally Focused Therapy [ICEEFT] Web site: http://www.iceeft.com). Learning an experiential model from the observation of practice is essential in furthering a therapist's ability to recognize a client's experience and foster the exploration of this experience.

In response to increasing questions as to how to best learn EFT, ICEEFT has created a systematic process for earning certification as an EFT therapist. While no therapist need be certified in EFT to use the approach, the process of developing mastery in broad use of the model is systematically addressed in the certification process. The process of learning EFT builds on a combination of resources, which include the following:

- Frequently offered 28- to 30-hour externships (presented in various cities in North America and increasingly in other countries)

- Advanced core skills training (48 hours in groups of 10–12 attendees) meeting four weekends spread out over a year to focus on specific steps/skills in the EFT approach; advanced externships are also offered
- Individual and group supervision from EFT-certified supervisors (including the use of live and recorded feedback based on the moment-to-moment review of EFT practice)
- Teleconferences (certified EFT trainers or supervisors lead group consultation via phone)

CONCLUSION

EFT offers the couple therapist a model of change based on a clear scientific theory of love. The practice of EFT provides therapists with a map to the emotional terrain of a couple's interaction and history and their efforts to deal with distance and distress and to regain a meaningful connection. More than a communication approach, EFT enables couples to engage in compelling new experiences together, using the potent language of attachment and emotion. A growing and robust empirical literature supports EFT's efficacy, and a series of process research studies offers unique insight into its practice. This book and studies reviewed in this chapter illustrate the broadening application of EFT and its relevance to couples facing physical and psychological adversity. This casebook project also represents an ongoing attempt to provide resources to therapists endeavoring to put this model into practice with the couples they serve. We also believe this volume will spur on new research, new ideas, and the application of EFT to new populations, as well as to relationship problems not previously considered.

REFERENCES

Baucom, D. H., Shoham, V., Mueser, K. T., Daiuto, A. D., & Stickle, T. R. (1998). Empirically supported couple and family interventions for marital distress and adult mental health problems. *Journal of Consulting and Clinical Psychology, 66,* 53–88.

Bowlby, J. (1969). *Attachment and loss: Vol. 1. Attachment.* New York, NY: Basic Books.

Bowlby, J. (1988). *A secure base.* New York, NY: Basic Books.

Bradley, B., & Furrow, J. L. (2004). Toward a mini-theory of the blamer softening event: Tracking the moment-by-moment process. *Journal of Marital & Family Therapy, 30,* 233–246.

Byrne, M., Carr, A., & Clark, M. (2004). The efficacy of behavioral couples therapy and emotionally focused therapy for couple distress. *Contemporary Family Therapy, 26,* 361–387.

Chambless, D. L., & Ollendick, T. H. (2001). Empirically supported psychological interventions: Controversies and evidence. *Annual Review of Psychology, 52,* 685–716.

Cloutier, P. F., Manion, I. G., Walker, J. G., & Johnson, S. M. (2002). Emotionally focused interventions for couples with chronically ill children: A 2-year follow-up. *Journal of Marital and Family Therapy, 28,* 391–398.

Dalton, J., Johnson, S. M., & Classen, C. (2010). Treating relationship distress and the effects of childhood abuse with emotion focused couple therapy: A randomized controlled trial. Manuscript submitted for publication.

Dandeneau, M. L., & Johnson, S. M. (1994). Facilitating intimacy: Interventions and effects. *Journal of Marital and Family Therapy, 20,* 17–33.

Denton, W. H., Burleson, B. R., Clark, T. E., Rodriguez, C. P., & Hobbs, B. V. (2000). A randomized trial of emotion-focused therapy for couples in a training clinic. *Journal of Marital and Family Therapy, 26,* 65–78.

Denton, W. H., Johnson, S. M., & Burleson, B. R. (2009). Emotion-focused therapy–therapist fidelity scale: Conceptual development and content validity. *Journal of Couple and Relationship Therapy, 8,* 226–246.

Denton, W. H., Wittenborn, A. K., & Golden, R. N. (2010). Augmenting antidepressant medication treatment of depressed women with emotionally focused therapy for couples: A randomized pilot study. *Journal of Marital and Family Therapy.*

Dessaulles, A., Johnson, S. M., & Denton, W. H. (2003). Emotionally focused therapy for couples in the treatment of depression: A pilot study. *American Journal of Family Therapy, 31,* 345–353.

Dunn, R. L., & Schwebel, A. I. (1995). Meta-analytic review on marital therapy outcome research. *Journal of Family Psychology, 9,* 58–68.

Duplassie, D., Macknee, C., & Williams, M. A. (2008). Critical incidents that help and hinder learning emotionally focused therapy for couples. *Journal of Couple and Relationship Therapy, 7,* 1–18.

Fredrickson, B. L. & Losada, M. (2005). Positive affect and the complex dynamics of human flourishing. *American Psychologist, 60,* 678–686.

Goldman, A., & Greenberg, L. (1992). Comparison of integrated systemic and emotionally focused approaches to couples therapy. *Journal of Consulting and Clinical Psychology, 60,* 962–969.

Gottman, J. M. (1998). Psychology and the study of the marital processes. *Annual Review of Psychology, 49,* 169–197.

Greenberg, L., Ford, C., Alden, L., & Johnson, S. (1993). In-session change in emotionally focused therapy. Special section: Couples and couple therapy. *Journal of Consulting and Clinical Psychology, 61,* 78–84.

Greenberg, L. S., & Goldman, R. S. (1988). Training in experiential therapy. *Journal of Consulting and Clinical Psychology, 56,* 696–702.

Greenberg, L. S., & Johnson, S. M. (1988). *Emotionally focused therapy for couples.* New York, NY: Guilford Press.

Greenberg, L. S., & Pascual-Leone, A. (2006). Emotion in psychotherapy: A practice-friendly review. *Journal of Clinical Psychology, 62,* 611–630.

Greenberg, L. S., Rice, L. N., & Elliott, R. (1994). *Facilitating emotional change: The moment-by-moment process.* New York, NY: Guilford Press.

Halchuk, R., Makinen, J., & Johnson, S. M. (2010). Resolving attachment injuries in couples using emotionally focused therapy, A 3-year follow-up. *Journal of Couple and Relationship Therapy, 9,* 31–47.

Hazan, C., & Shaver, P. (1987). Romantic love conceptualized as an attachment process. *Journal of Personality and Social Psychology, 52,* 511–524.

Huston, T. L., Caughlin, J. P., Houts, R. M., Smith, S. E., & George, L. J. (2001). The connubial crucible: Newlywed years as predictors of marital delight, distress, and divorce. *Journal of Personality and Social Psychology, 80,* 237–252.

Jacobson, N. S., & Margolin, G. (1979). *Marital therapy: Strategies based on social learning and behavioral exchange principles.* New York, NY: Brunner & Mazel.

James, P. S. (1991). Effects of a communication training com-
    ponent added to an emotionally focused couples therapy.
    Journal of Marital and Family Therapy, 17, 263–275.

Johnson, S. M. (1986). Bonds or bargains: Relationship para-
    digms and their significance for marital therapy. *Journal of
    Marital and Family Therapy, 12,* 259–267.

Johnson, S. M. (2003). Introduction to attachment. In S. M.
    Johnson & V. E. Whiffen (Eds.), *Attachment processes in
    couple and family therapy.* New York, NY: Guilford Press.

Johnson, S. M. (2004). *The practice of emotionally focused
    couple therapy: Creating connection* (2nd ed.). New York,
    NY: Routledge.

Johnson, S. M. (2009). Emotionally focused couple therapy. In
    A. S. Gurman (Ed.), *Clinical handbook of couples therapy*
    (4th ed.; pp. 107–137). New York, NY: Guilford Press.

Johnson, S. M., & Best, M. (2002). A systematic approach to
    restructuring adult attachment: The EFT model of couples
    therapy. In P. Erdman & T. Caffery (Eds.), *Attachment and
    family systems: Conceptual, empirical and therapeutic
    relatedness* (pp. 165–192). New York, NY: Springer.

Johnson, S. M., Bradley, B., Furrow, J. L., Lee, A., Palmer, G.,
    Tilley, D., & Wooley, S. (2005). *Becoming an EFT therapist:
    The workbook.* New York, NY: Brunner/Routledge.

Johnson, S. M., & Greenberg, L. S. (1985a). Differential effects of
    experiential and problem-solving interventions in resolv-
    ing marital conflict. *Journal of Consulting and Clinical
    Psychology, 53,* 175–184.

Johnson, S. M., & Greenberg, L. S. (1985b). Emotionally focused
    couples therapy: An outcome study. *Journal of Marital and
    Family Therapy, 11,* 313–317.

Johnson, S. M., & Greenberg, L. S. (1988). Relating process to
    outcome in marital therapy. *Journal of Marital and Family
    Therapy, 14,* 175–183.

Johnson, S. M., Hunsley, J., Greenberg, L., & Schindler, D.
    (1999). Emotionally focused couples therapy: Status and
    challenges. *Clinical Psychology: Science & Practice, 6,*
    67–79.

Johnson, S. M., Maddeaux, C., & Blouin, J. (1998). Emotionally
    focused family therapy for bulimia: Changing attachment
    patterns, *Psychotherapy, 35,* 238–247.

Johnson, S. M., & Talitman, E. (1997). Predictors of success in
    emotionally focused marital therapy. *Journal of Marital
    and Family Therapy, 23,* 135–152.

Lebow, J. L., Chambers, A., Christensen, A., & Johnson, S. M. (in press). Marital distress. In D. Sprenkle & R. Chenail (Eds.), *Effectiveness research in marriage and family therapy.* Washington, DC: AAMFT.

MacIntosh, H. B., & Johnson, S. (2008). Emotionally focused therapy for couples and childhood sexual abuse survivors. *Journal of Marital and Family Therapy, 34,* 298–315.

MacPhee, D. C., Johnson, S. M., & Van Der Veer, M. C. (1995). Low sexual desire in women: The effects of marital therapy. *Journal of Sex & Marital Therapy, 21,* 159–182.

Makinen, J., & Johnson, S. (2006). Resolving attachment injuries in couples using emotionally focused therapy: Steps toward forgiveness and reconciliation. *Journal of Consulting and Clinical Psychology, 74,* 1055–1064.

Mikulincer, M., & Shaver P. (2007). *Attachment in adulthood: Structure, dynamics, and change.* New York, NY: Guilford Press.

Mikulincer, M., & Shaver, P. R. (2005). Attachment theory and emotions in close relationships: Exploring the attachment-related dynamic of emotional reactions to relational events. *Personal Relationships, 12,* 149–168.

Mikulincer, M., & Shaver, P. R. (2009). An attachment and behavioral systems perspective on social support. *Journal of Social and Personal Relationships, 26,* 7–19.

Minuchin, S., & Fishman, H. C. (1981). *Family therapy techniques.* Cambridge, MA: Harvard University Press.

Montagno, M., Svatovic, M., & Levenson, H. (2010). Short-term and long-term effects of training in emotionally focused couple therapy: Professional and personal aspects. Manuscript submitted for publication.

Naaman, S., Johnson, S. M., & Radwan, K. (in press). Evaluation of the clinical efficacy of emotionally focused therapy on psychological adjustment of couples facing early breast cancer. *Psychiatry: Biological and Interpersonal Processes.*

Palmer, G., & Johnson, S. M. (2002). Becoming an emotionally focused therapist. *Journal of Couple and Family Therapy, 1,* 1–17.

Rogers, C. (1951). *Client centered therapy.* Boston, MA: Houghton–Mifflin.

Sandberg, J. G., & Knestel, A. (2010). The experience of learning emotionally focused couple therapy. Manuscript submitted for publication.

Shadish, W. R., & Baldwin, S. A. (2003). Meta-analyses of MFT interventions. *Journal of Marital and Family Therapy, 29,* 547–570.

Walker, J. G., Johnson, S., Manion, I., & Cloutier, P. (1996). Emotionally focused marital intervention for couples with chronically ill children. *Journal of Consulting and Clinical Psychology, 64,* 1029–1036.

Wood, N. D., Crane, D. R., Schaalje, G. B., & Law, D. D. (2005). What works for whom: A meta-analytic review of marital and couples therapy in reference to marital distress. *American Journal of Family Therapy, 33,* 273–287.

Zuccarini, D. (2010). *The attachment injury resolution model in emotionally focused couple therapy: A psychotherapy process study of in-session client performances and therapist behaviors.* Ottawa: University of Ottawa.

Two

The Attachment Perspective on the Bonds of Love
A Prototype for Relationship Change

SUSAN M. JOHNSON

INTRODUCTION

John Bowlby was perhaps the very first family therapist. He wrote his paper, "Forty-four Juvenile Thieves," in 1944. In it, he noted that "behind the mask of indifference is bottomless misery and behind apparent callousness, despair." He pinpoints here the emotional drama behind the negative actions of his young clients. He also suggests that, if you understand a person's relational context, all their responses, no matter how seemingly bizarre or dysfunctional, are eminently reasonable, even if, at first, they appear "exaggerated or distorted" (Bowlby, 1988, p. 81).

Bowlby was also, I suggest, the first person to integrate a systems approach with a focus on individual informational and emotional processing. He tells us that we need to focus on the interaction between the "inner ring" of emotional processing that maintains "physiological homeostasis" with the "outer ring" of response patterns in a person's closest relationships (Bowlby, 1973). Attachment theory offers the couple therapist the first holistic integrated model that links dancer and dance, self and system, the intrapsychic and interpersonal elements of a couple's relationship. It is also the first theory of love that offers depth and specificity as well as research studies—thousands focusing on parent–child bonds and now hundreds focusing on the bond between partners (Johnson, 2003a). Just like John Bowlby (1969), every couple therapist grapples with the drama of "love and hate, anxiety and defense, attachment and loss" (p. xxvii). Due to his legacy, however, therapists now have a secure base of understanding, a prism through which to see, shape, and transform close relationships.

It seems significant to me that the study of adult attachment started in the 1980s with researchers who were engaged in the study of loneliness, helplessness, and trauma (Mikulincer & Shaver, 2007). Perhaps the most fundamental message of attachment theory is that emotional and physical isolation is inherently traumatizing for human beings and is coded by the human brain as danger, while soothing closeness to others is coded as safety. This offers the couple therapist a broad existentialist vision of relationship problems, as well as a specific way of understanding the significance of the everyday, specific complaints that partners bring to therapy—the most basic of which is that partners are together but fundamentally alone.

This chapter will not summarize attachment theory per se (Mikulincer & Shaver, 2007) nor provide a comprehensive overview of attachment as it relates to the practice of EFT; a number of other articles and chapters offer this to the reader (Johnson, 2003b, 2003c; Johnson & Greenman, 2006). There is also literature that specifically describes the natural links between the experiential and systemic roots of EFT and attachment theory (Johnson, 2009a). This chapter will focus on four key ways that attachment theory and research help the EFT therapist to formulate and address the tasks of therapy with a typical distressed couple. This offers the reader a base from which to explore, in the other chapters in this book, how the attachment frame and EFT can then be adapted to less typical couples with specific needs.

SETTING YOUR SIGHTS

The first key insight offered by attachment theory concerns the goal of couple therapy as a modality. As Yogi Berra remarked, "If you don't know where you are going, you will wind up somewhere else." The goals of couple therapy have most often been formulated in terms of conflict containment, the creation of better sets of communication skills or individual insights as to how past relationships impact present ones. This is logical if we assume that conflict is the primary generator of relationship distress. A key prospective study, however, found that decreases in affectional expression and responsiveness marked couples who would later divorce, rather than increases in negativity (Huston, Caughlin, Houts, Smith, & George, 2001).

Attachment theory posits that relationship distress begins with the absence of specific kinds of responsive intimate interactions, which then lead to negative interactions and unmet needs (Roberts & Greenberg, 2002). The goal of couple therapy has then to be the creation of safe emotional connection, of "felt security" arising from mutual emotional responsiveness. This responsiveness enables couples to resolve and repair conflicts and to disclose and deal with emotions and needs in an optimal fashion that naturally leads to intimacy and satisfaction.

Understanding adult love and how this love is shaped is crucial if we are to "hit the nail on the head"—if, as couple therapists, we are really to make a difference. Researchers point out, for example, that little evidence exists that happy couples use any form of "empathy" responses in conflict situations (Gottman, Coan, Carrere, & Swanson, 1998). However, attuned, contingent empathic responses seem to be absolutely critical to relationship satisfaction in the context of the disclosure of emotional needs or vulnerabilities. Process research on EFT suggests that when this responsiveness occurs in key sessions in Stage 2 of EFT, it creates a more secure emotional connection that provides an antidote to negative interactional patterns and predicts lasting positive change in the quality of a relationship (Johnson & Talitman, 1996). Understanding love tells us what matters and when it matters; it offers us a compass in the reshaping of dance between partners.

One criticism of couple therapy is that it simply focuses on relieving superficial symptoms of distress; it does not, in fact, offer couples what they come to therapy for: the creation of a happier, more loving relationship. Clients repeatedly tell us that cognitive explanations and more "skilled" practiced interactions do not get to the heart of the matter in a love relationship. But the creation of a secure, emotional bond, where partners can reach for each other, share attachment needs and fears, and offer mutual comfort and reassurance, is a substantially more ambitious goal than conflict containment or increasing general positive interactions such as going on dates.

The attachment perspective explicitly charges the couple therapist with the task of helping a distressed couple to evoke and shape love and loving, a task that has traditionally been left to poets and dreamers. This constitutes what systems theorists would term a "second-order change"—that is, a change

that reorganizes a system rather than simply modifying specific components. Even more than this, an attachment-oriented
couple therapist is actively promoting *effective dependency* in
each partner. Attachment theory is clear that dealing with key
emotional needs in ways that lead to more secure bonds promotes each partner's individual growth and healing. This is
supremely relevant when we consider the application of any
form of couple therapy to different kinds of distressed couples
facing individual problems, as in this casebook.

The attachment perspective offers couple therapists a specific model, an operationalization of the key ingredients of a
healthy love relationship that goes far beyond teamwork or
friendship or collaborative problem solving. Study after study
tells us that more securely attached partners are more able to

- Retain emotional balance, even when feeling momentarily disconnected or stressed, rather than becoming
  flooded with anxiety or anger
- Tune in to their emotions and remain open, offering
  coherent, direct, and explicit messages about their
  needs to loved ones in a way that encourages these
  loved ones to respond
- Trustingly take in comfort and care when it is offered,
  return to physiological homeostasis, and maintain
  positive tolerant perspectives on others' behavior
- Deal with ambiguous responses from others with less
  defensiveness and catastrophizing
- Turn back into the world, actively explore, learn, and
  adapt to new situations
- Turn toward and respond to the other with empathy and
  caring in a way that constantly renews loving bonds

This model of a secure bond then translates into a list of tasks
for the couple therapist and a map that aids in directing interventions. An EFT therapist, for example, will specifically ask a
client, "What does it feel like when your partner leans toward
you like this and offers you caring?" and will help a client
address blocks to opening up to such caring. The EFT therapist will also focus on any inability to form or express attachment needs. Shame at being perceived as "needy" that blocks
the open expression of needs will be actively addressed.

As previously stated, attachment theory integrates self
and system. Lovers are seen as engaged in a neural duet
(Goleman, 2006); as regulators of each other's physiological

responses—especially those associated with anxiety; and as cocreators of each other's construal of the world and sense of self (Johnson, 2009a). This perspective offers us a clear model for the ways in which specific interactional changes foster intrapsychic change. For example, when partners experience their relationship as a safe haven, they learn to regulate potentially chaotic emotions better and so find it easier to engage in metacognition and reflect on different perspectives (Jurist & Meehan, 2009). In relationships, they can then stand back and comment on patterns in negative interactions. ("I think we are caught in that place where I begin to feel rejected and shut you out. Then you get freaked out.")

This not only affords them more control over negative patterns, such as blame–withdraw, but also helps them make sense of their relationship drama and create a coherent story of specific negative life events. Securely attached partners are able to create narratives of traumatic events such as imprisonment and torture (Solomon, Ginzburg, Mikulincer, Neria, & Ohry, 1998) or the events of 9/11 (Fraley, Fazzari, Bonanno, & Dekel, 2006) that integrate these experiences in the most positive way possible, ordering them so that they are less overwhelming and toxic in their implications. A secure attachment is the ultimate coping strategy and personal source of resilience.

Attachment not only impacts how we encode and organize negative information and events, but also plays a crucial part in positives such as the creation of an articulate and positive sense of self (Mikulincer, 1995). Secure partners who know they can turn to another for support and have internalized this felt sense that others will be there for them are also able to be more separate and autonomous; they are more confidant that they can solve problems on their own and tend to be better at reaching their goals (Feeney, 2007).

Perhaps the effect of secure bonding that speaks most eloquently to the power of attachment-focused interventions to create both personal and relationship change is that a felt sense of security creates openness. Emotional perceptions and responses can then be experienced fully without distortion or constriction and expressed to others in adaptive ways. More secure partners show increased curiosity and flexibility in their beliefs and are more able to deal with ambiguity. This openness allows for a deep engagement with and awareness of moment-to-moment living; Carl Rogers (1961) called this "existential living."

Spontaneity and the ability to revise beliefs and responses in the light of new information as well as the ability to trust one's experience and choose from alternatives in a responsible way are also part of this orientation. Rogers, like Bowlby, believed that safe connections with others offer not just more freedom from anxiety but also the chance for "more sensitive living, with greater range, greater variety, greater richness" (1961, pp. 195–196). The ultimate goal of an attachment-oriented couple therapy such as EFT is then to create not just less distressed but also more alive partners who engage in a more engaged and dynamic relationship that constantly offers opportunities for further growth and development.

To have a clear goal and a bright image of a destination allows a therapist and his or her clients to travel more hopefully and with more focused direction. Sharing this image of what a loving relationship looks like is itself transforming for partners who very often are trying to create a loving relationship with no model at all or with only negative models.

SNAPSHOT

When James and Margaret come to see me, they tell me that over the last 20 years they have occasionally had big fights, but that since the kids have gone off to college the problem has been hard to define. Margaret, who "hunkers down and withdraws" when there is a problem, finally tells me, "There is a giant emptiness in the middle of this relationship." Sad random thoughts of "What's the use anyway? Life wouldn't be much different if we just split up. This is just the way it goes after years of marriage" go through her head. James angrily interrupts and says that he has now "given up" trying to get his wife to talk to him and spends hours "staring at screens" (TV and computer). His doctor has just suggested to him that he is "chronically depressed." "We don't really understand the problem here," he tells me. "And I don't even know why I get so enraged. I am either hopping mad or just turned off."

There are a myriad of ways that the problem can be framed here and the goals of therapy set. However, this is best done in a way that is supremely relevant to the couple—a way that directly reflects their pain and their longings. I follow the emotion in the room, asking about the tears in Margaret's eyes in an evocative way. She sighs and says, "I guess the real issue for me is that I am lonely. So lonely." James responds with a look of surprise and irritation. "Well, then, why don't you try talking more?" he snaps. The negative pattern of withdrawal and angry criticism followed by sullen shutdown is obvious. I reflect this pattern and James says, "So then tell us how just to stop doing that and everything will be fixed." Margaret rolls her eyes.

As I look at this couple, my goal is to help them see and contain this negative pattern. More than this, it is to change their ability to tune in to and regulate their attachment emotions, especially their fears, and give clear signals that can address the longings and needs that they cannot as yet articulate. James hits it on the head when he murmurs, "We are strangers. I have lost her." As he expresses it here, this is a problem of distance and separateness—a problem that can only be remedied by a new kind of emotional connection. He then offers another insight. "Maybe this distance is where my darkness comes from—this kind of hopelessness or whatever the doctor calls it." He reminds me that my goal is to help him and Margaret find and address the deeper attachment longings hidden by their cycle of distress, creating a connection that empowers both of them and offers them a safe haven from helplessness and hopelessness.

SAFE HAVEN SESSIONS

The goal of more secure attachment requires that the therapist's absolute ongoing priority is the creation and maintenance of a safe haven and secure base with both partners in therapy sessions. The therapist is a consultant who collaborates with partners in accessing, ordering, and restructuring both their construction of ongoing emotional experience and cognitive models and their habitual steps in the relational dance. This restructuring mostly occurs from the bottom up, as experience or interaction occurs, rather than the top down. This requires that the therapist display a transparent emotional presence, a sensitive responsiveness that creates trust and a sense of safety in the same way as this occurs in an attachment bond.

Bowlby echoes the teachings of humanists such as Rogers when he suggests that therapists need to empathize with and validate a client's reality—for example, a widow's rage and "unrealism"—before guiding a client forward (1979, p. 94). The therapist's validation and compassion offer partners a secure base from which to explore warded off experience and learn to

integrate this new experience into their relationship and sense
of self. The map of the emotional realities of bonding relationships offered by attachment theory aids the therapist in his or
her attempts to be accurate and empathetic. The framework of
attachment helps the therapist see the logic in apparent rage or
lack of responsiveness or the fear behind willfulness or hostility. This helps therapists to step past their own frustration or
need to pass judgment and to stay on base with each partner.

Attachment theorists suggest that the client–therapist relationship—while not a true secure bond, curtailed as it is by
the limits of the therapist's role—specifically offers a secure
base to clients (Farber & Metzger, 2009; Parish & Eagle, 2003)
where they can enact habitual attachment behaviors and then
explore and reflect on them. The more securely attached a
client is in general, the higher the levels of self-disclosure and
exploration are likely to be with the therapist in the session
(Grabill & Kerns, 2000).

In couple therapy, the presence of a "real" (not just therapeutic surrogate) attachment figure, who may be constantly
evoking a person's attachment fears, will likely impact these
factors. This suggests that it is important that the therapist
provide safe, predictable emotional support and also show
himself or herself assertive and skilled enough to contain and
redirect hurtful responses from the other partner. The EFT
therapist will then "catch the bullet" (Johnson 2004), blocking
responses like hostility between partners.

Thus, when James states that his wife's feelings are "pathetic
and ridiculous," I will turn to him, block this interaction, and
frame his response as, "You do not know how to respond when
Margaret says these things. They are hard for you to listen to.
So you naturally push them away and want to tell her that her
response is not valid. I think she is trying to tell you…"

There is also some evidence that, in individual therapy at
least, more secure therapists find it easier to maintain a strong
working alliance over the course of therapy and tend to be more
empathic than anxiously attached therapists (Sauer, Lopez, &
Gormley, 2003). Holmes (2009) points out that the attachment
literature offers descriptions of secure mother–child interactive sequences that can also guide therapists. These sequences
involve affect expression by the caretaker and empathic resonance, followed by affect regulation where emotion is turned
up or down to engage the child, ending in mutual playfulness
or "enlivenment." The result is focused active engagement in

a joint process of exploration. Timing, tone of voice, and the identification of feelings are key, as is the engagement in "a conversation about a conversation."

Validation is the cornerstone of EFT as a therapeutic approach and is essential in creating a therapeutic alliance (Johnson, 2004). To engage with and explore unfamiliar emotional territory, partners have to know that their experience will be seen as valid and legitimate. In particular, the EFT therapist will help partners to acknowledge stuck places, especially when this is an alternative to blaming the other ("I don't know how to respond" contains more positive possibilities than "You are too difficult to respond to"). The essence of EFT and of the EFT vision of attachment is that the therapist first focuses on and acknowledges the legitimacy of where the client IS as a person before considering how this person might move to solve his or her problems.

The therapist will validate the fact that many partners have no model and no systematic knowledge of how to be loving or how to be loved. Most importantly, therapists explicate and legitimize attachment needs and fears by putting these into the framework of the survival code that is human attachment. Both men and women often express shame about needing others or being vulnerable to abandonment or rejection. The cultural creed of adult self-sufficiency is actively and directly countered by the therapist, who places these needs in the framework of the survival code of attachment in the session. Male clients, in particular, seem to respond to the cognitive understanding of love offered here and to the validation of their need for connection. This may explain the paradox that, in a culture that decrees maleness to be synonymous with cool self-sufficiency, an approach that focuses on the edges of emotional awareness and emotional signals and on deeper needs for connection seems to be so popular with and so applicable to male partners (Greenman, Faller, & Johnson, in press).

The creation of a safe haven in session also helps clients deal with the fact that interactions between attachment figures are key contexts for the definition of self. As James tells me toward the end of therapy:

> Couples sessions are perilous, you know. In individual therapy you have more control. Here you might find that all your worst fears about how your partner sees you are true—that you have not only lost out on her love, but that it's because of you—you are fatally flawed.

Session 3 with James and Margaret begins with James telling me in an irritated voice that it seems as if he is being
labeled as abusive here. We focus on this issue and I reassure James that while, in their negative cycle of demand
and withdrawal, Margaret has seen him as angry, this is
not the same as abuse. We talk about this for as long as necessary to mend the alliance and to put James's "irritation"
in the context of the negative cycle that has separated him
from Margaret and the "discomfort" that this creates for
him. James then becomes critical of himself, stating that
he is a "more than competent communicator" at work but
with his wife he is a "disaster." I block his criticism by
normalizing that love relationships are different and evoke
such strong emotions in us that we all have more difficulty
accessing "skills" and get stuck in negative responses.

In the process I also find ways to validate that Margaret,
while not seeing James as abusive, is beginning to access
that she becomes "alarmed" by his anger and also by his
"cold shutdown" after their fights. When she makes comments that in any way might evoke shame in James, I "catch
the bullet" by framing these comments in terms of the cycle.
The normalizing, the validation of attachment needs and
fears, reframing of critical comments, and accurate empathy, as well as the clarity of the attachment framework that
translates their "chaos" into understandable order, create a
sense of safety and hope in the session.

DEALING WITH THE DANGER

The most basic tenet of the attachment view of love is that
emotional connection is coded by the brain as safety, especially when cues of uncertainty or threat arise in the world
or in the relationship. This safety promotes flexibility and
openness. Distance and separation are coded as danger, and
if this danger cannot be alleviated by the primary attachment
strategy of reaching for another and receiving comfort, a neural response of "primal panic" ensues (Panksepp, 1998). This
fear response is part of an ancient survival code originating
from the vulnerability of the human infant who, if unable to
evoke caring responses from others, would surely die. It is

then amazingly powerful and easily able to disrupt other cues, rational thoughts, and logical skill sets.

Strong emotions have "control precedence" (Tronick, 1989), especially in relationships with those upon whom we depend. From an EFT point of view, how this fear of abandonment or rejection is cued and handled is *the* pivotal issue in determining whether a relationship moves toward secure connection or slides into ever-deepening insecurity, conflict, and distance. Attachment is a transactional theory of affect regulation and the interpersonal consequences of different modes of emotional engagement with others.

Bowlby (1991) noted that the main function of emotion was to communicate one's needs, motives, and priorities to oneself and others. He would have resonated with the EFT concept that being tuned out of emotional experience is like navigating through life without an internal compass. He believed that less than effective affect regulation is the core mechanism underlying constricted responses in personal problems and distressed relationships. Emotion is seen as the vital element in guiding perception, cueing internal models of self and other and shaping or "moving" people into specific interactional responses. Emotion comes from the Latin word *emovere* (to move).

The concept of emotion has become more differentiated and its role in therapy more articulated than was the case when attachment theory was formulated. It now seems to be clear that there are six or seven main universal emotional responses (Frijda, 1986) recognized and understood across humans as a species. In couple therapy, therapists mostly work with reactive anger—what Bowlby called the anger of despair—*with* shame, which cues withdrawal and lack of transparency and, most of all, with different versions of fear or attachment panic.

While *some* attachment theorists (Holmes, 2001) talk mostly of insight into emotion as a primary change mechanism in therapy, an EFT therapist shapes new corrective emotional experiences rather than creating insight per se and also helps clients to integrate these experiences into a coherent whole. This ability to engage in moment-to-moment emotional experience, explore it, and then integrate it into a coherent whole has been shown in research to be part and parcel of secure attachment (Main et al., 1985). It is worth noting here that in the large NIMH study of depression, a collaborative approach to helping clients explore emotion was positively related to outcome irrespective of model of intervention (Coombs, Coleman, & Jones, 2002), whereas an educative approach to emotion and coping with it was not found to be related to outcome.

The EFT therapist notes how emotion arises and is dealt with in key situations when attachment fears are present and compelling. In the first steps of EFT, the therapist will focus on how each partner's responses become automatic and narrowed in order to protect the self, either by shutting down and mini-mizing emotions or heightening emotional signals and push-ing the other for a response. These responses reflect the two universal ways to deal with attachment needs and fears when a sense of safe connection is missing. The essence of EFT as an attachment intervention is for distressed partners to discover how their ways of dealing with their emotions send signals to their partner that tend to perpetuate attachment panic and insecurity in the other.

The therapist reflects patterns of interaction, such as demanding and withdrawing, as they occur. He or she notes how a partner can pull the other close, opening up the options for responsiveness, or drive the other away and cue defen-sive strategies. These negative patterns of interaction that arise from and evoke attachment panic are framed as the couple's joint enemy (Johnson, 2004, 2008). Each partner begins to have a felt sense of how he or she sends out incongruent or unclear or conflicting signals that reduce the other's sense of safety. This process then creates a platform of relative safety in the relationship so that new levels of risk and learning become possible and new emotional experiences and signals begin to take shape.

The regulation of attachment emotion is not taught so much as shaped collaboratively by therapist and by partners *as it occurs in the moment*. Survival-oriented emotion is encoded with lightning speed by the brain. Once it is encoded, it is not easily let go of or modified. The evidence is that once a neural fear pathway is laid down in the amygdala (the center in the brain for the processing of fear), it is very difficult to eradicate this pathway. It can be added to or modified by powerful new experiences, however (Ekman, 2003). The EFT therapist mostly validates and then develops an emotion further so that, for example, reactive anger recedes and the more primary threat that is a vital part of that anger comes to the forefront. The speed of an emotional response also means that suppression is a difficult and often ineffective strategy that often increases arousal and also leaks out to a partner in cues such as facial expressions and tone of voice. Understandably, then, the suppression of emotion in one partner has been found to increase tension in the other (Gross, 2001).

The EFT therapist hones in on pivotal emotional moments— focusing on specifying cues; body responses; associated thoughts and meanings about self, other, and the relationship; the actions prompted by the emotions; and the resulting cycles of interaction. Coan (2008) suggests that this kind of immediate, bottom-up, and interpersonal experience of affect regulation is more effective than solitary or more logical attempts, which are more top-down. The latter happens later in the process of experiencing and requires more effort. The empathic presence of the therapist allows for a new engagement with experience *as it is being encoded in the brain.* This may promote reshaping of neural circuits as they are being challenged (Coan, 2008). As a result of this kind of active processing of emotional experience, partners move from surface-reactive feelings of frustration or numbness to deeper emotions, such as fear over abandonment and rejection, shame at perceived unworthiness, sadness, and loneliness.

Attachment research validates the fact that key factors such as sensitivity to negative cues arising in interactions can be heightened by past experiences in attachment relationships, either the present one or with other lovers or parents. These relationships have also shaped habitual emotion regulation strategies adopted when reaching and sharing are not perceived as bringing a loved one closer. Secondary strategies such as avoidant numbing and withdrawal (to disengage from attachment needs and fears) or anxious, strident, intensified protest at another's perceived lack of responsiveness (to maximize signals and compel a response) can be functional at times, but in distressed couples, these strategies take over and become part of the problem that they are designed to solve.

These strategies can be thought of as styles or traits or as states that can vary in a relationship and across relationships; they can be conscious or latent, general or specific to a relationship. For a couple therapist, it seems most useful to think of these individual differences as habitual ways of engaging loved ones when attachment fears and needs arise. History does matter. There is continuity in our experience with and shaping of our closest relationships. Assessing how safely connected 1-year-olds are to their mothers in the "strange situation" allows one to predict how socially competent these children will be in elementary school and how close their friendships will be in adolescence. These things, then, in turn, predict the quality of these kids' love relationships at age 25 (Simpson, Collins, Tran, & Haydon, 2007).

However, research also shows that, with new experiences of relatedness, such sensitivities and habitual strategies can and do change (Davila & Cobb, 2004). Cognitive working models and strategies of engagement with others can be thought of as prototypes—a set of "if this, then that" programs. These programs can differ in different relationships and can shift and change across time. Most importantly for the couple therapist, these prototypes are formed, elaborated, maintained, and revised through emotional communication (Davila, Karney, & Bradbury, 1999). In fact, to be optimally useful, they must be constantly revised and kept up to date as changes occur in interpersonal contexts. In this context, the therapist has to help couples step out of the patterns that constantly confirm their worst fears and cement their less than optimal ways of dealing with these fears, blocking trust and responsiveness to the other.

SNAPSHOT

Once James and Margaret are able to identify their negative pattern—a dance of demand–distance followed by mutual withdrawal—they begin to see that it leaves them both alone and in a state of emotional starvation. With the therapist's help they begin to touch on the attachment emotions that underlie this pattern. Margaret is able to talk about how lonely she feels and how she expresses this in a "silent seethe." She feels ashamed that she is not "able to stand on my own two feet," but needs closeness so much, even though her friends tell her that after years of marriage this is "just not the way things are." James then senses the tension and "badgers" her with questions about what is wrong. When she stays silent, he "loses it" and "rants" about how difficult women are before storming off and going to watch TV. Both agree that they have many strengths in their long relationship: They are great managers of their family, finances, and friends on many levels. However, they agree that this lack of connection is slowly and surely eating away at their bond. Margaret has even started to add a "why don't I just leave?" question hanging in the air. They begin to see how they are both victims of this dance of silence, rage, and separateness that leaves them both alone, helpless, and hopeless.

As they are able to access the deeper, softer emotions, Margaret is able to piece together her experience of the times when James goes into one of his "rants." She needs considerable empathic support, validation, and focused evocative questions before she can access that she is indeed very afraid at these moments. James becomes reactive here and protests that he is not fearsome, but Margaret is able to tell him that when she hears his frustration, an old fear that she is inherently unacceptable arises. All she can do then is to "hide out" and wait for his rage at her obvious flaws to blow over. As she tells him this, his resentment dissolves into amazement and then compassion.

James is able to explore his emotions and identify that he indeed goes into "terror" when she cannot help him under-stand her tension and then turns away from him. He finally withdraws as well and goes to a "deep dark place of hopeless-ness." In this place he tells himself that she no longer needs him or cares for him and that their previous happiness was an illusion. This naturally leads to the depression response that attachment research finds is part of separation distress. James also berates himself for getting so angry. I validate that becoming angry and demanding or shutting down are really the only ways we have to deal with strong needs and fears when we cannot connect with a loved one. His anger reflects his anxiety that he cannot reach his partner. Attachment fills in the blanks in the emotional drama of toxic interac-tion patterns that have been found to predict divorce.

As each partner is guided by the therapist to expand the range of his or her emotions and clearly articulate them to the other, the couple begins to create a secure base. They have then begun to do what secure couples can do—that is, to hear the other's protest at emotional separation for what it is: a desperate cry for connection. The therapist constantly prioritizes and normalizes attachment fears and longings and offers them to partners as new ways into grasping their own needs and connecting with their partner.

SHAPING SECURE BONDS

The attachment view of love dictates that once a couple has contained the negative cycle that perpetuates their insecurity and thus *shaped the beginnings* of a secure base, it is time to help them create a positive cycle of emotional responsiveness that addresses their need for secure connection and intimacy. Such a positive cycle involves a pattern of interactions where withdrawers become reengaged and are able to assert their needs and tune in to their partner; blaming partners "soften" in that they are able to ask for their needs to be met from a position of vulnerability that evokes caring from their partner. Softening events in best sessions have been shown to predict recovery from distress and stability of positive relationship changes across time (Bradley & Furrow, 2004).

However, secure connection occurs on a continuum; not every partner will reach an optimal sense of felt security with the other. The minimal level occurs when each partner can begin to share his or her fears and the other side of those fears—their longings, asking for their needs to be met in a basically congruent fashion that evokes some level of responsive compassion and caring in the other. This then lowers the two dimensions of attachment insecurity (anxiety and avoidance; Fraley & Waller, 1998) to the point where partners can connect, even if this connection is not always optimal or consistent. With the help of the therapist, interactions occur where the answer to the question "Are you there for me when I need you?" is positive. These interactions are characterized by ARE: *a*ccessibility, *r*esponsiveness, and *e*motional engagement (Johnson, 2008).

What does the optimal level of felt security look like in clinical practice? As Schore (1994) notes, contact with a supportive, safe attachment figure "tranquillizes the nervous system" (p. 244). A safe relationship promotes optimal affect regulation and vice versa (Fosha, 2000), and each partner learns that emotional hurt and isolation indeed have a "solution." Moments of disconnection are then less overwhelming.

More than this, if attuned, safe connection becomes a road that both partners can reliably find, and if this trust and felt security then become integrated into their models of self and other, then a state of resonance seems to occur. Physicists speak of "resonance" as a sympathetic vibration between two elements that allows these elements suddenly to synchronize signals and act in a new harmony. This can be observed in the tight mutual coordination between infant and mother in free play. The timing of responses is exquisite, facial expressions are synchronized, emotions are shared, and the intentions of the other are anticipated. There is a correspondence, a flow that is beyond empathy and has been suggested as the source of a deep engagement with the other, or intersubjectivity (Stern, 2004). Each person knows the other's mind and recursively knows that he or she exists in this mind.

Some modern theorists speak of this kind of connection as a human need over and beyond that of secure attachment. This kind of connection can also be viewed as the flowering of the attachment process (Johnson, 2009b). As Fonagy has suggested (Fonagy & Target, 1997), secure attachment is knowing that you exist in the mind of the other. Partners in optimal softening episodes appear to resonate with each other in this fashion, to be totally present and able to synchronize moves and responses in an entirely new way. This is not just calming, but experienced as intensely rich and rewarding. Mirror neurons that fire in our brains when we watch another act intentionally, allowing us literally to feel their experience and actions in our own bodies and respond with empathy, have been proposed as a key mechanism in this kind of state.

One clinical implication here is that partners should be facing each other and paying attention to the other's nonverbal cues to create this kind of attuned connection. As a clinician, it seems to me that these moments of resonance, albeit that they have to be recreated and sustained, are the promise behind our species' obsession with romantic love. These states are characterized by intensely positive emotion and an absorption in the dance with the other. Partners speak of this in terms that remind me of the concept of flow, as defined by Csikszentmihalyi (1990).

An EFT therapist does not imagine that every couple will be able to shape this kind of bond. However, it is important to understand the enormous significance and power of the natural process that an attachment-oriented therapist is tapping into. When, for example, partners can safely focus their attention on the other and resonate with this other, we find a natural wellspring of empathy and sensitive caring even in those who, on a cognitive level, do not know "how" to be close and how to respond in a loving way. Indeed, recent attachment research finds that accessing images of loving attachment figures reliably primes softer emotions such as compassion for others (Mikulincer et al., 2001; Mikulincer, Shaver, Gillath, & Nitzberg, 2005).

The neurochemical base of attachment is also becoming clearer and helping us understand the powerful impact of key change events such as softenings. Recent research (Carter, 1998) shows that in moments of responsive emotional engagement, our brains are flooded with the "cuddle hormone" oxytocin. This neurotransmitter is produced only by mammals and is associated with states of calm, joy, and contented bliss. It seems to create a cascade of pleasure and comfort and offers a physiological basis for the safe haven that Bowlby outlined. Kerstein Uvnas-Moberg, a Swedish neuroendocrinologist, discovered that merely thinking about loved ones can trigger a release of oxytocin (1998). The administration of oxytocin also appears to increase the tendency to trust and interact with others.

How does the therapist help a couple shape powerful moments that create more secure bonding interactions, resonance, and empathy? The therapist continues to create safety and works to resolve blocks to trust, such as specific traumatic attachment injuries (Makinen & Johnson, 2006) where one partner has been abandoned or betrayed at a crucial moment of need and this unhealed injury then makes the risk of putting oneself again in another's hands untenable. The EFT therapist tracks and guides the moment-to-moment experience and interactional process, heightening partners' awareness of and ability to articulate their attachment fears and needs in enactments with their partners. The therapist also then helps the other partner to stay engaged and respond to the expression of these fears and needs. These key change events are discussed in more detail in the following chapter.

SNAPSHOT

The therapist focuses on helping Margaret, the more withdrawn partner, tune in to and articulate her deeper attachment fears, using empathic reflection, evocative questions, and interpretations to heighten Margaret's engagement in this process. By unpacking a moment in the session where she feels herself shutting down and shutting James out, Margaret is able to connect with her aloneness and her fear that she is not acceptable to her husband. At the end of her emotional exploration, she says:

I think I just feel so very separate and so deeply lonely. And that is so sad, so sad after all these years. And I am afraid. If I open up and tell you, you will get angry and that scares me. I just wither like a leaf in an icy wind. I hear that you are fed up with me. I am not whom you want. And worst of all is when part of me agrees that I am not verbal enough, strong enough, sexy enough and shouldn't even need you the way I do. This is so hard; I just put my head down and go into this shell. But I am all alone in there and that hurts.

I ask her to tell James directly the most important part of this message and she turns to look at him and says, "I am just so alone, that is why I seethe and huff. But then I can't tell you. I am so afraid of your anger and disapproval." James tears and reaches across to her. "I don't want you to feel that way," he says softly. "I am alone too." She smiles. I validate James's openness and then ask Margaret to tell him directly what she needs from him to help her with her fear and aloneness. She is able to tell him that she needs him to be less "loud and pushy" when she is trying to tell him about this and to reassure her that she is indeed precious to him. As she is able to articulate this in more detail, her voice becomes firmer and her stance more assertive.

The process of withdrawer engagement is outlined in many chapters and articles to be found on the EFT Web sites (www. eft.ca; www.iceeft.com) and in the core literature on EFT (Johnson, 2004). In general, the risks involved in voicing these fears and longings to one's partner have to be sliced thinner with couples dealing with comorbidities such as posttraumatic stress (Johnson, 2002) and this process is easier with couples who have not become mired in rigid negative patterns and are seeking to enhance their relationship (Johnson, 2008).

James has already identified that he feels "terror" when Margaret turns away from him and this "giant space" opens up between them. He is now able to engage with this feeling more deeply but has difficulty expressing this to Margaret. He believes that she will see him as "weak" and not "in control" if he does this. She is able to be encouraging and supportive. He is able to turn and tell her about the sense of "helplessness" that comes up into his throat like bile and spurs him into demanding answers and flinging stinging remarks at his wife. He tells her that he does not know what to do at this point. She is behind a wall and he has lost her. He then explores his sense of "bitter resignation" that results in him storming off to another part of the house and comes up to paralyze him whenever he begins to ask her to make love. He is then able to ask for reassurance that she will not leave him and wants to be with him. He tells her in ways that are new in their 25 years of marriage how much he needs her. She weeps and responds.

When they come in for the next session, they can give me an integrated account of these new interactions and responses and what they mean for their relationship. They also tell me that they have been able to reach for each other at home and are experiencing a sense of emotional and physical connection that is new to them. Watching them, they seem to be in synch and able to be fully engaged with each other. The levels of change here are myriad, emotional, cognitive, and behavioral as well as reshaping the relational system as a whole. James talks about how he feels empowered by his new relationship with his wife and has decided not to fill the prescription for antidepressants that is sitting on his shelf. Margaret also talks of seeing herself and James in a different light and feeling more confident and able to articulate her needs in general. Secure interactions grow a positive and resilient sense of self. People who are securely attached can generally reappraise situations, symbolically transform threats into challenges, hold onto an optimistic sense of self-efficacy and attribute undesirable events to temporary, or context dependent causes. In brief, they have learned that distress is manageable.

This kind of result fits with the now sizable body of research on the relevance of attachment theory to adult relationships (Cassidy & Shaver, 2008; Mikulincer & Shaver, 2007). Secure attachment has been found to predict such positive aspects of relationship functioning as greater commitment, trust, and satisfaction in couples; higher levels of support seeking and providing; greater intimacy and less withdrawal and verbal aggression; more sensitive and appropriate caregiving behaviors; and less jealousy. Individuals with insecurely attached spouses also report lower satisfaction and couples where both are securely attached report better adjustment than couples in which either or both partners are insecurely attached (Lussier, Sabourin, & Turgeon, 1997). This research parallels the recent findings that stress the pivotal importance of soothing and supportive responses in defining close relationships and the absolute requirement for safe emotional engagement (Gottman, 1994; Pasch & Bradbury, 1998).

NEW FRONTIERS OF ATTACHMENT
AND COUPLE INTERVENTIONS

What New Frontiers of Attachment Theory
Are Relevant for the Couple Therapist?

First, one obvious new development is the new understandings
of the physiology associated with attachment. Mirror neurons
and the cuddle hormone oxytocin have already been mentioned. The role of attachment in affect regulation can be seen
in a recent study by Coan, Schaefer, and Davidson (2006). In
this study, women were placed in an MRI machine and told that
when a light flashed they would sometimes be shocked on their
feet. Researchers could then see how the brain lit up in response
to this stressor. Being left alone in the machine maximized the
stress response in the brains of these women and the subjective
experience of pain from the shocks. When a stranger held their
hand, the stress response and pain intensity lessened. The most
significant decrease occurred when spouses were present to
hold the women's hands. This effect was directly proportional
to the women's experience of the positive quality of their connection with these partners. A sense of secure connection also
helps people process more everyday emotional experiences and
to process emotion in a way that promotes positive relationship
behaviors such as confiding or assertiveness.

On the other hand, research tells us that loneliness can
increase blood pressure to the point where the risk of heart
attack and stroke is doubled (Hawkley, Masi, Berry, & Cacioppo,
2006) and that, in men and women with congestive heart failure, the state of the patient's marriage is as good a predictor of
survival after 4 years as the severity of symptoms and degree
of impairment (Coyne et al., 2001). Also, the more belligerent
and contemptuous a partner's conflicts are, the higher the levels of stress hormones tend to be and the more depressed the
immune system is. This seems to impact processes such as
wound healing directly (Kiecolt-Glaser et al., 2005). The seemingly sentimental images of the positive and negative effects
of loving and being loved, broken hearts, and wounded bodies
are apparently more than simply images.

This kind of research increases my confidence in the power
of the interactional changes that I am working hard to create in couple sessions and makes me pay exquisite attention
to physiological changes in session or in partners' described
experiences of the relationship.

Second, Bowlby viewed love relationships as containing three basic elements: attachment, caretaking, and sex. Caretaking has been touched on in this chapter, but the links between the experience and expression of sexuality are becoming clearer and clearer (see Mikulincer & Shaver, 2007, for summary of research; Johnson & Zuccarini, in press). Securely attached partners enjoy sex more and can communicate about sexual needs and fears. Perhaps the most crucial point to come out of this new focus is that it reinforces the concept that, while attachment seems to override all other motivations, a loving relationship based on secure attachment involves an integration of bonding, caretaking, and sexuality. The attachment focus suggests that any addressing of sexual problems begin with these problems being placed in an attachment context, and that the best recipe for improved sexuality is a more secure bond.

Third, as we are able to become more and more articulate about adult love, what it means to us, how it goes wrong, and how to put it right, this framework can be used not just as a map for therapeutic change in distressed relationships but also as a guide to relationship education and enhancement. Clinical practice in EFT suggests that educating clients about the nature of love (Johnson, 2008) encourages their involvement in the therapy process and accelerates their progress toward a more secure bond. Simply because attachment theory is both a broad theory of personality development and a relational theory of love, it has the power to expand the field of couple therapy in general, allowing it to create interactions that address individual problems—such as depression, for example. It also has the same power to provide a new focus and direction for the field of relationship education. Understanding how love works also has huge significance for other aspects of love relationships, such as parenting (Neufeld & Matte, 2004; Siegel & Hartzell, 2003).

In this chapter, I have suggested that attachment theory and research clarify the goals of couple interventions. Researchers studying the stability of romantic love have challenged our field to have "higher expectations" regarding the impact we can have (Acevedo & Arons, 2009). Attachment theory gives us the same message and shows us a way to get there. Attachment deepens our awareness of the context that is necessary to support change. We do not simply need a good alliance with our clients; we also need to create a safe haven for them. This perspective also focuses the therapist on the fear and insecurity, the emotional music that dictates the dance in love relationships, and offers us a guide as to how to sculpt that dance in a therapy session so that deprivation and despair give way to resonance and resilience.

We and our families do not have to pay the price of defining love as a mystery anymore. As the French Christian mystic Pierre Teilhard de Chardin (1936) suggests, after mastering winds and waves, tides and gravity, one day "We shall harness the energies of love. And on that day, for the second time in the history of the world we shall have discovered fire." (pp. 86–87) This fire, offering light and warmth, can perhaps guide us to a new era in close relationships and a more humane society in general.

REFERENCES

Acevedo, B., & Arons, A. (2009). Does a long-term relationship kill romantic love? *Review of General Psychology, 13,* 59–65.

Bowlby, J. (1944). Forty-four juvenile thieves: Their characters and home life. *International Journal of Psychoanalysis, 25,* 19–52; 107–127. Reprinted as monograph. London, Bailliere, Tindall & Cox.

Bowlby, J. (1969). *Attachment and loss: Vol. 1. Attachment.* New York, NY: Basic Books.

Bowlby, J. (1973). *Attachment and loss: Vol 2. Separation, anxiety and anger.* New York, NY: Basic Books.

Bowlby, J. (1979). *The making and breaking of affectional bonds.* London, England: Tavistock.

Bowlby, J. (1988). *A secure base.* New York, NY: Basic Books.

Bowlby, J. (1991). Postscript. In C. M. Parkes, J. Stevenson, R. Hinde, & P. Morris (Eds.), *Attachment across the life cycle.* London, England: Routledge.

Bradley, B., & Furrow, J. (2004). Toward a mini-theory of blamer softening. *Journal of Marital and Family Therapy, 30,* 233–246.

Carter, S. (1998). Neuroendocrine perspectives on social attachment and love. *Psychoneuroendocrinology, 23,* 779–818.

Cassidy, J., & Shaver, P. R. (2008). *Handbook of attachment: Theory, research and clinical implications.* New York, NY: Guilford Press.

Coan, J. (2008). Toward a neuroscience of attachment. In J. Cassidy & P. Shaver (Eds.), *Handbook of attachment: Theory, research and clinical implications,* 2nd ed. (pp. 241–268). New York, NY: Guilford.

Coan, J., Schaefer, H., & Davidson, R. (2006). Lending a hand. *Psychological Science, 17,* 1–8.

Coombs, M., Coleman, D., & Jones, E. E. (2002). Working with feelings: The importance of emotion in the NIMH Treatment of Depression Collaborative Research Program. *Psychotherapy: Theory, Research, Practice, Training, 39,* 233–244.

Coyne, J., Rohrbaugh, M. J., Shoham, V., Sonnega, J., Nicklas, J. M., & Cranford, J. (2001). Prognostic importance of marital quality for survival of congestive heart failure. *American Journal of Cardiology, 88,* 526–529.

Csikszentmihalyi, M. (1990). *Flow: The psychology of optimal experience.* New York, NY: Harper & Row.

Davila, J., & Cobb, R. J. (2004). Predictors of changes in attachment security during adulthood. In W. S. Rholes & J. A. Simpson (Eds.), *Adult attachment: Theory, research and clinical implications* (pp. 133–156). New York, NY: Guilford Press.

Davila, J., Karney, B. R., & Bradbury, T. N. (1999). Attachment change processes in the early years of marriage. *Journal of Personality and Social Psychology, 76,* 783–802.

Ekman, P. (2003). *Emotions revealed: Recognizing faces and feelings to improve communication and emotional life.* New York, NY: Times Books.

Farber, B. A., & Metzger, J. A. (2009). The therapist as secure base. In J. H. Obegi & E. Berant (Eds.), *Attachment theory and research in clinical work with adults* (pp. 46–70). New York, NY: Guilford Press.

Feeney, B. C. (2007). The dependency paradox in close relationships. Accepting dependence promotes independence. *Journal of Personality and Social Psychology, 92,* 268–285.

Fonagy, P., & Target, M. (1997). Attachment and reflective function and their role in self-organization. *Development and Psychopathology, 9,* 679–700.

Fosha, D. (2000). *The transforming power of affect.* New York, NY: Basic Books.

Fraley, R. C., Fazzari, D. A., Bonanno, G. A., & Dekel, S. (2006). Attachment and psychological adaptation in high exposure survivors of the September 11th attack on the World Trade Center. *Personality and Social Psychology Bulletin, 32,* 538–551.

Fraley, R. C., & Waller, W. G. (1998). Adult attachment patterns: A test of the typological model. In J. A. Simpson & W. S. Rholes (Eds.), *Attachment theory and close relationships* (pp. 77–114). New York, NY: Guilford Press.

Frijda, N. H. (1986). *The emotions.* Cambridge, England: Cambridge University Press.

Goleman, D. (2006). *Social intelligence.* New York, NY: Bantam Books.

Gottman, J. (1994). *What predicts divorce?* Hillsdale, NJ: Lawrence Erlbaum Associates.

Gottman, J., Coan, J., Carrere, S., & Swanson, C. (1998). Predicting marital happiness and stability from newlywed interactions. *Journal of Marriage and the Family, 60,* 5–22.

Grabill, C. M., & Kerns, K. A. (2000). Attachment style and intimacy in friendship. *Personal Relationships, 7,* 363–378.

Greeman, P. J., Faller, G., & Johnson, S. M. (in press). Finding the words: Working with men in emotion focused therapy for couples. In D. Shepard & M. Haraway (Eds.), *Working successfully with men in couples counseling: A gender-sensitive approach.* New York, NY: Brunner Routledge.

Gross, J. (2001). Emotional regulation in adulthood. Timing is everything. *Current Directions in Psychological Science, 10,* 214–219.

Hawkley, L., Masi, C. M., Berry, J., & Cacioppo, J. (2006). Loneliness is a unique predictor of age-related differences in systolic blood pressure. *Journal of Psychology and Aging, 21,* 152–164.

Holmes, J. (2001). *The search for a secure base: Attachment theory and psychotherapy.* London, England: Routledge.

Holmes, J. (2009). From attachment research to clinical practice: Getting it together. In J. H. Obegi & E. Berant (Eds.), *Attachment theory and research in clinical work with adults* (pp. 490–514). New York, NY: Guilford Press.

Huston, T. L., Caughlin, J. P., Houts, R. M., Smith, S. E., & George, L. J. (2001). The connubial crucible: Newlywed years as predictors of marital delight, distress and divorce. *Journal of Personality and Social Psychology, 80,* 237–252.

Johnson, S. M. (2002). *Emotionally focused couple therapy with trauma survivors: Strengthening attachment bonds.* New York, NY: Guilford.

Johnson, S. M. (2003a). The revolution in couple therapy: A practitioner–scientist perspective. *Journal of Marital and Family Therapy, 29,* 365–385.

Johnson, S. M. (2003b). Introduction to attachment: A therapist's guide to primary relationships and their renewal. In S. M. Johnson & V. Whiffen (Eds.), *Attachment processes in couples and families* (pp. 3–17). New York, NY: Guilford Press.

Johnson, S. M. (2003c). Attachment theory: A guide for couple therapy. In S. M. Johnson & V. Whiffen (Eds.), *Attachment processes in couples and families* (pp. 103–123). New York, NY: Guilford Press.

Johnson, S. M. (2004). *The practice of emotionally focused couple therapy: Creating connection* (2nd ed.). New York, NY: Brunner Routledge.

Johnson, S. M. (2008). *Hold me tight: Seven conversations for a lifetime of love*. New York, NY: Little Brown.

Johnson, S. M. (2009a). Attachment theory and emotionally focused therapy for individuals and couples: Perfect partners. In J. H. Obegi & E. Berant (Eds.), *Attachment theory and research in clinical work with adults* (pp. 410–433). New York, NY: Guilford.

Johnson, S. M. (2009b). Extravagant emotion: Understanding and transforming love relationships in emotionally focused therapy. In D. Fosha, D. Siegel, & M. Solomon (Eds.), *The healing power of emotion: Affective neuroscience, development and clinical practice* (pp. 257–279). New York, NY: Norton.

Johnson, S. M., & Greenman. P. (2006). The path to a secure bond. *Journal of Clinical Psychology: In Session, 62,* 597–609.

Johnson, S. M., & Talitman, E. (1996). Predictors of success in emotionally focused marital therapy. *Journal of Marital and Family Therapy, 23,* 135–152.

Johnson, S. M., & Zuccarini, D. (2010). Integrating sex and attachment in emotionally focused couple therapy. *Journal of Marital and Family Therapy, 36,* 431–445.

Jurist, E. L., & Meehan, K. B. (2009). Attachment, mentalization and reflective functioning. In J. H. Obegi & E. Berant (Eds.), *Attachment theory and research in clinical work with adults* (pp. 71–93). New York, NY: Guilford Press.

Kiecolt-Glaser, J. K., Loving, T. J., Stowell, J. K., Malarkey, W. B., Lemeshow, S., Dickinson, S., & Glaser, R. (2005). Hostile marital interactions, proinflammatory cytokine production and wound healing. *Archives of General Psychiatry, 62,* 1377–1384.

Lussier, Y., Sabourin, S., & Turgeon, C. (1997). Coping strategies as moderators of the relationship between attachment and marital adjustment. *Journal of Social and Personal Relationships, 14,* 777–791.

Main, M., Kaplan, N., & Cassidy, J. (1985). Security in infancy. Childhood and adulthood: A move to the level of representation. In I. Bretherton & E. Waters (Eds.) Growing points of attachment theory and research. *Monographs of the Society for Research on Child Development, 50,* 66–104.

Makinen, J., & Johnson, S. M. (2006). Resolving attachment injuries in couples using emotionally focused therapy: Steps towards forgiveness and reconciliation. *Journal of Consulting and Clinical Psychology, 74,* 1055–1064.

Mikulincer, M. (1995). Attachment style and the mental representation of the self. *Journal of Personality and Social Psychology, 69,* 1203–1215.

Mikulincer, M., Gillath, O., Halevy, V., Avihou, N., Avidan, S., & Eshkoli, N. (2001). Attachment theory and reaction to others needs: Evidence that the activation of the sense of attachment security promotes empathic responses. *Journal of Personality and Social Psychology, 81,* 1205–1224.

Mikulincer, M., & Shaver, P. R. (2007). *Attachment in adulthood: Structure, dynamics and change.* New York, NY: Guilford Press.

Mikulincer, M., Shaver, P. R., Gillath, O., & Nitzberg, R. (2005). Attachment, caregiving and altruism: Boosting attachment security increases compassion and helping. *Journal of Personality and Social Psychology, 89,* 817–839.

Neufeld, G., & Matte, G. (2004). *Hold on to your kids: Why parents matter.* Toronto, Canada: Alfred A. Knopf.

Panksepp, J. (1998). *Affective neuroscience. The foundation of human and animal emotions.* New York, NY: Oxford University Press.

Parish, M., & Eagle, M. N. (2003). Attachment to the therapist. *Psychoanalytic Psychology, 20,* 271–286.

Pasch, L. A., & Bradbury, T. N. (1998). Social support, conflict and the prediction of marital dysfunction. *Journal of Consulting and Clinical Psychology, 66,* 219–230.

Roberts, L., & Greenberg, D. (2002). Observational windows to intimacy processes in marriage. In P. Noller & J. Feeney (Eds.), *Understanding marriage: Developments in the study of couple interaction* (pp. 118–149). Cambridge, England: Cambridge University Press.

Rogers, C. (1961). *On becoming a person.* Boston, MA: Houghton Mifflin.

Sauer, E. M., Lopez, F. G., & Gormley, B. (2003). Respective contributions of therapist and client adult attachment orientations to the development of the early working alliance: A preliminary growth modeling study. *Psychotherapy Research, 13,* 371–382.

Schore, A. N. (1994). *Affect regulation and the origin of self.* Mahwah, NJ: Lawrence Erlbaum Associates.

Shaver, P. R., & Mikulincer, M. (2009). An overview of adult attachment theory. In J. Obegi & E. Berant (Eds.), *Attachment theory and research in clinical work with adults* (pp. 17–45). New York, NY: Guilford Press.

Siegel, D., & Hartzell, M. (2003). *Parenting from the inside out.* New York, NY: Tarcher/Putnam.

Simpson, J., Collins, A., Tran, S., & Haydon, K. (2007). Attachment and the experience and expression of emotions in romantic relationships: A developmental perspective. *Journal of Personality and Social Psychology, 92,* 355–367.

Solomon, Z., Ginzburg, K., Mikulincer, M., Neria, Y., & Ohry, A. (1998). Coping with war captivity: The role of attachment style. *European Journal of Personality, 12,* 2710.

Stern, D. N. (2004). *The present moment in psychotherapy and everyday life.* New York, NY: Norton.

Teilhard de Chardin, P. (1975). *Toward the future.* New York, NY: Harcourt Brace Jovanovich.

Tronick, E. Z. (1989). Emotions and emotional communication in infants. *American Psychologist, 44,* 112–119.

Uvnas-Moberg, K. (1998). Oxytocin may mediate the benefits of positive interactions and emotions. *Psychoendocrinology, 23,* 819–835.

Three

New Insights Into Change in Emotionally Focused Couple Therapy

BRENT BRADLEY

INTRODUCTION

The process of change in emotionally focused couple therapy (EFT) is being strenuously researched in ongoing process studies (Bradley & Furrow, 2004, 2007; Makinen & Johnson, 2006; Naaman, Pappas, Makinen, Zuccarini, & Johnson-Douglas, 2005). These studies are removing any veil of vagueness and erroneous suggestions that EFT is a "personality-specific" or "guru" model. The recently unearthed processes of change identified in the resolution of attachment injuries and softening events, for example, provide uniquely detailed maps for focused intervention. These new "minitheories" (Bradley & Johnson, 2005) tap into therapist and client responses and bring to light the precise interventions used to navigate successfully through transforming shifts in individual responses and interactional patterns in EFT.

The process research base in EFT stands in stark contrast to other couple therapy approaches. These studies serve to hold a reflective mirror up continually to the EFT moment-to-moment change process. This kind of research adds, refines, and tweaks the approach as more is learned about what is effective across a litany of complaints and clinical populations. The approach also shares an emphasis on emotion and attachment theory with other experiential individual and family therapy approaches such as attachment family therapy (Hughes, 2007) and accelerated experiential dynamic psychotherapy for individuals (Fosha, 2000). The EFT process research aimed at how change happens sets it apart from those and all other couple therapy approaches.

This zest for research, however, does not end with process research. Since its inception in the mid-1980s, this model has been quantitatively examined repeatedly. Further setting it apart, EFT (Greenberg & Johnson, 1988; Johnson, 2004) is now one of only two empirically validated approaches to couple therapy (Lebow, Chambers, Christensen, & Johnson, in press). (For a thorough review of the empirical and process research in EFT, please see Chapter 1 in this volume.) EFT therapists can go forth with a healthy sense of confidence, utilizing detailed, researched maps of the difficult and bumpy terrain on the road named "change."

This chapter is written within and adds to the rich tradition of identifying key elements of change in EFT. To work with emotion successfully, it is paramount to understand exactly what emotion is and the critical role it plays in creating change. The first section of this chapter offers a clear definition and explanation of emotion and how it is utilized in EFT. An understanding of emotion, however, is not sufficient to practice this approach effectively. Attachment theory, with its systemic emphasis on affectual bonds, the nature of relational distress, and the declaration of healthy interdependence from cradle to grave, is the conceptualizing force that steadily guides the EFT therapist. Attachment theory and EFT, along with recent findings in neuroscience, are explained in the second section of this chapter.

There are certain emotion-laden constants in the effective practice of EFT. These constants are vital throughout the duration of therapy. The third section identifies three key constants, or fundamentals, and places them under the microscope, specifying how to utilize them immediately in practice. The real bread and butter of change in EFT is the "within" and "in-between" sequence underlying this systemic or relational approach. The therapist in this model is constantly moving into one's primary emotion or affect, processing this deeply, and then moving the focus to the other partner, replaying with feeling what just emerged into awareness, and diving into the other partner's immediate experience of being impacted by it. The fourth section captures a recurring emotional interactional sequence in which the EFT therapist anchors to create intrapersonal (inside) and interpersonal (in-between) lasting change.

IN THE BEGINNING: EMOTION AND CHANGE IN EFT

In the early days of EFT, long before any research studies, this approach emerged from the detailed observation of session recordings and an active search for how change occurred and what worked across a range of experiential and systemic interventions. Johnson brought to the equation an increasing respect for the work of John Bowlby and attachment theory, although at the time of this model's formulation, this theory was not extensively applied to adult relationships.

The first process study on EFT (Johnson & Greenberg, 1988) found that the presence of high levels of client experiencing of emotion—that is, a deepening of emotion—and the presence of new, more engaged interactions based on the expression of deeper, "softer" emotions keenly mediated success in the approach. Johnson and Talitman (1997) also found that the element of the alliance that indicated the relevance of the key tasks of EFT to partners and their willingness to engage in these tasks—namely, exploring and deepening emotions and engaging in new enactments—predicted success in the approach. Consistently, high levels of experiencing and the presence of more open and responsive interactions appear to be crucial to change in EFT. Bradley and Furrow (2004, 2007) have since examined the moment-by-moment process of change in crucial Stage 2 "softening" events. Similarly, Coombs, Coleman, and Jones (2002) found that, in individual therapy for depression, the collaborative exploration of emotion—rather than educative and coaching ways of working with emotion—predicts success across models of therapy.

It would seem that any approach to working with couples has to have a systemic understanding of how to conceptualize and handle negative and positive in session emotion (Johnson, 2009). Emotion in EFT is viewed as a verb. It is an active, ongoing construction, created by an individual from elements such as perceptions, bodily sensations, thoughts, meanings, and action tendencies. It is a powerful motivational force in human lives, especially in key human relationships. When we slow down enough to pay attention to what our emotions are telling us, we tap into a uniquely adaptive built-in guidance system. This emotional system takes into account all of our lived experience and changes us as new experiences occur. We now know, for example, that infants partake in an emotional neural moment-by-moment interactional dance with their primary caretakers long before the brain is able to form words or beliefs. The engagement in this dance actually shapes the brain and the manner in which we learn to relate to our ongoing experience (Stern, 2000; Trevarthen, 2009).

Emotion is a profound, powerful, and potent agent of change. When properly used, emotion generates hot new meanings that motivate us to action and usher in new, fresh ways of seeing ourselves and those we love (Johnson, 2009). Bowlby (1988) referred to these as internal models of self and other. He found that we relate to others from within an affective state of more or less felt security. When felt security is missing we tend to regulate our emotions by anxiously intensifying them or by avoiding and dismissing them. Attachment theorists also find, however, that we can deploy different emotion regulation strategies with different attachment figures. It seems that the other person's messages in relational interactions have the power to impact the strategy employed.

In EFT, the focus is not only on cognitive models cued by affective signals but also on delineating the automatic procedural maps for affect regulation—that is, how one deals with, integrates, pushes away, or acts upon one's own affect in times of relational distress. This has significant consequences for how therapists both conceptualize and treat couples. In EFT, rather than seeing a client as being "avoidantly attached," as if this strategy defines a person, therapists focus on how each partner seems to use a certain attachment/emotional strategy *with the significant other* at specific times of distress. Although Bowlby did not talk extensively on how to work with emotions in his writings, he did state that emotion was essentially about communication. Emotion comprises a set of signals to the self and to others about one's own state and basic survival needs. Adult attachment theorists Mikulincer and Shaver (2007) refer to attachment strategies as the *emotional regulating features* of adult attachment.

Emotion can be broken into three categories: primary or core; secondary or more surface reactive emotions, such as reactive anger; and instrumental or manipulative expressions (Greenberg & Johnson, 1988; Johnson, 2004). Primary emotions (often referred to as "affect" or "attachment affect") are the initial "gut felt" experiences or tinges that course through us almost instantaneously. Attachment affect is especially compelling in situations of perceived threat or distress. When Robert's wife, for example, sits down next to him and calmly says, "I'd like for us to talk about our relationship for a minute,"

Robert can immediately feel his body stiffen. In an instant, Robert's brain and body are in a state of red-hot alert.

Panksepp (2009) refers to this panic or fearful state as a "raw affective consciousness" that has a mind of its own and can steamroll over cognitive awareness (p. 18). This initial, raw, felt sense is home to Robert's primary emotional experience. The EFT therapist is not looking simply to "name" primary emotion (as in choosing a label from a word list of feelings, for example). Rather, the road to change is paved by experientially processing the primary emotion from within this core affective state. The vague rawness becomes much clearer, allowing for new sensations and meanings to surface and for new associated responses or action tendencies to emerge that motivate the client toward healthy change. Robert realizes that the panic coursing through his veins represents a real fear that his wife might actually say that she is unhappy in the relationship, and that she is uncertain about her future with him. "I really had no conscious idea that my fear was about that," Robert later said to the therapist. "I think it's just always been this powerful fear reaction to her, and I've learned to say something that would throw her off-track."

Robert would then respond in reaction to his fear. His secondary emotional reaction would usually be one of irritation centered around a content issue, such as being frustrated with his wife because her expectations of him are too high. "I pick up our daughter from school every day," Robert typically would say. "But it's never enough." Robert's wife then typically would respond to what he revealed to her (which is his reactive/defensive secondary state) and this then pulled her into either attack or defend responses. This couple, like so many others, then would fall into a negative interactional cycle based on content differences and disagreements that, in fact, had little to do with the core attachment issues in their relationship.

Instrumental emotion refers to using emotion to manipulate others. For example, sometimes Robert gets upset with his wife when she begins to ask him if they can talk about their relationship. Robert does not like the initial strong affective state that this conversation brings forth, but on some level he's also learned that, if he gets angry or frustrated, he throws the conversation off-track. In these scenarios, when Robert shows frustration, it leads to his wife reacting to his frustration, which then takes the couple into a totally different place where a negative interactional cycle is fueled by secondary emotional reaction. At times Robert uses a show of emotion to manipulate his wife out of talking about their relationship in serious ways. He intentionally plays a role of being frustrated or angry for the benefit it brings, which is a sidetracking of a much more serious attachment-based conversation with his wife.

In EFT, the immediate, often unacknowledged primary affective states of sadness, fear, panic, and shame (Bradley & Furrow, 2004, 2007; Johnson, 2004; Panksepp, 2009) hold the key, when processed, to changing negative interactional cycles into positive bonding cycles. The new ensuing positive bonding cycles are laced with powerful positive emotions (Fosha, 2000). Thinking "about" one's emotions is not enough to produce change (Trevarthen, 2009). Furthermore, deep processing of attachment affect with each partner individually is not enough to create relationship change. It is the *within* and *in-between* deep processing of attachment affect that, in turn, unleashes transforming positive emotions that leads to lasting change (Johnson, 2004, 2009).

For example, when Robert "experientially understands" his fear and panic that his wife might find him deficient, the therapist helps him move toward alleviating this fear by risking and confiding in his wife, which then pulls her to reassure Robert that he is the one she wants. They find each other in a new, safe place, replete with positive emotions that serve as a kind of bonding glue as they flow into new positive cycles of interaction. In this process, Robert changes his procedural map for how to work with his emotions, finds out that they are indeed workable and to be trusted, and experiences new, positive emotions with his wife and in relation to himself.

EMOTION, ATTACHMENT, AND NEUROSCIENCE

We have entered into a new era of understanding what emotion is, how it is processed, and how it shapes and is processed by the brain. We are now learning how emotional states are mediated by the presence of those emotionally close, safe, and accessible to us—be it in person or in mind. Physical contact with a safe loved one can, for example, change how we perceive and respond to threat and pain (Coan, Schaefer, & Davidson, 2006).

Neuroscientists describe our brain as a distinct social organ, requiring engagement with others for proper social development and modulation (Goleman, 2006; Schore, 1994).

Our limbic system, in the midpart of our brain, processes sensory information from the world and body-based information in two distinctly significant ways: fast and slow (Cozolino, 2002; Le Doux, 2002). The fast system typically operates on nonverbal signals and is relatively automatic, fast acting, and mostly unconscious. This processing is especially oriented to the fear response, which allows for rapid response to signals related to survival. This system readies an individual for fight or flight. Conversely, the slower system operates by allowing us to use our higher cortical functions to consider and think about the stimulation occurring. This slower process is more deliberate and more conscious. Mated couples are in a constant neural duet, transmitting their emotional states right brain to right brain on a moment-to-moment basis. Schore (1994) suggests that this physical and emotional synchrony and coordination are an innate part of interpersonal connection and bonding.

Neuroscience provides a conceptual framework that gives the EFT therapist a deeper understanding of what is actually being transmitted between partners during enactments and states of profound emotional dysregulation (Johnson, 2009). It also suggests that attempts simply to go around or "control" these responses by instructions or cognitive frames are unlikely to be successful. As Gross (2001) suggests, suppression of emotions is hard work and, as such, actually heightens arousal. This arousal is then conveyed to a partner; this, in-turn, heightens this person's arousal.

Moreover, neuroscientist Jim Coan's (2008) recent imaging research demonstrates that the brain starts from a baseline that *assumes social networks and relational partners* rather than a unit of one. The "baseline" human emotion regulation strategy is most likely *social* in nature rather than individually based. Additionally, this research suggests that distance from relational partners increases threat sensitivity. These findings seem to provide additional evidence for the central place of attachment-related fear in couple therapy.

From an attachment perspective, the goal of effective psychotherapy is the facilitated integration of emotion, which then allows for a coherent sense of self and a way of being in the world (Siegel, 2009). As we are "seen" (which gives a feeling of being real and connected with another—of not being alone) and "safe" (when we have the sense of emotional connection with another), we develop a sense of "inner security." Painful or negative emotional states, such as feeling unsafe, closed off, or well defended, diminish our level of emotional integration and "paralyze" our thinking. If we are not "seen" at times of increased arousal, emotions such as anger, fear, sadness, and shame overwhelm us and can, over time, lead to negative internal views of self and others. Entrenched, negative perceptions can serve to lock us into rigid and repeated patterns of behavior. Every couple therapist is familiar with these fixed, looping patterns of thought, perception, feeling, and action that can lock us in, shut us down, and shut others out.

According to EFT, the restructuring of emotional responses and interactions leads to increased emotional safety, openness, and shared vulnerability in the relationship. This process results in a shared sense of safety for the couple—a secure base—that is demonstrated by mutually increased emotional accessibility and responsiveness. This secure base fosters autonomy and the confidence needed to be separate. Individuation is placed in the context of and arises from integrated needs for connection with others. Concepts such as enmeshment and differentiation are seen through the lens of attachment fear and insecurity.

To conclude, EFT views effective emotional regulation and integration and the resulting increased emotional accessibility and responsiveness to others as the basic building block of loving relationships and personal effectiveness. The sequence of processing emotion, clarifying, and shifting emotional signals between partners starts early in EFT. The following section presents three important fundamentals that significantly intensify the impact of working with attachment affect. Because the central issue in any short-term approach to therapy is finding and keeping a clear focus that allows the therapist to stay on target and build momentum for change, it is important now to explain these organizing fundamentals.

FUNDAMENTALS OF EFT: HARNESSING THE POWER OF EMOTION

Comprehending and applying the following fundamentals provides the EFT therapist a set of guidelines to harness the power of emotion throughout the course of treatment. While these are referred to as fundamentals, they are not basic or elementary. If these fundamentals are not mastered, EFT becomes stunted and effectiveness is limited. Just as the hurdle-sprinter, with practice and grit, eventually commits the necessary strides and leaps to muscle memory, so too must the EFT therapist commit the following organizing fundamentals to therapist muscle memory:

1. Attachment theory paves the way.
2. Emotional processing is the "yellow brick road." Follow it.
3. The therapist's emotional presence and use of self step into and make sense of powerful core affect states.

Fundamental 1. Attachment Theory Paves the Way

Attachment theory provides EFT with a constant focal point. In every session, attachment theory points out what is important. Attachment is also the common human denominator between therapist and couple. Joe and Rebecca come to couple therapy, for example, with "communication problems." In the first session Joe reports that he is upset because Rebecca does not care about his career and how hard he works. "All she talks about is her job, and how she works and how she takes care of the kids," Joe said. "I appreciate that, you know...but I feel like I am on an island with my career. I get no credit. Maybe we need to negotiate what chores I do. Maybe that will solve this problem."

Using an attachment lens, the therapist will assess how Joe's career seems to leave him feeling shut out from the family, alone, and emotionally disconnected from Rebecca. This leaves him questioning whether he is a good husband and father. This, in turn, scares him. On the other hand, the therapist will be interested in how Rebecca seems to be the parent in charge of daily care of the children. Rebecca appears exhausted, with too many plates spinning in the air simultaneously. This situation leaves her also feeling alone in caring for the children, and she cannot shake this fear that if Joe really saw how she does not have it all together, he may not like that, and he may be disappointed in her as a wife. The prospect of this scares her.

To use EFT effectively, processing attachment affect must be at the core of the therapeutic process. All of therapy, including therapist's mind-set and interventions, targets the bonding aspect of the relationship. The following transcript exemplifies the attachment implications underlying the practice of EFT. This dialogue takes place in session six, with the couple still in Stage 1.

Rebecca: Oh, I feel it there too. (Tears run down her cheek.)

Therapist (softly): Yeah? What's happening inside now? I see your tears; what's happening inside as we talk about this? (*evocative responding*)

Rebecca: I feel bad because he sees me as a nag. But I need his help. I can't carry this much of the load anymore. And I am afraid that he won't change to help me more.

Therapist: You really need him to help you more. But you're afraid that he won't do that, that he won't really get how tired you are...how this overwhelms you....how sad it leaves you...and how much you need him, right? (She nods yes.) It's him you need. (*heightening, attachment reframe*)

Author comment: The therapist reframes emotion from an attachment perspective. Rebecca is not just sad, for example. She is sad because she misses him, and she needs him and his help.

Rebecca: I am sad. And I do feel so far from him.

Therapist: You said you were afraid that he won't heed your calls for help. Can you tell me more about that fear, please? (*evocative responding*)

Rebecca (more tears): I am scared that this will not reach him. I am afraid that he won't come to me and help me.

Therapist: You're afraid that he won't take this seriously...That he won't see your pain? (*reflecting underlying emotion*)

Therapist (to Joe): What happens inside right now as you see your wife so sad...crying because she's afraid that you might not see how much she needs your help? She's afraid that right now you might not see her pain...might not respond to her call...might turn away. (*evocative responding, heightening*)

Author comment: The therapist "sets the table" by replaying with emphasis how she needs him, how she is in pain, etc. This attachment affect focus begins to pull empathy from him and begins to pull him to see her need and move into helping her.

Joe: I feel sad for her.

Therapist: You hear her now and you feel sad? Tell me more, please, about this sadness. Is this new for you, this sadness? (*reflecting primary emotion, evocative responding*)

Author comment: The therapist focuses in on her present experience of sadness.

Joe: Well, I've heard her nag me before about helping. I've heard that a lot. But I don't think I ever realized that it...scared her this much or that she was afraid that I would never come and help her. I think before I just saw it as her nagging me. And that made me feel like I wasn't being a good husband and father. I never really understood the deepness of this.

Author comment: The therapist is careful always to focus dialog with each individual partner in the context of the other partner. This is another example of an attachment focus.

Therapist (to Joe): OK, I think I see. Before you just saw her as criticizing you as a parent and husband. You didn't see her pain. (Therapist speaks slowly.) But now...as she sits and *really* shows you her vulnerability, this helps you see how overwhelmed she is, and how much she *really* needs you? (*heightening, evocative responding*)

Author comment: Her needing his help with the kids and dinner is placed within an attachment focus of her needing his help—the "him" is heightened even more than the chores. Used in this manner, her sadness and fear pull for him to offer support and comfort to her. Support and comfort in this scenario are tied to helping with the children and with dinner.

Joe: I had no idea that you were so burdened by this. No idea that you were afraid like this. I am so sorry honey... so sorry. (He tears up.)
Therapist: You want to help her more? You want to let her know that you will be there for her in this? (*heightening*)
Joe: Yes. I will.
Therapist: Share this with her please, now, in your own words. (*restructuring interactions*)

Author comment: The idea is that her sense of being overburdened, overwhelmed, and afraid of having always to do this all alone **pulls** *the husband to move toward her with his help and support.*

Fundamental 2. Emotional Processing Is the Yellow Brick Road. Follow It.

The practice of EFT involves moment-by-moment tuning in and attending to bodily movements such as shifts in a chair, eye movements, sighs, deep breaths, watering eyes, and such. These slight movements are seen as invites into unacknowledged affect, which is believed to be sending messages of healthy needs and wants (Johnson, 2004). When these messages are blocked from current awareness, trouble ensues. Key words emerge that the therapist has to note, hold, and use as handles to open the door into deeper feelings at appropriate moments or when clients cannot move into these feelings. If a client speaks of feeling a "dark dread," for example, the therapist uses this phrase again and again to evoke emotions and work with them.

An attachment perspective gives priority to fear and strategies for handling fear. Attachment affect is often couched in terms of fear—fears concerning the relationship itself (perhaps loss and abandonment) and fears surrounding how people feel about themselves in their cores (rejection and despair at the apparent unworthiness of the self). In attachment theory, models of self and models of other are saturated with primary emotion (Bowlby, 1988). New and more integrated emotional experience in Stage 2 of EFT fosters the revision of these models. The therapist learns to sit comfortably *in emotion* with clients without always knowing where this emotion will lead. The EFT therapist has to learn to trust the logic behind emotional exploration. Both attachment theory and EFT stress the central belief that *impaired affect regulation is the core issue underlying most constricted responses seen in therapy* (Johnson & Bradley, 2009).

The following is a transcript from a session taking place within Step 5 of EFT—the most individually oriented intrapersonal step in this approach. It illustrates tracking, evoking, and heightening emotion, which allows for the integration of attachment affect into present experience and awareness.

Session 7

Joe: I keep saying how sorry I am for having this affair...but I get to a place where *saying* it fails to show how sorry I really am.

Therapist: You say it and say it, and yet that comes up short for you. (*heightening*)

Joe (nods head in agreement): Yeah. It's frustrating. (He sighs deeply, looks down, and tears start to well up in his eyes.)

Therapist (softer and with emphasis): You *really* want her to get how sorry you are. (*heightening*)

Joe: I really do.

Therapist (more slowly and softly): And as you say this, I see tears welling up in your eyes...What's happening inside right now for you? (*heightening, evocative responding*)

Author comment: Immediate bodily-felt experiences are signposts or "entry points" into attachment-related affect.

Joe: I feel stuck. What else can I do?

Therapist: Let's stay with the tears for right now. What's happening inside? Do you feel it somewhere? (*evocative responding*)

Joe: Yes. I feel it in my throat and chest. It gets real tight. (He begins to tear again.)

Therapist: It's in your throat and chest, and there are the tears again. (He nods.) What's going on? What is the tightness in your chest and throat, and tears—what are they saying? What are they about? Help me understand here. (*reflecting underlying emotion, evocative responding*)

Joe (takes a deep breath): I know I've done a terrible thing. And I feel bad about that every single day. I also long for her to begin to trust me again. Just a little.

Therapist: OK. When you are still, and you allow yourself to really feel—the message is about feeling terrible about the affair on the one hand, and on the other there's a longing for her to begin trying to trust you again—just a little bit—is that close? (*tracking and reflecting primary emotion*)

Joe: Yes. That's right on. I think if she could trust me a little, I wouldn't let her down, and it would make things easier on her, too, because I know she worries.

Therapist: You want her to begin risking trusting you again, even if just a little to start off with. And you're saying, "I won't let you down," right? "I want and need some of your trust. That would mean so much to me...give me hope." Is that close? (*heightening*)

Joe: Yes. I do. And it would mean a lot to me.

Therapist: Right. And when you allow yourself to really feel, you feel these things in your chest...and in your throat, right? (He nods.) It's like these bodily things are signs for you...Like they point to something important for you. (*heightening*)

Joe (takes a deep breath): Yes, they do.

Therapist: Can you turn and share this experience with her now? Share with her how painful this is for you, and how you really want her to risk beginning to trust you again? In your own words, please share with her now. (*heightening, restructuring interactions*)

Author comment: The therapist trusts the emotional unfolding. She stays with it, nicely reflects, heightens, and then asks him to turn to his wife and speak from it.

Fundamental 3. The Therapist's Emotional Presence and Use of Self Step Into and Make Sense of Powerful Core Affect States

Sometimes the client has difficulty finding attachment affect or may be unclear of his or her internal emotional experience. Clients have different levels of emotional intelligence. There are times when the therapist must step *farther into* a client's experience and heighten attachment affect to help the client experience it more vividly. Therapists need to learn to use themselves as emotional "weather vanes" of sorts. At best, therapists can move into the kind of emotional resonance with a client that a responsive mother moves into with a confused or dysregulated child. The therapist then connects with her own range of experience to put herself in a client's shoes. She asks herself, "What must it feel like to be this person in this situation right now?" and then finds the answer within herself. This is not a cool cognitive search; it is an emotive search.

Subsequently, it is often helpful for the therapist to relay his or her own present internal experience back to the client in a style that describes and explores emotion rather than labeling it. The therapist then describes the experience of *being* sad, or *being* alone, or *being* afraid, etc. The therapist "tastes" just a little of that affective state to feed it back to the client tentatively. This is done with the hope of taking the client *one step farther into* the experience (Johnson, 2004). The following transcript is an illustration of the therapist doing this well.

Session 12

Rebecca: Yeah, I get afraid that if he really sees the real me, he won't like it much. You know, like when you see things on TV and you don't like it, you turn the channel. (She laughs nervously.)

Therapist: It's that light for you? As easy as turning a channel? You take it that lightly that he may not like what he sees? (*evocative responding*)

Rebecca: Well, no. I mean, if he left me it would hurt. We both know that.

Therapist: What's it like for you to consider that he may leave you if he really sees you? (*evocative responding*)

Rebecca: I don't really go there much. It's not helpful to worry, you know?

Therapist: Well, I agree, it's not really helpful to worry. But I am not sure he has any idea of what happens inside you...of how much he means to you...of how afraid you get. (*heightening*)

Rebecca: No, he probably doesn't.

Therapist: I need to understand that. Can you help me here please? What's it like inside when you get afraid that if he sees you, he may not like what he sees? (*heightening, evocative responding*)

Rebecca: He just might not like it. That's all. That's all there is to it.

Author comment: The therapist uses heightening and evocative responding to move farther into the client's emotional experience, but to no avail. The therapist must stay with it.

Therapist: That's all there is to it? I don't know...I am trying to understand this, trying to feel it in myself... Help me out here, but if I am afraid that if my partner sees me, and I mean *really* sees me, the parts I don't show *anyone*...and I am afraid that he will not like that, won't like *me* if he *really* sees *me*...I don't know how you live with that. I mean, to me, that feels like it would be amazingly scary. (*heightening, empathic conjecture/interpretation*)

Rebecca: It is. (She looks down.)

Therapist: Yeah. Can you please tell me more about this scary place? (*evocative responding*)

Rebecca: You spend your whole life hiding. There's always this part of you that you know not to show...to anyone. And you're right, it is amazingly scary.

Therapist: This is a place you've spent a lot of your life in hiding from anyone. (*heightening*)

Rebecca: Oh yeah. I've learned not to show it. People don't like it.

Therapist: You're saying, "I don't dare let him see that part of me. He'll despise it. Everyone else has." Right? And what would it be like if you risked showing him this part? And he did despise it? What would that be like for you? (*heightening, evocative responding*)

Author comment: When the therapist moves to his own internal felt sense to feel what may be going on inside the client, he is using his own sense of self. EFT describes this as the attachment affect being allowed into one's experience in the moment so that the associated "hot meaning" becomes clear and the client fully senses his or her attachment fears and wants. Clients can tolerate this experience with the help of the empathic presence of the therapist. The client can then risk owning and showing this unlovable part to the partner. This kind of interpersonal resonance and emotional integration imprints the experience of attachment security into our very being. It potentiates mental health and adaptive responding (Siegel, 2009).

INTERACTIONAL CHANGE IN EFT: THE ABCS OF PROCESSING EMOTION WITHIN AND IN-BETWEEN

While in Stage 1 the de-escalation of a couple's negative cycle is a crucial first step, the most impactful work in EFT is the successful completion of the Stage 2 change events of withdrawer reengagement and blamer softening. These two change events foster emotional engagement and secure bonding. The within and in-between contour in these key change events is the culmination and intensification of a similar generic emotional process starting in early sessions and continuing throughout treatment. An understanding of this generic sequence of tracking, exploring, and expressing attachment affect to restructure attachment responses is vital to success in EFT. While the sequence presented here is not meant to replace the Step 7 withdrawer engagement or blamer softening minitheory (see Bradley & Furrow, 2004; Johnson et al., 2005), those culminating events only become possible through the continual use of the generic sequence presented here.

The EFT therapist continually works to

1. Distill and deepen attachment affect
2. Guide a client into sharing and expanding this attachment affect with a partner
3. Focus the client on and explore this experience of sharing
4. Encourage the other partner to stay engaged and process this new message
5. Structure engaged congruent responses by this other partner
6. Reflect and integrate this sequence of new responses into the self of partners and the relationship system

What follows is a case scenario and transcript vignettes illustrating each move in the sequence and key associated interventions.

CASE SCENARIO

Robert and Connie had been married for 12 years. They came to therapy because Connie was worried about their relationship:

> We've gotten stuck in just taking care of the day-to-day things. We do that well. We take care of the kids well. We are good parents. But the "us" in this marriage has suffered. I love him, but I don't know him like I used to. It seems everything I do pisses him off and he walks away. I am at my wits end!

In Stage 1 of EFT, the couple got a good taste of their cycle, with Connie touching her anger easily, and slowly easing into her primary sadness and loneliness. Robert found this surprising, as he had no idea that Connie missed him. Robert had fallen into a rut of listening to Connie's frustration, defending himself, and then retreating as Connie overwhelmed him with her anger. The therapist slowed things down with Robert and was able to access the sense of inadequacy underlying his sensitivity to Connie's frustration.

The key to cycle de-escalation in Stage 1 is the slow tracking of the cycle so that both partners *repeatedly experience the affect underlying the positions* they take in the cycle.

As they both entered into Stage 2, the cycle had de-escalated, they felt closer, and the stage was set for work in Steps 5 and 6.

The therapist now went deeper into Robert's sense of feeling inadequate as a husband, which came to the surface during and after times of conflict between the two. The reason for deepening attachment affect is twofold: First, by sitting in his attachment affect, Robert will become experientially clearer of his feelings of inadequacy, and how this keeps him withdrawing. This will bring his attachment needs and wants to the surface, and his emotions will galvanize him toward getting his attachment needs met, and thus assuage his negative affect. Second, Connie will "get" how powerful these feelings are for Robert and how painful it is for him to feel like he is inadequate for her. This will impact her ability to respond positively to him.

As is the case most of the time in EFT, what is being processed with one partner simultaneously sends strong messages and has a powerful impact on the other. In EFT, partners change and grow each other (Johnson, 1999). When deepening attachment affect, the therapist often uses empathic conjecture, evocative responding, heightening, and restructuring interactions through choreographed enactments (Johnson, 2004).

1. Distill and Deepen Attachment Affect (Session 9)

Therapist: Robert, what happens to you when Connie gets so frustrated with you? (*evocative responding*)

Robert: Well, once again, on some level I start to stiffen, you know, like I just want to protect myself and get out of here.

Therapist: Yes, a part of you says, "Oh no. Here we go again," right? (He nods.) "I am not pleasing her. I've done something to disappoint her yet again." (*heightening*)

Author comment: The therapist takes a "first-person stance" when using parts language, speaking as the client, in the client's voice. This has the effect of "stepping in" to the client's experience more.

Robert: Yep. I hate that feeling.

Therapist: You hate it. Can you tell me more about this please? What's it like for you to be in this place? (*evocative responding*)

Robert: I've failed again. (He looks down to the floor.)

Therapist: You failed her once again. It's never enough. You always come up short. (*heightening*) Robert, what is it like to be a husband in this place? A place in which you find yourself coming up short with your wife... Failing her as a husband. (*evocative responding*)

Author comment: There is something very helpful in not just processing attachment affect, but actually moving a step forward and into what it is like being in such a position as a husband, wife, or partner. This often further intensifies immediate experiencing.

Robert: It's terrible. I always wanted to be a good husband. That's always been my dream. And here I am, failing at it...Disappointing her. Disappointing myself.
Therapist: You've always dreamed of being a good husband, and yet here you are, failing her. And failing yourself. It's like one of the worst things that could happen has come to fruition. (*heightening, empathic conjecture*)

2. Guide Sharing and Expanding Attachment Affect With Partner

Therapist: Robert, would you be able to turn to Connie and tell her a little bit about how hard it is for you when you start to touch these feelings of inadequacy? Could you begin to let her into this a little now, in your own words? (*evocative responding, restructuring interactions*)
Robert: Somehow I knew you'd ask me to do that! (He smiles.)
Therapist: It's not easy, huh? A little scary? (*validation, empathic conjecture*)

Author comment: If the client is unable to turn toward the partner and share attachment affect, it may be necessary to stop here and further process blocks to or fears of sharing and, in turn, share these first before moving on.

3. Focus on Exploring the Experience of Sharing

Robert: Yeah...Yeah, it is. But I can do it. (He turns toward Connie.) We don't argue as often as we used to before we started coming in to therapy. And we aren't as... hard on each other either, so I don't want you to hear this as criticism. But it really is true that when we fight, at some point I start to feel these feelings of inadequacy. I start to feel like...like I am a failure as a husband (tears up). I hate that feeling, man. It's...

like...this sounds weird but...I feel almost frightened. I freeze up.

Therapist: That was awesome Robert (*validation*). What was
that like for you, to tell her that you get frightened?
This is why you withdraw. You are really feeling this
right now? (Robert nods.) It takes courage to dig deep
and say, "I hate feeling like this...like I am failing as
a husband." What was that like for you? (*evocative
responding, heightening*)

Robert: It was hard but it feels good. It feels good to say it.
Better. It's real. It's a relief.

*Author comment: Robert starts to experience positive emotions
such as feeling relieved and feeling authentic as a result of the
processing of attachment affect.*

4. Encourage Processing by the Other Partner of the Shared Message

Therapist: Connie, what happens to you inside as you hear
Robert really sharing deep parts of himself with you
right now? He really risked sharing with you like
that. What happens inside as you experience him in
this way? (*evocative responding, heightening*)

*Author comment: Note how the therapist validates Robert's
risk taking. This increases the likelihood of Connie responding
positively to Robert.*

Connie: I really had no idea that Robert felt this way.

Therapist: He rarely shows you his softer...underbelly, right?
(*attachment reframe*)

Connie: That's right. I've never understood what's really going
on with you. (She looks at Robert.)

Therapist (to Connie): This is a little bit new to you? (*evocative responding*)

Connie: Very new. (She looks at Robert again.) I've never felt
you were a failure. I would never think that. I really
didn't know. I thought you couldn't care less. It is
strange to hear this. It puts me off balance.

Therapist: He doesn't show you this side of him much? This
side that starts to feel inadequate. It's confusing for
you to hear this? (*evocative responding*)

Connie: I wouldn't say confusing. I understand what he's saying. It's just that I didn't know.

Therapist: Right. You didn't know that a part of him at times feels such despair...like he's failed you. He doesn't risk showing this part, yeah? I see...how could you know!? (*heightening, validation*)

Connie: Exactly. (She looks again at Robert.)

Therapist: Can you let it in? What do you feel toward Robert right now? I notice you're looking earnestly at him; what's happening inside? (*evocative responding*)

Connie: I feel compassion for him. I feel sorry for him.

Therapist: When he shows you this vulnerable part—you like that? You feel compassion for him? (*evocative responding*)

Connie: Yes.

Author comment: The therapist now prompts for reach back with support.

5. Structure an Engaged Response by This Other Partner

Therapist: Could you tell him that now? My sense is he's really not sure what to expect, because when he begins to feel like he's failing you, he never shows that part to you. Could you share with him now how you feel compassion toward him? (*evocative responding, restructuring interactions*)

Connie: It hurts me to see that you feel like a failure. I feel sad and sorry for you. I don't want you to feel like a failure to me, Robert.

Therapist: You don't see him as a failure. You don't want him feeling that way. It actually hurts you to see him feel like a failure. (*reflecting attachment affect*)

Connie: It does hurt. I get upset with him, but I never want him to feel like a failure. (She looks at him.) I didn't know my words hurt you this badly. I will be more careful, Robert. I am sorry.

Author comment: If Connie cannot reach back without negativity, the therapist will catch any "bullet" she fires off and help her process the secondary and primary emotions that are triggered here. She will then be able to own her inability to respond to this new cue, rather than dismiss or blame her partner.

6. Reflect and Integrate This Sequence of New Responses Into Self and System

The therapist now reflects the process that has just occurred.

Therapist: So what just happened here? Robert, you realized
that you are frightened of getting this message that
you are disappointing your wife and that this sparks
your moving away from her. You shared this and,
Connie, you were able to hear it, even though it was
a bit strange and new. When Robert reaches down
deep and takes the risk to confide, you appreciate it.
You don't see him as failing you. Also, when he risks
and shares like this, your feelings for him change.
You don't want him to hurt. You have just been trying to reach him, right? (Connie nods.). Robert, you
really stepped out. You basically invited her to see
your core emotion and fears, correct? (He nods.) You,
like, lead the way toward a new kind of relating...
You invited her into a new relationship dance—a
dance of vulnerability, openness, where each of you
is "real." And when he does that, Connie, you find
your soft caring feelings for him again. That is pretty
powerful stuff guys!

The preceding sequenced moves and interventions run all
through the EFT process as expanded emotion shapes new
responses to each partner. While this outlined sequence is
not proposed as the only way to process affect with two partners or as capturing the whole nature of EFT intervention,
it does provide a map to the use of newly shaped emotions
and emotional signals in the service of changing attachment
interactions. A key to this work is the reliance not only on
affect to touch and move someone and shape new meanings
and responses, but also on the power of attachment affect to
have a strong, positive impact on the observing partner simultaneously. Over time, the coherent expression of attachment
affect pulls for partners to comfort and reassure each other.
This process offers an intrapsychic (within) and interpersonal
(between) corrective emotional experience of tuning in to and
ordering inner experience. Following this sequence allows
partners to connect emotionally with a loved one in a new and
more secure way.

CONCLUSION

Emotion, once viewed as disorganizing and unimportant in
facilitating change, is increasingly being recognized as adaptive and crucial to promoting lasting change in psychotherapy.

Attachment theory, long respected in developmental psychology, is now impacting neuroscience, social psychology, clinical psychology, and marriage and family therapy. EFT is distinct in that it has a strong base in emotion and attachment and is exemplary in its focus on both process and outcome research. The science of how partners relate and revise their relationships is at the heart of EFT. The practice of EFT is also, however, an art.

This chapter presented key fundamentals and a generic sequence for processing attachment affect within and between partners. With a clear focus and a map of the moves in the therapy tango, the therapist can, like an artist, improvise and stay in the present, discovering and creating new realities with couples. This is a process of mutual growth, however, for clients and therapists alike. This "tango" explores the most basic drama that defines us as human beings: the drama of attachment and primary emotion.

REFERENCES

Bowlby, J. (1988). *A secure base: Parent–child attachment and healthy human development.* New York, NY: Basic Books.

Bradley, B., & Furrow, J. L. (2004). Toward a mini-theory of the blamer softening event: Tracking the moment-by-moment process. *Journal of Marital and Family Therapy, 30,* 233–246.

Bradley, B., & Furrow, J. L. (2007). Inside blamer softening: Maps and missteps. *Journal of Systemic Therapies, 26,* 25–43.

Bradley, B., & Johnson, S. (2005). Task analysis in family therapy: Reaching the clinician. In D. Sprenkle & F. Piercy (Eds.), *Research methods in family therapy* (2nd ed.). (pp. 254–271). New York, NY: Guilford Press.

Coan, J. (2008). Toward a neuroscience of attachment. In *Handbook of attachment: Theory, research, and clinical applications,* 2nd ed. (pp. 241–265). New York, NY: Guilford Press.

Coan, J., Schaefer, H., & Davidson, R. (2006). Lending a hand. *Psychological Science, 17,* 1–8.

Coombs, M., Coleman, D., & Jones, E. E. (2002). Working with feelings: The importance of emotion in both cognitive behavioral and interpersonal therapy in the NIMH treatment of depression collaborative research program. *Psychotherapy: Theory, Research, Practice and Training, 39,* 233–244.

Cozolino, L. J. (2002). *The neuroscience of psychotherapy: Building and rebuilding the human brain.* New York, NY: W. W. Norton and Co.

Fosha, D. (2000). *The transforming power of affect: A model for accelerated change.* New York, NY: Basic Books.

Goleman, D. (2006). *Social intelligence: The new science of human relationships.* New York, NY: Bantam Books.

Greenberg, L., & Johnson, S. M. (1988). *Emotionally focused therapy for couples.* New York, NY: Guilford Press.

Gross, J. (2001). Emotion regulation in adulthood: Timing is everything. *Current Directions in Psychological Science, 10,* 214–219.

Hughes, D. A. (2007). *Attachment-focused family therapy.* New York, NY: W. W. Norton & Co.

Johnson, S. (1999). *Emotionally focused couple therapy: Straight to the heart. Short-term couple therapy* (pp. 13–42). New York, NY: Guilford Press.

Johnson, S. (2009). Attachment theory and emotionally focused therapy for individuals and couples: Perfect partners. In J. H. Obegi & E. Berant (Eds.), *Attachment theory and research in clinical work with adults* (pp. 410–433). New York, NY: Guilford Press.

Johnson, S., Bradley, B., Furrow, J. L., Lee, A., Palmer, G., Tilley, D., & Woolley, S. (2005). *Becoming an emotionally focused couple therapist: The workbook.* New York, NY: Brunner–Routledge.

Johnson, S., & Greenberg, L. (1988). Relating process to outcome in marital therapy. *Journal of Marital and Family Therapy, 14,* 175–183.

Johnson, S. M. (2004). *The practice of emotionally focused marital therapy: Creating connection* (2nd ed.). Philadelphia, PA: Brunner/Mazel.

Johnson, S. M., & Bradley, B. (2009). EFTHERAPIST: Emotionally focused couples therapy. In J. H. Bray & M. Stanton (Eds.), *Clinical handbook of family psychology* (pp. 402–415). Hoboken, NJ: Wiley–Blackwell Publishers.

Johnson, S. M., & Talitman, E. (1997). Predictors of success in emotionally focused marital therapy. *Journal of Marital and Family Therapy, 23,* 135–152.

Lebow, J. L., Chambers, A., Christensen, A., & Johnson, S. M. (in press). Marital distress. In D. Sprenkle & R. Chenail (Eds.), *Effectiveness research in marriage and family therapy.* Washington, DC: AAMFT.

LeDoux, J. (2002). *Synaptic self: How our brains become who we are.* New York, NY: Penguin.

Makinen, J., & Johnson, S. (2006). Resolving attachment injuries in couples using emotionally focused therapy: Steps toward forgiveness and reconciliation. *Journal of Consulting and Clinical Psychology, 74,* 1055–1064.

Mikulincer, M., & Shaver, P. (2007). *Attachment in adulthood: Structure, dynamics, and change.* New York, NY: Guilford Press.

Naaman, S., Pappas, J., Makinen, J., Zuccarini, D., & Johnson-Douglas, S. (2005). Treating attachment injured couples with emotionally focused therapy: A case study approach. *Psychiatry: Interpersonal and Biological Processes, 68,* 55–77.

Panksepp, J. (2009). Brain emotional systems and qualities of mental life: From animal models of affect to implications for psychotherapeutics. In D. Fosha, D. Siegel, & M. Solomon (Eds.), *The healing power of emotion: Affective neuroscience, development & clinical practice* (pp. 1–26). New York, NY: W. W. Norton & Co.

Schore, A. N. (1994). *Affect regulation and the origin of the self: The neurobiology of emotional development.* Hillsdale, NJ: Lawrence Erlbaum Associates.

Siegel, D. (2009). Emotion as integration: A possible answer to the question, what is emotion? The healing power of emotion: Affective neuroscience, development & clinical practice. In D. Fosha, D. Siegel, & M. Solomon (Eds.), *The healing power of emotion: Affective neuroscience, development & clinical practice* (pp. 145–171). New York, NY: W. W. Norton & Co.

Stern, D. N. (2000). The interpersonal world of the infant: A view from psychoanalysis and developmental psychology (2nd ed.). New York, NY: Basic Books.

Trevarthen, C. (2009). The function of emotion in infancy: The regulation and communication of rhythm, sympathy, and meaning in human development. In D. Fosha, D. Siegel, & M. Solomon (Eds.), *The healing power of emotion: Affective neuroscience, development & clinical practice* (pp. 55–85). New York, NY: W. W. Norton & Co.

II

APPLICATION OF EMOTIONALLY FOCUSED COUPLE THERAPY

Four

Depression
Enemy of the Attachment Bond

WAYNE H. DENTON AND ADAM D. COFFEY

INTRODUCTION

Depression is the leading cause of disability worldwide (World Health Organization, 2001). It is estimated that during a given year, nearly 7% of adults in the United States will experience a serious episode of depression and nearly 6 in 10 of those will experience severe or very severe impairment (Kessler et al., 2003). Over a 15-year span, people with unipolar depression have been found to be virtually unable to carry out their work functions for 21% of the time (Judd et al., 2008). In the United States, less than a quarter of people with serious depression receive adequate treatment, whether medication or psychotherapy (Kessler et al., 2003). Clearly, there is a great need for effective treatments of depression. Emotionally focused therapy (EFT) for couples (Johnson, 2004) offers a unique approach to alleviating the suffering of those struggling with depression and their partners, who share in this isolating journey.

IMPROVING THE TREATMENT OF DEPRESSION

Sadly, it is widely accepted that the results from studies to date with treatments of depression, while highly effective for some, are generally disappointing. Results from the STAR*D study, one of the largest studies of depression treatments ever conducted in real-world practice settings (Rush et al., 2004), illustrate this concern. Over 4,000 patients suffering with major depressive disorder were enrolled in the study from multiple clinical sites across the United States. If participants did not reach remission from an initial treatment, they received up to three additional courses of treatment. Treatments were primarily medication, although a relatively small number of participants received cognitive therapy. Overall rates of remission from depression were 37% for Step 1, 31% for Step 2, 14% for Step 3, and 13% for Step 4 (Warden, Rush, Trivedi, Fava, & Wisniewski, 2007). With each ensuing step, a lower percentage of patients reached the desired goal of freedom from depression. Overall, 30% of patients who remained in the study through all four levels of treatment—a period of nearly 1 year—never achieved remission (Warden et al., 2007).

A person receiving state-of-the-art depression treatment with either medication or psychotherapy has less than a 50% chance of being free of depression upon completion of treatment. Discouraging statistics have recently led the director of the National Institute of Mental Health (NIMH) to conclude that "with optimal care...too many people will not recover" (Insel, 2009, p. 129). In response, the NIMH has developed a new strategic plan charting a research course that may hold promise for new approaches (National Institute for Mental Health, 2008). The strategic plan lists four opportunities for progress, including the development of personalized treatment approaches (as opposed to studies where everyone receives the same treatment) and fully harnessing the untapped power of psychosocial treatments (Insel, 2009).

Not every person with serious depression is in a relationship and not all in a relationship are experiencing relational discord. However, for those people experiencing both serious depression and relational discord, evidence is emerging that emotionally focused couples therapy may be a useful addition to a personalized approach to treatment selection (Denton, Wittenborn, & Golden, 2010; Dessaulles, Johnson, & Denton, 2003).

Relationship Discord and Depression Go Hand in Hand

Depression can be devastating on relationships, and relationship discord can have deleterious effects on mood. The association between depression and relational discord is well established (Whisman, 2001). There is evidence to support the belief that depression can lead to relational discord and, conversely, that relational discord can lead to depression. Relational distress puts individuals at risk for depression. In a random community sample of 904 people, those with relational discord were nearly three times more likely to be in a major depressive episode 1 year later than those without relational discord (Whisman & Bruce, 1999). The authors also found that when all participants were included—those without relationships and those with nondiscordant relationships—nearly 30% of new major depressive episodes over the course of the year were associated with marital dissatisfaction.

People who have experienced an episode of major depression are significantly more likely to experience divorce (Kessler, Walters, & Forthofer, 1998). Relationships with a depressed partner are often characterized by more negative communication, such as blame, withdrawal, and verbal aggression. These relationships also exhibit less positive communication, such as self-disclosure, problem solving, smiling, and eye contact (reviewed in Rehman, Gollan, & Mortimer, 2008). Depressive symptoms such as irritability, loss of motivation, loss of the ability to experience pleasure, and loss of sexual interest can create serious strain in any relationship. Living with a depressed person can itself lead to depression (Coyne et al., 1987). The impact of depression on a couple's relationship and the higher incidence of relational distress suggests that couple therapy would be useful to many people suffering from depression, yet few clinical treatments focus on the unique issues couples face in dealing with depression.

How Depression Is Diagnosed

The current standards for diagnosing clinically relevant depression focus on symptoms such as disturbed sleep or appetite, loss of energy, poor concentration, etc. In the *Diagnostic and Statistical Manual of Mental Disorders, Fourth Edition, Text Revision* (DSM-IV-TR) (American Psychiatric Association, 2000), which is widely used in the United States, this condition is referred to as "major depressive disorder." Other parts of the world may use the *International Classification of Diseases,* which utilizes a similar symptom-based classification (World Health Organization, 1992).

It would be more accurate to say "major depressive syndrome" than "disorder" because the classification describes, but does not explain, the phenomenon of serious depression. There is evidence to support that the same clinical condition may be associated with different brain abnormalities (Walsh et al., 2008) and, undoubtedly, the symptoms of depression have different etiological sources in different people. Nonetheless, a term is needed to distinguish clinically relevant depression from ordinary depressive feelings not requiring professional intervention. We will use the term "major depressive disorder" here due to common professional usage.

The Many "Causes" of Depression

The "cause" of major depressive disorder in final analysis is unknown. Undoubtedly, it results from the interplay of environmental/psychosocial and genetic/biological factors. Understanding depression is an emerging area of neuroscience research that has moved beyond simplistic notions of "chemical imbalance." Current conceptualizations focus on understanding altered functioning within complex neuronal networks (Insel, 2007). These efforts are hampered, however, by our limited ability to study the functioning of the brain, even with the most advanced brain imaging technologies currently available. Thus, it appears that it will still be years before neuroscience research will add meaningfully to our ability fully to understand and treat depression.

This is not to say that depression is "caused" by brain problems; indeed, stressful life events often precede an episode of major depression (Kendler, Karkowski, & Prescott, 1999). Further, it is increasingly recognized that the environment can change the brain. Only in the last 10–20 years have scientists accepted that the adult human brain grows new functional neurons—a process referred to as neurogenesis (Gross, 2000). There is evidence to suggest that impaired neurogenesis in the hippocampus is associated with depression (Eisch et al., 2008; Thomas & Peterson, 2008) and stress has been found to cause impairment in hippocampal neurogenesis (Mitra, Sundlass, Parker, Schatzberg, & Lyons, 2006).

Studies such as these suggest a mechanism by which psychosocial stress, such as relationship discord, can be translated into the experience of depression (Dranovsky & Hen, 2006). This research also does not mean that only biological treatments will be indicated in the future—take exercise, for example. Exercise is a behavioral intervention that has antidepressant activity found to increase hippocampal neurogenesis (Ernst, Olson, Pinel, Lam, & Christie, 2006). For our purposes, consider couple therapy with EFT. Might it be that strengthening the attachment bond leads to the growth of new brain cells in partners struggling with depression? This is an intriguing speculation that we hope will be tested someday.

Fortunately, even though the cause or causes of depression are unknown, there are treatments that can help people with depression, and EFT is one of them (Denton et al., 2009; Dessaulles et al., 2003).

Attachment Issues Are Related to Both Relational Distress and Depression

Attachment separation or distress and a partner's habitual ways of regulating this distress play a major role in an EFT understanding of the creation and maintenance of relationship problems (Johnson, 2004). For example, when Darrell feels Sherri's loss of interest in him, he becomes flooded with anxiety and then masks his initial vulnerable feelings of loss by hurling angry and demeaning comments at her. These responses push Sheri away and her withdrawal, coupled with threats of divorce, increases Darrell's desperate rage and his sense of loss. He feels helplessness fueling deeply held fears about his own adequacy. This then triggers a depressive episode. As Darrell either explodes or withdraws into depression, the relationship slides toward divorce.

Attachment injuries in childhood or adolescence (e.g., trauma, neglect, or loss) are a risk factor for the later development of major depression (Kendler, Kessler, Neale, Heath, & Eaves, 1993; Sjoholm, Lavebratt, & Forsell, 2009). If Darrell is also a survivor of childhood abuse, the threat to his connection to Sherri is even more likely to trigger an onset of depressive symptoms. Depression is more common among persons with more anxious and avoidant attachment styles as compared to control groups (Lemmens, Buysse, Heene, Eisler, & Demyttenaere, 2007; Mickelson, Kessler, & Shaver, 1997). Attachment distress is a lynchpin in the strong association between relationship distress and depression.

EFT Impacts Depression

There have been two randomized clinical trials utilizing EFT in the treatment of couples where one partner is diagnosed with major depressive disorder (Denton et al., 2010; Dessaulles et al., 2003). These studies provide preliminary but promising evidence for the efficacy of the use of EFT with couples as a depression treatment. There is also emerging evidence that emotion-focused therapy for individuals is an efficacious treatment of depression (Greenberg & Watson, 1998; Watson, Gordon, Stermac, Kalogerakos, & Steckley, 2003). While EFT for individuals will not be covered in this chapter, it is an empirically supported option for individuals seeking psychotherapeutic treatment of depression.

Both studies utilizing EFT in the treatment of couples were of women with major depressive disorder who were also experiencing relational discord. In the first study, participants were randomly assigned to either EFT alone or antidepressant medication (Dessaulles et al., 2003). Twelve participants completed the study and were included in the analysis. EFT treatment consisted of 14 conjoint sessions and one individual session for each partner, for a total of 16 weekly sessions. Participants randomly chosen to receive medication were treated for 16 weeks with desipramine, trimipramine, or trazadone. At the end of treatment, women in both groups had experienced a significant improvement in their level of depressive symptoms. The women in the EFT group actually had a lower level of depressive symptoms than the women receiving medication, but, due to the small sample size, this difference did not reach statistical significance.

The women were reevaluated 6 months after completing treatment and again there was no significant difference between the two groups. The women in the EFT group, however, experienced a significant improvement in depressive symptoms during this post-therapy period. The women in the medication group had no change in symptoms during these months and actually had a nonsignificant trend toward worsening of their depressive symptoms. (It should be noted that medication was stopped at the end of the 16 weeks.) Thus, it appears that the benefits of EFT for depression were continuing to build even after treatment was over.

In a second study, EFT was examined as an adjunctive treatment to antidepressant medication (Denton et al., 2010). Twenty-four women with both major depressive disorder and relational discord were randomized to either antidepressant medication alone or antidepressant medication combined with EFT. Medications utilized were bupropion sustained release, escitalopram, sertraline, and venlafaxine extended release. Medications were selected clinically and could be changed during the course of the 6-month treatment if they were not efficacious or tolerable. EFT was delivered in 15 weekly conjoint sessions. Both groups significantly and equally improved in depressive symptomatology. Women receiving EFT, however, experienced significantly greater improvement in relationship quality than did the women receiving medication alone

(Denton et al., 2010). Because relationship discord at the end of depression treatment predicts a worse long-term outcome, it may be that EFT will have preventive effects for these women, although that hypothesis was not tested in this study.

CONCEPTUALIZATION

Using an EFT lens, we conceptualize depression as a response to attachment distress based on a perceived loss of connection to, abandonment by, or rejection by another who is of attachment significance. The intrapsychic consequence of this loss is a sense of inadequacy and isolation. This does not negate other ways of describing depression because there can be multiple factors involved in the onset of depression. In targeting depression, it is particularly important to frame depressive symptoms as part of the couple's negative interactional cycle. Both partners are impacted by and struggle with depression's symptoms in their own way. Yet, depression can be externalized as the common enemy of both partners.

James Coyne (1976) has also proposed a systemic model of depression that integrates patterns of negative interaction and symptomatology. Coyne outlined how depressive symptoms can trigger relationship distress and how depression and relationship distress interact to reinforce each other mutually. He proposes that when people are stuck in depression, their partners initially try to provide support and to "cheer them up." When these efforts have little or no impact, resentment and hostility may eventually begin to develop. These partners will feel guilty about these feelings and rather than sharing these negative feelings with their depressed partners, try to hide them and continue to offer support and encouragement. The depressed partners, however, sense the insincerity of the support (which may be tinged with hostility) and may begin to feel rejected by their partner. Their feelings of depression worsen and the other partner's attempts at helping are even less effective, and so the cycle goes (Coyne, 1976).

The interactional model has received empirical support in the context of marital relationships (reviewed in Rehman et al., 2008). This cycle is not always seen in couples with depression, but it is seen often enough to serve as a useful guide for the EFT therapist. These negative feedback loops of depression and relationship distress also have another step—namely, that often the partner who was initially not depressed also begins to develop depression.

In general, EFT with couples is beneficial to partners struggling with depressive symptoms. EFT explicitly addresses the
common issues associated with depression, including emotional isolation and a sense of not being valued by others, loss
and a sense of helplessness that often arises as part of this isolation, and doubts about the competence and acceptability of
the self. Positive bonding interactions provide opportunities in
which the self is experienced as agentic, lovable, and connected
to another. Helping couples make these emotional connections
would seem to be a natural positive antidote to depression.

ASSESSMENT

Indications and Contraindications for Use
of EFT in Treatment of Depression

A person in a committed relationship presenting with depression and relational distress at a primary care or mental health
clinical setting should be considered as a candidate for EFT.
Clinical judgment suggests that if there is no evidence of
couple distress and one may assume that the couple remains
responsive to one another in the face of a depressive episode,
then individual intervention is appropriate rather than EFT.

If a person with depression has sought treatment from his
or her primary medical care provider, engaging the partner
in couple therapy can be a challenge. This is one of the challenges faced in applying couple therapy to this population. In
our clinic it is not unusual for a woman to call reporting that
she is depressed and is also in a relationship that is distressed.
Often she is interested in coming for couple therapy only to
find that her partner will not attend with her. (We often speculate that his unwillingness to participate in her treatment may
help explain her depression!) There seems to be a gender difference here in that if a depressed man calls for couple therapy
it is much more likely that his female partner will eventually
come in with him.

Therapists interested in learning more about the assessment
of major depressive disorder can refer to the structured clinical interview for the DSM-IV (SCID) (First, Spitzer, Gibbon, &
Williams, 1997) for examples of questions that can be used.
Self-report or clinician-administered inventories can be used
to assess severity of depressive symptoms and to monitor progress. The inventory of depressive symptomatology is particularly attractive because it has well-established psychometric

properties (Biggs et al., 2000; Rush, Gullion, Basco, Jarrett, & Trivedi, 1996; Rush et al., 2003) and is available in the public domain (www.ids-qids.org).

A therapist must make a clinical judgment that the depressed person is able to tolerate the negative emotions that are explored in Stage I of EFT. Individual psychotherapy for depression is usually experienced as a supportive process. In initial EFT sessions, however, depressed people may hear their partners discuss frustration and possibly even resentment for them. EFT therapists must assess the ability of the depressed person to tolerate the other partner's complaints without becoming excessively distressed. Therapists can control the intensity of the session through standard session management techniques (e.g., the types of questions asked, directing who should speak, who the partners should speak to, blocking arguments, etc.). Therapists also modulate the focus on underlying emotions and attachment needs. Distress can be observed by a depressed person's nonverbal communication or the therapist can simply ask, "How is it for you hearing this?" The goal is to maintain an engaged and productive level of emotional intensity without its becoming overwhelming or emotionally invasive.

In our pilot study, the women treated with medication alone had greater improvement in their depressive symptoms initially than the women receiving medication combined with EFT (Denton et al., 2010). While this difference did not reach statistical significance, it is a reminder to EFT therapists that the expression of negative affects in the early sessions of EFT has the potential to be experienced as stressful by a depressed partner.

Whenever a therapist is working with people experiencing depression, suicidality must always be a concern. Major depression is the major risk factor for having suicidal ideation (Goldney, Dal Grande, Fisher, & Wilson, 2003) and it is estimated that between 3.4 and 6% of all people with major depressive disorder will eventually die from suicide (Nierenberg, Gray, & Grandin, 2001). The EFT therapist must assess for suicidality at the beginning of therapy and as clinically indicated throughout the course of therapy. It is beyond the scope of this chapter to review the basic clinical skill of suicide assessment and readers are referred to other sources (Jacobs, Brewer, & Klein-Benheim, 1999; Patterson, Williams, Grauf-Grounds, & Chamow, 1998).

Similarly, the therapist must make a judgment about whether the person with depression can tolerate the intensity of EFT sessions without an increase in suicidality. Finally, the usual contraindications to EFT apply, such as intimate partner violence or any situation (e.g., emotional abuse) where a partner does not feel safe, or where the therapist would not want to ask one or both of the partners to make themselves vulnerable to the other (Johnson, 2004).

Treatment

Emotional distance and isolation in the relationship were prominent themes in our study. Depressed women partners often reported feeling very lonely; by comparison, male partners reported feeling frustrated and defeated because they could not "fix" their wives' depression. This frustration typically gave way to withdrawal. Our strategy was to place depression into the negative interaction cycle and externalize the cycle and depression as the common enemy of both partners and their relationship. While the cycle is normally externalized in EFT, with this population we highlighted the externalization of "depression." This began to help bring the couple back together as a team. The following example illustrates what a therapist might say when externalizing depression in the context of a cycle:

> Aiden, it hurt you to see Emma suffering, so you made suggestions of things she might do to lift her spirits. But, Emma, you didn't have the energy and motivation to do these things and experienced frustration from Aiden and sometimes it felt like he was actually "disgusted" with you. Aiden, you felt you weren't able to help her and eventually quit trying to cheer her up and turned your attention to your own life and the kids. Emma, you felt Aiden pulling away, which made you feel even worse about yourself and even more alone and unvalued. Now you are at a point where both of you feel very alone and disconnected from each other even though neither of you had bad intentions. Am I understanding your pattern? What I see, guys, is that the enemy here is not either of you; it is the depression. Depression is hurting both of you and depression is what you have to fight together. That is what we are going to work on here.

Once the couple accepted the negative interaction cycle and its relationship to depression, the cycle became the focus of treatment as in traditional EFT. Over the course of successful therapy, the couple would reengage as a male partner felt less inadequate and the other felt less lonely—and less depressed. In short, EFT with depressed couples looks very much like regular EFT except for the additional attention given to depressive symptoms and the part they play in the couple's cycle and the fact that these symptoms are framed in attachment terms.

We have not found a need to refer depressed partners to adjunctive individual therapy or schedule additional individual sessions. However, many people with major depressive disorder will need more than one type of treatment. If relationship issues resolve with EFT, but depressive symptoms continue, the use of experiential individual therapy (Watson et al., 2003) or cognitive therapy, which are empirically supported treatments, may be helpful. Cognitive therapy teaches depression-fighting skills that can alleviate depressive symptoms and prevent relapse (Jarrett et al., 2001; Segal, Williams, & Teasdale, 2002). These can all be options for a "next-step" treatment if needed. All of the women in our study were on antidepressant medication. This did not prove to be a problem because the women and their partners did not focus on the medication.

If an EFT therapist is the first health professional seeing a couple with a depressed partner, a decision will have to be made whether to refer for medication evaluation. Evidence suggests that people with more severe and recurrent episodes of major depression may do better with the combination of psychotherapy and medication, while people with mild to moderate episodes may not need combination treatment (Keller et al., 2000; Thase et al., 1997). Indications for referral for medication evaluation include patient preference, severe level of symptoms (e.g., a score of 16 or greater on the self report quick inventory of depressive symptomatology found at www.ids-qids.org), clinically concerning levels of suicidality, and lack of response in EFT sessions.

As noted before, even though the EFT therapist works to create a safe and calming environment that enhances affect regulation, EFT sessions can be emotionally intense and may exacerbate depressive symptoms. In this case the therapist should monitor and "check in" as needed with the depressed partner during the session with questions such as, "How is this for you?" "Is this OK?" "Too much?" The therapist should leave time before the end of the session to prepare the couple for "reentry" into their life outside the therapy room. The therapist will want to inquire how the session has been for the couple and if they have any concerns about leaving the session. The therapist may wish to inquire of depressed partners who struggle with suicidality where they are with these thoughts and process them as indicated.

For example, with Emma and Aidan, the therapist always ended the session with questions such as, "We're going to end in a few minutes, but I want to check first how this has been for you all today. Emma, where are you with those thoughts of not wanting to exist any longer? Does either of you have any concerns about how the rest of the day and week will go?"

CASE EXAMPLE

Terry is a 27-year-old female in a 7-year marriage to Mike, who is a 29-year-old male. Both partners are Caucasian. Terry called for treatment of depression after learning about our study in a newspaper advertisement. At initial presentation Terry reported that she had been in an episode of depression for "about 2 years." She had one prior episode of depression while in high school that passed without treatment. Family history of mood disorder consisted of an older sister who had recently started an antidepressant for depression. Terry's symptoms before treatment included depressed mood, trouble falling asleep, waking up in the night with trouble returning to sleep, early morning awakening, low energy, loss of usual interests, and decreased appetite. She did not have any suicidal ideation.

Terry has a son (age 9) from a previous marriage that had lasted less than 3 years. Terry and Mike have an 8-year-old son. Neither partner reported having received mental-health services prior to this treatment, nor did they report a history of drinking problems or heavy drug use. Both denied any past incidence of physical abuse. The couple met when Terry was 18 and Mike was 20; they soon became seriously involved, and decided to marry. During their first 3 years of marriage, Terry shared that she felt that they "couldn't be in the same room together" because they both had numerous grievances and could become quite embattled in their arguments. From her perspective, she grew tired of feeling alone in her position as mother and wanted to spend more time with Mike. Although she learned that Mike had once been unfaithful early in their marriage, she stayed with him and eventually it seemed their relationship did improve until about 1 year prior to couple therapy, when they began "fighting" once or twice a month.

In couple therapy, Terry expressed disapproval of some of Mike's behaviors, especially his angry outbursts. She stated that she believed that she did not please him or meet his expectations. Overall, Mike expressed less concern but did share about his frustrations regarding Terry's spending and responsibility for household tasks. His main goal was to communicate better, "without blowing up," and he admitted to avoiding conversations with Terry for fear that they would fight and "things would continue to get worse." Terry's goals were to feel more comfortable with Mike, hoping that he would understand that she could not always please him and for them both to be happy together. Both reported that their commitment level to working on their marriage was high.

As part of this research project, Terry was treated with antidepressant medication and EFT couple therapy. She was initially started on sertraline and began having improvement in her depressive symptoms; however, she experienced loss of sexual interest, so sertraline was discontinued after 1 month of treatment and escitalopram was initiated. She was able to tolerate this medication and experienced a return of sexual interest.

At the beginning of therapy, Terry was interviewed with the SCID and found to meet the DSM-IV criteria for major depressive disorder, recurrent, moderate. Terry's score on the inventory of depressive symptomatology (30-item, clinician-rated version; IDS-C) (Rush et al., 2003) was 26, which corresponds to a moderate level of severity. Mike's score on this instrument was 4, which is considered to represent "no depression." Terry's score on the quality of marriage index (QMI) (Norton, 1983) was 25, which is in the relational discord range. Mike scored 33 on the QMI, which is in the nondiscordant range. The QMI is a brief, self-report assessment of relational quality commonly used in relationship research and available at no cost from the original article (Norton, 1983).

Description of the Cycle/Key Change Events/ Turning Points

Terry and Mike attended EFT couple therapy for approximately 4 months for a total of 12 sessions. Their dominant distressing cycle was a female pursuer–male withdrawer pattern: Terry might begin to feel alone and then become suspicious that Mike might be seeing another woman. She would then angrily question him and Mike would become defensive and deny her accusations. Terry would become angrier and revoice her concern. Mike would then counter by offering a grievance related to her not meeting his expectations around chores and also become angry. Terry would begin to doubt herself (i.e., "I don't think I please him").

Their conflict would escalate; Mike would stop talking and retreat to a place away from her and Terry would feel more depressed. Later, they would both make repair attempts, wherein they offered apologies and/or tried to correct the concerns, but generally these attempts stayed focused on pragmatic (rather than attachment-focused) solutions, cognitive (superseding emotional) talk, and more surface secondary (rather than deeper primary) emotional experiences. As noted earlier, Mike presented their problem as less significant than did Terry. Terry's primary complaint was her doubts about Mike's love for and commitment to her and the power of his angry outbursts; Mike's primary complaint was Terry not meeting his expectations around tasks and the arguments that often ensued when he raised his complaints.

Despite these problems, throughout therapy the couple revealed their love and desire to be closer to each other. For example, Terry was able to identify how she wanted to please Mike and feared that she would not be enough for him; Mike identified the importance of wanting to do something different with his experience of anger so as to prevent her upset. To explore the reconnection process with this couple, summaries of key moments from their most relevant sessions are examined.

Stage 1: Cycle De-Escalation

The first sessions addressed their initial meeting, initial (beyond physical) attraction for each other, commitment to the therapeutic process on a scale of 1 to 10, presenting concerns, goals, some relevant context, and distressing cycle. Mike soon noted that he was "trying to avoid doing the silent thing" even though Terry did not notice a difference. To help discern their existing attachment to each other and potentially strengthen this attachment, the therapist (ADC) gave a homework task to notice and begin to be aware of *significant moments* in which they were communicating well and/or felt comfortable with each other. (Note: EFT couple therapy promotes experiential, in-session shifts for couples; therefore, this kind of task can be used to heighten in-session experiences as well as intensify the faintest appearances of what will become a consolidated, secure base.)

In the second session, the therapist linked some of Terry's depressive symptoms, such as obsessing about losing Mike, to the couple's distressing cycle:

Terry, you are on guard and you worry about losing Mike and you feel so alone. So you question him and he counters by getting mad and telling you that you don't do chores and then moves away. This leaves you more alone and more unsure of his love and commitment and more depressed and worried. Mike, you see Terry not being able to focus on her tasks and coming at you with questions all the time. So it's hard, then, to relax and give her the support she needs—to help her with her depression. You both end up alone and discouraged here. We need to change this dance.

The therapist worked at reengaging Mike in the session and he began to share about his past affair, noting his desire to maintain faithfulness to Terry. As Terry felt more comfortable in therapy, she began to talk about her "hurt" around this and the doubts that it left her with and how her fears escalated when Mike was unwilling to talk with her about this. The therapist set up a partner-to-partner enactment to provide a small reconnecting experience and support Terry to express her raw-spot feelings rather than accusing and then sinking into depression.

Therapist: I am wondering if sitting here with me right now... if you would be able to talk with Mike about this "uncertainty" that triggers your sense of hopelessness and how much it hurts you to have him get upset and not be willing to talk to you about what's happened in your history with him.

Terry (turns to Mike, speaking softly): It really hurts when you get mad at me and you try to change subjects on me when I ask you questions about this. It really does hurt. I want to be enough for you and (Her voice becomes hard here.) you're just not showing that I am.

Terry starts softly but ends with an accusation, which is typical of Stage 1. A long pause follows, then Mike looks at her and then at the therapist, and the therapist starts to speak, using a soft tone.

Therapist: Terry, it's hard to stay with the hurt and uncertainty and not protest Mike's silence. (She nods.) And, Mike, what is it like hearing what Terry is saying to you?

Mike: I understand that it hurts and stuff. Like I said, I am trying to avoid any issues like that. It's, I think, more the fact when you do bring it up and stuff, it's more accusatory and not—I understand you wonder, but it comes out accusatory that I'm doing something when I'm not. So I get mad and accuse back or shut down. (Mike has a somewhat defensive response in reaction to Terry's accusation.)

Therapist: And when that happens, Terry feels alone again and worries that you don't see her as enough—and the depression floods back in. Is that right? The cycle sort of happened in a small way right here.

This session ends with Terry expressing relief as Mike's typical anger was replaced with the beginnings of his actually listening to her experience.

As they continued to de-escalate in Session 3, Mike became more aware of Terry's emotional pain and depression about his past affair. Terry expressed her ongoing worries about his interactions with women and she connected these worries and the associated fears about her own acceptability leading to her slide into depressive thoughts and feelings. Rather than showing her that he understood, Mike responded in a tit-for-tat fashion, countering that he had similar concerns about her contact with men. After reflecting his defensive response and struggle to accept Terry's connection of her underlying fears and depressive symptoms, the therapist helped the couple begin to move beyond their escalating reactive responses about possible "other men" and "other women" to outlining their underlying attachment fears.

Therapist: You're telling her, "Terry, when I get mad or turn away it's because you mean so much to me that I want to know that we can solve everything—fix this so that we can keep our marriage because you mean so much to me." (Here the therapist heightens Mike's vaguely stated attachment-related longings in response to Terry's fear rather than getting stuck in the content of the past.)

Mike (pause): Yes, very much so.

Therapist: I didn't hear you talk about your fear of losing her…

Mike (interrupting therapist in midsentence): I have the fear that she'd want to leave me. I have a fear that eventually she's just going to want to give up, because we've had that talk before. (Mike speaks softly, with concern, looking down at the floor.)

Therapist: You're saying, "Hey, underneath all of this clutter that we get caught up in, underneath all of that there is a part of me that really gets scared that you may in fact get fed up and leave me." Am I hearing you right Mike? (Mike nods.) And this scared part of you is powerful, right? You don't dare risk opening up this scared part of you to her. You are so afraid that she may leave and hurt you that you keep this "afraid" part sealed off and show her your angry response to this fear. Am I hearing you right, Mike?

Mike: That's it. That's exactly it. (He looks down to the floor.) I run from this fear. It's huge.

Therapist: Could you now begin just to describe this fear for her, Mike? I'd like for you to risk some. Could you begin to tell her a little about how big this fear is?

Mike (to Terry): I'm afraid when we discuss and you say you're tired of being upset or tired of crying and you just want to go off—I'm afraid of that happening. I'm extremely afraid of anything coming between us that especially would affect the boys and our relationship. You and the boys are what's the most important to me. So, I'm definitely afraid of pushing you away enough that it couldn't be corrected. And I know at times that you've expressed that you're at that point, and that you're tired of it and it does scare me. (There is a long pause). But I'm still hopeful for the future (with a grin). (After exploring his fears, Mike makes a subtle attachment bid.)

Terry: Me too.

Therapist (to Terry): He just risked with you right here. He never shows this part to you. What's it like for you right now when he begins to risk and show you his fears of losing you?

Terry: It's really great. It lets me know that he does care about me. It's new, though; it's still hard to trust it.

Mike starts to risk more by deepening his engagement with Terry by more openly sharing his fears about losing her. He is now able to step away from his anger and move toward his softer emotions. Additionally, Mike self-identifies as a "problem solver," so as he steps slowly and deeply into his fears he does not stay with this experience for long. Instead, he becomes more of a "problem solver" for himself and Terry, adaptively moving into optimism. At moments like this and depending on a therapist's clinical discernment, she or he can slow a client down to allow for the possibility of an experiential shift through a longer embracing of fear and new, more emotionally engaged interactions with the other partner.

Throughout Sessions 4 through 7, Mike clearly identified his struggle to share more vulnerable emotions with Terry. This was something he had never done in any previous relationship. As he began to move away from his withdrawn position and moved toward Terry, he recognized how unfamiliar this was for him. As he reengaged into the relationship, Terry was able to be more open about her lingering vulnerability: "Can you show/tell me that I'm enough for you?" she asked.

Predictably, some of these new conversations went miserably awry and Mike turned to his anger. In these times, Terry felt disappointed, sad, depressed, and like a failure. The therapist would slow down this process, track their "depression cycle," and help each of them contact their attachment affect underneath their secondary responses. This cycle left them both feeling alone and emotionally disconnected; depression was indeed the enemy. In time, this experiential process brought the couple toward each other increasingly, which served to de-escalate their negative interactional cycle and create a secure base in their relationship.

Stage 2: Restructuring Interactions

In Session 9, Terry and Mike, who could now exit from their negative cycle even when discussing difficult topics (e.g., finances), were able to take more risks with each other. Mike was able to ask Terry not to threaten to leave and to help him learn to be more supportive. In the example that follows, the therapist works with Terry to deepen an understanding of her yearning for Mike during those times when her doubts come up and he retreats to his anger and distancing. Terry is softening in her approach to Mike, and Mike is able to stay engaged with her.

Therapist: Like he's shut down, he's not going to listen to me, he's not going to hear me, he's not going to understand, he's not going to care, and I'm over here all alone having to deal with this. (Therapist heightens the attachment fears so that they are alive and explicit in the room as Terry nods in agreement.) What do you do with all that, Terry?

Terry: I don't know—it's hard. (Therapist agrees.) Eventually we both get over it—we end up talking eventually. But,

I want it fixed; I want it fixed now, not later. And he doesn't want—he just wants to cool it off a little bit. I understand where he's coming from with that, but at times, when it's heated, I just want to get it fixed.

Therapist: Sure, sure. You want to get things resolved and feel connected to him again and have him hug you or hold you or something. You get desperate for this. (Therapist keeps an attachment focus.)

Terry: Uh-huh—feel like he wants to be next to me—that he wants me.

Therapist: Yeah. It feels like he really wants to be with you.

Mike: And I think I've improved in that I may shut down some, but I'll actually hold her or put my arm around her or something to try to calm her down. I think that's been improving quite a bit. (She agrees.)

Therapist: You want that too. It's like you want him to know that you need him when you are afraid, when all these depressing doubts come up. But it is really scary for you to say, "I need you to come close when I am afraid. I need you to reassure me." (Terry nods, in tears.) When he holds you or puts his arm around you—this soothes you? Reassures you?

Terry: Yes. Absolutely it does. I need his help here.

Here we see the effects of their potential distressing cycle dismantled by Terry sharing some of her fear and wanting Mike's reassuring touch when these fears begin to overwhelm her. Mike's responsiveness toward her is very significant for this couple as well because he is not becoming flooded by his own helplessness and tendency to shut down. The therapist walks with Terry through her fears of abandonment and rejection and the helplessness they trigger while normalizing her urge to "fix" things and force answers out of Mike. Terry shares about the value of Mike's touch and how he can calm her fears while simultaneously morphing his anger into a tenderness and closeness. Mike is now able to stay connected even during the intensity of an argument. Mike is aware of his progress in this area, recognizing that even when he feels angry or dismissed, he can soothe both himself and her with reassuring contact.

Throughout Sessions 10 and 11, Terry reveals that she is continuing to feel better, more empowered, and closer to Mike. Further, Terry's depressive symptoms have decreased. In EFT language, this has happened: As Mike and Terry experience less relational distress and are increasingly able to risk showing their more vulnerable attachment fears and wants, she becomes less depressed. As Mike witnesses these compelling attachment longings, he struggles with his own feelings of insecurity and fears of abandonment (e.g., by asking, "Am I enough for her?"), but is able to stay with her and offer comfort; in turn, this allows him to stay engaged and not get stuck in secondary anger. In effect, this couple is learning to co-regulate their attachment affect. This is not a cognitive or problem solving process; it is an experiential, in-the-moment attachment dance of mutual risk, reassurance, and comfort. The attachment fears and signals become clear and both partners experience increased accessibility and responsiveness while in these emotional states.

In the following exchange, the therapist heightens Mike's reemerging fear, as Mike struggles with Terry's socializing.

Therapist: To me, that [experience of talking to her about his fears] makes the "mad" feel very different. If you're mad at Terry and she's out at a bar, and you call her six times, and you're saying, "F___ this, f___ that" (Therapist is using Mike's words.) or whatever you're saying, then that's going to come across very differently to Terry than if you talk before she goes out, and you tell her about your fears and doubts and distrust. I mean that sounds very different, like (proxy enactment), "Sometimes Terry, I want you to have this freedom—I want to support you, because I know this is good for you. And, at the same time, sometimes I get scared to death when you go out like this, because I'm scared that you'll end up doing what I did. And sometimes, when I get scared in that way, I don't know what to do, and I begin to panic, and I begin to call, or I begin to do anything I can do to try to make sure that you're not doing that" (pause). Does that fit for you Mike?

Mike: For the most part.

Therapist: Well, help me here. Add to it, if you need to.

Mike: It's definitely a fear—a fear of what could happen. I discuss the jealousy part of it regarding people—I don't discuss the fear part. I'm not—I just don't talk about how fearful it is—how weak it makes me or how it makes me feel vulnerable. But, I project it more as a macho type thing.

Therapist: I appreciate your being a man and being that way in
this relationship. I also wonder how it would be for
you to show her more tenderness and to tell her, on a
more vulnerable level, what's really going on for you.
I wonder how that would be for you. I wonder if you
could tell her about this fear that takes over.

Here, the therapist uses empathic conjecture and validation
to help Mike understand what his vulnerable expression does
for their relationship. Using a proxy enactment, the therapist
asks him to imagine what showing his tenderness to Terry
does in their relationship. Mike acknowledges that his anger
covers the vulnerability he feels when he feels jealous and his
fears get the best of him. Jealousy then also becomes a mutual
problem this couple shares and can help each other with.

Session 12

In the final session, Terry and Mike continued to discuss how
they were dealing with rebuilding marital trust. Mike realizes that when his anger emerges, it pushes her away and that
concealed beyond the anger is that soft part of him that he
struggles to express. Terry realizes that she can be more open
to Mike's emotional expressions and is now less likely to fall
into her "not-enough" state. The triggers for Terry's depression have been lessened and her way of dealing with these
triggers has expanded. Also, the new safety she is able to create with Mike reinforces her security in the relationship and
her positive sense of self and hopefully offers further protection again relapse.

Even though this couple had more work to do, they began
the formation of a secure base that would allow them to move
beyond much of their negative cycle and history of relational
woundedness. By the end of treatment, Terry scored a 3 on the
IDS-C, which is in the range of "no depression." (Mike scored
a 7 and he continued to be in the "no depression" range.) Terry
scored 42 on the quality of marriage index (Norton, 1983),
which is well into the nondistressed range. Mike's score was
similar to his pretreatment score (and also in the nondistressed
range). Scores on the initiator style questionnaire (Denton &
Burleson, 2007) indicated that they felt that they were both
engaging in the discussion of relationship problems more than
they had before therapy.

CONCLUSION

Relational discord often accompanies serious depression and it would seem rational that treatment of relational issues might not only be helpful but perhaps even necessary for improvement and for relapse prevention. With EFT's focus on strengthening the attachment bond between partners, this treatment offers a strong and logical candidate for a couple therapy approach to depression. Indeed, emerging evidence is supporting this assumption. We have found that EFT is readily applicable to couples where one or both partners are suffering from depression.

In applying EFT to the treatment of depression, we identified the negative interaction cycle, which included depression and externalized depression, as the mutual "enemy" of the couple. We were sensitive to the fact that depressed people might have diminished ability to tolerate the negative affects that can arise in EFT and modulated the intensity of the sessions accordingly. Where there was fragility, we went slower than with traditional distressed couples where there is no individual impairment.

Additional research on the use of EFT in the treatment of depression is needed. Larger samples, studies of mechanisms of change, and determining the optimum place for EFT in the range of depression treatments are just a few of the topics waiting to be studied. All preliminary evidence, however, does point to the effectiveness of EFT in the treatment of depression and there is no evidence that it is not useful or is harmful. While we do not expect EFT to be a "miracle" treatment of depression, we are able to recommend EFT as one intervention that can be valuable in helping people with this troubling and potentially devastating condition.

REFERENCES

American Psychiatric Association. (2000). *Diagnostic and statistical manual of mental disorders, fourth edition, text revision*. Washington, DC: American Psychiatric Association.

Biggs, M. M., Shores-Wilson, K., Rush, A. J., Carmody, T. J., Trivedi, M. H., Crismon, M. L., et al. (2000). A comparison of alternative assessments of depressive symptom severity: A pilot study. *Psychiatry Research, 96,* 269–279.

Coyne, J. C. (1976). Toward an interactional description of depression. *Psychiatry, 39,* 28–40.

Coyne, J. C., Kessler, R. C., Tal, M., Turnbull, J., Wortman, C. B., & Greden, J. F. (1987). Living with a depressed person. *Journal of Consulting and Clinical Psychology, 55,* 347–352.

Denton, W. H., & Burleson, B. R. (2007). The initiator style questionnaire: A scale to assess initiator tendency in couples. *Personal Relationships, 14,* 245–268.

Denton, W. H., Wittenborn, A. K., & Golden, R. N. (2010). Augmenting antidepressant medication treatment of depressed women with emotionally focused therapy for couples: A randomized pilot study. Manuscript submitted for publication.

Dessaulles, A., Johnson, S. M., & Denton, W. H. (2003). Emotion-focused therapy for couples in the treatment of depression: A pilot study. *American Journal of Family Therapy, 31,* 345–353.

Dranovsky, A., & Hen, R. (2006). Hippocampal neurogenesis: Regulation by stress and antidepressants. *Biological Psychiatry, 59,* 1136–1143.

Eisch, A. J., Cameron, H. A., Encinas, J. M., Meltzer, L. A., Ming, G. L., & Overstreet-Wadiche, L. S. (2008). Adult neurogenesis, mental health, and mental illness: Hope or hype? *Journal of Neuroscience, 28,* 11785–11791.

Ernst, C., Olson, A. K., Pinel, J. P., Lam, R. W., & Christie, B. R. (2006). Antidepressant effects of exercise: Evidence for an adult-neurogenesis hypothesis? *Journal of Psychiatry & Neuroscience, 31,* 84–92.

First, M. B., Spitzer, R. L., Gibbon, M., & Williams, J. B. W. (1997). *User's guide for the structured clinical interview for DSM-IV axis I disorders—Clinician version (SCID-CV).* Washington, DC: American Psychiatric Press.

Goldney, R. D., Dal Grande, E., Fisher, L. J., & Wilson, D. (2003). Population attributable risk of major depression for suicidal ideation in a random and representative community sample. *Journal of Affective Disorders, 74,* 267–272.

Greenberg, L. S., & Watson, J. (1998). Experiential therapy of depression: Differential effects of client-centered relationship conditions and process experiential interventions. *Psychotherapy Research, 8,* 210–224.

Gross, C. G. (2000). Neurogenesis in the adult brain: Death of a dogma. *Nature Reviews Neuroscience, 1,* 67–73.

Insel, T. R. (2007). Shining light on depression. *Science, 317,* 757–758.

Insel, T. R. (2009). Translating scientific opportunity into public health impact: A strategic plan for research on mental illness. *Archives of General Psychiatry, 66,* 128–133.

Jacobs, D. G., Brewer, M., & Klein-Benheim, M. (1999). Suicide assessment: An overview and recommended protocol. In D. G. Jacobs (Ed.), *The Harvard Medical School guide to suicide assessment and intervention.* San Francisco, CA: Jossey–Bass.

Jarrett, R. B., Kraft, D., Doyle, J., Foster, B. M., Eaves, G. G., & Silver, P. C. (2001). Preventing recurrent depression using cognitive therapy with and without a continuation phase—A randomized clinical trial. *Archives of General Psychiatry, 58,* 381–388.

Johnson, S. M. (2004). *The practice of emotionally focused couple therapy: Creating connection* (2nd ed.). New York, NY: Brunner–Routledge.

Judd, L. L., Schettler, P. J., Solomon, D. A., Maser, J. D., Coryell, W., Endicott, J., & Akiskal, H. S. (2008). Psychosocial disability and work role function compared across the long-term course of bipolar I, bipolar II and unipolar major depressive disorders. *Journal of Affective Disorders, 108,* 49–58.

Keller, M. B., McCullough, J. P., Klein, D. N., Arnow, B., Dunner, D. L., Gelenberg, A. J., et al. (2000). A comparison of nefazodone, the cognitive behavioral-analysis system of psychotherapy, and their combination for the treatment of chronic depression. *New England Journal of Medicine, 342,* 1462–1470.

Kendler, K. S., Karkowski, L. M., & Prescott, C. A. (1999). Causal relationship between stressful life events and the onset of major depression. *American Journal of Psychiatry, 156,* 837–841.

Kendler, K. S., Kessler, R. C., Neale, M. C., Heath, A. C., & Eaves, L. J. (1993). The prediction of major depression in women: Toward an integrated etiologic model. *American Journal of Psychiatry, 150,* 1139–1148.

Kessler, R. C., Berglund, P., Demler, O., Jin, R., Koretz, D., Merikangas, K. R., et al. (2003). The epidemiology of major depressive disorder: Results from the National Comorbidity Survey Replication (NCS-R). *JAMA, 289,* 3095–3105.

Kessler, R. C., Walters, E. E., & Forthofer, M. S. (1998). The social consequences of psychiatric disorders, III: Probability of marital stability. *American Journal of Psychiatry, 155,* 1092–1096.

Lemmens, G. M. D., Buysse, A., Heene, E., Eisler, I., & Demyttenaere, K. (2007). Marital satisfaction, conflict communication attachment style and psychological distress in couples with a hospitalized depressed patient. *Acta Neuropsychiatrica, 19,* 109–117.

Mickelson, K. D., Kessler, R. C., & Shaver, P. R. (1997). Adult attachment in a nationally representative sample. *Journal of Personality and Social Psychology, 73,* 1092–1106.

Mitra, R., Sundlass, K., Parker, K. J., Schatzberg, A. F., & Lyons, D. M. (2006). Social stress-related behavior affects hippocampal cell proliferation in mice. *Physiology & Behavior, 89,* 123–127.

National Institute for Mental Health. (2008). *National Institute of Mental Health strategic plan.* Retrieved March 9, 2009 from http://www.nimh.nih.gov/about/strategic-planning-reports/nimh-strategic-plan-2008.pdf

Nierenberg, A. A., Gray, S. M., & Grandin, L. D. (2001). Mood disorders and suicide. *Journal of Clinical Psychiatry, 62,* 27–30.

Norton, R. (1983). Measuring marital quality: A critical look at the dependent variable. *Journal of Marriage and the Family, 45,* 141–151.

Patterson, J., Williams, L., Grauf-Grounds, C., & Chamow, L. (1998). *Essential skills in family therapy: From the first interview to termination.* New York, NY: Guilford Press.

Rehman, U. S., Gollan, J., & Mortimer, A. R. (2008). The marital context of depression: Research, limitations, and new directions. *Clinical Psychology Review, 28,* 179–198.

Rush, A. J., Fava, M., Wisniewski, S. R., Lavori, P. W., Trivedi, M. H., Sackeim, H. A., Thase, M. E., & Niederehe, G. (2004). Sequenced treatment alternatives to relieve depression (STAR*D): Rationale and design. *Controlled Clinical Trials, 25,* 119–142.

Rush, A. J., Gullion, C. M., Basco, M. R., Jarrett, R. B., & Trivedi, M. H. (1996). The inventory of depressive symptomatology (IDS): Psychometric properties. *Psychological Medicine, 26,* 477–486.

Rush, A. J., Trivedi, M. H., Ibrahim, H. M., Carmody, T. J., Arnow, B., Klein, D. N., et al. (2003). The 16-item quick inventory of depressive symptomatology (QIDS), clinician rating (QIDS-C), and self-report (QIDS-SR): A psychometric evaluation in patients with chronic major depression. *Biological Psychiatry, 54,* 573–583.

Segal, Z. V., Williams, J. M. G., & Teasdale, J. D. (2002). *Mindfulness-based cognitive therapy for depression: A new approach to preventing relapse.* New York, NY: Guilford Press.

Sjoholm, L., Lavebratt, C., & Forsell, Y. (2009). A multifactorial developmental model for the etiology of major depression in a population-based sample. *Journal of Affective Disorders, 113,* 66–76.

Thase, M. E., Greenhouse, J. B., Frank, E., Reynolds, C. F., III, Pilkonis, P. A., Hurley, K., et al. (1997). Treatment of major depression with psychotherapy or psychotherapy-pharmacotherapy combinations. *Archives of General Psychiatry, 54,* 1009–1015.

Thomas, R. M., & Peterson, D. A. (2008). Even neural stem cells get the blues: Evidence for a molecular link between modulation of adult neurogenesis and depression. *Gene Expression, 14,* 183–193.

Walsh, T., McClellan, J. M., McCarthy, S. E., Addington, A. M., Pierce, S. B., Cooper, G. M., et al. (2008). Rare structural variants disrupt multiple genes in neurodevelopmental pathways in schizophrenia. *Science, 320,* 539–543.

Warden, D., Rush, A. J., Trivedi, M. H., Fava, M., & Wisniewski, S. R. (2007). The STAR*D Project results: A comprehensive review of findings. *Current Psychiatry Reports, 9,* 449–459.

Watson, J. C., Gordon, L. B., Stermac, L., Kalogerakos, F., & Steckley, P. (2003). Comparing the effectiveness of process-experiential with cognitive-behavioral psychotherapy in the treatment of depression. *Journal of Consulting and Clinical Psychology, 71,* 773–781.

Whisman, M. A. (2001). The association between depression and marital dissatisfaction. In S. R. H. Beach (Ed.), *Marital and family processes in depression: A scientific foundation for clinical practice* (pp. 3–24). Washington, DC: American Psychological Association.

Whisman, M. A., & Bruce, M. L. (1999). Marital dissatisfaction and incidence of major depressive episode in a community sample. *Journal of Abnormal Psychology, 108,* 674–678.

World Health Organization. (1992). *The ICD-10 classification of mental and behavioral disorders: Clinical descriptions and diagnostic guidelines.* Geneva: World Health Organization.

World Health Organization. (2001). The World Health Report: 2001: Mental health: New understanding, new hope. Retrieved March 5, 2009, from http://www.who.int/whr/2001/en/whr01_en.pdf

Five

Emotionally Focused Therapy for Couples Living With Aphasia

KATHRYN STIELL AND GILLIAN GAILEY

INTRODUCTION

Stroke is the leading cause of disability in North America. While the percentage of patients receiving any type of therapy in the years after a stroke is estimated to be as low as 10%, research indicates those who do receive therapy report lower levels of disability and related problems (DeAngelis, 2010). The links between chronic illness and couple relationships and the use of emotionally focused therapy in particular have been described in the literature (Johnson, 2002; Kowal, Johnson, & Lee, 2003; MacIntosh & Johnson, 2008; Mikail, 2003; Naaman, Johnson, & Radwan, in press).

Emotion and emotional communication are critical to relationship security and resilience in the face of life-threatening and life-altering medical conditions such as stroke. In this chapter we explore the disability of aphasia (uh-fay'-zhuh) as it presents unique challenges to both couples and therapist alike. Imagine knowing what you want to say to your partner, but when you go to speak, the wrong words come tumbling out. Imagine not being able to say the name of your spouse or even calling him or her by the wrong name. Aphasia impairment—the loss of the ability to use language—results from a stroke and other neurological events. Aphasia compromises an adult's primary means for social interaction and threatens a couple's emotional connection at a time when a supportive relationship is needed most.

Although many therapists may not be familiar with this particular disability, we have combined our professional expertise and devoted our careers to working with families living with aphasia. Through our shared efforts, we established one of the first aphasia centers in North America in 1990. We have had the privilege to learn from hundreds of couples, some who were coping well and others who were not. Importantly, we have learned that a partner's ability to cope with another's aphasia plays a crucial role in successful treatment. We hope to encourage EFT therapists to consider combining their expertise with that of other professionals to make EFT more accessible to this and other special populations.

In this chapter we describe our cotherapy EFT approach, demonstrating the active collaboration of an EFT therapist with a speech-language therapist, and our shared work with couples living with chronic aphasia. We review relevant literature on aphasia and two important behavioral changes that impact couples' relationships. The process of coping with aphasia is conceptualized using an attachment framework and issues unique to this population are then discussed in the context of assessment and the appropriateness of EFT treatment. Finally, specific variations in treatment interventions related to communication difficulties and behavioral changes are highlighted using a case example.

UNDERSTANDING APHASIA

In North America, well over one million people live with chronic aphasia. These people come from all socioeconomic, cultural, and educational backgrounds. For an estimated 80% of this population, aphasia is a consequence of sudden, life-threatening, left-hemisphere stroke. The resulting losses are traumatic. These include the instantaneous loss of normal physical functioning and neuropsychological processing and, second, a loss in the ability to talk about it.

Aphasia is a complex and puzzling disability that is not well known or understood by the public or many professionals. As a first step, EFT therapists must understand the nature of aphasia within a trauma framework and recognize the unique coexisting behaviors that stem from the same neurological event. It is only from this starting point that therapists can begin to appreciate the full impact of aphasia on models of self and interpersonal relationships. The next step involves recognizing the special communicative needs of this population and the effective use of communication strategies developed by a speech-language therapist. In this cotherapy model, the EFT therapist and speech-language therapist integrate their respective expertise to create what we call a communication platform—a solid and safe place where couples can face the aphasia-related challenges together. As will be shown, these strategies rely heavily on working with nonverbal communication, which, fortunately, is a very familiar part of the EFT therapist's skill set and makes EFT well suited to this population.

A speech-language therapist describes aphasia as an acquired communication disorder caused by injury to the brain that affects a person's ability to process information involving the use of words. Often described as people who "know more than they can say" (Kagan & Shumway, 2003), which alludes to their reduced ability to express themselves using speech, individuals with aphasia also typically have at least some degree of difficulty in getting their ideas across through writing. Those with aphasia commonly face problems in understanding what others are saying, and reading ability only rarely remains unscathed by the disorder.

Overall severity of communicative impairment can vary greatly—from global aphasia, with profound losses in both receptive and expressive language modalities, to mild aphasia, with virtually no detectable difficulty in most day-to-day communication. Within this range, individuals with aphasia exhibit complex diversity and unique language processing profiles in which there is no simple, one-to-one correspondence between difficulties in one modality relative to others. For example, a person with aphasia might retain good ability to talk but suffer tremendous difficulty in tracking conversations that involve more than one other person. Another may face only moderate impairment in writing, yet find reading back what he or she has just written to be a significant problem.

Although aphasia does not directly affect an individual's thinking and reasoning skills, the loss of fluent speech and the inability to engage easily in conversation often foster the misperception of mental and verbal incompetence. People with aphasia are usually intelligent, competent individuals who still have the ability to think and make decisions. Sadly, aphasia often masks a person's intelligence and ability to communicate feelings, thoughts, and emotions. Aphasia treatment has been the domain of speech-language therapists, who traditionally focus on one-on-one linguistic ability. More recently, speech-language therapists have expanded treatment to address the psychosocial impact of aphasia (Kagan & Gailey, 1993). Broader approaches to treatment encompass concerns including a person's quality of life, social participation, and the importance of communication to sustaining a healthy identity. For more information, see "Life Participation Approaches to Aphasia" (LPAA Project Group, 2000).

APHASIA AND THE CHALLENGES THAT COUPLES FACE

Stroke and other neurological events that cause aphasia also result in behavior changes that have significant implications for interpersonal connections. The partner with aphasia may experience difficulties with executive functions (e.g., planning, organizing, and initiating). Those with aphasia may also experience emotional lability in the form of reactions that do not seem appropriate to a situation and that, by self-report, do not reflect the real feelings of the person with aphasia. Our focus here is on the partner with aphasia's own inability to initiate conversation (lack of initiation) and more extreme emotional reactions that are described as "catastrophic reactions" (Goldstein, 1939). Despite their neurological origin, it is the experience of these behavioral changes in close relationships that must be addressed in therapy.

Recognizing the importance of intact communication to all aspects of daily living and social interactions and the complex nature of aphasia, it is puzzling that some couples cope so well. Tim and Ann's story illustrates this point. Tim was a very successful financial executive who previously could multitask to an extreme level. His office was like a command center, where he could conduct several telephone conversations and computer conversations at the same time. One day, he suddenly collapsed onto his office floor. Initially he lost all ability to speak; unable to call for help, he lay helpless on the office floor for an unknown amount of time before being rushed to the hospital. His wife, Ann, soon arrived at the hospital and stayed by his bedside. She recalls her fear of losing Tim and being terrified when he tried to speak and only nonsense sounds came out.

Relating their story now, Tim and Ann describe this day as their "9/11"—the day their life changed forever. Two months later, Tim still has paralysis of his right arm and significant loss of the ability to communicate, but was discharged home to the care of Ann, who had left her job. Tim accepted that he could not return to work and was now on long-term disability. In contrast to his abilities before his stroke, Tim had great difficulty conducting even a single telephone call because he relied heavily on nonverbal cues such as facial expression to understand what people were saying. He would always turn to Ann for help finding the right words. Tim remained motivated to improve his ability to use language. A common family scene saw his teenage children doing their homework while Tim practiced his own reading skills—albeit, using children's books such as the Dr. Seuss stories.

Despite all these substantial life changes, Tim and Ann actively adapted to them and both were receptive to additional support. It did not matter to Ann whether or not her husband was reading Dr. Seuss or Charles Dickens. She was comfortable in her caregiving role and Tim was able to accept his new dependence on her. In fact, they were now doing more things together than ever before. Tim and Ann seemed to be able to confront the daily challenges of aphasia and coexisting behavioral changes together.

Unfortunately, not all couples do so well. Stroke and aphasia can have a devastating impact on both partners. Research and our own clinical experience indicate that coping does not get easier over time. Astrom, Adolfsson, and Asplund (1993) found major depression in 25% of stroke survivors during acute stages and then a reduction to 16% at 1 year. However, over the next 2 years, depression scores increased again to 29%.

Code and Herrmann (2003) report that depression among persons with aphasia in an acute stage is more likely to have an organic basis, with structural lesions leading to neurobiochemical changes. They note that this depression often persists into the chronic stages and years following the onset of aphasia. Over time, the full psychosocial and emotional impact of disability becomes increasingly clear, putting both the person with aphasia and his or her spouse at risk of reactive depression. In a study of spouses of people with aphasia, changes in lifestyle and loss of emotional support and sexual relationships were associated with lower rates of marital satisfaction (Williams & Freer, 1986).

In our clinical experience, it is not unusual for a couple like Tim and Ann to be referred for couple counseling 2 years after onset. The delayed impact of aphasia on a couple's relationship is not uncommon, as illustrated in the case of Joan and John, who were seen shortly after the second Christmas season following Joan's stroke. During their first Christmas after Joan's discharge, the family had gathered for a traditional Scrabble® tournament. Joan soon became aware that she was not able to play the game. She was disappointed but able to comfort herself by adding this as one of her therapy goals. However, when the same experience occurred the following Christmas, the experience was traumatic. She began doubting her competence, withdrawing, and feeling tearful much of the time. As John also started to withdraw in frustration after unsuccessful attempts to help, feelings of distance in the relationship increased.

APPROACHES TO TREATMENT

Therapists cannot expect a person with aphasia to pick up the telephone and call for an appointment or to ask his or her doctor for a referral. Communication difficulties and behavioral changes, such as lack of initiation, prevent accessing support through normal means. In turn, partners may not feel that couple counseling is an option because of the communication difficulties that they experience with their partner. Referrals to therapy typically come from speech-language therapists, who are the primary professionals working with this population. In our setting at the Aphasia Center of Ottawa, these specialists provide long-term communication therapy in a group setting and work proactively to identify problems and make appropriate referrals. They also share an attachment framework and recognize distress not only in terms of an individual's communication or behavior problems but also in the context of couple relationships.

The term "identity theft" was coined by Shadden (2005) and applied to both persons with aphasia and their partners. Aphasia has a devastating impact on both partners and a strong case for couple intervention becomes clear. Descriptions and research into different approaches to treating couples living with aphasia can be found. Solution-focused and narrative therapy applications with this population have been described by Stiell and Gailey (1995) and by Boles and Lewis (2000). Coaching, another problem-solving approach, is described by Holland (2007), who states that "family buy-in is essential to living successfully with aphasia." Research studies on various approaches to couple therapy involve small numbers of participants, which points to the challenge of working with this population. The impact of severe aphasia on both spouses was shown to be reduced in a study of five couples when speech-language therapy was provided to couples (Michallet,

Tetreault, & Le Dorze, 2003). Finally, positive changes were found in a study of two families who completed therapy given jointly by a family therapist and a speech-language therapist (Nichols, Vachevker, & Pring, 1996).

More recently, we conducted a study based on an attachment framework. In this study, EFT and physiotherapy (accompanied by the use of supportive communication strategies) were provided using a group format with 17 couples as part of a multidisciplinary community treatment program (Ryan, Stiell, Gailey, & Makinen, 2008). Results showed encouraging trends toward strengthening relationship bonds. For example, one partner, who was confined to a wheelchair and had moderate aphasia, commented at the conclusion of therapy: "If it is possible after 50 years of marriage, we feel closer now than ever."

EFT: APHASIA AND ATTACHMENT

Conceptualization

Attachment theory offers a distinct perspective to therapists and couples as they identify the varied relational impacts of aphasia on a couple's relationship. From this perspective, chronic illness unfolds in the context of an interpersonal relationship in ways that both impact the disease process and the dynamics it evokes in an ongoing reciprocal fashion (Stiell, Naaman, & Lee, 2007). Seeing aphasia through an attachment lens helps the EFT therapist and the speech-language therapist understand more fully the emotional impact of this disability on close relationships and how to proceed in therapy.

Our clinical experience suggests that it is not the severity of illness or disability that determines how well a person will cope but rather the ability to maintain close relationships. We observe that even with such a pervasive disability like aphasia, the severity of the disability does not typically correspond with the degree of a couple's distress. In fact, the level of attachment security is a better predictor of a couple's adjustment to the pervasive impact of aphasia. Attachment is a crucial source of resilience. In this regard, Johnson (2002) suggests:

> To be resilient in the face of trauma, people need not just friends and a sense of community, but close attachment bonds. The quality of such bonds is clearly linked with the ability to regulate emotions and develop an integrated concept of self, both of which have been associated with resilience in later life. (p. 27)

Following the assumptions of attachment theory, we suggest that more secure couples are more likely to cope better with the demands and impact of aphasia compared to less securely attached couples. More secure attachment is generally associated with resilience to stress, assertiveness, and effective caregiving (Mikulincer & Shaver, 2007). In our clinic, more secure couples seem to show a greater ability to focus and to engage the energy needed to adapt to the new playing field created by aphasia. These couples are also more receptive to outside support from others. This may include a speech-language therapist who actively promotes the acceptance of communication difficulties within the context of a relationship problem, rather than solely identifying the concerns as an individual problem (e.g., aphasia-related symptoms/impacts).

Working from their own resources along with the help of others, these couples are likely to find new, effective ways to interact and be less negatively impacted by related behavioral changes. Couples can then find new ways to have "hold me tight" (Johnson, 2008) conversations using supported conversation strategies. It is in the context of these more secure relationships that positive answers are given to fundamental attachment questions such as "Am I still loveable? Can I depend on my partner to respond?" (Johnson, 2002).

Couples with more insecure attachment and caregiving styles tend to struggle more with the challenges posed by aphasia. Their less supportive patterns of interaction are exacerbated by interruption in language ability and the need for increased flexibility. Such flexibility is necessary to establish new patterns of communication or to seek professional help from others. The patterns of insecurity and the partner's unmet attachment needs get in the way of effective caregiving (Collins, Guichard, Ford, & Feeney, 2006). On the one hand, individuals who are anxiously attached may become overinvolved in caregiving behavior to assuage their own needs to be close to their partners. On the other hand, avoidant caregivers may not respond to their partners' distress because of their own needs to deactivate attachment concerns.

This attachment framework helps explain different attitudes found in distressed couples and obstacles confronted in a speech-language therapist's efforts to get partners to use supportive conversation strategies effectively. For example, avoidant partners may refuse to adopt recommended strategies, fail to attend educational sessions, or struggle to acknowledge their partners' competence. On the other hand, anxiously attached partners may continuously seek out help and attend numerous education sessions but fail to adopt communication strategies effectively in the home setting. A partner's anxious responses can create a level of overprotection seen in one partner "speaking for" the other or constantly repairing or correcting behaviors that negatively impact a partner's communicative output (Croteau & Le Dorze, 2006).

After a stroke, even more secure couples can find themselves vulnerable and at risk for distress. Each partner is coping with the dual traumas of stroke and aphasia. In this context, there is increased risk of old negative cycles resurfacing or new negative cycles evolving as couples attempt to cope with this complex disability. Aphasia's low public profile makes it hard for partners to find successful role models within their community or learn from others' personal experiences.

Social isolation is a common consequence of the feelings of shame, embarrassment, and incompetence that accompany the changes that aphasia brings to a couple's life together. Clearly, feelings of incompetence arise for the person with aphasia as a response to the personal loss of language and the social impact of others treating the person with aphasia as less competent. Less apparent but equally damaging to relationship security are growing feelings of incompetence in the partner without aphasia as he or she faces a growing sense of inadequacy in the caregiving role.

From an attachment perspective, the onset of the illness threatens a couple's relationship security and activates the couple's attachment and caregiving systems. Partners can respond by becoming more aware of the other's needs and offering comfort and assistance. Successful activation of caregiving and care-receiving systems can restore relationship security.

Attachment and caregiving are described as two separate systems (Collins et al., 2006). The attachment system focuses on reducing the risk of the self coming to harm while the caregiving system focuses on reducing the risk of an intimate other coming to harm. Successful caregiving depends first on the caregiver's accessibility and responsiveness to his or her partner and thus being able to focus attention and resources on the partner. The caregiver's ability to be empathetic and responsive to another's needs is essential.

> Sensitivity includes attunement to, and accurate interpretation of, another person's signals of distress, worry, or need, and responding in synchrony with the person's proximity- and

> support seeking behavior. It also includes noticing both the
> needy person's implicit and explicit signals (George & Solomon,
> 1999)...Lack of sensitivity and responsiveness can cause a care
> seeker to feel misunderstood, disrespected, or burdensome,
> which exacerbates distress rather than providing a secure base
> (Collins et al., 2006). (Mikulincer & Shaver 2007, p. 327)

Failure to provide a secure base in turn increases feelings of
incompetence and emotional distress in the caregiver. The
distress renders the caregiver even less able to provide care.

A person with aphasia has difficulty expressing both
instrumental and emotional needs, making it harder for the
caregiver to provide appropriate care. At the same time, those
suffering from aphasia may be less inhibited in expressing
emotions through nonverbal gestures, including facial expression, crying, or angry outbursts. How a partner responds to
these emotions and expressions becomes critical to effective
caregiving. These nonverbal forms of communication may
cause more confusion and push the caregiver away.

At the same time, the caregiving spouse may withhold
expression of his or her own needs, contributing to a withdrawn position in an emerging negative cycle. This often happens in the context of a caregiver dealing with the traumatic
impact of aphasia on his or her life and at the same time assuming responsibility for the partner's recovery and preventing
another stroke. A caregiver may suppress his or her own needs
and concerns about the partner, fearing that this would be
inappropriate or even dangerous. These dynamics often contribute to a "withdraw–withdraw" pattern that appears to be
common for many couples coping with chronic illness.

Assessment

Equipped with both a speech-language therapist's lens and an
EFT therapist's attachment lens, it is now possible to turn to
assessment and some unique concerns that a therapist faces in
working with a couple confronting the impact of aphasia. Determining appropriateness of EFT treatment begins by exploring a
couple's willingness to take part in the cocreation of what we
have coined as a "communication platform." This platform is
an emotionally safe and communicatively even playing field
for both partners that represents the most significant innovation in using EFT therapy with couples and aphasia.

The person with aphasia often has become familiar with
some of the strategies used in creating a communication

platform in previous work in speech and language therapy. While this partner may be familiar with and open to the need of a platform, the caregiving partner may have less experience with the process and as a result be more hesitant to embrace the process. Cotherapists must be able to engage both partners by using their own interpersonal skills, empathetic and non-expert stance, and their knowledge of supportive communication strategies. Early sessions will give an indication of each partner's stance and flexibility in accepting a reframing of the problem in a relationship context. A couple's participation will also reflect the degree of secure versus insecure attachment and caregiving styles. This reframe represents a significant shift for the couple because the person with aphasia previously was primarily perceived as the problem.

Therapists identify contraindications for couples therapy in the early stages of constructing the communication platform. Frustration, increased vulnerability, and dependence on others increase the risk of abuse. We believe that it is important for therapists to identify aphasia-related abuse, which in our opinion need not rule out proceeding cautiously with therapy. Instances of abuse following the onset of aphasia are commonly forms of neglect. Perceptions of incompetence and some of the coexisting behavioral changes may result in neglectful behaviors that include being isolated from social activities, social conversations, important decision making, and financial affairs. Individual assessment sessions must clearly explore whether or not either partner is a victim of physical or emotional abuse. EFT should not proceed if physical abuse exists or if abuse existed prior to onset of aphasia. Safety remains a primary concern.

In the first session, the EFT therapist and speech-language therapist begin to "weave" together their respective areas of expertise to provide a communication platform. The "platform" is a term we use metaphorically to capture the concept of providing support to facilitate inclusion in conversation. For example, the platform offers an emotionally safe and even playing field for communication, where each partner is given voice to explore his or her experience and "aphasia-related challenges." These challenges commonly pose threats to the couple's emotional security. The communication platform evolves into a tangible object in the form of many sheets of paper and other communication resources used that serves a practical purpose in supporting conversation.

Throughout assessment, treatment, and consolidation, we actively capture on paper the transient words and nonverbal messages of both partners, as well as gist of our own input, using ad hoc diagrams, key words, multiple choices, and drawings. These initial couple-specific, pencil-and-paper "conversations" form an integral part of the communication platform, which in reality becomes increasingly thick and solid with ongoing layering of additional therapy documents cocreated by the couple and therapists. These documents become an active part of our interactions with couples and continue to serve to support and maintain the therapeutic alliance throughout treatment.

Therapy is conducted at round tables to facilitate this process and all therapy documents are kept readily accessible. The platform makes it possible to proceed with identifying negative cycles and continuing to deepen the engagement between partners. The tasks and interventions of EFT become possible through the use of communication strategies, which are continuously woven into the therapy sessions, thus maintaining a strong platform. Documentation helps to facilitate application of the skills and interventions that a typical EFT therapist uses to access and reformulate emotion. Reflection, validation, evocative responding, and heightening all become possible, even with limitations of aphasia. Restructuring interactions follows surprisingly easily; this is perhaps partly due to the positive experience of using the communication strategies. Discovering that they can communicate after all is a very powerful shared experience for the couple.

The scaffolding used in EFT to support the therapy process is an essential component of our communication platform. One can appreciate how writing out key words as a conversation unfolds fits well with the scaffolding components like RISSSC: repeat, image, simple, slow, soft, client's words (Johnson, 2004, p. 109). When normal verbal communication has been compromised, this solid communication platform sets the stage for exploration of more difficult and less easily accessible emotions. The development of a foundation of trust and customized communicative support requires significantly more time up front than for most other EFT applications. These efforts are critical to enable couples to become sufficiently comfortable to be able to forget about the aphasia, per se, and begin to focus on their relationship.

Adjunctive resources support the communication process and are included throughout therapy as a part of the communication platform. Use of a stickman (Figure 5.1), in combination

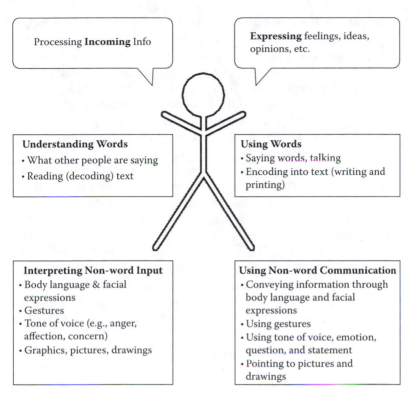

Figure 5.1 Stickman.

with other generic and/or commercially available pictographic materials (see, for example, resources available through the Aphasia Institute: http://www.aphasia.ca/), provides essential concrete, visual support for the therapists to proceed safely in therapy. In most first meetings with couples, the process of validating and normalizing a couple's experience of aphasia is supported through the introduction of stickman, which is a graphic depicting processes involved in communication and visually highlights the distinction between the four, word-based language modalities affected by aphasia. These include understanding what is being said, reading, talking, and writing and other receptive and expressive processes (represented in the lower half of the graphic in Figure 5.1) that are not based on the use of words.

As we review the graphic, we highlight the impact of tone of voice and body language, particularly in face-to-face communication, emphasizing that these communicative parameters are particularly relevant when the message being communicated

involves feelings and attitudes (Mehrabian, 1971). To further
illustrate the central role of nonverbal communication, we
role-play common social exchanges and the potential for confusion when the words being used do not seem to match the
apparent emotional state of the speaker. For example, saying
"just great" in response to the question, "How are you?" would
seem incongruent with the actual message being conveyed if
delivered in a flat tone or with the respondent simultaneously
rolling his or her eyes.

Typically, in previous individual sessions, the speech-
language therapist has already assessed the communication
difficulties experienced by the person with aphasia and brings
her knowledge of effective communication strategies into the
first session. Standardized measures are useful to determine
attachment styles (adult attachment questionnaire; Simpson,
Rholes, & Phillips, 1996), levels of depression (BDI-II; Beck,
Steer, & Brown, 1996), and relationship distress (dyadic adjustment scale; Spanier, 1976). However, verbal ability must be
taken into consideration in use of a self-report measure with a
person who has aphasia.

Balancing the implications for validation of measures with
the desirability of obtaining direct information, we have
adapted some measures to be "aphasia friendly"; in other
situations, we have facilitated self-reporting by the person
with aphasia through additional communication support.
We administer the caregiver questionnaire, developed by
Kunce and Shaver (1994), to the partner without aphasia as
a resource in assessing a partner's caregiving abilities and
motivation. This measure is also helpful in predicting how
successfully engaged a caregiving partner will be in what initially appears as a laborious therapy process.

Likewise, we assess the impact of aphasia on other immediate family members, including children. When acute issues in
the parent–child relationship are apparent, there is an urgent
need to provide supportive interventions. For example, one
mother with aphasia related that her most painful loss was the
loss of the role of mother. This loss became evident when her
son refused to bring home the announcement of the parent–
teacher interviews. Embarrassed, he did not want his teachers
or friends to meet his mother. In his words, "They will see how
stupid she is...she can't even talk to people." Through the process of therapy, a communication platform was constructed
and the mother's competence was revealed and seen by her

son. Further, the platform facilitated their sharing underlying fears about losing each other.

As with other families in distress, the EFT therapist must assess and decide which family dyad to work with and whether or not the distressed-couple and parent–child dyads can be treated concurrently. If concurrent treatment is not possible, we recommend reducing couple distress before turning to parenting issues, as suggested by Kobak and Mandelbaum (2003).

Treatment

Following assessment of the couple, it is possible to turn our attention to the treatment interventions that are unique to working with this population. Here we will expand further on the use of a communication platform and the interventions used to address the behavioral changes associated with aphasia and uncovering partners' underlying feelings and attachment needs. Two primary behavioral changes can threaten the couple's relationship security and may contribute to withdraw–withdraw cycles after onset of aphasia, even among the most securely attached couples.

The first behavioral change is a lack of initiation that is experienced as a loss of responsiveness and accessibility between partners. The second behavioral change involves unpredictable explosions of frustration and anger, which we label as catastrophic reactions. These explosive reactions pose a real threat to felt safety in the relationship and interfere with proximity seeking and closeness. Successful outcomes in treatment are related more to decreasing the negative impact the behaviors have on relationships than to the goal of increasing initiation or reducing catastrophic reactions.

Forming a Communication Platform

Our consistent approach begins by gently engaging the couple verbally as well as through the use of a full range of supportive communication strategies, including key wording, gesture, body language, and drawing. We maintain a focus on eliciting and validating the expression of each partner's emotional experience of the trauma of losing previously integral and automatic language skills. We are also seeking to create as many opportunities as possible for the partners to have the previously mentioned new experiences of communicating with each other, despite the aphasia, and setting the stage for replacing negative cycles with positive ones. Here the goal is to increase the security of the relationship through increased accessibility and responsiveness, focusing attention on each partner's attachment-related needs.

For example, we often review the stickman graphic with a couple in order to facilitate expression of each partner's perceptions of aphasia-related changes in each of the four language modalities: understanding what is being said, reading, talking, and writing. To facilitate this conversation, we "detour" to a new piece of paper and draw four visual analog scales, each simply anchored by 0 and 100% at either end of a therapist-drawn line and labeled with one of the modalities— for example, reading. Typically, with communicative support to convey the task, even persons who have severe aphasia are well able to indicate their perceived ability in reading by placing a mark on the line. Explicit discussion of losses frequently elicits tears from one or both spouses, and this emotional moment offers an opening for the therapists to explore sadness, anger, or other expressed emotions a bit further.

Throughout the steps of therapy, primary and secondary emotions are captured on paper in many different ways and are actively used to explore and expand emotions. Therapists have on hand a single page with a variety of faces depicting different emotions; the person with aphasia points to the one that fits most closely to his or her experience at any given moment. Even more effective are, in the moment, writing key words or making diagrams capturing emotions as they are being experienced. For example, in the case of sadness, the word SADNESS may be written in large letters on a single page, accompanied by the drawing of a face with mouth turned downward. The therapist may have the person with aphasia decide how much the mouth is turned down or have the person draw it on his or her own. The powerful visual concepts used in EFT that focus on interactions such as a cycle or pattern, distance and closeness, and moving away from or toward all lend themselves easily to graphics. One man expressed his feeling of isolation and hurt by marking over and over again using heavy lines between the names of his wife and daughter, while only a thin single line was drawn showing his connection to his wife.

At the same time, the success of the person with aphasia genuinely expressing how he or she feels enables the therapist to heighten this experience and to highlight attention to a sense of personal competence and the new possibilities for the couple's relationship. At this point, the therapist may refer back to the diagram of stickman and the lower portion of the diagram to capture further what ability has been lost and what ability is still intact.

Frequently, the sessions proceed with a couple's detailed description of their experience of the events at the time of the stroke. As they tell the story, the therapists use a time line to document the trauma from each partner's perspective while focusing on significant dates, actions, places, and recollections. Both partners are encouraged to place their own marks on the time line document in a way that makes sense to them. Kept in clear view throughout future sessions, the time line can be used as a reference to their story as many times as needed. The time line visually illustrates each partner's personal experience of the trauma and becomes a key means to help the couple access their emotional experience.

As the therapist focuses on times of acute trauma, the partner with aphasia may have little recall or awareness of the events around the stroke, but for the caregiving partner, this is an opportunity to share the traumatic experience of the stroke. This may be the first time the person with aphasia has heard his or her partner's version. It is a critical time to ensure a complete understanding of what has been told and to provide a means of responding to this story through supportive communication strategies. Validation from the therapist and then from the partner with aphasia can be a turning point, especially for a more withdrawn caregiving partner. The therapist can further strengthen this shared support by accessing and processing the caregiver's underlying fears of losing his or her partner and the experience of feeling helpless and alone.

The therapist team's efforts to establish a solid communication platform provide an experiential tool for restoring perceptions of communicative competence in both partners, although it has not enabled the couple to face the other neuropsychological changes in the person with aphasia. In our clinical experience, these changes frequently have a more profound negative impact on the partner without aphasia. The feelings of incompetence are more easily accessed and apparent in the person with aphasia because of the obvious communication difficulties. Unfortunately, a caregiver's struggle to retain a sense of competence is compromised over time as he or she struggles and unsuccessfully attempts to cope with the unusual aphasia-related behaviors.

Sometimes the aphasia partner's behaviors that we have labeled as lack of initiation and explosive or catastrophic

reactions are experienced as a significant loss or as an attachment injury. The caregiver's experience of these stressful events
appears to be unimportant or even lost in the challenges of
dealing with aphasia. Not surprisingly, relationship distress
can often be traced back to a gradual loss of caregiver confidence and a lack of acknowledgment of his or her experience.

As a result, the caregiver typically moves to a withdrawn
stance in the couple's pattern. The partner with aphasia
is already in an "imposed" withdrawn position. Thus, a
withdraw–withdraw cycle frequently unfolds, especially in
the years after onset; this helps to explain the unbearable pain
and isolation experienced by the most distressed couples. The
therapist's focus on processing the couple's behaviors in terms
of this cycle sets the stage for each partner to move from a
withdrawn position to explore further underlying feelings
that threaten a felt sense of relationship security.

Loss of Initiation

The "imposed" withdraw stance in the partner with aphasia is
due to language impairment per se and is experienced by the
partner as loss of initiation. Caregivers first identify the more
overt behavioral manifestations of the loss of initiation as key
sources of stress and dissatisfaction. Caregivers relate their distress to having to play "Twenty Questions" 24/7, the responsibility of having to "speak for" the partner with aphasia, and loss
of their partner's input in decisions. They also describe their
fatigue and frustration linked with the perceived/apparent
unwillingness of their partners to offer to help with any household chores, even those that are well within their capabilities.
Examples of areas of contention raised in our therapy sessions
have been as simple as straightening a curtain, filling the dog
bowl, or unloading the dishwasher.

How the caregiving partner makes sense of this pervasive inaction is crucial and in turn affects whether he or she
responds by turning away from or toward the partner. Once
the partner without aphasia's experience of living with "loss
of initiation" is validated, he or she is more easily able to
accept its neurological origin, like the language and physical
impairment. In turn, the caregivers are more open to adopting
a necessary initiating role using strategies that help cue their
partners. This is difficult work as the caregiver directly con-
fronts the linguistic/grammatical difficulty of verbally engaging his or her partner through the use of such social, almost
automatic questions. "What did you do today?" or "How are

you feeling?" are familiar prompts. The therapist assists the caregiver in finding prompts that are normal for each specific couple, using "turns of phrase" and expressions that help prompt communication.

The caregiver's experience of this "loss of initiation" results in a deep sense of loss that triggers attachment grief and fear. This loss means no longer hearing a loved one comment in previously intimate ways that express the uniqueness of their relationship. The caregiver is then also injured—wounded. In this new framework where their relationship, rather than the communicative barrier, is front and center, the meaning of this hurt can be validated and underlying emotions processed. The struggle to communicate is now reframed as a struggle to reconnect and the pattern that developed is framed as the couple's struggle to cope in the best way they could with this unfamiliar disability and frightening loss of emotional connection.

The couple's process of working through this injury becomes part of their developing competence and reengagement. The couple can be left with documentation to support further processing on their own or strategies to prevent future hurts and moments of disconnection. Importantly, we have learned that providing education and insight into the behavioral changes is not adequate to deal with the emotional aftermath.

For example, Mary and her husband Harry sought counseling several years after Harry's onset of aphasia. Mary had become discouraged and the early sessions revealed a withdraw–withdraw cycle that had recently evolved. Prior to the stroke, they had a secure relationship with both partners able to approach the other for physical affection. After the onset, Mary found herself in the new role of sole pursuer, initiating displays of affection in addition to dealing with all of the couple's day-to-day activities. When she started therapy, she was feeling distant from Harry and doubted he still desired her. When she thought of all the years she had devoted to supporting him, she went into hurt and angry withdrawal. Therapy revealed that her distress was related to a specific incident, which was framed as an attachment injury.

Before the stroke, the couple had a tradition in which Mary would model her new clothes and Harry would respond with great enthusiasm. However, when she attempted this ritual for the first time since the stroke, much to her shock, Harry showed no interest. In the safety of therapy session, Mary revealed how devastating this was for her. The therapist guided Mary to connect with her underlying fear that she no longer mattered to her husband. This provided an opportunity for the therapist carefully to set up an enactment in which Mary was able to turn to Harry and using verbal words, gestures, and written key words, share her fear and ask for reassurance.

With this population, the EFT therapist must be more active in facilitating the enactment. Here, the therapist first confirmed that Harry understood Mary's message by repeating it and writing key words. Then, the therapist facilitated his response by using a visual analog scale on which he was able to indicate how much he cared. Much to Mary's surprise, he took the pencil and made a mark beyond the end of the highest point on the scale! Harry was able to respond with compassion and share that he had not intended to hurt her. Mary felt, heard, and then comforted as Harry reached for her and held her hand. This prompted a bonding event for the couple and Mary was able to shift from her withdrawn position and gradually become reengaged in the relationship.

Catastrophic Reactions

Catastrophic reactions are another coexisting behavioral change that can have a negative impact on relationships. From our experience, reactions range from tears to white-hot anger and throwing objects. For our clients, the trigger for such "catastrophic reactions" is often the intensely frustrating and inexplicable inconsistency of their ability to communicate. In particular, the experience of being unable to convey a relatively simple, but important message, which he or she has been able to express in recent history, is a particularly strong trigger. Frustrations relating to physical therapy and slow recovery may also be a trigger. While emotional lability is distressing and perplexing for both partners, unpredictable catastrophic reactions can be frightening and have a long-lasting negative impact on the partner without aphasia. Adding to this hurt, the caregiver sees the partner quickly get over this painful and intense event with little recall of what occurred.

Couples are embarrassed and ashamed of these incidences and discussing these moments is often taboo, especially in the early stages of therapy. Change can occur through helping couples talk about these experiences, validating their experience, and processing underlying emotions. Using the communication platform couples can share the fears and their own needs after one of these catastrophic reactions. After taking safety into consideration, we have found that partners can be helped to turn to each other to cope with these explosive reactions. By reframing these reactions as the most dangerous "monsters" a couple faces in confronting aphasia, the therapist can heighten the couple's need to face these threats together. Like other behavior changes, catastrophic reactions play into feelings of caregiver incompetence and relationship insecurity, as we will illustrate in the following case example.

CASE EXAMPLE

Roger and Jane, a couple in their late 50s, sought help coping with the aftermath of Roger's stroke, which had occurred 2 years earlier. This stroke left him with aphasia and weakness in his right arm and leg. The couple self-referred under encouragement from their adult daughter, who became alarmed hearing her mother talk about separation. Roger had been a very successful executive whose job required him to travel internationally. Married 24 years, Jane had quit her job to be able to travel with Roger after their only daughter left home. They described their lifestyle as going from "full speed" to "dead stop" after his stroke. Thanks to a generous insurance plan, finances were not a problem. Roger was highly motivated in rehabilitation and worked hard in speech therapy and physical therapy, where his goal was a 100% recovery.

Unfortunately, the stroke resulted in significant communication difficulties. Roger needed support with both his receptive and expressive abilities (see Figure 5.1). The couple needed strategies to help him both process information and express his experience. He was not able to initiate conversation, ask questions, or respond to open-ended questions. When the pace of the conversation was slowed, more complex conversations were possible using a variety of supports that included repeating, key wording, diagrams, and visual analog scales. While it was evident that Jane had knowledge of these strategies, she confided that she had stopped using them.

When the couple was referred to therapy, Jane appeared despondent, describing their social life as nothing more than short visits from family. Friends had dropped off due to discomfort around Roger's communication difficulties and his unpredictable and embarrassing angry outbursts.

In the initial sessions, the therapists created a strong alliance with the couple and a communication platform was used to help Jane and Roger explore their past and present relationship issues. The couple's experience with supportive communication strategies enabled this process to move quickly.

It proved important that Jane be able to acknowledge to the therapist, and then to Roger, that she had stopped using these strategies to support conversation in recent months. She also stopped doing the extra things that she knew he liked. Touch was now reduced to only necessary physical care. As she related this change and the therapist put these messages down on paper, Jane became tearful. Roger responded with a puzzled look and uttered the words, "Why? Why?"

Together, the therapists portrayed the couple's interaction in terms of a cycle, one that had recently changed. Their old and new patterns were easily captured on paper. Early after Roger's onset of aphasia, Jane adopted the position of a pursuer, which played out in her role as his wife and caregiver. Roger was able to respond when she approached and cued him. In their cycle, if Jane did not pursue Roger, he essentially remained physically and seemingly emotionally disengaged. Roger's withdrawal was heightened by his imposed "loss of initiation." Despite Jane's previous knowledge of how actively to support communication with him, Roger's lack of ability and minimal response led her to withdraw as well.

His lack of response to her withdrawal confirmed to Jane that Roger did not notice or care about her. She began to feel that anyone could take her place as caregiver and, essentially, she did not matter to him. The therapists helped the couple to understand that Roger's apparently withdrawn position was one manifestation of his reduced ability to initiate that, like the aphasia, was another neuropsychological consequence of stroke. Delineating and validating both partners' positions in their destructive cycle—especially Roger's inability to initiate conversation or ask questions—was the beginning of a change event for the couple. The speech-language therapist led Roger in responding to Jane's fear that she no longer mattered to him. When asked more concretely, he confirmed that she could not be replaced by anyone in the world!

However, tension remained in their relationship and, as the process moved into Stage 2 of EFT, Jane was able to express her ongoing fear that she would not be able to continue in this relationship. Jane's withdrawn position was deeply rooted in her feelings of incompetence and failure as a caregiver and wife. These powerful feelings were frequently triggered by Roger's angry outbursts. By this point in therapy, Roger had increased self-confidence and was able to stay engaged. He resisted his usual angry defensive responses that dismissed Jane's concerns by arguing that she could not possibly know what he was going through.

The EFT therapist must carefully support the withdrawn caregiver, who not only may be reluctant to speak about her own needs but also may feel that sharing her needs will cause harm, and possibly another stroke. The following transcript illustrates that techniques used here to create the communication platform parallel general EFT interventions used to access and reformulate emotions. In this case, skills such as slowing down, repeating, heightening, and reflecting help the withdrawn caregiver feel heard and validated. The slow pace of conversation also helps her monitor her husband's reaction and provides much needed safety. The EFT therapist in turn "holds" the partner with aphasia through slowing the conversation down, writing, and softly checking out if he got the caregiver's message. For the first time since his stroke, Roger is hearing Jane's emotional needs being expressed and is able to respond in a positive way.

Therapist: So, Jane, you said sometimes you still don't have the energy. You need to stop.

Jane: It's hard, I still do the basics. Not the extras—like rubbing his affected leg. It's always about the stroke. I get up 2 hours earlier each morning just to have some nonstroke time by myself.

Therapist: You're very tired. (Jane nods.) It's like there is only one channel, the stroke channel. All day, every day you are always on the same channel.

Speech-language therapist (to Roger) draws a TV, writes "stroke channel," and draws a frown.

Jane: I don't like the channel. I can't handle his sudden bursts of yelling (turns to Roger). You pound the table like a Frankenstein and swear! The next minute you are calm but I...I stay totally rattled for a long, long time. I never get over it.

Speech-language therapist slows down and repeats Jane's message using key words and pictures, confirms that Roger got the message, and checks with Jane that this is her message.

Therapist: So when Roger gets angry, that makes you want to give up? His anger pushes you away?

Roger (to speech-language therapist): I have to get to 100%, maybe 90%, physical and speech. (He searches for the document with previous diagram in which he mapped out each year and what percent progress he needs to make.)

Jane (angry): See! He has to be physically perfect before he can be happy. Sometimes I see him laugh and then he just catches himself and stops. He can't be happy until he is perfect again, perfect speech, perfect body. I can't do any more. I can't wait that long to feel some joy around here. There are times when I do feel happiness...but it's like I am not supposed to feel this way.

Therapist: You need to be able to make him happy; that's what you're hoping for...just being able to feel a little joy. That is important for you? If both of you have some happiness, all your work has been worth it? (slowly and softly) Let's stay with this...See if we can figure this out some more.

The EFT therapist acknowledged that Jane's voice was trembling. Always the supportive caregiver who parked her own needs, she was now risking speaking out. Roger also picked up this different tone and kept a steady gaze on Jane. At this point, the therapist set up a communication-supported enactment using a drawing of two cups half empty and half full to help them turn to each other and evoke further emotion. The therapist asked the couple to indicate their desire for closeness and both drew a line at the top of their cup.

Next the couple indicated the degree of joy and happiness they felt. Jane showed she had some joy/happiness in her cup by marking a line a little way from the bottom and added arrows going up and down to indicate fluctuation in how much joy she felt. When Roger's turn came to represent joy, rather than making a line near the bottom of the cup, as everyone anticipated, he drew a hole in the bottom of the cup, indicating that any joy that comes to him just seems to run out.

This new dialogue was a turning point for Jane and helped her move out of a withdrawn position in the cycle. She was able to share her underlying fear of being a failure as a caregiver. This fear became acute when she could not make Roger happy and she wondered if they would ever really be happy as a couple. Recognizing Roger's inability to initiate conversation, both therapists actively led him in giving feedback that addressed her attachment needs. Skillfully, the two therapists worked together to facilitate a new conversation for the couple by tentatively suggesting that Roger could talk to Jane about his sadness. The therapist encouraged Roger that it might not be so scary to reach for Jane and that he might not need to get so angry, especially when he realized it pushed her away.

Roger's catastrophic reactions decreased but did not go away completely. It was apparent that the frustration of both his aphasia and physical impairment was too great to suppress his explosive responses consistently all the time. However, Jane's ability to be in touch with Roger's sadness helped to restore her felt connection. Jane reframed her experience of his anger and neglect in the context of Roger's other behaviors and impairments that were related to his brain injury. This allowed her to respond differently to his frightening outbursts. Rather than letting these behaviors push her away, she had the option of turning to Roger and using communication strategies to ask him for reassurance, which, in effect, restored reciprocity to their relationship. Jane now felt closer to Roger and more confident and able to assert herself. Also, she was able to reassure her daughter that separation was no longer an issue.

CONCLUSION

Supportive communication strategies developed by speech-language therapists and the skills of emotionally focused therapists can be woven together to make EFT powerfully accessible to couples living with chronic aphasia. Sharing a common attachment-based understanding of relationship distress, EFT therapists and speech-language therapists work together to address the unique emotional needs of both traumatized partners. The creation of a communication platform, as well as the experience of using it to address relationship issues, provides the couple a secure base and the foundation of a long-term support mechanism that can help partners stay connected in the face of future challenges. This platform facilitates the therapist's ability to explore and validate each partner's experience and reframe the problem of living with aphasia in the broader context of their relationship and attachment needs.

Most importantly, this cotherapy model provides an opportunity to address the emotional needs of the partner without aphasia, strengthening his or her ability to provide care and maintain relationship security. Because support of this person is one of the most important links to successful coping with chronic illness and disability, we believe that EFT should become an integral part of the array of support services provided to families in rehabilitation and community settings. The power of EFT to help couples reengage both the care and support they need, even when facing adversity, points to our timeless and universal longing for a secure and lasting relationship.

REFERENCES

Astrom, M., Adolfsson, R., & Asplund, K. (1993). Major depression in stroke patients—A 3-year longitudinal study. *Stroke, 24,* 967–982.

Beck, A., Steer, R., & Brown, G. (1996). *BDI-II Beck depresssion inventory* (2nd ed.). San Antonio, TX: The Psychological Corporation.

Boles, L., & Lewis, M. (2000). Solution-focused co-therapy for a couple with aphasia. *Asia Pacific Journal of Speech, Language and Hearing, 5,* 73–78.

Code, C., & Herrmann, M. (2003). The relevance of emotional and psychosocial factors in aphasia to rehabilitation. *Neuropsychological Rehabilitation, 13,* 109–132.

Collins, N., Guichard, A., Ford, M., & Feeney, B. (2006). Responding to need in intimate relationships: Normative processes and individual differences. In M. Mikulincer & G. Goodman (Eds.), *Dynamics of romantic love: Attachment, caregiving, and sex* (pp. 149–189). New York, NY: Guilford Press.

Croteau, C., & Le Dorze, G. (2006). Overprotection, "speaking for," and conversational participation: A study of couples with aphasia. *Aphasiology, 20,* 327–336.

DeAngelis, T. (2010). Today's generation of researchers is making stroke rehabilitation more effective, consumer-friendly and cutting-edge. *Monitor on Psychology, March,* 53–55.

George, C., & Solomon, J. (1999). Attachment and caregiving: The caregiving behavioral system. In J. Cassidy & P. R. Shaver (Eds.), *Handbook of attachment: Theory, research, and clinical applications* (pp. 649–670). New York, NY: Guilford Press.

Goldstein, K. (1939). *The organism: A holistic approach to biology, derived from pathological data in man.* New York, NY: American Book.

Holland, A. (2007). Counseling/coaching in chronic aphasia: Getting on with life. *Topics in Language Disorders, 27,* 339–350.

Johnson, S. M. (2002). *Emotionally focused couple therapy with trauma survivors: Strengthening the attachment bonds.* New York, NY: Guilford Press.

Johnson, S. M. (2004). *The practice of emotionally focused couple therapy: Creating connection.* New York, NY: Brunner-Routledge.

Johnson, S. M. (2008). *Hold me tight: Seven conversations for a lifetime of love.* New York, NY: Little, Brown & Company.

Kagan, A., & Gailey, G. (1993). Functional is not enough: Training conversation partners in aphasia. In A. Holland & M. Forbes (Eds.), *Aphasia treatment: World perspectives* (pp. 199–226). San Diego, CA: Singular.

Kagan, A., & Shumway, E. (2003). Communicating with patients/clients who know more than they can say: Introduction to supported conversation for adults with aphasia (SCAtm). PowerPoint Educational Module 1 and 2. Toronto, Canada: Aphasia Institute.

Kobak, R., & Mandelbaum, T. (2003). Caring for the caregiver. In S. Johnson & V. Whiffen (Eds.), *Attachment processes in couple and family therapy* (pp. 144–164). New York, NY: Guilford Press.

Kowal, J., Johnson, S., & Lee, A. (2003). Chronic illness in couples: A case for emotionally focused therapy. *Journal of Marital and Family Therapy, 29,* 299–310.

Kunce, L. J., & Shaver, P. R. (1994). An attachment-theoretical approach to caregiving in romantic relationships. In K. Bartholomew & D. Perlman (Eds.), *Advances in personal relationships: Attachment processes in adulthood,* Vol. 5 (pp. 205–237). London, England: Kingsley.

LPAA Project Group (in alphabetical order: Chapey, R., Duchan, J., Elman, R., Garcia, L., Kagan, A., Lyon, J., & Simmons-Mackie, N.). (2000). Life participation approaches to aphasia: A statement of values for the future ASHA Leader, 5, 4–6, American Speech-Language-Hearing Association.

MacIntosh, H., & Johnson, S. (2008). Emotionally focused therapy for couples and childhood sexual abuse survivors. *Journal of Marital and Family Therapy, 34,* 298–315.

Mehrabian, A. (1971). *Silent messages.* Belmont, CA: Wadsworth.

Michallet, B., Tetreault, S., & Le Dorze, G. (2003). The consequences of severe aphasia on the spouses of aphasic people: A description of the adaptation process. *Aphasiology, 17,* 835–859.

Mikail, S. (2003). Attachment and the experience of chronic pain: A couples perspective. In S. M. Johnson & V. E. Whiffen (Eds.), *Attachment process in couple and family therapy* (pp. 366–385). New York, NY: Guilford Press.

Mikulincer, M., & Goodman, G. (Eds.). (2006). *Dynamics of romantic love: Attachment, caregiving, and sex.* New York, NY: Guilford Press.

Mikulincer, M., & Shaver, P. (2007). *Attachment in adulthood: Structure, dynamics, and change.* New York, NY: Guilford Press.

Naaman, S., Johnson, S. M., & Radwan, K. (in press). Evaluation of the clinical efficacy of emotionally focused therapy on psychological adjustment of couples facing early breast cancer. *Psychiatry: Biological and Interpersonal Processes.*

Nichols, F., Varchevker, A., & Pring, T. (1996). Working with people with aphasia and their families: An exploration of the use of family therapy techniques. *Aphasiology, 10,* 767–781.

Ryan, C., Stiell, K., Gailey, G., & Makinen, J. (2008). Evaluating a family centered approach to leisure education and community reintegration following a stroke. *Therapeutic Recreation Journal, 42,* 119–131.

Shadden, B. (2005). Aphasia as identity theft: Theory and practice. *Aphasiology, 19,* 211–223.

Simpson, J. A., Rholes, S. W., & Phillips, D. (1996). Conflict in close relationships: An attachment perspective. *Journal of Personality and Social Psychology, 71,* 899–914.

Spanier, G. (1976). Measuring dyadic adjustment. *Journal of Marriage and Family, 13,* 113–126.

Stiell, K., & Gailey, G. (1995). Cotherapy with couples affected by aphasia. *Topics in Stroke Rehabilitation, 2*(3), 34–39.

Stiell, K., Naaman, S. C., & Lee, A. (2007). Couples and chronic illness: An attachment perspective and emotionally focused therapy interventions. *Journal of Systemic Therapies, 26,* 59–74.

Williams, S. E., & Freer, C. A. (1986). Aphasia: Its effect on marital relationships. *Archives, Physical Medicine and Rehabilitation, 67,* 250–252.

Six

Emotionally Focused Couple Therapy in Chronic Medical Illness
Working With the Aftermath of Breast Cancer

SANDRA NAAMAN, KARAM RADWAN,
AND SUSAN M. JOHNSON

INTRODUCTION

Breast cancer, currently the most prevalent female malignancy across all age groups, has become an important public health concern worldwide. Advances in screening technologies and treatments have resulted in increased survivorship; fortunately, women are living longer, but they have to contend with significant biopsychosocial sequelae (Sherman & Hossfeld, 1990).

Beyond the acute phase of illness, breast cancer patients face a number of challenges, including reckoning with just having been diagnosed with a potentially life-threatening illness, long-term effects of toxic treatments, the possibility of recurrence even after many years of apparently successful treatment, career interruptions, and financial strain. Adequate resolution of these concerns occurs within a preexisting family context, which affects and is affected by the disease and treatment processes. The pivotal role of the marital relationship has been receiving gradual recognition by researchers within the psychosocial oncology literature. Northouse and Peters-Golden (1993) redefine breast cancer as a "biopsychosocial

141

problem that occurs in the context of an intense personal relationship that affects, and is affected by, the disease process in circular reciprocity."

The goals of this chapter are threefold: to discuss the impact of breast cancer on the couple relationships; to review empirically established interpersonal processes shown to unfold in couples facing breast cancer, as well as identify risk factors associated with greater psychological distress; and to illustrate the process of relationship repair for couples impacted by cancer morbidity. Emotionally Focused Couples Therapy (EFCT) is presented as a useful treatment option for couples experiencing unremitting psychological and relational distress following diagnosis and treatment for breast cancer.

IMPACT OF BREAST CANCER ON THE MARITAL RELATIONSHIP

Following diagnosis of a life-threatening illness, patients often describe their spouses as a primary source of support. The illness experience and associated treatment regimens are potent enough, however, to provoke various forms of emotional disturbance—not only in patients themselves but also in patients' partners. These include anxiety, depression, and fears of recurrence and losing one's partner to death (Iqbal, Qureshi, & Saeed Siddiqui, 2001). As many as 29% of sampled couples who had been receiving cancer treatment report clinically significant levels of emotional distress (Rodrigue & Hoffman, 1994), and there is evidence for concordance between the levels of emotional distress experienced by patients and their partners (Northouse, Laten, & Reddy, 1995).

In the face of a cancer diagnosis, spouses experience levels of distress similar to or even greater than those of their affected partners (Ferrell, Ervin, Smith, Marek, & Melancon, 2002; Northouse, Mood, Templin, Mellon, & George, 2000). Northouse (1989) observed that, 18 months after treatment, both patients and their partners reported similar levels of psychological distress. More importantly from a coping perspective, husbands' and wives' levels of adjustment to breast cancer at 1 year after diagnosis seem to have a significant and direct effect on each other's adjustment (Northouse, Templin, & Mood, 2001).

Difficulties in psychosocial adjustment are not solely confined to the early phase of illness; they may persist over time for both patients and husbands in a consistent fashion. Dyadic adjustment problems and elevated emotional distress occurring well into the posttreatment phase have been reported in several studies (Hagedoorn, Bruunk, Kuijer, Wobbes, & Sanderman, 2000; Oberst & Scott, 1988). A longitudinal study of 43 newly diagnosed breast cancer patients, undertaken by Keitel, Zevon, Rounds, Petrelli, and Karakousis (1990), found that spouses' distress levels tended to decline over time and that those who continued to experience adjustment difficulties were more likely to be married to patients with relatively higher levels of physical symptoms. In another study by Omne-Ponten, Holmberg, Bergstrom, Sjoden, and Burns (1993) that compared the levels of adjustment among husbands of patients who had undergone either breast-conserving surgery or mastectomy, 48% were found to experience continued emotional distress up to 13 months after surgical treatment. This rate was similar to that reported in patients themselves. The reciprocal effect that partners have on each other when serious illness strikes is clear.

In general, dyads report similar levels of distress, suggesting some degree of congruence in their adjustment processes. While distress in couples appears to decline over time, for a sizeable proportion of couples, there continue to be elevated levels of unremitting distress even after the immediate shock and crisis of diagnosis and treatment have elapsed. The rates of dissatisfaction and divorce in couples facing breast cancer are not any higher than in couples in the general population, but there is evidence of more strain and conflict (Carter, Carter, & Siliunas, 1993; Northouse, Templin, Mood, & Oberst, 1998). Not surprisingly, couples who were at high risk for marital breakdown were those who faced the breast cancer experience with preexisting marital problems, where the illness had added further demands and strain on their relationship (Carter et al., 1993; Lewis & Hammond, 1992; Northouse, 1989).

INTERPERSONAL PROCESSES IN COUPLES FACING BREAST CANCER: EMPIRICAL FINDINGS

The emotional support provided by an intimate partner can have a profound buffering effect on the stress levels experienced by the breast cancer patient as she contends with both the psychological and physiological sequelae of her illness (Lewis & Deal, 1995; Northouse, 1984). Emotional support is conceptualized in the literature as communication of care, concern, empathy, comfort, and reassurance both verbally and nonverbally, such as through facial expressions and gestures (Helgeson & Cohen, 1996). Specifically, provision of emotional support by husbands has been linked to lower emotional distress, fewer depressive symptoms, and better role adjustment in their wives who were experiencing breast cancer (Tatelman, 1999).

In fact, emotional support, as opposed to informational or instrumental support (e.g., problem solving), emerged as the most preferred type of support cited by women facing breast cancer, particularly if they experience greater impairment from their illness and treatment course (Manne, Alfieri, Taylor, & Dougherty, 1999). Increasing feelings of vulnerability in the breast cancer patient were assuaged by intimate exchanges characterized by high empathy and low withdrawal from the spouse (Pistrang & Barker, 1995).

A woman's intimate relationship seems to provide a unique type of support that, if absent or experienced aversively in this particularly stressful period, will predictably lead to a greater likelihood of mood disturbance, according to a number of studies (Burg & Seeman, 1994; Carter & Carter, 1994). Facing breast cancer and its associated stressors, however, can unwittingly propel couples to interact with each other in unsupportive ways as each spouse attempts to cope and regulate perceived partner distress (Lyons, Sullivan, Ritvo, & Coyne, 1995). Spousal interactional patterns in the context of early breast cancer and their association with overall adjustment seem to be associated with three general international patterns: open engagement, mutual avoidance (also known as protective buffering), and pursue–withdraw (Manne et al., 2006; Zunkel, 2002).

The first pattern—couples who are openly engaged—is characterized by a high degree of emotional expressivity about the illness and this has been linked to positive adjustment, enhanced cohesiveness, and decreased destructive conflict (e.g., Northouse, 1989). Specifically, in a study of 92 women diagnosed with Stage 1 and 2 breast carcinoma, those found to cope using emotional expression around their diagnosis had fewer cancer-related morbidities, decreased distress, and enhanced health and vigor 3 months after assessment (Stanton, Kirk, Cameron, & Danoff-Burg, 2000). This open engagement style characterizes more secure attachment and the processes of communication shaped in emotionally focused couple therapy.

The second pattern—mutual avoidance or protective buffering in couples facing breast cancer—seems to evolve as a result of efforts not to upset each other, resulting in withheld feelings of distress and worries. This appears to undermine adjustment in both partners. The use of protective buffering was compared to open communication and active engagement in a study and the latter pattern of communication predicted higher marital satisfaction and better adjustment in the face of illness (Hagedoorn et al., 2000). Similarly, breast cancer survivors who confided in their partners during times of crises enjoyed better prognoses, as measured by survival (Weihs, Enright, & Simmens, 2002). These findings are particularly relevant in view of the positive relationship between quality of the marital relationship and adjustment responses in both partners, as well as recovery from disease in patients (Burman & Margolin, 1992; Rodrigue & Park, 1996).

Other studies have also examined the impact of unilateral avoidance—specifically, husbands' avoidance in reaction to their partners' illness, where wives desired more closeness. When wives undergo mastectomies, some men tend to adopt a "protector's role" while simultaneously avoiding any open expression of feeling. Such stereotypic male behavior is often experienced aversively by their spouses, in addition to being perceived as insensitive and rejecting. Avoidance of open discussion about the cancer experience and its association with greater distress is a recurring finding in the cancer literature. This also parallels findings from the noncancer literature linking husbands' withdrawal behavior to aversive states of emotion in their wives (Gottman, 1994; Noller, Feeney, Bonnell, & Callan, 1994).

Husbands' avoidance is arguably the most deleterious interactional pattern to marital functioning and adjustment. In the face of crisis, habitual patterns of relating to one another usually become intensified. Avoiding discussion of the cancer has been shown to lead to communication problems, even among those couples who initially reported high levels of marital satisfaction (Lichtman, Taylor, & Wood, 1987). For other couples, long-standing negative patterns of communication often escalate during the illness trajectory, directly impacting the extent of destructive conflict and strain on each partner.

The third interactional pattern observed in some couples facing breast cancer entails a cycle of criticism and withdrawal from the wife and husband, respectively (Manne, Taylor, Dougherty, & Kemeny, 1997). Where emotional support and open engagement are unavailable, some breast cancer survivors tend to engage in criticism, which is experienced as creating some semblance of engagement (Pistrang & Barker, 1995). This seems to be more tolerable than dealing with more complete withdrawal on the husband's part. Unfortunately, the pursuing wife's behavior propels further distancing and withdrawal from her husband, leading to lower marital satisfaction.

Withdrawing or distancing behavior of some husbands in reaction to their wives' illnesses has been examined by some studies. Because husbands, as previously mentioned, respond to their wives' diagnoses with their own increased mood disturbance (Baider & Kaplan De-Nour, 1988), withdrawal from engagement is one form of affect regulation, albeit sometimes a maladaptive one. Withdrawal, as previously mentioned, is related to an enhanced risk for mood disturbance in the ill spouse.

In summary, unsupportive patterns of relating predictably lead to greater marital distress, especially in the context of a life-threatening illness, which can further exacerbate depressive symptoms in women. In fact, the spousal relationship has been found to be of significant emotional potency that, if troubled, ensuing distress cannot be simply overcome by additional social support (Pistrang & Barker, 1995). Taken together, empirical studies examining interpersonal processes in the context of a potentially life-threatening illness converge on the centrality of the marital relationship in mediating coping and overall adjustment of both partners.

While many couples clearly possess the emotional resources required to weather the crisis of a cancer diagnosis, there is evidently variation in the manner in which couples cope with this difficult experience. Understanding normative processes as well as individual variation in emotional regulation, coping, and adjustment is important in relation to being able to identify couples at risk for adjustment difficulties, in addition to guiding suitable remediation. Clinical intervention, however, requires a theoretically informed framework to guide clinicians in working with such couples and the multitude of issues they face. Attachment theory arguably provides the most cohesive and well-articulated framework for understanding the intrapersonal and interpersonal processes that emerge in the face of the challenge of serious illness. Adult attachment theory provides the theoretical anchor for EFT, a couples-based intervention offered to couples experiencing adjustment difficulties following breast cancer.

ATTACHMENT THEORY

The attachment model of adult intimacy views a relationship between couples in terms of a bond with an irreplaceable other. This psychological tie is a function of emotional, cognitive, behavioral, and physiological processes that interact to optimize survival (Mikulincer & Shaver, 2007). An individual's response to any real or perceived separation from or loss of an attachment figure, particularly in the face of threat, has been shown to instigate a predictable series of responses designed to reinstill the bond and to facilitate an adaptive response to environmental demands (Bowlby, 1969, 1988).

For example, departure of one partner in a dyad is associated with a heightened overt display of proximity-seeking behaviors in the other (Fraley & Shaver, 1998). Similarly, adults demonstrate a tendency to seek others for support while experiencing or immediately following stressful events. Proximity-seeking behavior in the face of physical or psychological stress or threat has clear survival value in that comfort and security are obtained from an attachment figure, thereby restoring any psychological or physical homeostatic deviations from optimal states, which in turn enhance adaptation to or coping with the presenting stressor.

Central to attachment theory is the concept of internal working models, which accounts for the interpersonal differences observed in attachment behaviors (Bartholomew & Horowitz, 1991). These constitute organized internal representations of the self in relation to significant others and procedural scripts as to how to engage these others. Beliefs and feelings of oneself are partially dependent on perceived accessibility and responsiveness of an attachment figure to one's needs for security and comfort (Cassidy, 1988). Internal working models provide a cohesive framework from which attachment-related events are interpreted and revised (Bowlby, 1973).

These working models give rise to attachment strategies, which are essentially habitual forms of engagement that become particularly salient in times of fear or uncertainty, such as receiving a breast cancer diagnosis or having to undergo invasive treatments. Secure attachment is based on the perception that attachment figures are accessible and responsive to a vulnerable self facing an uncertain future. The unsure self is soothed through exchanges with a responsive and attuned attachment figure. Exchanges that are marked by congruent emotional engagement constitute the building blocks of secure bonding and these exchanges define the relationship as a safe haven.

In contrast, an unresponsive attachment figure will trigger separation distress and protest behaviors such as angry demands in an attempt to reinstill some connection with an irreplaceable other. Insecure forms of engagement can be organized along a two-dimensional model: anxiety and avoidance (Brennan, Clark, & Shaver, 1998). Adults endorsing elevations on attachment anxiety along with low attachment avoidance typically engage in emotionally intense pursuit of loved ones, marked by clinging and even aggressive behaviors. Adults who are low on anxiety and high on avoidance, on the other hand, cope with the aversion associated with a lack of safe connection by suppressing attachment needs altogether. Such individuals employ distancing strategies to avoid potentially distressing emotional engagement with attachment figures.

These habitual ways of engagement—secure, anxious, and avoidant (also known as attachment styles in the literature)—may be conceptualized as filters for construing attachment experiences that affect how people cope in the face of adversity. Two characteristic features distinguish attachment strategies from fixed cognitive schema: their interpersonal and reciprocally reinforcing quality and their emotional nature. Specifically, it is the emotional quality of attachment strategies that ultimately organizes dyadic interactions and also makes them open for revision following corrective emotional experiences (Johnson, 2002, 2004).

A THEORY OF AFFECT REGULATION AND COPING

Attachment theory is primarily a theory of affect regulation. Attachment strategies or habitual ways of engaging one's significant other in times of threat are manifestations of a biobehavioral control system that becomes particularly activated in the face of danger or uncertainty. Its activation serves to promote emotional and physical proximity to a loved one and thus a felt sense of security. Bonding has a protective impact on emotional and physical health, including fostering the restoration of immune competence, and mediating optimal coping with adversity, including chronic illness (Kiecolt-Glaser, Malarkey, Chee, & Newton, 1993). Secure connection promotes effective self-regulation, openness to experience and new learning, and the integration of information (McFarlane & Van der Kolk, 1996).

In contrast, emotional connection that is desperately needed from an attachment figure, but is not forthcoming, culminates in isolation and relational distress and is associated with symptoms of posttraumatic stress and depression (Whisman, 1999). In the context of such relationships, weathering a potentially traumatic experience, such as a life-threatening diagnosis and medical treatments, will be more difficult. Specifically, the absence of secure attachment often results in feelings of being flooded with fear and helplessness and an inability to cope adequately and to adapt to new situations. The relationship becomes defined as insecure and couples become readily consumed by absorbing and compelling states of negative affect that trap them in dysfunctional cycles of interaction that spiral into further stress and distress (Johnson, 2004).

Habitual ways of engaging one another in the context of close relationships that determine the extent of secure connection created seems to be one of the determining factors as to whether a couple can pull through in the face of trauma or not. Indeed, several studies have substantiated systematic differences in ways of coping with stress that are associated with different attachment strategies pulled for in the context of close relationships and overall adjustment. For example, Simpson, Rholes, and Nelligan (1992) observed that, among dating couples, secure women showed a tendency to seek partner support, whereas avoidant women showed the opposite pattern in response to experienced anxiety.

More securely attached adults evidence higher levels of social support and more effective support-seeking behavior in comparison to their anxious or avoidant counterparts (Mikulincer, Florian, & Weller, 1993). Anxious individuals are more prone to engage in coping that emphasizes more extreme negative emotions, whereas avoidants are more likely to adopt repressive or emotion-distancing tactics. Like avoidants, anxious individuals, while also attempting to connect with others, engage more in escape-avoidance maneuvers, such as smoking, drinking, eating, and drug use (Brennan & Shaver, 1995).

Taken all together, empirical research clearly supports the use of attachment theory as a theory of affect regulation that becomes activated in the face of danger and activates strategies that impact how an individual deals with stress and trauma. By filtering perceptual information, shaping emotional regulation, and guiding coping strategies, attachment strategies appear to hold important implications for adjustment and personal well-being, particularly in the face of chronic illness. Secure attachment is an "inner resource" (Mikulincer & Florian, 1995, p. 144) that enables an individual to cope more adaptively in the face of stress, thereby optimizing effective adaptation.

UNDERSTANDING COPING WITH BREAST CANCER FROM AN ATTACHMENT THEORY PERSPECTIVE

Bowlby (1969) maintained that attachment behavior is most likely activated in the face of three main types of conditions: dangerous external events (e.g., a terrorist attack), physical or emotional withdrawal of an attachment figure, and departures from homeostasis with respect to physical health, such as during pain, fatigue, or sickness. Breast cancer poses a substantial threat to a woman's existence and to the attachment bond existing between her and her partner that will result in the activation of the attachment behavioral system of both partners. This threat will also trigger the caregiving behavioral system, and more secure connection has also been linked to more effective and appropriate caregiving in intimate bonds (Mikulincer & Shaver, 2007).

Effective caregivers demonstrate sensitivity as to the type of support elicited by their partners (emotional versus instrumental) and attuning to partners' needs; in turn, this results in improved mood and felt security in the care seekers (Collins & Feeney, 2000). In general, secure caregivers offer more flexible and coordinated care (Pietromonaco, Greenwood, & Feldman Barrett, 2004). Similarly to their avoidantly attached counterparts, anxiously attached caregivers, on the other hand, tend to provide less than optimal support in response to their distressed partners (Carnelley, Pietromonaco, & Jaffe, 1996). Because they tend to be overwhelmed by their own anxiety, anxious partners have difficulty tuning in to the other who needs care; avoidant partners struggle as well because they tend to dismiss their partners' emotional cues or shut down to regulate their own distress.

Attachment theory, in summary, appears to provide the most comprehensive framework unifying both intrapersonal and interpersonal processes involved in coping and adjustment in the face of serious illness. Though its utility is thoroughly recognized in clinical, developmental, and personality research, application of attachment theory in the medical field, and particularly in chronic illness, has been relatively neglected (Schmidt, Nachtigall, Wuethrich-Martone, & Strauss, 2002), although three separate studies (Brennan et al., 1998; Hamama-Raz & Solomon, 2006; Schmidt et al., 2002) have examined patient coping and adjustment to chronic illness, including cancer, using attachment-based processes. All three supported the basic concepts articulated previously and validated the "inner resource" view of secure attachment.

The clear conceptual frame and research on attachment supports a focus on the attachment aspects of close relationships as a base for intervention and the lessening of insecure attachment behaviors and the promotion of secure attachment as an appropriate key goal in any couple intervention that fosters the ability to cope with an illness such as cancer. From this standpoint, there is an obvious fit between EFT and the needs and dilemmas of couples facing cancer.

In view of the mounting research on mutually elevated distress levels in the patient and significant others, as well as the inextricable involvement of partners in the adjustment process, the paucity of couples-based interventions within the cancer literature is conspicuous. Manne et al. (2005) aptly point out that intervention research does not "take advantage of the family context of cancer and a key source of support for patient, namely the partner" (p. 634). In response to this gap, these researchers developed and tested the efficacy of a couple-based group intervention targeting women with early breast cancer. Higher distress levels at study entry were associated with stronger treatment gains, and women describing their spouses as unsupportive benefited more compared to women with less critical husbands. A relatively small, but stable treatment effect was found for depression but not anxiety, general well-being, or trauma symptoms surrounding the cancer (e.g., avoidance and intrusion).

This study was the first to address a major gap in the psychosocial treatment literature by evaluating a short-term intervention that capitalizes on resources inherent to the dyadic unit; it aimed to recreate more supportive exchanges between partners. Notwithstanding, the trial was characterized by a high refusal and dropout rate, leading the study researchers to speculate about the "acceptability" of a group-based couples intervention among breast cancer dyads. A second study, using an emotionally focused couple therapy intervention, will be briefly described at the end of this chapter. The final goal of this chapter is to present EFT—an evidenced-based, time-limited, therapeutic approach based on attachment theory—as an effective intervention that can be offered to breast cancer couples experiencing difficulties in adjustment.

EFT AND MEDICAL ILLNESS

The overarching goal of EFT is to foster the creation of secure bonds between partners, which in turn facilitates emotional connection and resilience in the face of adversity. EFT accords emotion a key role in shaping dyadic interactions (Johnson, 2004). Specifically, emotion is viewed as a healthy and adaptive mechanism that guides perceptions, communicates needs to oneself and others, and organizes social interactions. In the context of intimate relationships, attachment behaviors are primarily guided and shaped by emotion. Predominant emotional experiences of felt insecurity or separation distress will therefore organize current interactions, typically leading to problematic cycles of relating. This perspective fits with Gottman's (1994) research with respect to distressed relationships. Specifically, he found that strained relationships tend to be characterized by partners' propensity to become stuck in absorbing states of negative affect that give rise to rigid interactional patterns, which lead to further aversive states.

EFT further posits that, whether in the form of negative affective states or rigid interactions, distressed couples are essentially manifesting a struggle for attachment security (Bowlby, 1969). Creation of secure emotional connections between partners is therefore achieved by eliciting and expanding the couple's core emotional experiences that give rise to their interactional positions and then effectuating a shift in these interactional positions.

One of the core assumptions of EFT is that emotional responses and interactional positions are reciprocally determined (Johnson, 2004). They are therefore equally addressed in treatment. Empirical evidence for the impact of EFT in creating more secure bonds for initially distressed couples has been reported (Makinen & Johnson, 2006). Secure bonds, in turn, have been shown to be powerfully associated with physical and emotional health and well-being, with resilience in the face of stress and trauma, and with optimal personality development (Mikulincer & Shaver, 2007).

Breast cancer is becoming increasingly recognized as a chronic illness that impacts the entire family. Interventions are needed that address the negatively charged interactions that have been shown to impact mental and physical health adversely (Salovey, Rothman, Detweiler, & Steward, 2000) as well as promote secure attachment bonds to significant others. Secure bonds have been clearly linked to emotional and physical health and well-being, as well as general resilience, particularly in the face of trauma. EFT offers a relevant and on-target treatment choice for couples facing adjustment difficulties following serious illness such as breast cancer. Grounded in attachment theory, the EFT therapist focuses on the quality of attachment interactions.

Specifically, in EFT, partners are helped to step away from reactive cycles of compellingly negative emotion, to express their needs more clearly, and to use one another as a source of support in regulation of the fear, helplessness, anger, and uncertainty often associated with breast cancer and its treatment. A couple's relationship then becomes a safe haven in which comfort may be sought when attachment needs are primed and a secure base is offered that helps both partners recover and take back their lives. By the end of successful treatment, the relationship essentially provides a necessary antidote against the feelings of vulnerability often experienced in the context of breast cancer. As the positive interactions consolidated in treatment become enacted over time, each partner's sense of felt security in relation to the other deepens, increasing a couple's ability to tolerate and cope with adversity.

The goals of the EFT therapist working with a distressed couple who are also dealing with the aftermath of cancer are to

- Assess the level of personal and relationship trauma that has resulted from the ongoing struggle with cancer, including possible attachment injuries.
- Identify the negative cycle of interaction that contributes to relationship distress and ongoing negative impacts of the survivor's illness. Use Stage 1 interventions to de-escalate this cycle and begin to create a safe base from which the couple can repair their relationship and deal with the aftermath of cancer together.
- Create a positive cycle in Stage 2 of EFT that fosters safe emotional engagement for both partners where their needs can be met and resilience restored.

A CASE STUDY

Cassy and Mike were referred by Cassy's physician, who believed that her distress in her 30-year marriage was interfering with her full recovery from her second-stage breast cancer. Cassy had been hassling her doctor to find another surgeon who would perform a second breast reconstruction because she was not satisfied with the results of the first. On the Davidson trauma scale (DTS; Davidson, 1996), Cassy reported that indeed she still had nightmares about her diagnosis and chemotherapy; was usually angry, irritable, and unable to sleep; and actively avoided all reminders and places associated with her cancer. She was highly vigilant about any physical cues that might suggest relapse and also exercised until she was "numbed out." She had stopped all sexual contact with Mike and become obsessed with household chores and rules. Her scores on the functional assessment of cancer therapy scale (FACT B), breast cancer version (Cella et al., 1993), were low on the functional, social, and emotional well-being scales.

This couple's relationship adjustment on the dyadic adjustment scale (DAS; Spanier, 1976) was also low (their mean score was 74; 70 is typical of divorced couples). Cassy had turned to her two grown daughters for support as Mike had become more and more taciturn and absorbed in his job and computer games.

The first challenge was to make an alliance with these partners. Mike was resentful of being in couple therapy and was talking about moving down to the basement in his house to get away from his wife's "constant nagging." Cassy was volatile, angry at the available times for therapy, and cynical about the effectiveness of couple therapy. She came because her doctor told her to.

This couple's cycle was very clear. Cassy would berate Mike for his "passivity" and neglect of household rules. Mike would throw up his hands and become more and more silent. Cassy would then weep and accuse him of ignoring her as he did "even when I was ill." The fact that he had not accompanied her to chemotherapy was a source of ongoing anger for her. Cassy was the oldest of many children and her alcoholic parents had taught her to be "tough" and never to "depend on anyone." She was running 5 miles a day and had kept up some kind of running schedule all the way through her cancer treatment. Mike had fallen in love with Cassy in school and courted her patiently until she had been ready to marry him. He was a solitary child and close only to his sister, who had died of heart disease when he was 16. He loved his job creating computer programs and worked or played games late into the night, coming to bed after Cassy was asleep.

The therapist here informed the authors that in the 22 sessions with this couple she particularly used reflection of ongoing interactions in the session, validation in the face of denial of feelings and attachment needs, and "catch-the-bullet" interactions (Johnson, 2004) in enactments when Cassy would attack even as Mike was opening up to her. Enactments were very structured and processed intently. In terms of attachment strategies, Mike appeared to be avoidant, dismissing emotions and problems, and Cassy seemed both anxious and avoidant. Her attachment strategy is best labeled as fearful avoidant, moving between hostile, angry protest and controlling demands and momentary tears and bids for support, followed by dismissal of any longings for closeness.

Summary of Key Moments and Interventions

This couple's progress in therapy is noted in the following key moments that illustrate the EFCT change process.

Key Moment 1

The therapist makes the cycle explicit (Step 2 in the change process). She reflects key moments of interaction where Cassy and Mike's negative cycle is apparent. At the end of Session 2, Mike comments:

> So, there are no bad guys here then. I thought I was going to hear what a smuck I was. But it's that we are stuck in this dance. The dance was there before Cassy's cancer—but then it got more extreme. I get overwhelmed and move away and she gets mad 'cause she can't find me and get me to listen. Is that it? But I never see her as "needing" anything from me. She just orders me around.

Mike now becomes engaged in therapy.

Key Moment 2

Cassy rages in therapy, listing all the times that Mike apparently "ignores and dismisses" her and telling him:

> Well, I am just here to tell you that I survived cancer 'cause I am tough and you can decide to live by my rules and my standards—like keeping a spotless house and eating on time—or you can get out. I like order. It makes me feel like I have some

control. So, that's it. I can tough things out but you are just a coward. You run away.

The therapist validates that, indeed, Cassy's standards give her a sense of control and her ability to tough things out has probably saved her life, but notes that as she says these things she has tears in her eyes. She suggests that these things still leave Cassy feeling alone. She frames rules and toughness as a starvation diet: not enough to fill you up. The therapist starts where Cassy is, framing her as a fighter, but also adds her underlying deeper emotions of sadness and desperation. At first, Cassy refuses these frames, but then she allows herself to express her underlying feelings of desperate aloneness and a need to control her world. She owns that she does "push Mike around" because that is the only way she can get him to do his "duty" as a husband and pay any attention to her. She also "pushes" her body in exercise, especially when she has images of relapse. Cassy begins to move into a metaperspective and acknowledge the negative cycle and her part in it and also move down into more primary emotions.

Key Moment 3
The therapist tracks Mike's responses and guides him with evocative questions so that he is able to pinpoint and unpack the elements in his emotional response to Cassy that has him "running away at the drop of a hat and hiding in the basement." He can tell her:

> I hear this edge in your voice and I get shaky inside. I hold my breath. I am going to hear that I am a complete failure in your eyes. I am already defeated, so I just give up. I let you scold me and give me orders and I zone out. I guess I run away and leave you behind and then you just get madder. This is happening right now—right here. I can't do this anymore. I want us to stop this.

This is Step 4 of EFT. Mike catches the cycle as it happens, elaborates his part in it, frames his steps in the dance in terms of his underlying emotions, and, in doing this, steps out of the dance, inviting his wife to do the same. The therapist also has to confront Cassy continually as she negates Mike's attempts to open up with reflections of the present interactions and statements like, "This is hard for you to hear; it seems different from how you have seen Mike and your relationship but I think he is saying...But when he says this, you don't see him trying to confide and connect with you, so you turn him down. Yes?"

Key Moment 4

As the couple move into being able to de-escalate their negative cycle, the therapist slowly moves into Step 5, accessing deeper, underlying attachment emotions with each partner and turning them into powerful enactments. Mike is able to tell Cassy:

> I never see you as vulnerable. You seem so fierce to me, so hard. You treated cancer like an inconvenience. I feel like I can never measure up or meet your standards. So I guess I just get ashamed and crawl off into my hole and talk to my computer. I am terrified most of the time. All I hear is that I am defective— a wimp. So I shut you out.

After the therapist has helped her to tune in to and distill her attachment fears, Cassy is able to tell Mike:

> I do get enraged; it's like no matter what I do, I can't get your attention. So I rant and rave. But inside I am so small, so scared, and so alone. Especially when I suddenly get reminded—it's like the cancer is always there in the background. My friend relapsed. It came back. All my exercise is my way of refusing to bow down to it. I exercise to prove I can. And you are right. I never showed you I needed you. What am I, a wimp? I shouldn't need you. I can do this on my own. All my life, I have never admitted I needed anyone. Needing someone scares me too. Needing you scares me.

Key Moment 5

As Mike becomes more engaged, he is able to step forward and assert his needs to Cassy. He is coherent, clear, and open (this characterizes the disclosures of more securely attached individuals). He states:

> I don't want to be always living by your rules. I don't want to be anxiously putting my shoes away, always doing stuff to dodge your anger. I want you to give me some space to breathe here. I feel lonely too and I do want to be there for you. I want to learn how to do that. And I want to stand with you against the great "C."

Cassy hears him and talks of her fears of recurrence and allowing herself to "rely on" Mike. She tells him that she "knows" that if she counts on anyone, this person will let her down and then she will "dissolve" and be so hurt and weak that she will not be able to "get up again." He is compassionate and tender with her. She tells him that she does need his comfort and support, but that there is a "big hurt"—a specific injury that blocks her turning to him. She also speaks of her shame about her "mutilated" body. Throughout these enactments, the therapist first helps to deepen a speaker's emotion and distil it and then to shape these "new" emotions into new signals sent to the partner. Second, the therapist helps the other partner to process and respond to these disclosures. Third, the therapist helps the speaker to take in and integrate the other's positive response and places this response in the context of attachment.

Key Moment 6

Cassy and Mike move through the steps of forgiving an attachment injury that occurred when Cassy went to her first chemotherapy session alone. She "refused to admit" that she wanted Mike to come; in fact, she had blithely said that she wanted to go alone, but had been longing for him to offer to support her. He had "played it safe" and avoided going with her. He shared with her that on that day his memories of his sister going to the same hospital and dying of heart disease had been triggered and he had "wimped out."

The couple proceeds through a process of forgiveness outlined in EFT, at the end of which Cassy is able to ask Mike for the support that she had longed for on that day—and every day since. This constituted an EFT forgiveness event (Makinen & Johnson, 2006) and allowed for a renewal of trust. Cassy was then able to address her great vulnerability around Mike seeing her body. They had not had sex since her fight with cancer, 3 years before, and she would not let him see her naked. As she disclosed her fears that he would find her "disgusting," Mike was able to remind her that he had seen her naked at a doctor's appointment he attended with her and that he found her beautiful and desperately missed their lovemaking. She began to believe him.

Cassy and Mike showed marked improvement on measures of trust, marital adjustment, mood disturbance, and trauma symptoms. The therapist helped them create a coherent story of the transformation of their relationship and a plan for a loving and healthy future.

CONCLUSION

In a recent small EFT study of second-stage breast cancer patients who were also experiencing relationship distress (Naaman, Johnson, & Radwan, in press), five out of nine couples made significant gains in marital adjustment, mood disturbance, and total trauma symptoms on the DTS and assessment of cancer therapy scales in the FACT-B measure. Two more couples, while still experiencing some distress in their relationship, also significantly improved on all these measures. None of the couples in a control group offering psychoeducation on cancer and relationships improved on any measures. Relationship adjustment, as measured at 3-month follow-up, continued to improve.

These results support our clinical experience that EFT offers a coherent and inclusive approach for the treatment of relationship distress that occurs in the context of recovery from traumatic illness and the resulting posttraumatic stress problems and depression that are often part of that recovery. These mental health problems are the ones that most often accompany and are exacerbated by marital distress (Whisman, 1999). With both partners, the EFT therapist specifically shapes accessibility and responsiveness—the key elements of a secure bond. Such a bond is associated with mental and physical resilience (Johnson, 2008), even in the face of the dragons and demons of traumatic experience. Such bonds offer us a safe haven and a secure base—that is, a place where we can "stand and face dragons" with courage (Johnson, 2002, p. 206).

REFERENCES

Alter, C. L., Pelcovitz, D., Axelrod, A., Goldenberg, B., Harris, H., Meyers, B., et al. (1996). Identification of PTSD in cancer survivors. *Psychosomatics, 37,* 137–143.

Baider, L., & Kaplan De-Nour, A. (1988). Breast cancer: A family affair. In C. L. Cooper (Ed.), *Stress and breast cancer* (pp. 155–170). New York, NY: John Wiley & Sons.

Bartholomew, K., & Horowitz, L. M. (1991). Attachment styles among young adults: A test of a four category model. *Journal of Personality and Social Psychology, 61,* 226–244.

Bowlby, J. (1969). *Attachment.* New York, NY: Basic Books.

Bowlby, J. (1973). *Attachment and loss, Vol. 2. Separation, anxiety and anger.* New York, NY: Basic Books.

Bowlby, J. (1988). *A secure base.* New York, NY: Basic Books.

Brennan, K. A., Clark, C. L., & Shaver, P. R. (1998). Self-report measurement of adult attachment: An integrative overview. In J. A. Simpson & W. S. Rholes (Eds.), *Attachment theory and close relationships.* New York, NY: Guilford Press.

Brennan, K. A., & Shaver, P. R. (1995). Dimensions of adult attachment, affect regulation, and romantic relationship functioning. *Personality and Social Psychology Bulletin, 21,* 267–282.

Burg, M. M., & Seeman, T. E. (1994). Families and health: The negative side of social ties. *Annals of Behavioral Medicine, 16,* 109–115.

Burman, B., & Margolin, G. (1992). Analysis of the association between marital relationships and health problems: An interactional perspective. *Psychological Bulletin, 112,* 39–63.

Carnelley, K. B., Pietromonaco, P. R., & Jaffe, K. (1996). Attachment, caregiving, and relationship functioning in couples: Effects of self and partners. *Personal Relationships, 3,* 257–278.

Carter, R., & Carter, C. (1994). Marital adjustment and effects of illness in married pairs with one or both spouses chronically ill. *American Journal of Family Therapy, 22,* 315–326.

Carter, R. E., Carter, C. A., & Siliunas, M. (1993). Marital adaptation and interaction of couples after a mastectomy. *Journal of Psychosomatic Oncology, 11,* 69–81.

Cassidy, J. (1988). Child–mother attachment and the self in 6-year-olds. *Child Development, 59,* 121–134.

Cella, D. F., Tulsky, D. S., Gray, G., Sarafian, B., Linn, E., Bonomi, A., et al. (1993). The functional assessment of cancer therapy scale: Development and validation of the general measure. *Journal of Clinical Oncology, 11,* 570–579.

Collins, N. L., & Feeney, B. C. (2000). A safe haven: An attachment theoretical perspective on support seeking and caregiving in intimate relationships. *Journal of Personality and Social Psychology, 78,* 1053–1073.

Davidson, J. (1996). *The Davidson trauma scale.* North Tonawanda, NY: MHS, Inc.

Ferrell, B., Ervin, K., Smith, S., Marek, T., & Melancon, C. (2002). Family perspectives of ovarian cancer. *Cancer Practice, 10,* 269–276.

Fraley, R. C., & Shaver, P. R. (1998). Airport separations: A naturalistic study of adult attachment dynamics in separating couples. *Journal of Personality and Social Psychology, 75,* 1198–1212.

Gottman, J. (1994). *What predicts divorce? The relationship between marital processes and marital outcomes.* Hillsdale, NJ: Lawrence Erlbaum Associates.

Hagedoorn, M., Bruunk, B. P., Kuijer, R. G., Wobbes, T., & Sanderman, R. (2000). Couples dealing with cancer: Role and gender differences regarding psychological distress and quality of life. *Psycho-oncology, 9,* 232–242.

Hagedoorn, M., Kuijer, R. G., Buunk, B. P., De Jong, G., Wobbes, T., & Sanderman, R. (2000). Marital satisfaction in patients with cancer: Does support from intimate partners benefit those who need it most? *Health Psychology, 19,* 274–282.

Hamama-Raz, Y., & Solomon, Z. (2006). Psychological adjustment of melanoma survivors. The contribution of hardiness, attachment, and cognitive appraisal. *Journal of Individual Differences, 27,* 172–182.

Helgeson, V. S., & Cohen, S. (1996). Social support and adjustment to cancer: Reconciling descriptive, correlational, and intervention research. *Health Psychology, 15,* 135–148.

Iqbal, A., Qureshi, A., & Saeed Siddiqui, K. (2001). The incidence of anxiety among spouses of breast cancer patients. *International Journal of Psychosocial Rehabilitation, 6,* 13–20.

Johnson, S. M. (2002). *Emotionally focused therapy with trauma survivors. Strengthening attachment bonds.* New York, NY: Guilford Press.

Johnson, S. M. (2004). *The practice of emotionally focused couples therapy: Creating connections.* New York, NY: Brunner/Mazel.

Johnson, S. M. (2008). *Hold me tight: Seven conversations for a lifetime of love.* New York, NY: Little Brown.

Keitel, M., Zevon, M., Rounds, J., Petrelli, N., & Karakousis, C. (1990). Spouse adjustment to cancer surgery: Distress and coping responses. *Journal of Surgical Oncology, 43,* 148–153.

Kiecolt-Glaser, J., Malarkey, W., Chee, M., & Newton, T. (1993). Negative behavior during marital conflict is associated with immunological down-regulation. *Psychosomatic Medicine, 55*(5), 395–409.

Lewis, F. M., & Deal, L. W. (1995). Balancing our lives: A study of the married couple's experience with breast cancer recurrence. *Oncology Nursing Forum, 22,* 943–953.

Lewis, F. M., & Hammond, M. A. (1992). Psychosocial adjustment of the family to breast cancer: A longitudinal analysis. *Journal of the American Women's Medical Association, 47,* 194–200.

Lichtman, R. R., Taylor, S. E., & Wood, J. V. (1987). Social support and marital adjustment after breast cancer. *Journal of Psychosocial Oncology, 5,* 47–74.

Lyons, R. F., Sullivan, M. J. L., Ritvo, P. G., & Coyne, J. C. (1995). *Relationships in chronic illness and disability.* Thousand Oaks, CA: Sage.

Makinen, J., & Johnson, S. (2006). Resolving attachment injuries in couples using emotionally focused therapy: Steps toward forgiveness and reconciliation. *Journal of Consulting and Clinical Psychology, 74,* 1055–1064.

Manne, S., Taylor, K., Dougherty, J., & Kemeny, N. (1997). Supportive and negative responses in the partner relationship: Their association with psychological adjustment among individuals with cancer. *Journal of Behavioral Medicine, 20,* 101–125.

Manne, S. L., Alfieri, T., Taylor, K. L., & Dougherty, J. (1999). Spousal negative responses to cancer patients: The role of social restriction, spouse mood, and relationship satisfaction. *Journal of Clinical and Consulting Psychology, 67,* 353–361.

Manne, S. L., Ostroff, J. S., Norton, T. R., Fox, K., Goldstein, L., & Grana, G. (2006). Cancer-related relationship communication in couples coping with early stage breast cancer. *Psycho-oncology, 15,* 234–247.

Manne, S. L., Winkel, G., Grana, G., Ross, S., Ostroff, J. J., Fox, K., et al. (2005). Couple-focused group intervention for women with early stage breast cancer. *Journal of Clinical and Consulting Psychology, 73*(4), 634–646.

McFarlane, A. C., & Van der Kolk, B. A. (1996). Trauma and its challenges to society. In B. A. van der Kolk, A. C. McFarlane, & L. Weisaeth (Eds.), *Traumatic stress: The effects of overwhelming experience on mind, body, and society* (pp. 24–45). New York, NY: Guilford Press.

Mikulincer, M., & Florian, V. (1995). Appraisal of and coping with a real-life stressful situation: The contribution of attachment style. *Personality and Social Psychology Bulletin, 21,* 406–414.

Mikulincer, M., Florian, V., & Weller, A. (1993). Attachment styles, coping strategies, and post-traumatic psychological distress: The impact of the Gulf War in Israel. *Journal of Personality and Social Psychology, 64,* 817–826.

Mikulincer, M., & Shaver, P. (2007). *Attachment in adulthood: Structure, dynamics, and change.* New York, NY: Guilford Press.

Naaman, S., Johnson, S. M., & Radwan, K. (in press). Attachment processes in couples facing early breast cancer. *Psychiatry, Biological and Interpersonal Processes.*

Noller, P., Feeney, J. A., Bonnell, D., & Callan, V. (1994). A longitudinal study of conflict in early marriage. *Journal of Social and Personal Relationships, 11,* 233–252.

Northouse, L., & Peters-Golden, H. (1993). Cancer and the family: Strategies to assist spouses. *Seminars in Oncology Nursing, 9,* 74–82.

Northouse, L. L. (1984). The impact of cancer on the family: Overview of the literature. *International Journal of Psychiatry in Medicine, 14,* 87–113.

Northouse, L. L. (1989). A longitudinal study of the adjustment of patients and husbands to breast cancer. *Oncology Nursing Forum, 16,* 511–516.

Northouse, L. L., Laten, D., & Reddy, P. (1995). Adjustment of women and their husbands to recurrent breast cancer. *Research in Nursing and Health, 18,* 515–524.

Northouse, L. L., Mood, D., Templin, T., Mellon, S., & George, T. (2000). Couples' patterns of adjustment to colon cancer. *Social Science Medicine, 50,* 271–284.

Northouse, L. L., Templin, T., & Mood, D. (2001). Couples' adjustment to breast disease during the first year following diagnosis. *Journal of Behavioral Medicine, 24,* 115–136.

Northouse, L. L., Templin, T., Mood, D., & Oberst, M. T. (1998). Couples adjustment to breast cancer and benign breast disease: A longitudinal analysis. *Psycho-oncology, 7,* 37–48.

Oberst, M. T., & Scott, D. (1988). Post-discharge distress in surgically treated cancer patients and their spouses. *Research in Nursing Health, 11,* 223–233.

Omne-Ponten, M., Holmberg, L., Bergstrom, R., Sjoden, P., & Burns, T. (1993). Psychosocial adjustment among husbands of women treated for breast cancer: Mastectomy vs. breast conserving surgery. *European Journal of Cancer, 29A,* 1393–1397.

Pietromonaco, P. R., Greenwood, D., & Feldman Barrett, L. (2004). Conflict in adult close relationships: An attachment perspective. In W. S. Rholes & J. A. Simpson (Eds.), *Adult attachment: New directions and emerging issues* (pp. 267–299). New York, NY: Guilford Press.

Pistrang, N., & Barker, C. (1995). The partner relationship in psychological response to breast cancer. *Social Science and Medicine, 40,* 789–797.

Rodrigue, J. R., & Hoffman, R. G., III. (1994). Caregivers of adults with cancer: Multidimensional correlates of psychological distress. *Journal of Clinical Psychology in Medical Settings, 1,* 231–244.

Rodrigue, J. R., & Park, T. L. (1996). General and illness specific adjustment to cancer. Relationship to marital status and marital functioning. *Journal of Psychosomatic Research, 40,* 29–36.

Salovey, P., Rothman, A., Dotwoiler, J., & Steward, W. (2000). Emotional states and physical health. *American Psychologist, 55*(1), 110–121.

Schmidt, S., Nachtigall, C., Wuethrich-Martone, O., & Strauss, B. (2002). Attachment and coping with chronic illness. *Journal of Psychosomatic Research, 53,* 763–773.

Sherman, C. D., & Hossfeld, D. K. (1990). Breast cancer. In D. K. Hossfeld, C. D. Sherman, R. R. Love, & F. X. Bosch (Eds.), *Manual of clinical oncology* (pp. 253–271). New York, NY: Springer–Verlag.

Simpson, J. A., Rholes, W. S., & Nelligan, J. S. (1992). Support seeking and support giving within couples in an anxiety-provoking situation: The role of attachment styles. *Journal of Personality and Social Psychology, 62,* 434–446.

Spanier, G. (1976). Measuring dyadic adjustment. *Journal of Marriage and Family, 13,* 113–126.

Stanton, A. L., Kirk, S. B., Cameron, C. L., & Danoff-Burg, S. (2000). Coping through emotional approach: Scale construction and validation. *Journal of Personality and Social Psychology, 78,* 1150–1169.

Tatelman, S. S. (1999). Social support, marital status in relation to psychological symptoms among survivors of breast cancer. *Dissertation Abstracts International, 60*(3-B), 1318 (UMI no. 9921296).

Weihs, K. L., Enright, T., & Simmens, S. J. (2002). High-quality spousal or long term partner relationships predict time to recurrence of breast cancer, after control for disease severity. *Psychosomatic Medicine, 64,* 107.

Whisman, M. A. (1999). Marital dissatisfaction and psychiatric disorders: Results from the national comorbidity study. *Journal of Abnormal Psychology, 108,* 701–706.

Zunkel, G. (2002). Relational coping processes: Couples' response to a diagnosis of early breast cancer. *Journal of Psychosocial Oncology, 20*(4), 39–55.

Seven

Dancing With the Dragon of Trauma
EFT With Couples Who Stand in Harm's Way

SUSAN M. JOHNSON AND GEORGE FALLER

INTRODUCTION

Creating and maintaining a close, satisfying relationship may be especially challenging for couples where one partner's work routinely places him or her in harm's way. These life-threatening conditions put couples at risk as struggles to cope with traumatic experiences disrupt partners' felt sense of security and, at the same time, increase the ongoing need for comfort and support. Couples therapists working with first responders (e.g., firefighters, police) and military personnel confront the debilitating impact of posttraumatic stress disorder (PTSD) and related conditions such as depression. Partners struggle to relate as their relational conflict and emotional distance exacerbate anxiety; this anxiety then adds to the inability to deal with the emotional costs of trauma exposure. This chapter explores the use of emotionally focused therapy (EFT) for couples with partners whose professions constantly place them in harm's way. A clinical example illustrates how EFT is effectively used with a firefighter couple.

The psychological demands for professionals facing routine exposure to traumatic events are significant. The impact of episodic or chronic exposure often results in depression, substance abuse, general anxiety disorders, or symptoms consistent with full or partial PTSD. These first responders are more likely to confront greater risk of functional impairment, including interferences with occupation, family, school, and leisure activities (CDC, 2004). Elevated rates of PTSD have been reported in a number of studies involving rescue workers and returning veterans (CDC, 2004; Difede, Apfeldorf, Cloitre, Spielman, & Perry, 1997; Gross et al., 2006; Hoge et al., 2004; Perrin, DiGrande, Wheeler, Thorpe, & Brackbill, 2007; Tapp et al., 2005). Stellman et al. (2008) found that rates of PTSD (11.1%) among World Trade Center disaster rescue and recovery workers were similar to those for soldiers returning from Afghanistan (11.5%) and more than double those of the general population (3–4%).

These numbers most likely dramatically underestimate the actual impact of trauma exposure because the work culture surrounding these professions encourages the minimization and denial of stress responses. The stigma associated with mental health issues in this culture is also a significant factor. Frontline responders are most often expected to manage, contain, and suppress their fears, and the acknowledgement of vulnerability and the expression of any form of fear are shunned. This stigma and the lack of skills in communicating emotionally within this insulated culture lead to emotional isolation and heightened distress for those who serve and their relationships with those they love.

COUPLES THERAPY AND TRAUMA

There is limited empirical evidence concerning the outcome of couple therapy with trauma couples. There is one pilot study of cognitive behavioral couple therapy (CBCT) for couples facing PTSD from military deployment (Monson, Schnurr, Stevens, & Guthrie, 2004). At this study's completion, a veteran's relationship satisfaction remained unchanged. Studies of EFT have found more promising results with couples dealing with the effects of trauma (Dalton, Johnson, & Classen, in press; Macintosh & Johnson, 2008; Naaman, Johnson, & Radwan, in press). However, in two of the studies noted, couples were coping with stress disorders arising from past physical and sexual abuse in their families, and in some their symptoms seemed to be most appropriately considered as complex PTSD (see MacIntosh & Johnson, 2008).

There is also one ongoing study of EFT with 10 couples enrolled in treatment with the VA system where one partner has faced combat and has a PTSD diagnosis. An educational postdeployment preventative program has also been developed based on the steps of EFT (Johnson & Rheem, 2003). If we consider disorders often associated with PTSD, such as depression, there is evidence of effectiveness for both CBCT and EFT (Denton, Wittenborn, & Golden, in press; Dessaulles, Johnson, & Denton, 2003; Jacobson, Dobson, Fruzzetti, Schmaling, & Salusky, 1991).

Until very recently, couple interventions were not seen as part of the treatment of trauma. This has now begun to change. Posttraumatic stress disorder is a multidimensional problem that often requires different kinds of interventions to address different aspects of the problem. The three core symptoms of PTSD—intrusive reexperiencing, numbing and avoidance, and hyperarousal—all cause problems in survivors' relationships. Hyperarousal resulting in irritability and hypervigilance for threat skew everyday interactions—not only resulting in negative exchanges but also escalating these exchanges to the point of creating secondary traumatic stress symptoms in the partner (Nelson & Wampler, 2000).

Emotional numbing has been found to best distinguish victims with PTSD from those without it (Foa, Hearst-Ikeda, & Perry, 1995). There seems to be a growing consensus that this response is at the heart of PTSD and is also very difficult to treat in traditional individual and group therapies (Foa & Rothbaum, 1998). Numbing certainly cuts off emotional connection with a partner and quickly erodes any kind of attachment security in a relationship. A couple intervention such as EFT, however, holds great promise in that therapists are experts in dealing with numbing strategies and they also have a potent emotional trigger—namely, the other spouse present in the therapy room. As couple interventions in general have become more systematic and as we recognize more and more clearly that a secure bond is the primary defense against trauma-induced problems, couple interventions—specifically, EFT—have begun to take their place as a recognized part of trauma treatment.

A RATIONALE FOR EFT AND COUPLES WITH PTSD

Apart from the evidence of the previously mentioned studies, over the last two decades EFT has been used extensively in clinical practice with different kinds of trauma survivor couples, and EFT clinicians and clients regularly report successful outcomes. Conceptually and clinically, EFT seems to be particularly suited to working with trauma couples. It is useful to list the obvious ways in which this approach fits with the task of addressing relationship problems in trauma survivors.

First, interventions in EFT and the steps in the process of change are explicit, tested, and systematic. There are several studies of the process of change detailing key interventions and predictors of recovery from distress in EFT. The three stages of EFT—de-escalation, restructuring, and consolidation—are very similar to the three stages of treatment described in the treatment of trauma: stabilization, working through and building self and relational capacities, and integration (McCann & Pearlman, 1990). In the chaos of a distressed relationship further complicated by the overwhelming aftermath of traumatic experience, EFT offers the therapist a clear map for intervention (Bradley & Furrow, 2004; Johnson, 2002, 2004).

Second, EFT explicitly addresses the impact of emotions on the quality of close relationships and actively regulates and processes emotional cues. Affect regulation, processing, and integration are central to all posttraumatic stress difficulties. All three of the key symptoms of traumatic stress disorder—intrusive reexperiencing, avoiding and numbing or becoming "dead to the world" (Kardiner, 1941, p. 249), and hypervigilance that involves agitation and the generalization of threat—reflect disorders of affect regulation. The world, others, and even the self often become sources of threat, resulting in extremes of overreactivity or freeze responses. In chronic hyperarousal, the person's own disorganizing and extreme physiological response becomes itself a source of anxiety (van der Kolk & McFarlane, 1996).

In terms of which symptom is most predictive of outcome in the treatment of trauma, it seems clear that numbing is the most destructive because it cuts off the victim from his own experience, which then cannot be revised or integrated, and from others who may be able to offer support and consolation. It also predicts distress in a survivor's relationships (Riggs, Byrne, Weathers, & Litz, 1998). Clinicians and researchers alike have noted that numbing is a core problem and interventions should focus on that symptom directly (Cook, Riggs, Thompson, Coyne, & Sheikh, 2004). The competent EFT therapist is well equipped to deal with both numbing and reactive, exaggerated emotions.

Third, EFT is based on a clear and research-based conceptualization of adult bonding (Mikulincer & Shaver, 2007). The relevance of attachment theory to the trauma field has long been recognized. As noted by van der Kolk, Perry, and Herman (1991) and reflecting the seminal work of Bowlby (1969, 1988), the best predictor of trauma recovery is not trauma history per se but rather whether it is possible to seek comfort from others who offer solace and a safe haven. Secure bonds promote resilience and healing from traumatic stress. After 9/11, those in the vicinity of the towers who reported being able to turn to others and find comfort and reassurance were the ones who recovered well from their trauma and even reported a sense that they had grown as a result of their traumatic experience (Fraley, Fazzari, Bonanno, & Dekel, 2006). EFT directly addresses the security of the bond between survivors and their partners and how insecurity actively perpetuates the long-term effects of trauma or, conversely, how a felt sense of increased security can provide a healing environment.

Fourth, EFT is an experiential humanistic approach that is deliberately collaborative and focuses on validating and affirming clients. This nonpathologizing approach is essential and particularly restorative in a client population where a sense of "bad things happen to bad people" often becomes part of the frame for understanding how a trauma unfolded. Self-blame, stigmatization, and other negative cognitions seem to be a natural part of the aftermath of trauma and to cause profound changes in schema about self and others in the world, usually in a negative direction (McCann & Pearlman, 1990).

The inability to regulate one's own experience after trauma is also a source of humiliation: Survivors lose confidence in their ability to deal with and order their own experience and count on themselves. The commitment of the EFT therapist to creating a safe haven and secure base in each therapy session and to offering active, ongoing emotional presence and responsiveness is also obviously relevant to the treatment of survivors and their partners, who can be flooded with shame, helplessness, and terror in session as they work with traumatic experience.

ATTACHMENT PROCESSES AND TRAUMA

An attachment-oriented therapist is used to working specifically with the constricting and disorganizing results of chronic fear. As Slade (2008) points out, a key aspect of attachment is the "privileging of fear in the development of all psychopathology." Indeed, the essence of insecure attachment can be considered to be overwhelming fear that has no "solution." Attachment figures are seen as unresponsive, emotionally absent, or even dangerous. In the case of insecure attachment, as in the case of traumatic crises experienced later in life, "solutions" that allow for immediate coping often have long-term consequences that lead to emotional distress and themselves become toxic. Strategies such as cutting one's body to exit states of numbness or exploding at one's partner to take back a sense of control become, in themselves, a trap that perpetuates traumatic stress and disconnection from others (Shalev, 1993). One set of symptoms and way of dealing with these symptoms blocks routes to healing and self-regulation on other levels. After a while, all routes and strategies simply lead back into fear and insecurity about the self and others.

Secure attachment acts as a protective shield against PTSD (Mikulincer, Shaver, & Horesh, 2006), activating hopeful internal representations of self and others, restoring emotional balance, and allowing victims to cry for help and obtain comfort from others. Variations in habitual, more insecure attachment strategies also impact the specific form that PTSD takes. Anxious hyperactivating strategies seem to facilitate the development of intrusive symptoms such as nightmares and flashbacks, while avoidant strategies incline a person to deny trauma and avoid trauma cues but also to show more somatization and hostility (Mikulincer, Florian, & Weller, 1993). Even if habitual, global attachment strategies are negative, increasing the general likelihood of traumatic stress reactions, the evidence is that, in the context of a specific attachment relationship, a daily sense of being connected to others weakens hyperarousal and reexperiencing symptoms for that day (Mikulincer, Shaver, & Horesh, 2004).

A sense of attachment security on a given day with a loved one leads to positive changes in PTSD symptoms for avoidant and for anxiously attached soldiers, although avoidance is still associated with more severe symptoms, even on days when these soldiers feel relatively well supported. Anxiously attached individuals seem to be more responsive to support from a loved one. For the more avoidant survivor, practiced impermeability and the minimizing or dismissing of support when it is offered mires this survivor in more symptoms and perpetuates his or her isolation.

TREATMENT ISSUES SPECIFIC TO WORKING WITH TRAUMATIZED COUPLES

How does couple therapy with traumatized couples differ from regular couple therapy? We must now consider the main issues that arise in couple therapy when dealing with traumatized couples.

Assessment and Contraindications

The therapist must be more aware of contraindications for couple therapy, such as degree of violence or threats of violence; screen for them at the beginning of therapy and take them into account throughout the therapy process. It is not possible to conduct effective EFT if partners cannot feel a basic sense of safety in therapy (Bograd & Meredos, 1999; Holtzworth-Munroe, Marshall, Meehan, & Rehman, 2003; Johnson, 2004). If a partner is fearful in therapy and cannot risk being honest or there is a real threat of physical harm, conjoint therapy is not appropriate. For therapy to be effective, the partner who has used or threatened physical aggression against the other or the self must be able to acknowledge the problem and be taking steps to deal with this. The therapist must also structure a containment plan so that if one partner becomes in any way fearful or self-harming, both partners have an agreed-to plan for how to deal with a potentially dangerous situation.

Another contraindication for couple therapy is active engagement in addictive behaviors that undermine progress in therapy, especially the creation of increased trust and responsiveness. If a survivor turns to the bottle or to drugs every time he or she needs comfort, this will actively undermine progress in couple sessions. The EFT therapist will use an attachment frame here, suggesting that an addictive substance is used as a substitute safe haven, an alternative that will inevitably terrify and alienate the other partner. It makes sense from an attachment point of view that a partner who is caught in a negative cycle might go outside a relationship to get immediate needs for comfort met. Of course, this short-term solution only reinforces mistrust and strengthens the negative cycle. For treatment to be successful, these kinds of addictions have to be acknowledged, contained, and actively addressed by the addicted partner before or concurrently with couple sessions (see Chapter 8, this volume).

The clinical implications of these issues include the need for attention to pragmatic arrangements, such as the necessity to liaise with individual therapists or addiction counselors, and a thorough assessment in which these issues are directly addressed. Individual sessions are part of the standard EFT assessment procedure but are especially crucial with regard to these matters.

Explicit Education About Traumatic Stress Is Necessary

An educational focus on the nature of traumatic stress and specific symptoms has to be added to the traditional EFT couple model. In particular, it is usually the case that both partners have little or no knowledge about psychological trauma and its effects and do not recognize associations between prior trauma and problematic behavioral and emotional sequences. Additionally, the partners of trauma survivors often know only the barest of sanitized facts about the survivor's traumatic history, whether it is the civilian massacre witnessed by a peace-keeping soldier or a missed shot by a police officer that resulted in the death of a colleague. Survivors avoid disclosing past experiences of trauma for fear of being seen as failures or labeled as crazy or because of anxiety about contaminating their partner with their own memories and suffering. In particular, men in dangerous professions believe in being strong and silent and protecting their loved ones from the horrors that they have seen. In EFT, we have learned that the non-traumatized partner needs to know enough about the trauma so that he or she has "seen the face of the dragon" that comes for her partner; otherwise, attunement to this person's pain is almost impossible.

Education, in the EFT model, is offered in an experiential manner, from the bottom up rather than in a didactic top-down fashion. It is offered as trauma symptoms arise in the therapy process and impact interactions between partners; this "catch it as it happens" approach is the best way to make educational comments and reframes meaningful for both partners. Symptoms such as agitation or inability to sleep will be normalized and related to the trauma and to negative interaction cycles. Even simple facts, such as that the word "trauma" comes from an ancient Greek word for "wound," can provide a validating context for a survivors' symptomatic responses. Thus, a survivor's irritation with his wife may be reframed in terms of hypervigilance—an alert amygdala scanning for danger and his sense of traumatic helplessness. He can then explore the impact of his trauma-driven responses—the dragon's breath—on his wife with less defensiveness.

Demystifying trauma and offering strategies to enhance safety, security, and trust lay the foundation for recovery. Gaining insight into the interdependent web of emotional responses and coping behaviors allows cognitively oriented professionals like soldiers, police officers, and firefighters logically to understand the benefits of increased emotional awareness and engagement before they experientially confront the blocks to their emotional vulnerability. Providing new information about the survival benefits of emotional engagement is necessary to reframe and counter the unfailing messages of the traditionally masculine culture (military, police, and firefighters), which systematically discourage emotional expression, especially fear. Reducing fear is identified as the most important treatment goal in working with PTSD survivors (Foa et al., 1995), but it is hard for frontline professions to discuss fears when there is so little liberty in their professional lives to share these feelings. Being given permission to trust and express fears without shame is a huge first step forward toward mitigating a survivor's PTSD symptoms.

Complex Negative Interactional Cycles

The complex negative interactional cycles in survivors' relationships may reflect the fact that attachment needs are chronically high due to the constant sense of threat. Emotional responses in traumatized couples are often extreme, swinging from volatile reactivity to various levels of disassociation, and trauma symptoms also actively interfere with processes such as attunement to and empathy for the other. When a traumatic event shatters someone's worldview, it is difficult to find safety anywhere. This mistrust pervades both inner experience and interpersonal interactions. As each partner's range of possible behaviors constricts and becomes more defensive within the relationship, the negative cycle grows more reactive, intense, rigid, and intractable. The therapist has to be able to track each partner's steps in the "demon dialogues" of conflict and disconnection (Johnson, 2008) and create a coherent formulation of the couple's negative patterns, relating these patterns to attachment realities and to the echoes of trauma.

Cycles tend to be particularly complex if both partners have a trauma history or if recent trauma is complicated by a traumatic childhood history, where a person was abused by an attachment figure and thus demonstrates a fearful avoidant style, demanding connection and then recoiling when it is offered, or refusing to trust it and be comforted. The evidence is substantial that individuals who have experienced a "violation of human connection" (Herman, 1993) and who might be considered to suffer from complex or developmental trauma (Courtois & Ford, 2009) are more likely to develop PTSD as a result of traumatic experiences as adults.

This may, in part, reflect the impact of early trauma on the brain. There is evidence, for example, that severe stress damages the hippocampus (Gilbertson et al., 2002) and this then becomes a risk factor for future dysfunction. These individuals are also more likely to have trouble trusting others, to show more insecure attachment and thus have distressed relationships prior to and as the result of a trauma sustained as an adult. The couple therapist is sometimes in the position of helping partners deal with long-term emotional starvation and very seminal early experiences that have taught them that to open up and depend on others is exquisitely dangerous. Others are not framed as even a potential source of reliable comfort, and more recent traumatic events are then especially toxic because they are experienced in the context of emotional isolation.

Emotional Storms Are Inevitable

The essential focus of EFT is first to arouse or track emotion within the scaffold of a safe therapeutic relationship in which the therapist is an active moment-by-moment co-regulator and processor of emotion, and then to order and distil it, placing it in an attachment and interactional context. Once clarified, the implications of the more clearly defined emotional moment are explored and action tendencies reflected on. If this is done continually, the engagement with emotional experience is deepened. As this occurs, the therapist supports, validates, reframes if appropriate, and helps clients make sense of their emotions so that their experience becomes less overwhelming and more and more coherent and integrated. This newly shaped and expanded emotional experience then translates into an ability to send new signals to the other partner.

The range of emotion in traumatized partners is larger, danger cues are more generalized, and the ability to regulate or reflect on emotional experience is less. The therapist must be prepared to be more active in the regulation of a client's emotions. Four strategies are important here: First, the therapist must be able to ground and contain strong panic and anger responses; second, the therapist must take more time to sort through disorganized emotional "soups" and find a clear focus; third, the therapist must be more aware of repeatedly going over emotionally loaded moments and experiences as they occur in the session and helping clients to take in and integrate them; and, lastly, heightening emotions is done more carefully and emotional change events in Stage 2 of EFT often have to be "sliced thinner" so that risks are more manageable. This is especially true if the survivor has a history of abuse by an attachment figure.

Therefore, in working with a policeman on disability due to PTSD arising from a drug bust in which his colleague and a child were killed, the therapist might actively consult with this client's individual therapist as to the process of this therapy, reinforcing the awareness of rage cues and the ability to label them and not "talk up" the rage, as practiced in his individual therapy sessions. The EFT therapist will also block this client's outbursts of rage when they are directed toward his wife in session, reflecting the process, stopping the interaction, and, if possible, helping this client move into underlying feelings such as helplessness and grief. The therapist also slowly and carefully "unpacks" disorganized responses that occur when this client's wife reaches for him and he freezes and agitatedly begins to flick lint from his coat, his eyes begin to tear, and he then turns his chair away, toward the door.

The therapist helps him pinpoint reactive anger: "If I let myself lean on her, she will wham me"; sadness: "I can't let her touch me. I am alone in this"; and different kinds of fear and shame: "When she really gets what happened, she will spit at me. I don't deserve her comfort anyway" and "If I let my guard down, I will be naked when the shakes—when that dragon comes for me." Then, after reflecting all this so that the chaos of this experience is lessened and depending on where this couple is in the process of change, the therapist will choose to work with one response that clearly impacts attachment processes between the couple, as in: "Can we just stay with how dangerous it feels for you to let your wife comfort you right now? It's scary to think of just resting in her arms and being comforted, yes?"

This process might move into this client being able to tell his wife, "Right now, it's too scary to let my guard down and let you in. I am trying, but it is hard." The therapist will then go over this unpacked experience at the end of the session, summarizing it and making it into a coherent story. He or she will also play it back in the next session, exploring how both partners have processed this event and how it has impacted the level of their emotional engagement. The EFT therapist uses all these skills in regular EFT practice; here, they are simply honed and applied more deliberately.

Safety Is Everything: The Slow Pace of Therapy

Couple therapy with survivor couples takes longer. Traditional EFT can be completed in anything from 8 to 20 sessions. In the first series of seminal studies in EFT, therapists were given ongoing clinical supervision, which allowed the process to be completed in 10–12 sessions. When working with survivors of serious trauma, however, couples generally take 30–35 sessions unless the trauma is very circumscribed and the relationship was relatively happy and secure before its occurrence.

There are many reasons why the change process is more protracted here. One is that it often takes longer to form a strong alliance with traumatized partners, especially if they have a history of abandonment and betrayal with those they depended on. The alliance has to be monitored with even more attention than usual. It may need to be explicitly addressed and healed if necessary. The therapist has to be more careful to be transparent and collaborative. A second reason is that relapses and crises are more common with these couples during the process of change. The beginning of Stage 2, when the therapist is asking couples to take more significant risks with each other, can reactivate symptoms. For example, in one couple already described in the literature (Johnson & Williams Keeler, 1998), when the husband began to move out of withdrawal and actively offer comfort to his wife in session, she began to have a flashback of her abuse at the hands of her apparently comforting but very abusive father, and to numb out. It takes an unhurried, patient approach to allow trauma survivors the time and space needed to expand their experience, access cutoff parts of themselves, and ultimately challenge their emotional constriction.

Self of Therapist

To work with traumatized clients and offer them the safety they need, it is also necessary for the therapist to keep his or her emotional balance. There is now an extensive literature on the compassion fatigue and vicarious trauma (Pearlman & Caringi, 2009) that can occur when working with traumatized couples. The EFT therapist, in particular, is committed to staying emotionally present, open, and responsive to both partners. It is pertinent here to note that if one person in a relationship has any significant level of PTSD, the impact on the other partner is so great that this person is most often also symptomatic. Because the interpersonal drama in such couples is also more intense, the therapist does have to be aware that it is easier to become momentarily overwhelmed by these cases; thus, he or she needs to be able to step back, returning to the secure base of his or her understanding of attachment processes and the steps in a couple's change process.

There are many ways in which an EFT therapist keeps his or her balance when working with complex and very distressed couples. The collaborative nature of EFT takes the pressure off the therapist to be an all-knowing expert who always has an answer to difficult impasses and dilemmas. Thus, an EFT therapist can say, "I am so sorry, there is so much happening here. I am a little lost. Can we please go back to...?" Robert Karen suggests (1998) that the important thing in an attachment relationship (or a surrogate therapeutic attachment relationship) is not necessarily to be clever but to be "there." The transparency that is part of the EFT experiential approach also allows therapists to share their own emotions and thus regulate them. An EFT therapist might say, "This is so sad; it makes me want to weep with you" or "I am getting caught up in becoming frustrated here, even irritated. I want to listen to you, so can we go back to...?" Survivors with their fine-tuned vigilance will pick up on the therapist's emotional cues in any case and may misinterpret them if they are not acknowledged.

If a therapist is working with many clients facing trauma, it is also invaluable to have a community of supportive colleagues to whom the therapist can turn for support and consultation. The EFT therapist also has the secure base of the frame, steps, and systematic interventions to turn to. In complex, potentially chaotic sessions, this allows the therapist to stay calm, focused, and flexible in terms of intervention. The model orders and organizes the drama that is occurring in the session so that it remains workable.

How a therapist handles his or her emotional response also directly impacts the treatment process. EFT is most effective when the therapist is curiously walking, side by side, in the client's world. This radical attunement from the bottom up is crucial and the therapist has to show that he or she is interested in the client's emerging story more than in top-down cognitive labels or lists of facts. Given the unpredictable and chaotic nature of trauma, it is more difficult for therapists to stay focused and present with their clients. It is normal for therapists to get nervous, not knowing when the dragon will enter the room. Fear makes it difficult to go slowly and be open. When the therapist's own anxiety is triggered, it causes the predictable attachment responses of coming forward to fix the feelings or moving away to avoid them.

Either way, the therapist introduces his or her own agenda, which leaves clients unsupported at a time when they most desperately need help. It is highly unlikely that a trauma survivor will touch cutoff parts of himself or herself when the therapist is so far away from this experience. Therapists need to be tuned into their own anxiety, which is accurately signaling that they are missing the mark. Staying on the leading edge of the client's experience is the only way to help the client find words to express these hesitant feelings lying just outside awareness.

Healing

Caught in inner and outer recursive spirals of negative emotions, traumatized couples desperately need hope that they can find a way to face the dragon and hold on to each other. For the therapist, the challenge of working with trauma couples is to continue to believe in each partner's ability to heal from trauma and to forge a more secure bond in spite of setbacks, struggles, and relapses. The therapist holds out the hope for healing and growth, just as a responsive parent does when a child hurts, falls, has a tantrum, refuses to try, sulks, pushes the parent away, and then hurls himself at a task so hard that he hurts himself. The parent stays present and deals with whatever comes up. The value of a systematic map for change, for inner emotional realities, and for the territory of human bonds is invaluable here. The therapist's ability to trust the model is essential. The practice of EFT repeatedly shows the therapist the power of attachment longings to spur growth and the capacity of attachment responses to heal.

EFT therapists realize that, in seeing a negative cycle, they are getting a distorted image of a couple at their worst and that creating a more secure attachment has the power to transform this picture. In EFT, as attachment fears are calmed and disconfirmed in positive interactions and as positive responses are enacted, the partners change each other. A corrective emotional experience (Johnson, 2009) offers an antidote to shame, fear, and grief.

Thus, Karen, a withdrawn partner who is the victim of childhood abuse and a recent rape, tells her partner, Jim, about her sense of being "flawed" and "permanently damaged" and needing then to "hide" from him. In Stage 2 of EFT, rather than being critical and demanding, Jim is able to respond to her hurt with compassion and caring. He tells her, "I never see you that way. You are mine. These things that happened are not about you. I choose you for my partner. I want to hold you so you don't hurt anymore. I want you to let me close so I can do this."

This message and others in the same vein help Karen to begin to revise her defective model of self, empower her to accept and struggle with her pain, and change her faith in her loved one's ability to respond to her and her right to receive care.

CASE EXAMPLE

Paul, age 38, and Maureen, age 35, have been married for 10 years and have two young children. Paul, a lieutenant in the NYC Fire Department, survived the collapse of the World Trade Center on September 11, 2001. Maureen was an elementary school teacher. They began couple's therapy in 2003 following escalating marital discord and the growing fear of separation. Paul began individual therapy in 2002 and was diagnosed with PTSD. Maureen was also diagnosed with depression.

The EFT therapist fostered an alliance with the couple and sought to help them see the vicious cycle of Maureen's pursuit and Paul's withdrawal as the problem that had come between them. Paul's traumatic experience of 9/11 was tied to their cycle because this event had radically altered their relationship and their ability to address its impact. The therapist discussed the repercussions of the 9/11 event on the couple and the negative interactional pattern that had become so powerful between them. The couple described how the echoes of this trauma had pushed them farther apart in a general way, without talking about the specific details of that fateful day. The therapist framed the relationship as the victim and the trauma of 9/11 as the villain. A more general and cognitive recounting of their 9/11 experience provided a safe starting point for the couple. This safety sets the stage for accessing their more emotionally charged trauma experiences in Stage 2 of EFT.

From the initial session, Paul was adamant that discussing his experience on 9/11 was off limits. The therapist validated Paul's frustration about delving into the past and his concern that sharing his story would only cause harm to others. Paul coped with this potentially harmful experience by withdrawing and becoming emotionally numb. Maureen tried to respect his avoidance of 9/11, but she could not understand why he would not address pressing issues like his ailing health related to his exposure at Ground Zero. The therapist validated Maureen's frustration when she offered her concern and received Paul's rejection in return. Her anger made sense when she offered support but he was only able to respond with increased distancing.

The very mention of 9/11 triggered this couple's cycle, with Paul becoming increasingly defensive and Maureen feeling shut out. Repeated attempts to come together and address this distress in the months before therapy had failed, fostering an ongoing sense of mistrust and doubt. The therapist began to counteract this couple's negative cycle by helping them begin to grasp their impact on each other in the session and how each pulled the other into a negative cycle, which then spun out of control. The couple's predictable responses to each other, in these moments of distress, were framed as their best efforts at survival. De-escalation came slowly, showing up not just as a reduction of fighting and reactivity but also as the development of a new way of seeing and experiencing their relationship.

Paul explored how he typically shut down emotionally when faced with emotionally threatening experiences. Whether at work or at home, he relied on his ability to shut down to cope with emotional intensity. This response made total sense to him as a fireman faced with dangerous environments that require a cool, cognitive focus to assure the best chance of survival in life-threatening situations. The therapist empathized with this professional survival skill and its value to Paul and the esteem it won him among his fellow firefighters. The traditional masculine values of toughness, assertiveness, task orientation, logic, fearlessness, and confidence under pressure have become the measuring stick of competence for these first-responder professions. Firefighters who are able to control their emotions during stressful conditions are rewarded with accolades, citations, and promotions.

A therapist may invalidate a withdrawer's experience when the therapist lacks a context for the survival benefits of numbing and task performance under duress. A withdrawer's distress and corresponding defenses can be heightened as therapists push too quickly for emotional engagement. The EFT therapist's appreciation of the unique culture and training of the first responders provides a greater awareness of challenges faced in a therapy process that values the direct processing of emotions. In the field, first responders must work as a group and rely on one another. Individual experience is then secondary to the welfare of the unit and strong bonds of professional loyalty discourage deviation from these values. Therapists must respect the significant change required in putting aside years of training and experience to risk focusing on and sharing more experiences of vulnerability. These professionals on the frontlines will only risk vulnerability when they feel they can trust the therapist and have a framework for understanding the cost and benefits of such openness in therapy and in their relationship.

Paul's emotional withdrawal provided immediate safety for him but his distance increased Maureen's fears of rejection and abandonment. Over the course of 14 sessions, the therapist worked slowly in tracking the cycle, validating Maureen's frustration and anger before trying to go deeper. He normalized the mistrust that reinforced this couple's negative cycle and provided educational information to expand their perspectives and empower the couple to unite against the trauma. He also planted images of what a positive cycle of stepping out of the demand–withdraw dance and moving into sharing and responsiveness could look like. Paul and Maureen began to be able to step out of their cycle, demonstrating a shift in their awareness and moving from blaming each other to pinpointing the moments when the echoes of 9/11 and their negative dance would take them both over and leave them alone and exhausted.

The following example is taken from their 15th session of therapy as Paul began to share the details of his experience of 9/11. At the onset of Stage 2, the therapist invited Paul to begin to risk sharing some of his experience as a step toward accessing his underlying needs, fears, and model of self.

Therapist: In previous sessions you both mentioned never really talking about what happened on September 11, 2001. I was wondering, now that you both feel closer, is it something you want to discuss?

Maureen (looking at Paul): I really want him to turn to me and let me into his secret world.

Paul: I don't really see the need. What is done is done.

Therapist: Paul, it seems pointless for you to go back and revisit that day?

Paul: There is no point; nothing will change. We did the best we could and now we must move on. Why discuss it and bring up bad feelings for Maureen?

Therapist: Going back to the site brings back bad memories for both of you. It makes sense why you don't discuss it. Talking to Maureen about work in general is not something you are used to doing. Despite your good reasons not to talk, we know from your work here that excluding Maureen makes her feel unimportant. Paul, I am wondering what is happening to you when you think about talking about 9/11 to Maureen? (Therapist is validating the defenses while seeding possible risk.)

Paul (fidgeting in his chair): Nothing much. I really don't think about it much.

Therapist: OK, so you don't think about telling Maureen anything. I noticed when I asked you about talking about 9/11, you were moving around in your chair. What is that about? (Therapist focuses on the present body experience.)

Paul: I guess I feel uncomfortable, like I want to get away.

Therapist: Right. So this is really difficult for you. It seems easier to avoid going back there.

Paul: It seems easier not to talk but I know it just makes it worse (shaking his head).

Therapist: Paul, what's happening as you shake your head? (Therapist uses evocative responding to access emotional experience.)

Paul: I get angry at the whole situation. It seems pointless to go back in time.

Therapist: It is very frustrating to revisit that day. It's like your body is telling you there is no point. Am I getting that right? (Therapist normalizes secondary anger while heightening the perception of pointlessness.) (Paul nods in agreement.) Do you feel anything else in your body besides the anger and frustration?

Paul (pause): My stomach feels like it's in knots.

Therapist (slow voice): Your stomach hurts, like it is full of knots? (Therapist slows down to heighten emotion.)

Paul: It is a crappy feeling. I guess I never pay much attention to it. It reminds me of how my stomach felt when I was down there.

Therapist: Right now your stomach feels just like it did at the site. (Paul nods his head as he looks off into the distance.)

Paul (looking at the floor): It is pretty weird, something like being on another planet (shaking his head). I had a job to do so I didn't waste much time soaking it all in.

Therapist: When you talk about being on another planet, it almost seems like you are seeing it in the room right now. Is that correct, Paul? What are you seeing?

Paul: Yeah. Sometimes the smell of the smoke jumps right back into my head. I just wait for it to pass. (Paul's body tenses up as he closes his eyes, experiencing flashback.)

Therapist: What's going on Paul?

Paul: It's the sound. The building collapsing sounds like a freight train about to hit me. (Paul stops talking as his body turns sideways in the chair and his hands reach for something.)

Therapist (speaking in a very slow voice): Paul, it's all right; you are safe here. Do you know where you are? Can you feel your feet on the floor? (Therapist contains and grounds Paul's overwhelming emotional experience.)

Paul: (Trying to focus after going off—disassociating.) I'm sorry (clearing his throat and shaking his head again). This is why I don't want to talk about it.

Therapist: It always makes sense when we don't want to talk about it. Our bodies are trying to protect us. Do you want to stop or can I ask you another question about that day? (Therapist validates and normalizes Paul's response, educates about typical trauma responses, and assesses Paul's emotional reactivity.)

Paul (looking at Maureen skeptically as he half-heartedly replies): We've come this far, why quit now?

Therapist: Paul, as you talked about hearing the building collapse, I noticed your hands were reaching for something. Do you know what it was?

Paul (looking surprised): I just did that now? That is amazing. (Paul closes his eyes.) I was reaching for my radio; I had to let others know what was happening.

Therapist: So you were trying to reach out to others?

Paul: I guess so. That's why I don't want to talk about it. The whole thing reminds me of how powerless I am. Some of the greatest firemen in the world died that day. Good or bad, it made no difference. Who the hell wants to dwell on that? The whole thing sucks.

Therapist: So when you see the images of twisted steel and smoke, the whole thing sucks and you feel helpless with nowhere to go. Am I getting that right?

Paul (talking slowly): It could have so easily been me. I have
    never seen such a sight. They never had a chance. I
    feel so bad for them. Losing everything. Never see-
    ing their families again. So much twisted steel and
    smoke. I shouldn't be here (shaking his head, with
    tears in his eyes).

Therapist: Right. So much senseless loss and you feel you
    should have died with the others. (Therapist feeling
    sad while nodding his head to give permission for
    Paul's sadness.)

Paul (shaking his head again): My stomach hurts. It is such
    a shame. I am the lucky one. I shouldn't be feeling
    bad. I have my family. I should be doing so much
    better. I don't know why I can't get rid of these memo-
    ries. There must be something wrong with me.

Therapist: So when you see images of the smoke and twisted
    steel, you feel like there is something wrong with
    you. You tell yourself that you should be happy to be
    alive but these bad feelings won't go away. (Therapist
    stays emotionally present and does not try to talk
    Paul out of feelings of shame.)

Paul: I never thought of it that way but it seems right. I should
    have been stronger (tears in his eyes). I failed to
    measure up. It's not right to feel so bad. I'm disgrac-
    ing their memories.

Maureen (reaching over to put an arm around Paul): You didn't
    fail, honey; you did your best.

Paul (pulling away): My best just isn't good enough. Everyone
    calls us heroes. The only heroes died that day.

At the end of the session, an irritable Paul withdrew as the
therapist validated and normalized his feelings. This was
the first time that Paul shared the images of his 9/11 experience with Maureen and in the process he uncovered primary feelings that were previously outside awareness. The
therapist worked slowly to focus on Paul's emotions, which
allowed him to access different levels of emotion associated
with the trauma. Staying focused enabled the therapist to help
Paul move past avoidance and anger and touch sadness, failure, and shame. Paul showed Maureen a glimpse of his hidden
insecurities and fears. When she reached out to Paul, he did
not know how to receive her support, so he withdrew into his
anger and frustration. The therapist then reflected and outlined this predictable response and used this to frame their

problem pattern again. The therapist and the couple learned to tolerate the tension between expressions of vulnerability and exits to their familiar pattern.

In future sessions, Paul's approach to handling his fears and his sense that he was not entitled to comfort became tangible and clear. He grasped that he spent endless time and energy keeping his sense of helpless and shame in "lock down" and this left only the most surface parts of him accessible to his wife. Both partners saw how their continued fighting only reinforced Paul's fears that he was inadequate, powerless, and undeserving of Maureen's comfort. Paul was able to express how he experienced his relationship as a minefield and explore how he cautiously moved about so as not to set off Maureen's explosions. He shared how he constantly scanned the outside environment, looking for signs of danger and that he was "consumed and exhausted" by his "vigilance" for inner echoes of his trauma and for signs of Maureen's frustration in the relationship. Paul could not access his longing for Maureen because he was too busy managing his fear and his sense of failure as a firefighter and as a husband.

As the therapist normalized emotional avoidance as a professional survival tactic, Paul became increasingly less defensive and with this he began to own the weight of his "failings" with Maureen. He felt stuck between needing his wife's support and not having a way to acknowledge this need that fit with his sense of his professional and personal self. Paul was finally able to express his grief and helplessness, acknowledging his core fears and risking reaching out with them to Maureen. Maureen responded with empathy and with relief that her husband did indeed need her and that she was able to offer him reassurance and comfort.

Together, Paul and Maureen were able to replace their problem pattern with new cycles of emotional engagement. Paul continued to confront his 9/11 experiences with Maureen and he continued to seek and receive her support. Over time, their individual PTSD and depressive symptoms waned. However, the couple's successfully uniting against the trauma of 9/11 did not signal the end of treatment. Paul's continued struggle with his 9/11 experiences proved a formidable challenge for their relationship, but their negative pattern was also informed by Maureen's unspoken fears.

After Paul's reengagement, Maureen risked softening her more demanding stance with Paul by sharing her fears of being "deserted" and finding herself "left and broken." As Paul heard that her fears were not centered on his "failings" but rather on their negative cycle and sensitivities from her past, he leapt at the opportunity to comfort her. After 30 sessions, Paul and Maureen ended treatment confident in their abilities to maintain a safe and secure relationship.

SECURE ATTACHMENT AND HEALING OF TRAUMA

What does healing mean for a traumatized couple and for their love relationship? At the very least, couple interventions should lower the family tension and hostility that tend to trigger a survivor's symptoms and impede improvement (Tarrier, Sommerfield, & Pilgrim, 1999). EFT aims to do more than this. The new science of relationships suggests that attachment figures such as adult partners can have a stunning impact on each other (Coan, Schaefer, & Davidson, 2006); they are, in fact, the hidden regulators of key aspects of each other's physiology, especially in the face of threat. Emerging research (Uvnas-Moberg, 1998) on neurotransmitters such as oxytocin—the so-called "cuddle hormone" that induces calm and contentment when safe attachment figures are physically close or even imagined—suggests that therapists reconsider the power of interpersonal affect regulation.

By its very nature, trauma changes one's life and identity. Nevertheless, we as humans are able, especially if we have more secure attachments, not only to survive trauma but also to grow from it (Tedeschi & Calhoun, 2004). One could ask: What should a traumatized couple look like at the end of EFT? The answer would be that the treatment of trauma should result in decreased isolation, increased social competence, positive coping, and more supportive relationships (Harvey, 1996). At the end of therapy, the EFT therapist expects to see this kind of change.

More specifically, the process of EFT fosters the integration of memory, meaning, and emotion so that the survivor has more control around traumatic memories, as well as the ongoing impact of these memories, and is able, with the partner's help, to create a sense of closure. The meaning of memories as they emerge in session is cocreated and revised by the survivor, the other partner, and the therapist. As John, a war veteran, remembers the brutal acts he committed to survive, and the deep self-loathing these memories trigger, his wife takes his hand and reminds him that he brought all his men home, that he was caught in a whirlpool where choice was nonexistent, that he has already nobly borne the weight of these acts for 40 years, and that she loves him because he is a good man (Johnson, 2008). Instead of silent shame, this vet then turns toward his wife, weeps, and promises to turn to her when these "guilt voices" torment him. She tells him that he does not have to turn away and fight this dragon alone anymore.

As the preceding example suggests, EFT also addresses other key desired outcomes of trauma treatment as outlined by writers such as Harvey (1996). Two key desired outcomes—increased affect regulation, demonstrated in the ability to tolerate emotional moments without undue panic, and lessened impulsive reactivity or numbing—are constantly addressed in the EFT process. Also, the validation offered by the EFT therapist and the responsive interactions between partners builds self-esteem and a cohesive sense of self. In general, more securely attached individuals demonstrate a more positive, articulated, and cohesive sense of self (Mikulincer, 1995). The creation of new meaning around the trauma itself and the often less than optimal coping strategies that it has evoked is also a natural part of the EFT process, as is the ability to trust others more and to turn to others to help regulate emotions and deal with traumatic stress.

CONCLUSION

Professionals who stand in harm's way adopt tactics that are battle tested. After September 11, 2001, EFT earned credibility in the NYC Fire Department by successfully helping trauma survivors reconnect to their wired-in need for connection and support. Traumatic incidents indiscriminately assault a survivor's intrapsychic world and bonds with others. In general, the use of an attachment-oriented couple therapy, such as EFT, aims to create new levels of effective dependency for both partners. Effective dependency involves not just being able to turn to actual or internalized others for care and thus become stronger and more resilient, but also the creation of a more integrated inner world and more integrated relationships where attachment, caretaking, and sexuality can come together as a positive whole. This is the ultimate antidote to the fragmentation and chaos that is carried on the dragon's breath. Standing together creates a felt sense of security that we carry into all aspects of life—not just adversity. Hope is eternal when we are not alone.

REFERENCES

Bograd, M., & Meredos, F. (1999). Battering and couples therapy: Universal screening and selection of treatment modality. *Journal of Marital and Family Therapy, 25,* 291–312.

Bowlby, J. (1969). *Attachment & loss: Vol. 1. Attachment.* New York, NY: Basic Books.

Bowlby, J. (1988). *A secure base.* New York, NY: Basic Books.

Bradley, B., & Furrow, J. L. (2004). Toward a mini-theory of the blamer softening event: Tracking the moment-by-moment process. *Journal of Marital & Family Therapy, 30,* 233–246.

CDC (Centers for Disease Control and Prevention). 2004. Mental health status of World Trade Center rescue and recovery workers and volunteers—New York City, July 2002–August 2004. *Morbidity and Mortality Weekly Report, 53*(35), 807–815.

Coan, J., Schaefer, H., & Davidson, R. (2006). Lending a hand. *Psychological Science, 17,* 1–8.

Cook, J. M., Riggs, D. S., Thompson, R., Coyne, J., & Sheikh, J. (2004). Posttraumatic stress disorder and current relationship functioning among World War II ex-prisoners of war. *Journal of Family Psychology, 18,* 36–45.

Courtois, C. A., & Ford, J. (2009). *Treating complex traumatic stress disorders: An evidence-based guide.* New York, NY: Guilford.

Dalton, J., Johnson, S. M., & Classen, C. (in press). Treating relationship distress and the effects of childhood abuse with emotion focused couple therapy: A randomized controlled trial. *Journal of Marital and Family Therapy.*

Denton, W. H., Wittenborn, A., & Golden, R. N. (in press). Augmenting antidepressant medication treatment of depressed women with emotionally focused therapy for couples: A randomized pilot study. *Journal of Marital and Family Therapy.*

Dessaulles, A., Johnson, S. M., & Denton, W. H. (2003). Emotionally focused therapy for couples in the treatment of depression: A pilot study. *American Journal of Family Therapy, 31,* 345–353.

Difede, J., Apfeldorf, W., Cloitre, M., Spielman, L., & Perry, S. (1997). Acute psychiatric responses to the explosion at the World Trade Center: A case series. *Journal of Nerve Mental Disorders, 185,* 519–522.

Foa, E. B., Hearst-Ikeda, D., & Perry, K. L. (1995). Evaluation of a brief cognitive behavioral program for the prevention of chronic PTSD in recent assault victims. *Journal of Consulting and Clinical Psychology, 63,* 948–955.

Foa, E. B., & Rothbaum, B. O. (1998). *Treating the trauma of rape: Cognitive behavioral therapy for PTSD.* New York, NY: Guilford Press.

Fraley, C., Fazzari, D., Bonanno, G., & Dekel, S. (2006). Attachment and psychological adaptation in high exposure survivors of the September 11 attack on the World Trade Center. *Personality and Social Psychology Bulletin, 32,* 538–551.

Gilbertson, M., Shenton, M., Ciszewski, A., Kasai, K., Lasko, N., Orr, S., & Pitman, R. (2002). Smaller hippocampal volume predicts pathologic vulnerability to psychological trauma. *Nature Neuroscience, 5,* 1242–1247.

Gross, R., Nerla, Y., Tao, X., Massa, J., Ashwell, L., Davis, K., et al. (2006). Posttraumatic stress disorder and other psychological sequelae among world trade center clean up and recovery workers. *Annual New York Academy of Science, 1071,* 495–499.

Harvey, M. (1996). An ecological view of psychological trauma and trauma recovery. *Journal of Traumatic Stress, 9,* 3–23.

Herman, J. L. (1993). Complex PTSD: A syndrome in survivors of prolonged or repeated trauma. *Journal of Traumatic Stress, 5,* 377–391.

Hoge, C., Castro, C., Messer, S., McGurik, D., Cotting, D., & Koffman, R. (2004). Combat duty in Iraq and Afghanistan, mental health problems, and barriers to care. *New England Journal of Medicine, 351,* 13–22.

Holtzworth-Munroe, A., Marshall, A., Meehan, J., & Rehman, U. (2003). Physical aggression. In D. K. Snyder & M. A. Whisman (Eds.), *Treating difficult couples* (pp. 201–230). New York, NY: Guilford Press.

Jacobson, N. S., Dobson, K., Fruzzetti, A. E., Schmaling, K. B., & Salusky, S. (1991). Marital therapy as a treatment for depression. *Journal of Consulting and Clinical Psychology, 59,* 547–557.

Johnson, S. M. (2002). *Emotionally focused couple therapy with trauma survivors: Strengthening attachment bonds.* New York, NY: Guilford Press.

Johnson, S. M. (2004). *The practice of emotionally focused couple therapy: Creating connection* (2nd ed.). New York, NY: Brunner/Routledge.

Johnson, S. M. (2008). *Hold me tight: Seven conversations for a lifetime of love.* New York, NY: Little Brown.

Johnson, S. M. (2009). Extravagant emotion. Understanding and transforming love relationships in emotionally focused therapy. In D. Fosha, D. Siegel, & M. Solomon (Eds.), *The healing power of emotion: Affective neuroscience, development, clinical practice* (pp. 257–279). New York, NY: Norton.

Johnson, S. M., & Rheem, K. D. (2006). *Becoming a couple again: A post-deployment retreat for military couples.* Washington, DC: Strong Bonds, Strong Couples.

Johnson, S. M., & Williams Keeler, L. (1998). Creating healing relationships for couples dealing with trauma. *Journal of Marital and Family Therapy, 24,* 25–40.

Kardiner, A. (1941). *The traumatic neuroses of war.* New York, NY: Hoeber.

Karen, R. (1998). *Becoming attached: First relationship and how they shape our capacity to love.* New York, NY: Oxford University Press.

MacIntosh, H., & Johnson, S. M. (2008). Emotionally focused therapy for couples and childhood sexual abuse survivors. *Journal of Marital and Family Therapy, 34,* 298–375.

McCann, I. L., & Pearlman, L. A. (1990). *Psychological trauma and the adult survivor.* New York, NY: Brunner Mazel.

Mikulincer, M. (1995). Attachment style and the mental representation of self. *Journal of Personality and Social Psychology, 69,* 1203–1215.

Mikulincer, M., Florian, V., & Weller, A. (1993). Attachment styles, coping strategies and posttraumatic psychological distress: The impact of the Gulf War in Israel. *Journal of Personality and Social Psychology, 64,* 817–826.

Mikulincer, M., Shaver, P., & Horesh, N. (2004). Attachment basis of emotional regulation and posttraumatic adjustment. In D. K. Snyder, J. A. Simpson, & J. N. Hughes (Eds.) *Emotional regulation in families: Pathways to dysfunction and health*, pp. 77–99. Washington, DC: American Psychological Association.

Mikulincer, M., & Shaver, P. (2007). *Attachment in adulthood: Structure, dynamics and change.* New York, NY: Guilford Press.

Mikulincer, M., Shaver, P., & Horesh, N. (2006). Attachment bases of emotion regulation and posttraumatic adjustment. In D. Snyder, J. Simpson, & J. Hughes (Eds.), *Emotional regulation in couples and families* (pp. 77–99). Washington, DC: APA Press.

Monson, C., Schnurr, P., Stevens, S., & Guthrie, K. (2004). Cognitive behavioral couple treatment for posttraumatic stress disorder: Initial findings. *Journal of Traumatic Stress, 17,* 341–344.

Naaman, S., Johnson, S. M., & Radwan, K. (in press). Evaluation of the clinical efficacy of emotionally focused therapy on psychological adjustment of couples facing early breast cancer. *Psychiatry: Biological and Interpersonal Processes.*

Nelson, B. S., & Wampler, K. S. (2000). Systemic effects of trauma in clinical couples: An exploratory study of secondary trauma resulting from childhood abuse. *Journal of Marital and Family Therapy, 26,* 171–183.

Pearlman, L. A., & Caringi, J. (2009). Living and working self-reflectively to address vicarious trauma. In C. Courtois & J. Ford (Eds.), *Treating complex traumatic stress disorders* (pp. 202–224). New York, NY: Guilford Press.

Perrin, M., DiGrande, L., Wheeler, K., Thorpe, L., & Brackbill, R. (2007). Differences in PTSD prevalence and associated risk factors among World Trade Center disaster workers. *American Journal Psychiatry, 115,* 1154–1159.

Riggs, D. S., Byrne, C., Weathers, F., & Litz, B. (1998). The quality of intimate relationships of male Vietnam veterans: problems associated with posttraumatic stress disorder. *Journal of Traumatic Stress, 11,* 87–101.

Shalev, A. Y. (1993). Stress versus traumatic stress: From acute homeostatic reactions to chronic psychopathology. In B. A. van der Kolk, A. C. McFarlane, & L. Weisaeth (Eds.), *Traumatic stress* (pp. 77–101). New York, NY: Guilford Press.

Slade, A. (2008). The implications of attachment theory and research for adult psychotherapy. In J. Cassidy, & P. Shaver (Eds.), *Handbook of attachment: Theory, research and clinical applications* (pp. 262–282). New York, NY: Guilford Press.

Stellman, J., Smith, R., Katz, C., Sharma, S., Charney, D., Herbert, R., et al. (2008). Enduring mental health morbidity and social function in World Trade Center rescue, recovery, and cleanup workers: The psychological dimension of an environmental health disaster. *Environmental Health Perspectives, 116,* 1248–1253.

Tapp, L., Baron, S., Bernard, B., Driscoll, R., Mueller, C., & Wallingford, K. (2005). Physical and mental health symptoms among NYC transit workers after WTC attacks. *American Journal Industrial Medicine, 47*, 475–483.

Tarrier, N., Sommerfield, C., & Pilgrim, H. (1999). Relatives expressed emotion (EE) and PTSD treatment outcome. *Psychological Medicine, 29*, 801–811.

Tedeschi, R. G., & Calhoun, L. G. (2004). Posttraumatic growth: Conceptual foundations and empirical evidence. *Psychological Inquiry, 15*, 1–18.

Uvnas-Moberg, K. (1998). Oxytocin may mediate the benefits of positive social interaction and emotions. *Psychneuroendocrinology, 23*, 819–835.

van der Kolk, B., & McFarlane, A. C. (1996). The black hole of trauma. In B. van der Kolk, A. C. McFarlane, & L. Weisaeth (Eds.), *Traumatic stress* (pp. 3–23). New York, NY: Guilford Press.

van der Kolk, B. A., Perry, C., & Herman, J. L. (1991). Childhood origins of self-destructive behavior. *American Journal of Psychiatry, 148*, 1665–1671.

Eight

Emotionally Focused Couple Therapy and Addiction

**MARTIN LANDAU-NORTH, SUSAN M. JOHNSON,
AND TRACY L. DALGLEISH**

INTRODUCTION

Relationship problems and addiction go hand in hand. Addictions are toxic for relationships and negative relationships make individuals vulnerable to stress and less functional coping styles and thus more likely to turn to addictive substances and behaviors. Distressed relationships are also predictive of a poor prognosis in alcohol and drug abuse programs (Fals-Stewart, Birchler, & O'Farrell, 1999, 2003). Reviews of the best evidence-based treatment approaches to substance disorders indicate that most of them emphasize a focus on family or social networks as a key "active ingredient" of successful therapy (Miller & Wilbourne, 2002).

In spite of the fact that EFT practitioners report working successfully with couples who struggle with addictions, there is a paucity of material on the use of EFT with these couples. This chapter represents a modest start in addressing the growing use of EFT in the context of addictions. The word "addiction" comes from the Latin *addictionem,* the literal meaning of which is "a devoting." It appears to have been first used in its negative modern sense in the early nineteenth century to describe the opium addict's obsession with this drug. Romantic love has also been called an "addiction" (Fisher, 2004), although recent research has found that when this love lasts, the obsession or infatuation aspect that we might most associate with addictions disappears (Acevedo & Aron, 2009).

Stated similarities between romantic love and addiction hinge on the power of love as a motivating force, the "hunger" generated for contact with the beloved, and the distress that arises when this hunger is not satisfied. The exploration of the neurochemical correlates of love, especially the discovery that romantic love turns on dopamine, the brain's reward system, has also been used to link it to addiction. Viewing a photograph of a deeply loved partner seems to create brain activation patterns similar to those seen after an infusion of cocaine or opiates (Bartels & Zeki, 2000). The process of affect regulation does indeed appear to be inherent in an attachment view of romantic love and in the process of addiction; one man turns to images of contact with his wife for comfort while another turns to cocaine.

Thus, perhaps the ultimate goal of the EFT therapist working with an addicted couple is to help the addict substitute an "addiction" to emotional connection with a loved one for his or her attachment to a negative obsession with drugs, alcohol, or activities such as gambling or internet porn. As EFT therapists, we do use this metaphor with couples in reframes. We might say to an addict, "Your wife does get upset with your obsession with poker. It takes you away from her. It's like poker is your mistress and you put this mistress first. You turn to this mistress for pleasure and comfort." Metaphors can be useful as communication tools, but it is dangerous to take them literally. Although there are similarities, it seems to us that the addiction label can only seriously be applied to love if we focus on the initial infatuation phases of romantic love and also hold to a pathologizing view of adult dependency.

A more accurate way to place EFT as an attachment-oriented approach into the context of addictions is to suggest that the EFT process can help to address addictions precisely because it offers the opportunity to shape effective dependency (Bowlby, 1969). Addiction is a form of compulsive behavior that involves an ever increasing constriction of a person's behavioral repertoire (Insel, 2003). Secure, effective attachment involves the promotion of a broad and flexible response set and relationships where individual partners are stronger, more able to make choices, feel better about themselves, and become less focused on regulating negative emotions and more open to learning and growth.

Secure attachment, where individuals can turn to others as a safe haven and to provide a secure base that allows for resilient coping in the world, is the ultimate goal of EFT. This kind of bond makes us stronger and less vulnerable to becoming caught in the web of addictive substances and activities. Secure attachment fosters a positive and functional way of dealing with our hunger for comfort, positive emotions and sensations, soothing and relief from pain, and a sense of ourselves as valuable and strong. As such, it can perhaps be thought of as an antidote to addiction.

SUGGESTED MODEL FOR EFT PRACTITIONERS

If we take heavy drinking as an example of addiction, it is clear that there is no simple single pathway into addiction (Molnar, Sadava, Decourville, & Perrier, 2010). Some people drink heavily for social reasons, such as to fit into their social group. This main pathway to addictive drinking is, however, an emotional one. People drink to move into positive affect and alleviate emotional distress (Cooper, Agocha, & Sheldon, 2000).

Once the initial motivation leads into habitual addictive ways of regulating negative emotions, the second question becomes, how is this habit maintained, in spite of obvious negative consequences? First, we suggest that rather than focusing on the physical dependence model of addiction (where the pain of withdrawal triggers further use), an alternative positive-incentive theory of addiction (Pinel, 2006) is most useful. Pinel pinpoints the problems associated with the physical-dependence theories of addiction. These theories essentially state that addicts become ensnared in a substance-driven cycle whereby they are either taking drugs or struggling with terrible symptoms of withdrawal, thus having what is called a physical dependence on the drug itself.

However, some drugs, such as cocaine or amphetamines, do not produce severe withdrawal distress. Detoxified addicts, with no drugs in their system and who are no longer undergoing withdrawal, mostly regress to their former addictive behaviors even after long periods of abstinence. Also, addicts often find sufficient "reward" in drug-related cues alone. Alcoholics will fool around with an empty wine bottle, drool over it, and show behaviors that mimic intoxication. Needle addicts have been known to become euphoric by merely inserting empty hypodermics into their limbs even though there is no drug present.

The positive-incentive theory postulates that addicts are first and foremost caught in a web of expectation. This expectation of escape, release, and a positive shift in emotions in reality provides a more intense high than the pleasure addicts experience when actually drinking or taking a drug. Addictive behaviors are driven by anticipatory pleasure, and thus cravings are disproportionate to the actual pleasure ultimately derived from taking a drug or substance. Robinson and Berridge (1993) emphasize that it is not the pleasure of the drug that is fundamental to addiction. Rather, it is the wanting, the anticipation of a joyful high, or the release and disinhibition of drunkenness.

An example familiar to many may be that of underage binge drinkers. After planning intensively for a week, there is a party organized for a Saturday night. The excitement is palpable. Once at the party, they knock back their beers and after 10 minutes they are "out of it." The day after, they remember very little of what occurred the previous night. The pleasure is in the anticipation of the drinking than in the actual act, which was quick, numbing, and followed by vomiting and an unpleasant hangover. They then swear off ever having another drink, but within days, high on anticipation, they anticipate their next foray into substance abuse.

With pornography addiction, one of the authors of this chapter has found that the planning, secrecy, and anticipation of viewing sexually explicit materials maintains a quasi-persistent state of arousal, which lasts much longer than the actual viewing of pornography or the pornography-induced orgasm. Anecdotally, that author has had six male patients report that the persistent prodromal sexual arousal is, in many instances, more intense than the rapid or spontaneous ejaculation that occurs when the pornography is in fact viewed.

While the physical-dependence model cannot be dismissed in its entirety (withdrawal hurts), there is evidence to suggest that the positive-incentive theories pertaining to drugs, alcohol, and, in the one author's experience, also pornography elegantly capture the primary factor in addiction (Cardinal & Everitt, 2004; Everitt, Dickinson, & Robbins, 2001). In terms of relapse into addiction, the three causes seem to be rising stress, priming (a single exposure to the formerly abused substance), and exposure to environmental cues associated with the addiction.

For the EFT therapist, acceptance of the positive-incentive model leads to productive implications for the role of EFT in treating addictions and ties into an attachment approach to addiction. It emphasizes that it is not just the addictive behavior itself that is problematic for relationships. Once distracted by the anticipatory pleasure, the distracted and addicted member of the dyad becomes progressively and chronically more emotionally absent. Over time, this absence erodes romantic attachment, and in response the nonaddicted partner, while remaining attached, sends more and more cues of disappointment and anger.

This perspective also stresses that addiction is not just about altering, escaping, or coping with negative emotions; it is about seeking pleasurable mood-enhancing experiences and how the reliable expectation of these can be used as a constant emotional defense and regulator in everyday life, much as a felt sense of secure connection operates in positive relationships. In general, people attribute risk-taking behaviors to conscious efforts to pursue positive emotions and to escape from negative ones (Cooper, Flanagan, Talley, & Micheas, 2006). This implies that any relationship intervention with couples facing addiction has to focus not only on coping and conflict reduction but also on the creation of predictable positive emotional experiences and perhaps on bonding experiences that release pleasurable "cuddle" hormones such as oxytocin (Carter, 1998).

Addiction is also a systemic process—a set of interacting intrapsychic and interpersonal variables that impact and shape each other. As relationships become more negative and the addictive behaviors become more all encompassing, the addicted partner naturally turns more and more to the addiction as a primary predictable source of pleasure and as a reliable escape from his or her sense of alienation. Addicts become more and more disengaged with others as they become obsessed with the release and pleasure of future indulgences. Once the drug has been taken, the alcohol imbibed, or the pornography viewed, the inevitable consequences in the couple when the actual addictive act is discovered create a situation where alternative routes to positive emotion are lessened, negative emotion is heightened, and the addictive behavior gains in incentive value. The addictive substance becomes the only "solution" to negative emotions and a surrogate source of pleasure and soothing.

In key studies of behavioral marital therapy (BMT), this approach, which focuses on teaching communication and problem-solving skills, has been used in combination with individual treatment for drug addiction; this combination has been found to be more effective than stand-alone individual treatments (Fals-Stewart, O'Farrell, & Birchler, 2001). Studies of alcohol-related problems with BMT also show a consistent pattern of more abstinence and happier relationships for clients who receive BMT rather than only individual treatment (Fals-Stewart et al., 2003).

This behavioral intervention, its proponents note, has not been widely used. They suggest that this may be because it does not subscribe to the dominant disease model of addiction. Any couple approach to the treatment of addiction, while acknowledging the physiological impact of addictive substances and the power of the painful physical withdrawal process to trigger relapse, has also to pinpoint the power of specific relationship factors in the generation and persistence of addiction and the recovery process. EFT has a very specific, rich, and well-researched theory of adult love in the form of attachment theory and this offers a specific perspective on addiction and its treatment in couple therapy.

ADDICTION AS AN ATTACHMENT DISORDER

It is easy to frame addiction in attachment terms (Flores, 2001). Securely attached individuals are more into self-protective health behaviors and therefore less prone to damaging behaviors such as heavy drinking (Brennan & Shaver, 1995; Thorberg & Lyvers, 2006). Attachment is essentially a theory of affect regulation. Addiction can be seen as a consequence of and dysfunctional solution to the absence of satisfying close relationships and particularly as a seeking after comfort and positive emotion in a context of the experience of emotional isolation. The addiction becomes a substitute place of momentary security and pleasure and relief from this pain. Addiction is also associated with a particularly negative and shameful view of self as being inadequate and undeserving (McNally, Palfai, Levine, & Moore, 2003). The drug of choice then functions as a source of self-aggrandizement providing temporary relief from these negative models of self.

Higher levels of attachment anxiety and avoidance in close relationships result in less ability to regulate and manage internal distress and to reach out to others for support (Mikulincer, 1998). In general, anxious and avoidantly attached adults are more likely to use dysfunctional strategies to soothe, distract, and excite, such as engaging in risky sexual activity. For example, avoidant individuals are more likely to choose one-night stands as a sexual strategy (Gillath & Schachner, 2006; Stephan & Bachman, 1999). Anxiously attached adults drink more, explicitly drink to cope, and drink with greater negative consequences (Molnar et al., 2010). Some studies suggest that the anxiously attached indulge in problem drinking more than secure or avoidantly attached individuals (Kassel, Wardle, & Roberts, 2007; McNally et al., 2003).

Other studies (Cooper, Shaver, & Collins, 1998) find that both avoidant and anxiously attached young people consume more alcohol. It seems that sometimes anxiously attached individuals drink specifically to reduce negative affect and that dismissing individuals drink more to enhance positive affect. Another study (Doumas, Blasey, & Mitchell, 2006) found that anxious and fearful-avoidant attachment (both of which they note are characterized by a negative sense of self) were overrepresented in alcoholic and drug-dependent groups.

Attachment theory would predict that those of us who did not experience a safe haven and secure base relationship as children would be more vulnerable to the impact of stress and trauma, less able to cope with this stress by turning to others for support and caring, and thus be more likely to turn to addictive substances and behaviors to regulate emotions. These factors then release a cascading feedback loop where negative relationships forge negative views of self and other and more isolation and more stress result in more addictive coping behaviors, more conflict and distance in the relationship, and more attachment insecurity.

In therapy, a vicious cycle often appears where relationship distress triggers addictive behaviors or relapse into these behaviors and addictive behaviors trigger or maintain alienation and conflict. The addictive substance or activity, rather than the partner, becomes the addict's safe haven and secure base. Partners feel replaced and abandoned as well as betrayed by an addict's use of lies and evasions to hold onto his or her habit. So-called "codependent" responses that accommodate to the addict's habit are attempts by these partners to hold onto the tatters of their attachment bond with the addicted partner.

For example, Louis, in the case example offered later, grew up in a "cold" and extremely reserved and formal family. He could not remember ever being held or even playing in an intimate way with his siblings. Task performance and work were the focus of family life. As part of his adolescent rebellion, he had begun to play cards with boys in his neighborhood. At the card table he felt competent, "powerful," and admired. He won easily. This activity grew into a consummate skill in and obsession with poker and he played poker all through university into his early adulthood. He was a shy, introverted man who had few friends or girlfriends. He married Anne, his first serious girlfriend, and in the first years of their relationship, he developed his career as an accountant and stopped playing poker altogether.

However, 10 years later, after setbacks in his career, the arrival of twin boys, and growing alienation in his marriage, he joined a local poker club and within a year he was playing poker at tournaments on the weekend, two nights a week at a local club, and on the Internet every night. His wife objected more and more strenuously and they began to fight regularly over this issue. The more they fought, the more he turned to poker. He denied that his love of poker was in any way a problem; he pointed out that he won constantly and made significant money for the family this way and increased his involvement in the game.

The crisis occurred when he was playing on the Internet one night and his son fell down the stairs and knocked his head. Anne was alarmed and called for him to come, to which he replied, "Not now, I am winning!" Later that week, Anne discovered that on a few occasions Louis's poker club had invited a prostitute to come and offer favors at the end of the late-night games. She announced that she was leaving and moved with her sons into her mother's house. Louis's brother confronted him and Louis sought out therapy for his "problem." Two months later, Anne moved back in and they came for couple therapy.

The absence of secure attachment in this dyad triggered a propensity to turn toward addiction as the solution to distress in what Flores (2004) calls a *faux* attachment. This faux attachment also becomes integrated into the individual's self-concept, which then undermines the addicted partner's reengagement in the strengthening of the weakened attachment bonds (Johnson, 2004). This sense that addiction is inextricably tied into attachment bonds has also been noted as one of the reasons that the 12-step programs work. The essence of these programs is a relationship with a group of similarly struggling companions and also with a mentor who offers a form of safe haven and a secure base to the addict.

An attachment orientation to addiction also implies (Flores, 2004) that just as medication or addictive substances can alter neurology and biochemistry, so can the experience of secure attachment (Lewis, Amini, & Lannon, 2000). It is already clear that a felt sense of attachment alters brain responses to threat (Coan, Schaefer, & Davidson, 2006) and triggers the release of the cuddle hormone oxytocin and the sense of calm contentment it elicits.

EFT AND COUPLES STRUGGLING WITH ADDICTION

This chapter will not address the question of whether total abstinence is the only way to address addiction successfully, as is promoted by Alcoholics Anonymous in the 12-step model of treatment, or whether moderation management and controlled substance use can work (Marlatt, 1998). There is evidence that prolonged use of addictive substances alters the production of neurotransmitters and brain functioning and leaves some users unable to use substances nonaddictively (Leshner, 2001) so that nothing less than a commitment to total abstinence is likely to help. We suggest, as in the case of couple therapy with survivors of trauma who show signs of PTSD, that the identified addict needs to take responsibility for the addiction and its consequences.

The best scenario, then, is that the individual addict acknowledges his problem and takes active steps to address his addiction before beginning couple therapy. If this responsibility is absent, then the therapist will not be able to create safety in the couple session or encourage the nonaddicted partner to increase his or her engagement in the relationship. The level and chronicity of the abuse also need to be taken into account in terms of the feasibility of couple therapy. The EFT therapist also needs to be clear about the nature of the treatment that the addicted partner is engaging in for his or her addiction so that conflicts with EFT are minimized.

The EFT therapist is a process consultant, so if the addiction is denied or not seen as an issue by the addict, the EFT therapist has to offer the perspective that couple therapy is unlikely to offer any benefit, that the compulsive attachment to the addiction is undermining the relationship in very specific ways and will continue to do so, and that the couple's relationship is, in essence, caught in the jaws of the addiction. Along with this "I don't think this will work" message, it is also possible to offer hope in the form of images of what a positive relationship looks like, how it might offer more effective solace and satisfaction, and what would have to happen for the couple to begin this journey.

There is also a need with addicted partners for added vigilance on the part of the therapist in the assessment phase of EFT regarding issues of violence and anger problems and issues of depression and self-harm. The individual sessions provide a place where the therapist can ask explicit questions about these issues and apply the practice principles laid down in EFT (Johnson, 2004) regarding criteria for excluding couples on the basis of violence. The therapist uses the fear level of the less aggressive partner as the benchmark for whether it is possible to create safety in sessions and thus implement EFT. As with a partner suffering from PTSD (Johnson, 2002), the therapist may set up a contingency containment plan with the couple so that if issues of aggression or self-harm arise, there is a clear way of dealing with them and protecting partners from harm. There is evidence that couple therapy is indeed effective with couples who exhibit mild to moderate physical aggression but want to preserve the relationship and end the aggression (Simpson, Atkins, Gattis, & Christensen, 2008).

For an attachment-oriented approach to addiction issues in a humanistic intervention such as EFT, the principles that add to and expand how this model is implemented are the following:

- The therapist takes a person-centered rather than a problem-centered approach (Rogers, 1951) and accepts that the addicted partner has good reasons for his or her addiction. Many of these reasons will involve problematic attachments and, as Bowlby suggests, in this context a person's less than functional attempts to deal with emotions and the dilemmas of connection and disconnection are "perfectly reasonable." At the same time, the therapist pinpoints the toxic impact of the addiction on the addicted person, the partner, and the relationship. It is worth noting that those who struggle with addictions are more likely to report having parents who were addicted and that the children of such parents report high levels of attachment insecurity with romantic partners (Brennan, Shaver, & Tobey, 1991; Kelley et al., 2005). This attachment perspective offers a specific bridge between a family history of alcoholism and impaired relationships that then renders the next generation vulnerable to addictions. This also reminds us as therapists that most addicts have never seen the kind of secure connection that they wish for and try (without any blueprint) to create with their partner. The speed with which they fall into hopelessness in relationships is then understandable.
- In Stage 1 of EFT, the therapist places problematic compulsive responses and patterns in the context of the recurring spirals of negative interaction patterns such as demand–withdraw that continually confirm

attachment insecurities and often trigger turning to addictive substances. An addiction is both cause and effect for relationship distress; both the addiction and relationship distress trigger and maintain each other. The addiction is framed as part of a couple's negative cycle and, like that cycle, as the enemy in the couple's relationship that they can best defeat together. Specific effects of the addiction, such as the partner's vigilance for cues that the addiction is still present, are outlined and put into a couple's general cycle of distress.

- The validation of the need for emotional safety as the essential foundation for emotional openness and responsiveness is key. Negative behaviors such as angry outbursts or potentially abusive responses must be contained as noted before.

- Before beginning Stage 2 of EFT, the therapist needs to make sure that the addiction is being contained. An experienced therapist noted that working with addicted couples is like being in a canoe. There is a need to balance the risks involved in working through issues and reaching for the other with the risks of emotional flooding and subsequent relapse into the addictive behavior. In Stage 2, deeper emotions are explored, distilled, and shared in ways that create more open, responsive interactions. When working with addictions, once negative cycles of interaction have been outlined and owned, the deeper primary emotions linked to addictive responses are explored and placed in the context of attachment needs and fears and expectations for or models of self and other. Thus, sadness, deep fears about rejection and abandonment, and fears and shame about the self as inadequate or flawed are explored and placed in the context of the fall into addiction and attachment needs. Key moments in a partner's exploration of experience that focus on addictive responses as apparent "solutions" to emotional starvation and despair will be focused on and explored so as to deepen emotional awareness. Emotion and attempts at the regulation of emotion are seen as a leading or organizing element in the addiction and in the couple's attachment system.

- As part of Stage 2, positive interactions are created in enactments and these enactments, where one person risks and reaches for the other, are framed as direct alternatives to the addictive behaviors and associated demand or withdrawal responses. Thus, at this point, Doug is able to tell his wife, "When this empty feeling comes for me, I just want to run. I run to booze or I badger you for sex. Anything not to feel this empti- ness. I haven't known how to ask for your caring. But I think this…this reassurance and closeness is what I need. Can I ask you…?" The therapist helps Doug and his wife make this response into a coherent acknowl- edgment that he is now choosing to turn to her rather than numbing out with a bottle. Loving connection is structured and framed as the antidote to addictive regulation strategies.

- As part of the consolidation stage of EFT, partners for- mulate a story of their relationship distress and repair. Couples are encouraged to create a coherent story of the addiction and how it impacted their relationship, including how problems related to the addiction still emerge and how they are now able to deal with them.
- The therapist will guide partners to formulate a plan to guard against relapse into the addiction and to note trig- gers into the emotional states that set up these relapses.

It may be useful also to note that while some commenta- tors see alcoholics and addicts as "notoriously counterdepen- dent" (Flores, 2004, p. 43) or extreme avoidant, we and other attachment theorists (P. Shaver, personal communication, Feb. 2010) view them most often as using fearful-avoidant or disor- ganized attachment strategies. This means that these partners tend to flip in a haphazard manner between anxious hyper- activating and avoidant deactivating attachment strategies. They distance others and are uncomfortable with closeness but they also continue to experience a longing for connec- tion. They cannot simply dismiss attachment and deny their need for support. They are high on attachment anxiety and avoidance.

This strategy arises from growing up in an abusive or highly neglectful family (Shaver & Clark, 1994) and is often seen in trauma survivors who have been violated in their families. It then results in extremely intense but ambivalent, ambiguous messages being sent to the partner, such as "Come here. Why aren't you supporting me?" followed by "Go away—I don't need you." Others are, at one and the same time, the source of and solution to fear. An addictive substance allows for the regulation of anxiety without the risk of interpersonal connection.

There is extensive evidence that those responding with a fearful avoidant strategy tend to experience the least security and trust in adolescence and adulthood (Shaver & Clark, 1994). They have especially negative representations of their romantic partners, show less empathy for distressed others, are more cognitively closed and rigid, and generally show the poorest mental health (Mikulincer & Shaver, 2007). As with traumatized clients (Johnson, 2002), the therapist may have to slow the pace of therapy and slice risks thinner as well as offer more support and structure to help these partners take risks and order their chaotic inner experience. For all of these reasons, couple therapy with addictive partners may take longer than the usual 12–20 sessions of EFT. It is also worth noting that while there are positive outcome studies (listed on www. iceeft.com) assessing the use of EFT with trauma populations, there are as yet no outcome studies completed specifically with couples facing addiction. This is obviously a project for future research.

CASE 1: "BUT I WIN AT POKER"

As described earlier, Louis and his wife, Anne, exhibited a typical withdraw–demand pattern in their extremely distressed relationship. Louis had just recently engaged in individual therapy for his addiction, although he was still denying the seriousness of his problem in initial couple sessions. However, after 6 weeks alone in his house, he was very clear that he did not want to lose his family. In terms of Prochaska, DiClemente, and Norcross's (1992) stages of change, Louis had gone through precontemplation and contemplation into preparation and was moving into the action phase of addressing his addiction; this is a particularly stressful phase where individuals rely on increased support from helping relationships.

This professional couple was seen by the second author 15 times over a 6-month period. In the interest of brevity, in this first case example, the pivotal events and turning points together with challenges and key interventions will be summarized. At first, Louis admitted that his "obsession with" poker had destroyed his wife's trust in him. They both agreed that they had become caught in a cycle where she would try to accommodate to his poker habit but then explode and accuse him. He would defend himself, "shut down," and then play even more poker. He saw his habit as "an escape" from the stress of his job. Anne called poker his "mistress." By the first session of couple therapy, Louis had been able to limit his poker to 2 hours, one night a week, with his wife's agreement. Anne would repeatedly angrily remind him of events such as, "On our 12th anniversary you played cards for 20 hours straight; I was never in your mind! And you lie to me all the time—to protect your card games!"

Louis would begin by trying to defend himself, "No. It was only 10 hours that time" and then would be able to admit, "You and the kids were together and I was on the outside. I got so I was oblivious. I was lost. I was absent. I guess the word 'addiction' is the right one after all." Anne was now triggered into "panic and rage" if Louis even suggested playing. He had a very hard time articulating any emotion, but his face was a constant picture of sadness, shame, and bewilderment. He and his individual therapist were also working on his "depression" and he commented, "I think, really, I have been depressed forever. The first few years with Anne are the only bright spot in my life."

Anne would then hiss, "You were the one who ended that. You left me for the high of winning." He agreed that the anticipation of winning was the drug that intoxicated him and told her, "I can control my playing." She would accuse, "You can't control anything. You were consumed by that habit. And you deceived me, like I didn't matter. I was robbed." He would reply, "I deceived me too."

A key challenge in Stage 1 was to create an alliance with Louis and help him articulate his experience of the relationship. He was very "logical" and spoke very fast, but was able to allow the therapist to guide him in slowing down, exploring, and pinpointing his experience. He tells Anne:

> I have been alone forever. I am trying so hard. But poker was always there. I went back to counting on it when we lost each other. You were always with the kids and I would get hopeless somehow. At the poker table, I was a winner and everyone told me I was such a genius.

The therapist would have to validate his turning to cards while still noting the damage this had done and Anne's feelings. It was also necessary to "catch the bullet" when Anne would attack him as he attempted to share. Empathic reflection, validation, and process reflection were the main ways here. Both partners were able to grasp their pattern: She would demand, "You are playing poker too much. Do you want to be my husband? Where are you?" He would "hide," reason, defend, and play even more poker. Louis was able to admit that he had gotten to the place where he realized that he "had no idea how to be married and just got sad and overwhelmed." He was able to tell her, "I hated my work. I felt like I had lost you. I was failing, failing, so I just got more and more caught in getting high at the table. It was my lifeline."

The underlying emotional music here was the same as that which we find in nonaddicted couples. The withdrawn partner struggles with a sense of inadequacy and worthlessness and shuts down (but in this case finds a substitute safe haven in his addiction), while the other becomes more "panicked, angry, and abandoned." It was a real struggle for Louis to grasp the impact of his addiction and his "absence" on his wife. The therapist constantly framed his actions in attachment language, helped her to confide the panic and abandonment she had felt for many years, and helped him tune in to and process it. The interlinked nature of addictive behaviors and the necessity for helping couples exit negative cycles is supported by the finding that perceived criticism from a partner can undermine self-efficacy and lead to relapse (Fals-Stewart, O'Farrell, & Hooley, 2001)

Key moments in Stage 2 of EFT were when Louis was able to reengage emotionally with his wife. The therapist had to work very hard here to keep him focused, specific, and concrete. He is able to weep for the aloneness that he has "always" felt and the huge sense that he is alone because of his deficits as a person. He tells her:

> I needed this catastrophe to wake me up. I don't want to lose you and I want to be a dad. But all I know is distance. I am terrified that I cannot win here. I don't know how to be a husband. But I want to learn—for you to risk and let me learn.

It is one of the routine miracles of EFT that his wife allows herself to be moved by his vulnerability and presence and thus reaches for him, even as he admits his "ineptitude." He does not need to "know"; he just needs to be there. This being said, his poker habit was an ongoing toxic irritant in the relationship as he pushed the boundaries of their agreement as to how often he could play. As he became more engaged with Anne, he was able to state limits that fit for him and to hold to them and was also able to tell her, "If I need never to touch another card again to hold onto you, I will do it." His involvement with his job also changed and he was able, with encouragement, to list "highs" in his everyday life with his job and family, as well as "wins" that carried him through his self-doubts and "nudges" toward poker.

Louis integrates his view of his addiction with his emotional life as a whole. He tells Anne:

> I compartmentalized and got lost between the rooms in my head. I hungered for that sense of invincibility cards gave me. I was numb. Hooked. Blind. I felt trapped in my job and as a husband. When you talked about my playing, I would just feel criticized. And now I am ashamed of how I let you down. I know you are watchful, vigilant, now and I accept that. I need to show you that I am safe to rely on. I never knew that I could tell my hurt to someone, that that was even possible.

Helping Anne soften and take small steps toward trust played out as classic EFT with the unpacking of secondary emotions such as rage, thus heightening core emotions such as her grief at years of "not feeling wanted or needed" and her confusion about whether she was entitled to her emotions and needs. (She came from a culture where the man defined the agenda in the home and was not questioned.) She realized that she usually "swallowed" her emotions and then exploded. However, her fear of being "duped again" and "hurt even more" was significant.

Anne (to Louis): It will grab you again and you will glaze over and become someone else. Then I don't matter. I dare not count on you. I keep remembering the night when Adam [her son] hit his head and you did not come. You did not come.

Therapist: This is a deep wound, an injury for you. That moment kind of gathered all the pain and fear of how he was lost to you and you were alone, abandoned, into a ball. You go back to it when part of you thinks about risking—putting yourself in his hands again?

Anne: We didn't matter. I was so, so terrified. My son's breathing was strange. You didn't come. How could you—choose "winning" over us? (She weeps.) It was like we didn't exist.

Therapist: You called to him, desperate, needing him and he was caught in winning and numbing. He didn't hear you. You are telling him: "I am so hurt that you did not come and so terrified to put myself into your hands again"—yes? Tell him.

Anne: That moment, I did not have a husband; our love had never happened. You were a stranger. The cards had won. (She starts to shiver.) I am cold. Fragile. I can never feel that way again. I have to matter more than that. Can you hear me, Louis?

Louis (weeping, turns toward her): I do. I do. I let you down. I wasn't there. I have no right to ask you to begin to trust me again. I got so mesmerized, so lost. I want to warm you, to hold you warm against me. I am so sad and ashamed. Can you forgive me? I want you. I want our family. I did not understand that you were scared all those years. I saw you as so strong and in charge. I will do whatever you need to begin to feel close again. I saw you as trying to control me. I didn't understand. I am ashamed of how I hurt you and our son.

Anne (sits up in her chair and looks out the window): I just want to slug you.

Therapist: What happened just then, Anne? Can you hear him? He is telling you that he feels your hurt now—he hears your call and he is grieving that he so let you down. He wants to earn your trust. Can you hear him?

Anne: It's too scary. (She weeps and turns back to him.) You might crush me again. How could you turn to that game and leave us? You turned into someone else. I was shattered. (He weeps.)

Therapist: Can you help her, Louis? She is hurting—in pieces.

Louis (leans forward and reaches for her): I want to take care of you. To help you feel safe. I do not want to lose you. I want to reach for you for comfort and have you do the same. I will show you I am here now. (She cries and he gets up and holds her.)

This excerpt is part of the process of addressing the attachment injury that Louis's dedication to poker had created in this relationship. Anne cannot soften and become accessible and engaged with Louis until this traumatic injury (Johnson, Makinen, & Millikin, 2001) is addressed. He has to offer an antidote for her pain and fear in the form of explicit responsiveness and caring. At the end of therapy, both partners see the negative patterns they created as the enemy and his addiction as a trap that has almost defeated them.

Louis could recognize the addictive sequence of "isolation, helplessness, tension, craving to play, release, soothing, high, numbing, and then repeat" that trapped him in the past. He noted that this "compulsion" for poker seemed to have gone and that he felt much closer to his wife. Anne described herself as gradually feeling safer and more trusting in spite of having periods of vigilance, anxiety, and sadness. He was able to tell his wife when he experienced her as in "distant administration mode" and turn to her when he felt the "warning signs" of poker craving as well as when he just wanted to be close. This couple saw the poker obsession as something they could deal with together and Anne was able to tell him, "It's still so hard sometimes to ask for your comfort and attention, but I see you turning away from gambling and we are so much closer. I think we can do this, you and I."

CASE TWO: "IT TAKES AWAY THE PAIN"

An only child, Paula is a 25-year-old accounting graduate. She and Peter, a 29-year-old attorney, met at a speed-dating evening at a local hotel and were married after a 5-month courtship. They had been married just over 2 years when Paula's physician referred her for couple therapy after she had shown signs of depression due to her husband's insistence on using pornographic movies as a key part of their sexual life. Peter suggested that she try to be more like the women in the DVDs because she was his wife and should want to please him and that, if she would not do this, then she had broken her marriage contract and did not really love him. She asked that he talk more to her and cuddle her more. He stated that he could only really talk after sex.

As Peter saw the relationship, he gave Paula "everything she wanted, flowers, dogs, everything," so was a good partner. Peter also constantly complained of bad back pain and often requested to be taken to emergency care at the hospital. As therapy unfolded, it became clear that Peter had been addicted to Vicodin, a narcotic analgesic, since he was 15 years old. His physician father had originally prescribed them for him after he had broken his leg, and he quickly became addicted. After many years, the local physician who had been prescribing this drug for him finally cut him off. Presenting himself at urgent care with excruciating back pain, he had found a loophole in the system. Often he would be kept overnight and discharged with a prescription for as many as 90 Vicodin tablets.

Both partners agreed that Peter had become more and more disengaged from their relationship. Paula also disparaged his propensity to cry at the slightest upset. She said his tears had become a manipulative tool and saw him as lacking in judgment, citing his erratic driving as an example. She would throw him out of the house after arguments about his addiction, his driving, and his need for porn.

The first author, who has expertise in addictions, conducted 10 sessions with Peter focusing on his addiction and getting him into an addiction program before returning to couple sessions with both partners. These sessions offered an emotional way station to gauge properly the severity, etiology, and impact of Peter's addiction on the couple. Peter's history was one colored by neglect and attachment deprivation. His mother had suffered a stroke at his birth and become blind. Peter was given to his maternal grandparents for 2 years. When his grandmother died, he then went to live with his mother, who had returned home from rehabilitation.

He described his father as "busy all the time" and his mother as "remote and scary." He could never remember her holding him and she openly blamed her blindness on his birth. He could not remember his mother ever touching him, although he did admit that she might have tried when he was older, but that he had "recoiled." His father, a busy surgeon, would only relate to him if he mentioned that he had some sort of medical problem. Peter would invent aches and pains to get his father's attention; as a child, he was given sleeping pills almost every night. His father's offer of chemical soothing seemed to be his only experience of caring and he would "invent" physical hurts to get this soothing. He referred to his parents as "strangers" and was essentially raised by housekeepers.

Peter now described himself as an addict who was also an insomniac, distrustful and angry. He had tried to get his father to ask his colleagues to prescribe Vicodin in many manipulative ways and saw this as a test of his father's love because it "took away the pain." He called his relationship with his dad, "the prescription dance." Peter stated that for many years it was the anticipation of the high that gave him the most pleasure and that the actual taking of the drug became less of a euphoric experience. He stated that he distanced from his father and his wife to punish them (as his mother had punished him) and so that they would suffer rather than him. Peter had been to rehab in his late teens and had been so engulfed by anxiety that he had only "survived" by turning to porn sites and finding a way to soothe himself there—although, again, as suggested by the "positive incentive model" of addiction, it was now the anticipation of relief that was most potent for him and controlled his anxiety. He now repeatedly expressed the desire that his wife should lose weight to prove her love and look more like the women he saw in pornographic materials.

In their relationship, Peter realized that his anticipatory arousal and obsession with painkillers and porn was experienced as withdrawal by Paula, who would then attack or finally withdraw herself. The couple seemed to be stuck in a blame and withdraw cycle that later evolved into a mutual withdrawal. As when working with trauma couples (Johnson, 2002), the negative cycle in couples facing addiction tends to have more steps—that is, to be more complex and more extreme. As Peter was more and more able to control his addiction, this couple was able to see their negative cycle and the role of Peter's habits of emotional regulation in this cycle. Paula was also able to acknowledge that her rage and threats to leave were part of this cycle. As he struggled with relapse, Paula's threats and refusal to be near him when he had "relapsed" merely drove him into his faux attachments, into the soothing smoke and mirrors of Vicodin and pornography.

The challenge with Peter was to facilitate reengagement that then would allow his wife to soften toward him. Peter was able to talk about his urge to punish his wife for not loving him by shutting her out. Periods of anticipatory soothing, offered by images of Vicodin or pornography, had allowed him to distance from Paula without becoming massively anxious. In Stage 1 of EFT, Peter was able to weep at his wife's "rejection" of him and to acknowledge that his experience of her was colored by his inability to trust and his hurt and rage at his parents. His crying, however, did not "touch her heart" because she was unsure of his sincerity. The therapist was able to help him tolerate her ambivalence. Key snapshots of Peter's reengagement in Sessions 15 and 16 of EFT are seen in his following words:

> I know I kind of flip between pleading and demanding, crying and asking for a certain kind of sex to prove you love me and then turning away and shutting you out. I get that this drives you crazy. And I have deceived you—the pills were easier to rely on. Then I would feel kind of powerful when I turned away

and you couldn't hurt me anymore. I don't know how to do this connection thing. I never had it.

I am so, so scared of you leaving me. Of your anger. I get anxious when we make love that I won't be sexy enough, aroused enough, so I push for the porno. When you do cuddle me, I hold my breath just waiting for it to stop. Then when you threaten to leave, I just go into meltdown. And my brain tells me, "Only the drug is really there when you need. It takes away the pain and the fear." I have been scared and alone my whole life. [Paula is able to respond with compassion here.]

I can't believe that you want to be with me. I am such a desperate screwup. It's hopeless. Even my mother didn't want me. All I have learned to do is try to get my dose of comfort from you, from my dad. I see now how I have hurt you. I am so afraid that I am just defective. How can I ask you to love me? I can't even look in your face here. I will see disgust—contempt—so I crawl off into my hole. I can't ask you to love me.

I don't want to spend my life running like this—looking for a high to pick me out of the mud that is sucking me under. I want to learn to love you. It's so hard for me to trust—I want to come into your arms—I need your comfort. I want you to forgive me. I want to turn to you when my demons and fears and sadness come for me.

Paula was able then to move into her own softening and the couple came together against the addiction—their mutual enemy. This process involved the healing of several attachment injuries involving Paula's sense of abandonment resulting from Peter's deception and his "choosing" of porn over his wife.

The further this couple got from addictive objects, the closer they got to each other, opening the door to a more secure and respectful relationship. Although both remain vigilant and return for tune-up therapy, that certainly has been the case for Peter and Paula.

Walant (1995) suggests that our society has contributed to the rise of addictions by creating cultural norms that pathologize dependency and make expressing needs shameful. She emphasizes the need for therapy to provide "immersion" moments of deep understanding between therapist and client as a means of countering the alienation from self and others that typifies addictive individuals. The EFT therapist might concur, but add that in successful couple therapy, partners change each other and the moments of deep connection between partners seem to us to offer the best healing arena for and natural antidote to the compulsive behaviors of addiction.

9

REFERENCES

Acevedo, B. P., & Aron, A. (2009). Does a long-term relationship kill romantic love? *Review of General Psychology, 13,* 59–65.

Bartels, A., & Zeki, S. (2000). The neural basis for romantic love. *NeuroReport, 11,* 3829–3834.

Bowlby, J. (1969). *Attachment and loss: Vol. 1. Attachment.* New York, NY: Basic Books.

Brennan, K. A., Shaver, P. R., & Tobey, A. E. (1991). Attachment styles, gender and parental problem drinking. *Journal of Social and Personal Relationships, 8,* 451–466.

Brennan, K. A., & Shaver, P. (1995). Dimensions of adult attachment, affect regulation, and romantic functioning. *Personality and Social Psychology Bulletin, 21,* 267–284.

Cardinal, R. N., & Everitt, B. J. (2004). Neural and psychological mechanisms underlying appetitive learning: Links to drug addiction. *Current Opinion in Neurobiology, 14,* 156–162.

Carter, S. (1998). Neuroendocrine perspectives on social attachment and love. *Psychoneuroendocrinology, 23,* 779–818.

Coan, J., Schaefer, H., & Davidson R. (2006). Lending a hand. *Psychological Science, 17,* 1–8.

Cooper, M., Agocha, V., & Sheldon, M. S. (2000). A motivational perspective on risky behaviors: The role of personality and affect regulatory processes. *Journal of Personality, 68,* 1058–1088.

Cooper, M. L., Flanagan, M. E., Talley, A. E., & Micheas, L. (2006). Individual differences in emotion regulation and their relation to risk taking in adolescence. In D. Snyder, J. Simpson, & J. Hughes (Eds.), *Emotion regulation in couples and families: Pathways to dysfunction and health.* Washington, DC: APA Press.

Cooper, M. L., Shaver, P. R., & Collins, N. L. (1998). Attachment styles, emotion regulation and adjustment in adolescence. *Journal of Personality and Social Psychology, 74,* 1380–1397.

Doumas, D., Blasey, C. M., & Mitchell, S. (2006). Adult attachment, emotional distress and interpersonal problems in alcohol and drug dependency treatment. *Alcoholism Treatment Quarterly, 24,* 41–54.

Everitt, B. J., Dickenson, A., & Robbins, T. (2001). The neuropsychological basis of addictive behavior. *Brain Research Reviews, 36,* 129–138.

Fals-Stewart, W., Birchler, G. R., & O'Farrell, T. J. (1999). Drug abusing patients and their partners: Dyadic adjustment, relationship stability and substance use. *Journal of Abnormal Psychology, 108,* 11–23.

Fals-Stewart, W., Birchler, G. R., & O'Farrell, T. (2003). Alcohol and other substance abuse. In D. K. Snyder & M. A. Whisman (Eds.), *Treating difficult couples* (pp. 159–180). New York, NY: Guilford Press.

Fals-Stewart, W., O'Farrell, T. J., & Birchler, G. R. (2001). Behavioral couples therapy for male methadone maintenance patients: Effects on drug using behavior and relationship adjustment. *Behavior Therapy, 32,* 391–411.

Fals-Stewart, W., O'Farrell, T. J., & Hooley, J. M. (2001). Relapse among married or cohabitating substance abusing patients. The role of perceived criticism. *Behavior Therapy, 32,* 787–801.

Fisher, H. (2004). *Why we love. The nature and chemistry of romantic love.* New York, NY: Henry Holt.

Flores, P. J. (2001). Addiction as an attachment disorder. *International Journal of Group Psychotherapy, 5,* 63–81.

Flores, P. J. (2004). *Addiction as an attachment disorder.* New York, NY: Jason Aronson.

Gillath, O., & Schachner, D. A. (2006). How do sexuality and attachment interact? Goals motives and strategies. In M. Mikulincer & G. S. Goodman (Eds.), *Dynamics of love: Attachment, caregiving and sex* (pp. 337–355). New York, NY: Guilford Press.

Insel, T. R. (2003). Is social attachment an addictive disorder? *Physiology & Behavior, 79,* 351–357.

Johnson, S. M. (2002). *Emotionally focused couple therapy with trauma survivors: Strengthening attachment bonds.* New York, NY: Guilford Press.

Johnson, S. M. (2004). *The practice of emotionally focused couple therapy: Creating connections.* New York, NY: Brunner/Routledge.

Johnson, S. M., Makinen, J. A., & Millikin, J. W. (2001). Attachment injuries in couple relationships: A new perspective in impasses in couples therapy. *Journal of Marital and Family Therapy, 27,* 145–155.

Kassel, J. D., Wardle, M., & Roberts, J. E. (2007). Adult attachment security and college student substance abuse. *Addictive Behaviors, 32,* 1164–1176.

Kelley, M., Nair, V., Rawlings, T., Cash, T., Steer, K., & Fals-Stewart, W. (2005). Retrospective reports of parenting received in their families of origin: Relationships to adult attachment in adult children of alcoholics. *Addictive Behaviors, 30,* 1479–1495.

Leshner, A. I. (2001). Addiction—A brain disease with biological underpinnings. *Voice, 6,* 1–3.

Lewis, T., Amini, F., & Lannon, R. (2000). *A general theory of love.* New York, NY: Random House.

Marlatt, G. A. (1998). *Harm reduction: Pragmatic strategies for managing high-risk behaviors.* New York, NY: Jason Aronson.

McNally, A. M., Palfai, T. P., Levine, R. B., & Moore, B. M. (2003). Attachment dimensions and drinking related problems among young adults: The mediational role of coping motives. *Addictive Behaviors, 28,* 1115–1127.

Mikulincer, M. (1998). Attachment working models and the sense of trust. An exploration of interactional goals and affect regulation. *Journal of Personality and Social Psychology, 74,* 1209–1224.

Mikulincer, M., & Shaver, P. R. (2007). *Attachment in adulthood: Structure, dynamics and change.* New York, NY: Guilford Press.

Miller, W., & Wilbourne, P. (2002). Mesa Grande: A methodological analysis of clinical trials of treatments for alcohol use disorders. *Addiction, 97,* 265–277.

Molnar, D. S., Sadava, S. W., DeCourville, N. H., & Perrier, C. P. (2010). Attachment, motivations and alcohol: Testing a dual path model of high-risk drinking and adverse consequences in transitional clinical and student samples. *Canadian Journal of Behavioral Science, 42,* 1–13.

Pinel, J. P. J. (2006). *Biopsychology.* Boston, MA: Pearson Educational.

Prochaska, J. O., DiClemente, C. C., & Norcross, J. C. (1992). In search of how people change: Applications to addictive behaviors. *American Psychologist, 47,* 1102–1114.

Robinson, T. E., & Berridge, K. C. (1993). The neural basis of drug craving: An incentive-sensitization theory of addiction. *Brain Research Reviews, 18,* 247–291.

Rogers, C. (1951). *Client centered therapy.* Boston, MA: Houghton Mifflin.

Shaver, P. R., & Clark, C. L. (1994). The psychodynamics of adult attachment, In J. Masling & R. F. Bornstein (Eds.), *Empirical perspectives on object relations theories* (pp. 105–156). Washington, DC: APA Press.

Simpson, L. E., Atkins, D. C., Gattis, K. S., & Christensen, A. (2008). Low-level relationship aggression and couple therapy outcomes. *Journal of Family Psychology, 22,* 102–111.

Stephan, C. W., & Bachman, G. F. (1999). What's sex got to do with it? Attachment. Love schemas and sexuality. *Personal Relationships, 6,* 111–123.

Thorberg, F. A., & Lyvers, M. (2006). Attachment, fear of intimacy and differentiation of self among clients in substance disorder treatment facilities. *Addictive Behaviors, 31,* 732–737.

Walant, K. B. (1995). *Creating the capacity for attachment: Treating addictions and the alienated self.* Northvale, NJ: Jason Aronson.

Nine

EFT for Sexual Issues
An Integrated Model of Couple and Sex Therapy

SUSAN M. JOHNSON AND DINO ZUCCARINI

INTRODUCTION

Masters and Johnson (1970), founders of modern-day sex therapy, understood the significance of treating sexual problems within a couple's relationship. The resolution of sexual issues, regardless of cause, required the participation of a supportive, cooperative partner in the treatment process. In an era where mechanistic, genital-focused behavioral and medical interventions were heralded as a panacea for sexual problems, this integrated approach to couple and sex therapy fell by the wayside. Recently, however, scholars in the field of sex therapy have again begun to call for a return to a more integrated approach to couple and sex therapy (Leiblum, 2007). In this chapter, we return to an integrative framework, describing an attachment-based approach to couples' sexual functioning that locates sexual problems and their remedies within the context of the couple relationship.

Attachment theory offers a compelling and relevant framework within which EFT couple therapy and sex therapy can be combined to map out a couple's intricate overlapping emotional, physical, and sexual responses. This combined model guides a therapist in accessing a couple's positive relational resources and offers an alternative to the individually oriented and problem-focused interventions that pervade the sex therapy field (Heiman, 2007). Using an attachment perspective, EFT focuses the therapist on each partner's habitual patterns of emotional engagement and how these patterns impact each partner's expression of emotional and sexual needs in a relationship (Johnson & Zuccarini, 2010). An EFT therapist works to engage couples in more emotionally secure bonds that promise greater sexual adjustment and satisfaction.

In this chapter, we explore a number of sexual issues faced by couples seeking EFT treatment. The most common sexual problems reported in North America include low sexual desire in women (Basson, 2007) and premature ejaculation or lax erections in men (McCarthy & McCarthy, 2003; Metz & McCarthy, 2004). From our perspective, when couple relationships are besieged by complaints related to sexual arousal, orgasm, or desire issues, these issues inevitably emerge in the context of a couple's growing sense of disconnection. Distressing emotions and cascading attachment distress are manifested in the couple's ongoing negative interactions outside and inside the bedroom. Partners' underlying emotions and self-protective attachment strategies complicate the couple's sexual relationship and sexual interactions must be understood within the context of a couple's general cycles of emotional connection and disconnection.

Assessment of these patterns may be challenging when partners take specific or unique positions in response to sexual issues. For example, a male partner who generally withdraws may pursue for sex, yet maintain a distant and avoidant emotional stance toward his partner in bed.

ATTACHMENT AND SEXUALITY IN ADULT ROMANTIC LOVE BONDS

Bowlby (1969) considered three behavioral systems of primary significance in the formation of adult romantic love bonds: the attachment, caregiving, and sexual systems. Each system was viewed as distinct from yet integrated with the attachment system playing an important role in shaping these other systems, given attachment's primary influence in early development. Sexuality typically plays a significant role in facilitating the development of attachment bonds between partners, but wanes in its influence in the later stages of a couple's relationship (Hazan & Zeifman, 1994). All through life, sexuality and caregiving are experienced and expressed differently by those in relationships characterized by secure versus insecure attachment (Diamond & Blatt, 2007; Mikulincer

& Shaver, 2007). In a reciprocal manner, a couple's experience of safety and felt security shapes each partner's sexual responsiveness and experience. A couple's sexual relationship may be a vexing source of distress and insecurity or a profound resource for fostering greater attachment security.

A couple's sexual dance is altered by partners' self-protection strategies, such as anxious pursuit or reactive numbing, which are employed to manage attachment distress. Attachment insecurity exacerbates the struggle to manage frustrations and differences in each partner's desire and arousal. Couples face the inevitable differences in desire, arousal patterns, and orgasm capacities throughout their history together. How these changes and possible frustrations are addressed will be influenced by a couple's level of attachment security. Sexual functioning and satisfaction will impact and be impacted by each partner's level of security and associated attachment strategies.

Sexuality is an affect-regulated interaction (Heiman, 2007). Ways of regulating and expressing emotion play a key part in how partners deal with sexuality within the relationship. How a couple manages emotional and attachment distress shapes sexual experience and may fix in place the negative and rigid sexual interactions that underlie a couple's sexual problems. Self-protective affect regulation strategies result in constricted sexual experiences and rigid, negative interaction cycles in the sexual relationship that often diminish a partner's capacity for arousal, orgasm, and desire. Optimal sexuality, on the other hand, involves communication of and responsiveness to emotional cues and sexual arousal and longings within self and in the other.

SECURE ATTACHMENT AND OPTIMAL COUPLE SEXUALITY

Secure attachment offers a *secure base* from which individuals can explore their world and adaptively and flexibly respond to internal and external cues. It allows partners to attune to each other, sensing each other's inner state and intention and responding to each other's shifting patterns of arousal in the same way that an empathic mother is attuned to her baby (Stern, 2004). Nonverbal cues, sighs, gaze, and touch carry exquisitely coordinated signals that, when responded to, form a sense of deep rapport and create a "synchrony" where emotional, physical, and sexual connection merge together. In a secure relationship marked by emotional accessibility and responsiveness, the three aspects of romantic love—attachment, caregiving, and sexuality—can be integrated. Emotional responsiveness, tender touch, and erotic playfulness then become a seamless whole. In such a spiraling feedback loop, each element then enhances the other; thus, passion enhances emotional bonding and bonding enhances caring touch and passion.

In these moments, emotional safety shapes physical synchrony and physical synchrony embodies emotional safety (Johnson, 2008, 2009). Touch—one of the most basic elements of sexuality—integrates the language of sexuality and attachment. Touch prompts arousal, offers soothing, and expresses comfort. The thrill offered through attachment security is the openness to moment-to-moment connection and the exploration that is possible with an engaged partner who is able to surrender to sensation without reserve or caution.

Couples with this level of felt security can adapt to shifts in sexual focus and each partner's sexual pleasure goals. Fears of abandonment or rejection do not arise to block the sharing of sexual needs and longings with one another. Secure partners can then flexibly tolerate variations in a partner's responses, including sexual desire and the emotional and physical aspects of sexuality. As a result of this attunement, securely attached partners can achieve a sense of connection and closeness in the sexual realm. For secure partners, this closeness is a primary reason for engaging in sex (Davis, Shaver, & Vernon, 2004; Schachner & Shaver, 2004).

INSECURE ATTACHMENT AND SEXUAL DYSFUNCTION

For many distressed couples, the avoidant deactivation or the anxious hyperactivation of their attachment system directly impacts their sexual functioning. Insecurely attached partners are generally less able to process unresolved emotional experiences, particularly in their sexual relationship. Couples experiencing more insecure attachment are likely to report more communication difficulties and to express fewer positive and more negative feelings regarding sex (Birnbaum, Reis, Mikulincer, Gillath, & Orpaz, 2006; Davis et al., 2006).

Sexual encounters become less fulfilling in the context of emotional insecurity. These negative emotional experiences are likely to distort a couple's perception, attentional focus, and meaning making during sexual contact. Insecure partners are more likely to experience reduced levels of physical attractiveness and sexual self-esteem and have a greater tendency to see sex as controlled by the other partner or by situational factors (Bogaert & Sadava, 2002; Feeney, Peterson, Gallois, & Terry, 2000; Shafer, 2001). In many insecure relationships, partners can become obsessed with sexual performance and extremely anxious in sexual contexts. Consequently, these couples express less willingness to experiment sexually (Birnbaum et al., 2006; Hazan, Zeifman & Middleton, 1994).

At more extreme levels of attachment insecurity, some male partners may revert to physical force and coercive strategies in sexual relations (Smallbone & Dadds, 2000). A partner's demanding sexual behavior can be a form of "protest" behavior triggered by unacknowledged attachment fears of rejection and abandonment. Overall, more insecure couples find it difficult to articulate their needs for love or sexual attention, and each partner's sexual responses can be understood either in terms of a hyperactivation or deactivation of the sexual system in the service of maintaining some form of attachment security or comfort.

Hyperactivation of the Sexual System

Hyperactivation involves overprocessing of cues about the partner's accessibility during sexual contact or seeking out sexual contact to regulate attachment-related distress. A partner's inaccessibility and unavailability heighten emotional distress and trigger proximity-seeking behaviors that may be expressed sexually. More anxiously attached partners are more likely to pursue sex in order to gain a partner's reassurance and avoid rejection (Davis et al., 2004; Schachner & Shaver, 2004). When sex is sought primarily to garner contact-comfort or reassurance, perceived inaccessibility by the other partner will likely trigger a predictable sequence of emotions based on separation distress, including angry protest, clinging, depression, and despair.

Separation distress then often manifests as a progression from chronic sexual demands based on attachment fears and needs to heightened angry, critical demands for sexual contact, followed by eventual despair and withdrawal from initiation and couple sexuality. When a couple's sexual contact is overfocused on the attachment needs of an anxiously attached partner, the other partner often feels pressured to sate the other's attachment fears in the sexual realm, which leads to more sexual constriction, rigid sexual enactments, and an over-focus on the anxiously attached partner's needs.

Hyperactivation may result in a preoccupation with the attachment-specific aspects of sexual contact. For these partners, seeking affection is often a primary focus, rather than the sexual activity itself (Gillath & Schachner, 2006; Hazan et al., 1994). Sexual dissatisfaction and complaints are organized around a lack of romance or emotional connection (Davis et al., 2006). A hypervigilant attention may be given to sexual behaviors and responses, including the anxious monitoring of a partner's sexual initiations, arousal response, and orgasm.

It is our clinical experience that anxiously attached partners often experience the lack of the other's sexual desire, arousal, orgasm, or satisfaction as a sign of imminent abandonment. These partners rely heavily on sex to meet their attachment needs. Yet, the pervasive nature of a couple's insecurity heightens emotional distress, leaving couples more vulnerable to sexual experiences that reinforce a more negative view of self and seeding fears about one's desirability as a partner.

Anxious patterns of sexual intimacy often differ in their impact on the relationship depending on gender (Birnbaum et al., 2006). For anxious men, just having sex seems to improve their view of their relationship; for women, the quality or positive experience of the sexual encounter is what matters. These findings seem to reflect the perennial dialogue between male and female distressed partners: Women want to feel close and then make love to express these feelings of closeness, whereas men want to make love, stating that the sex act itself will create feelings of connection and closeness.

Deactivation of the Sexual System

Deactivation or down-regulation of sexuality involves minimizing internal emotional and sexual cues and associated needs. Sex often becomes one dimensional and task oriented rather than more open and relationship oriented. This strategy diminishes the likelihood of painful rejection by one's partner. There is a constricted focus on one's own pleasurable sensations and on the performance aspects of sexuality or on the task of having sex to minimize conflict or maintain a relational status quo. A partner may also engage in "spectatoring," which includes monitoring sexual performances and behaviors without any emotional engagement.

For partners using more avoidant attachment strategies, the sexual experience of vulnerability (e.g., surrendering to arousing emotional and pleasurable sensations and feelings of closeness) can activate overwhelming fears of rejection and losing one's self. Suppression of internal bodily cues and sensations is adopted to avoid vulnerability and emotional closeness in sexual encounters. Negative affective experience and attachment distress related to sexual experiences are managed by attributing sexual difficulties to the other's neediness, demands, and unrealistic sexual expectations. When sexuality becomes a burden, emotionally avoidant men and women reported having sex less often and report trying to avoid sex with their partner (Brassard, Shaver, & Lussier, 2007).

Patterns of avoidance are often common in the sexual history of partners who respond to attachment distress using numbing or deactivating strategies. More avoidant adults are likely to endorse self-enhancement motives in sex in which they report having sex to fit into a group or so as to be able to brag about it (Davis et al., 2004; Schachner & Shaver, 2004). Those adopting more avoidant attachment strategies tend to report less frequency of intercourse and more solitary masturbation (Bogaert & Sadava, 2002). They also endorse more positive attitudes toward casual emotionless sex and tend to detach sex from love and commitment, instead favoring short-term mating strategies, including "one night stands" (Gillath & Schachner, 2006; Stephan & Bachman, 1999). More avoidant partners focus mostly on the physical aspects of sex and dislike the attachment aspects of sexuality, including affectional behaviors such as kissing and cuddling (Davis et al., 2006; Gillath & Schachner, 2006; Hazan et al., 1994).

In brief, anxious hyperactivation and avoidant deactivation of the attachment system predispose partners to construe and enact their sexuality rigidly in a manner that creates and maintains negative interaction patterns and interferes with positive, satisfying sex.

Attachment and Sexual Dysfunction

Emotional and sexual arousal share similar neurophysiological systems and structures. Lingering negative absorbing emotions and the resulting insecure attachment strategies employed to manage these emotions can alter perceptions of sexually arousing sensations, dampen sexual interest, and diminish sexual attunement to self and other. Without a secure base, insecurely attached individuals will not feel sufficiently safe to explore their sensations, desires, and erotic cues, which will affect all aspects of sexual functioning. From our perspective, unlike other authors who suggest that sex is only a window into the self (Schnarch, 1997), sexuality is a window into the attachment bond between partners.

The implication here is that safe attachment, characterized by attunement and responsiveness to emotional and physiological cues, is the primary foundation for satisfying sex. When partners are emotionally accessible, responsive, and engaged, sex can then become intimate play—a safe adventure (Johnson, 2008). Partners who are free from fears of abandonment and rejection are more able to be fully sexually and emotionally engaged and more responsive to their own and their partner's sexual needs.

SEXUAL DISORDERS AND ADULT ATTACHMENT

Problems of Sexual Desire

Sexual desire seems contingent upon numerous physiological, sociocultural, intrapsychic, and interpersonal factors, as well as whether sexual contact itself is emotionally rewarding and pleasurable. Due to the highly contextual nature of female desire (Basson, 2000), relationship context profoundly impacts women's levels of sexuality in this area. However, relationship context also influences male sexual desire (Johnson & Zuccarini, 2010). Partner emotional accessibility and responsiveness and physical intimacy outside the bedroom are arguably the greatest aphrodisiac in long-term couple bonds.

An attachment perspective on sexual desire sheds light on the significance of partner engagement as a mediator of sexual desire. As stated before, an anxiously attached sexual partner may initiate sexual contact to assuage attachment fears about partner accessibility. He or she may eventually become unaware of what is pleasurable in partnered sex outside this vigilant attention to the other partner's response. From this perspective, sexual desire is driven by heightened emotional and attachment distress and reinforced by the other's attention and sexual responses during sexual contact. Pleasure may not be able to be experienced for pleasure's sake. Sexual seeking is then infused with fears of isolation and rejection. The more anxiously attached partner's hypersensitivity to his or her partner's responses leads the couple into a sexual world that is increasingly constricted by desperate fears. Without emotional safety, the exploration of positive emotional experiences and pleasurable cues during sexual contact is limited and desire is lost.

The anxious partner's heightened sensitivity to any perceived inaccessibility on the part of the partner may quickly turn to anger and criticism. Frustration and hypervigilance to negative cues color the anxious partner's experience of any differences in expectations around sex, desire, and affection. For others, obsessive sexuality may be fueled by anxiety related to the other's perceived distance in the relationship. An anxious pursuer's excessive vigilance regarding the partner's sexual initiations and responsiveness infuses sexual interactions with tension and sets up conflict. Over time, an anxiously attached partner will often move beyond angry protest to hopelessness and eventual sexual withdrawal. Self-protection strategies divert attention away from emotional and sexual cues and prohibit sexual synchronicity, limiting the exploration of eroticism.

For an avoidantly attached partner, sexual interest is less focused on the relationship and more focused on sexual sensation and behavior. The pursuit of sex solely for physical pleasure or as a ritual performance maintains emotional distance. With this self-oriented view of sexuality, the aphrodisiac of an emotional connection cannot be experienced through partnered sex, and the deeper attachment-related meanings of sexuality are essentially lost. The other partner often then feels alone during sex and finds it difficult to remain fully engaged. Avoidance in the sexual realm involves the exclusion of important emotional and sexual cues that impact a couple's capacity for desire, arousal, or orgasm and significantly limit the physical and psychological satisfaction of sexual encounters. It is not hard to see how patterns of insecure attachment often lead to enduring levels of disappointment and distance in a couple's sexual relationship.

Avoidantly attached partners often speak of feeling inadequate and experiencing a sense of failure as lovers. They describe the sexual domain as pressure filled, overwhelming, or of little interest. Their sexual relationship often becomes a place of increasing detachment and boredom. Partners engage in dutiful sexual performances devoid of emotional engagement for months or years as a means to diminish conflict and maintain the status quo. For some, this ultimately results in a full withdrawal from partnered sex and a turning toward solitary activities such as masturbation and pornography.

In some couples, rigid, dispassionate sexual routines emerge that, at least at first, dampen each partner's immediate anxieties but also compound emotional insecurity and sexual dissatisfaction over time. For example, Mary was anxious about Tim's sexual responsiveness and this resulted in desperate sexual efforts on her part to garner particular sexual responses from him. She was vigilant about the rigidity of Tim's penis and the amount of time it took him to reach orgasm. Tim, the more emotionally withdrawn partner, initially enjoyed the pleasurable aspects of the sexual experience but eventually felt overwhelmed by her demands and just "went through the motions." Tim's lack of engagement continually fueled Mary's anxiety and vigilance. This rigid, negative cycle shut down mutual desire.

In general, sexual desire tends to become constricted in the face of attachment-related distress. Fear and tension dissolve spontaneity and sexual openness and pressure-filled routines foster sexual boredom and diminish emotional and sexual authenticity. In this context, partners cannot attend to other aspects of the sexual experience, including tender touch, positive emotional experiences of joy and excitement, and erotic wishes. Disconnection in the sexual relationship begins to mirror and exacerbate a growing sense of emotional disengagement in the relationship in general. Without safe emotional engagement, partners are unable to risk asking for the sex that they want or sharing erotic wishes that would promote greater passion during sex.

Problems of Arousal

High levels of anxiety dampen sexual arousal and divert attention to other stimuli (i.e., cognitions about performance). Pleasurable sensations and feelings of connectedness then fall out of awareness. Other approaches, such as cognitive-behavioral sex therapy, work primarily by restructuring anxious cognitions and offering strategies to reallocate attention to the pleasurable aspects of sex. This focus on top-down strategies may work for couples who have a supportive relationship, but it may also inadvertently reinforce a performance view of sexuality and promote more emotional and sexual disconnection.

From our perspective, what is missing here is an understanding of the interpersonal fears that permeate the sexual domain when emotional inaccessibility and nonresponsiveness are pervasive within the relationship. From an EFT perspective, both anxious and avoidantly attached individuals are more likely to have difficulties accessing and organizing sexual and emotional cues during sexual contact. Sexually arousing feelings and pleasurable sexual sensations are lost in a sea of fear and anger. Eroticism involves a deep sharing of internal emotional and sexual cues and wants in a manner that is both emotionally and physically arousing.

In terms of couple sexuality in long-term bonds, sexual arousal and recurring fear or anger seem to be uncomfortable bedfellows. The sexual system seems to be inextricably linked with the fear system in that sexual arousal is extinguished when the fight, flight, and freeze response predominates. The shutting down of sexual arousal in the face of fear may have adaptive value, given the need to reprioritize sexual goals when an internal and external threat exists (Bancroft, 1999). High levels of attachment threat, therefore, essentially shut down the sexual system. Fear redirects blood flow inward toward vital organs; desensitizes sensations, including heightening numbness and detachment from sexual and physical intimacy cues; and increases bodily tension.

Arousal requires relaxation to take in stimulation; otherwise, stimulation levels will have to be higher in order to facilitate sensory awareness to sexual cues. Psychological and physiological stimulation are required to maintain sexual arousal. More specifically, a partner's accessibility and responsiveness to internal emotional and physical pleasure cues during sex is essential to ongoing arousal. Taking the risk to express and to surrender to each other's sexual desires enhances arousal and a sense of connectedness during sexual contact.

The loving presence of a partner can often be the best antidote to lack of arousal, especially when this arousal is blocked by fear and traumatic experience. Claire "used to feel sexy, at least until we were actually having sex," when she first met Jeff, her partner, but now finds herself unable to put aside her suddenly intrusive memories of being raped as an adolescent. As she feels more vulnerable with Jeff, these memories have become more compelling and she is aware of "shutting off" at key moments and physically "turning away" from sexual contact.

When Claire is able to pinpoint and explore her trauma and fear with Jeff, she can then ask for the reassuring responses she needs from him in sexual contexts to stay in the present rather than numb out. Rather than feeling rejected and frustrated, Jeff understands that his partner needs his help, the help that perhaps only he can give, to deal with her fears and hurts. They agree that he will whisper Clare's name during foreplay to "keep her with me" and will stop and comfort her if her fear intrudes. Clare is gradually able to regain her desire, hold onto her arousal, and discover a safe and satisfying form of sexuality with her partner.

Part of an integrated approach to couple and sexual therapy includes dealing with situations where one partner's extreme sexual behaviors are actively interfering with another's ability to feel arousal or emotional connection. After he lost his job, Peter decided that only intercourse is proof of his wife's love and his desirability. He has become obsessed with sex and extremely demanding. His wife, Jane, is now scared and angry and has "lost all desire" for sex. Peter becomes enraged that his wife is not "passionate enough" and demands intercourse twice daily. He sees himself as "starved" and as "highly sexed." In therapy, he is guided not only to understand how these demands make it difficult for his wife to feel sexual and respond to him, but also to access his deep fear that he is about to be abandoned if he cannot attain his career goals. When he is able to find other ways to feel soothed and secure, rather than channeling all his attachment needs through sexuality, he can respond in a more balanced and flexible way in the sexual realm. His wife then becomes more "passionate" and aroused.

Problems of Orgasm

Orgasm requires both tension and psychological and physiological stimulation to achieve sufficient excitement, as well as the ability to relax, let go, and surrender to bodily sensations. By its very nature, therefore, an orgasm involves being able to tolerate a certain vulnerability in the presence of one's partner. Partners are defenseless once an orgasm takes hold of the body. Attachment insecurity has been associated with a lower rate of orgasms among women and lower rates of sexual satisfaction reported by both men and women (Birnbaum, 2007). Lower levels of anxiety seem to be associated with the ability to achieve orgasm and orgasm itself also appears to lower anxiety. Neuroimaging studies also show that orgasm, at least in women, involves deactivation of the hippocampal regions of the brain that are associated with anxiety (Bartels & Zeki, 2004). Further, couples who have attachment security are better able to direct attention both toward and away from sensory stimuli that can increase control over orgasm.

Orgasm and loving touch are also triggers for the "cuddle" hormone oxytocin (Carter, 1998), which is associated with bonding behaviors. This neurotransmitter induces pleasure, calm, and contentment and actively reduces the release of stress hormones such as cortisol. Orgasm is therefore extremely rewarding, particularly in the face of any heightened attachment anxiety.

Premature ejaculation is a more complex event that often combines high levels of arousal and heightened fears as to the security of the bond with the partner. Repeated experiences of premature ejaculation also reinforce a male partner's inability to regulate anxiety and arousal. Individually oriented techniques are used, such as the stop–start technique, where, after increasing awareness of the point of ejaculatory inevitability, the male partner is taught to stop penile stimulation and wait 15–60 seconds until the urge to ejaculate passes. This is learned first with manual stimulation and then during intercourse.

Metz and McCarthy (2003) make the point that this is a powerful technique, but that when relationship distress is a cause or a reaction to premature ejaculation, these men also need to focus on rebuilding intimacy. Resolving this problem needs the couple to work together as a team. This may include setting up a regular rhythm of sexual contact, which is the key to addressing this problem successfully, as well as being willing to try new sexual positions. These interventions are most effective when they are initiated and used with the help and support of a loving partner who is not overly reactive to this problem and is willing to explore different pathways to slower and more controlled lovemaking.

Avoidantly attached partners can find surrendering to sensations and moments of letting go especially challenging. Their efforts to control emotional and pleasure cues rely on a deactivating strategy that can inhibit their orgasmic release. Arousal can be lost and orgasm delayed. When surrendering to emotional and sexual sensations is difficult, sexual performances can also become void of any real sexual interest and orgasm becomes unattainable.

ASSESSMENT AND TREATMENT OF A COUPLE'S SEXUAL ISSUES USING EFT

The integration of sexuality and attachment has to start with the attachment system and the creation of safe emotional connection. A focus on emotional connection and disconnection is always the first level of intervention. This applies when a couple's sex life is an oasis of pleasure in an otherwise distress-ing relationship, a side issue that partners hope will improve as they feel happier together, a key part of their relationship distress, or a huge relationship issue exacerbated by a long-standing functional sexual problem.

The goals of EFT are to expand constricted emotional responses that prime negative interaction patterns, restruc-ture interactions so that partners become more accessible and responsive to each other, and foster positive cycles of com-fort and caring and sexuality. Within this renewed context of emotional safety, partners are better able to reintegrate physi-cal and sexual intimacy from a secure base of relational secu-rity and trust.

Stage 1 of EFT: Placing Sexual Interactions in the Context of the Cycle

In Stage 1, the EFT therapist must complete two important assessment tasks. First, the therapist identifies the couple's negative cycles of critical demanding and defensive with-drawal that underlie their relational distress. In EFT, the ther-apist explores a couple's pattern through a lens of attachment (i.e., seeking the other in a time of need), caregiving (e.g., emo-tional accessibility and responsiveness, reassurance, hugs, touch), and sexual interactions (i.e., interactions involving sexual pleasure). These three systems provide a way of pin-pointing and framing a couple's level of secure responsiveness. Partners' positions in their dance may reflect different strug-gles related to closeness and distance in different areas of the relationship. For example, a therapist may explore how Jane seeks out emotional contact and affection, while John with-draws from these same domains, but pursues her sexually.

Second, the therapist explores conflicts specific to sexual complaints and concerns. Partners caught in a cycle of distress, such as demand–withdraw, often experience sexual relations as one dimensional. For the more anxiously attached partner, the sexual focus may be on attaining reassurance and affec-tion, whereas the avoidantly attached partner often focuses on pleasurable stimulation and maintains distance by minimiz-ing the attachment aspects of sexual relations (Johnson, 2008). In some cases, he or she may overly control both emotional and pleasure cues during sexual contact for fear of losing con-trol. Difficulties in physical intimacy and sexual problems are understood as by-products of insecure attachment and a growing sense of emotional disengagement that erodes the capacity for openness relationally and sexually.

Aside from the typical EFT assessment, individual sessions should involve a sexual functioning assessment. The thoroughness of this assessment depends on the centrality of sexual issues in the presenting problem and cycles of negative interactions. It can include gathering information about sociocultural influence (e.g., scripts about sex from families of origin, culture, and religion), physiological functioning (e.g., hormones, diabetes, central nervous system, vascular, and organic issues), traumatic childhood and sexual experiences, current medical treatment (e.g., antidepressants, beta-blockers, and other medications that diminish functioning), and lifestyle factors (e.g., substance use, smoking). Underlying primary psychological issues, such as depression and anxiety, should be assessed and their impact on sexuality discussed. Whether these conditions stem from the attachment context or not, these issues should be addressed prior to addressing sexual problems. The underlying issues affecting sexuality extend beyond what has been listed here; ideally, the EFT couple and sex therapist should then receive training to assess the biopsychosocial dimensions of sexual functioning and/or work with a consultant who has expertise in these areas.

Once the EFT couple and sex therapist have a sense of whether underlying sexual issues are related to organic physical health problems, medication use, or psychological problems, these issues are placed in the context of the individual partner's present attachment relationship and attachment strategies. It is important to ascertain whether a particular sexual functioning issue is specific to a particular relationship or generalized. For example, some partners can achieve and sustain arousal, have an orgasm, and experience sexual desire, but not with their current partner.

Over time, partners and couples often experience overlapping and mutually generating sexual problems. For example, a husband's problem with arousal may trigger a loss of sexual desire, or a man with premature ejaculation may lose his capacity for arousal as his perceived sexual failures render sexual relations aversive. A woman's arousal difficulties may lead to sexual pain upon intercourse, which may then lessen her husband's interest in sex. On the other hand, a wife's plunging sexual interest may also result from her partner's premature ejaculation, which may further reduce his capacity for arousal and desire. The EFT sex therapist must track all of the emotional influences and coping strategies that shape the stuck patterns associated with sexual problems.

If a couple does not have specific sexual issues (such as long-standing premature ejaculation in the male partner) and their sex life has simply suffered as a result of relationship alienation and distress, their sex life usually begins to improve at the end of Stage 1 of EFT. Partners feel more hope for their relationship and can come together as a team against the incursions of their negative cycle in the bedroom and outside it. At times, sexual contact may be experienced as unsafe due to past trauma, generally high levels of emotional discomfort with closeness, or relationship-specific behaviors such as critical blaming on the part of one's partner.

When it becomes apparent that danger cues are deeply entrenched in a partner's sexual experiences, the couple will be encouraged to stop attempts at intercourse and other sexual contact. Sexual contact would typically only be fostered again in the context of Stage 2 of EFT when the de-escalation of negative interactions has been achieved and a form of secure base created. Partners are encouraged to engage in affectionate touch and holding prior to reengaging in sexual contact and to use their inner emotional reality as a guide in this process.

For couples experiencing sexual functioning issues, a first step is carefully to outline negative cycles of sexual interaction and to help each partner own his or her part in the cycle. The secondary emotional responses and self-protection strategies (such as numbing and withdrawal) underlying general relationship and sexual interactions are explored and placed in the context of attachment needs and fears. These strategies that block authentic sexual engagement and impede sexual functioning are validated as ways of regulating difficult emotions and their impact on the partner is explored. The validation of the need for emotional safety as the essential foundation for sexual openness and responsiveness is a key part of therapy. It is necessary to create a platform of safety in the session—a preliminary secure base from which to explore negative cycles of sexual interaction. Partners' conflicts about sexuality are embedded in an attachment narrative, created in collaboration with the therapist, about the loss of safe engagement across the domains of attachment, caregiving, and sexuality.

At the end of this first stage of therapy, the couple is able to disengage from their general negative cycle and their specific negative sexual cycle. They can see these cycles and the distance and insecurity they foster as the problem and can join together to stabilize their relationship. Partners begin to understand how a style of engagement underlies each partner's position in the sexual dance and how this has constricted the partner's own and his or her partner's sexual experience.

The therapist also places sexual responses in an attachment frame so that a partner's lack of desire and arousal is attributed to a lack of safety and need for self-protection. For example, Anne begins to understand that her angry, critical pursuing of Juan has contributed to Juan's increasing avoidance of physical contact, while Juan gains awareness of how his distancing strategy has exacerbated Anne's fears. Both partners begin to gain access to the underlying attachment fears that have motivated Anne's desperate efforts to solicit a response from Juan and the fears of failure and inadequacy that blocked Juan from authentically responding.

Phase 1 of EFT With a Low-Sexual-Desire Couple

Rhonda and Malcolm, a couple in their early 40s, present with pursue–withdraw dynamics related to long-standing sexual issues. For years, Rhonda has had increasing difficulty achieving sufficient arousal or having an orgasm and now expresses little desire for sexual contact. She is, however, able to be fully aroused and orgasmic while masturbating alone. Her withdrawal from the sexual realm of the relationship seemed to occur within the context of Malcolm's increasing emotional distance. Often she complained in session about how the "only way to his heart is through his penis."

Her quiet acquiescence to Malcolm's sexual overtures in the early years of the relationship eventually evolved into an increasing avoidance of any form of physical intimacy because she feared any physical contact would result in an increase in Malcolm pressuring her for sex. Over the years, Rhonda moved from feeling angry and abandoned to despair. Years ago, she had decided that Malcolm would never respond to her needs. He remained emotionally withdrawn, seeming to ignore her requests for more emotional connection, more affection, and foreplay in sex.

Malcolm's sexual initiations and angry demands for sex seemed to increase in direct response to Rhonda's withdrawal from physical intimacy. Her eventual lack of responsiveness to his sexual moves filled him with fears of rejection and fueled his physical clinging and sexual demands. In previous years, he had gained great satisfaction at being able to arouse

Rhonda and facilitate an orgasm. He seemed preoccupied by these responses as an indication of whether he was a sexual success or failure. Rhonda became increasingly aware of his lack of attunement to her experience and her needs for affection. Malcolm remained withdrawn emotionally in the relationship, unable to express his feelings, needs, and wants to her, all the while desperately pursuing Rhonda sexually.

A lack of emotional safety in the relationship had resulted in physical and sexual intimacy becoming a pressure-filled place. Sex was a self-alienating task for Rhonda, and sexual contact filled Malcolm with a sense of emotional despair and hopelessness. Their growing disconnection also became more visible and explicit as it played out sexually. Eventually, Rhonda's ability to achieve orgasm faded, along with her sexual interest and arousal. Malcolm's ongoing feelings of rejection and angry protest eventually slid into hopelessness, despair, and a reduction in his pursuit for sexual contact.

In early sessions, the therapist focused on increasing each partner's awareness about the negative interaction cycles that defined his or her intimate interactions and sexual relations. A map linking the partners' habitual manner of emotional engagement underlying the negative interaction cycle and sexual functioning issues was drawn.

Therapist: So, it seems that outside the bedroom, Rhonda, you've been pursuing Malcolm for more emotional contact, and Malcolm, for you, sexual contact with Rhonda seems to have been the place where you felt closest. Sexual contact was the way that you felt bonded. As Malcolm desired more sex, Rhonda, you quietly surrendered.

Rhonda: He had been so pushy with sex. I felt I should give him sex. And if I didn't have an orgasm, he'd get so pissed off.

Therapist: So he pursued you for sex and, somehow, you felt pressure. You felt pushed into sex, so eventually you withdrew. You had sex but were withdrawing from any awareness of any feelings of connection or pleasure in these moments. (Rhonda nods.)

Therapist: I want to spend some time here, guys, exploring the cycle we've been talking about. So at first, Rhonda, you were pursuing Malcolm for more closeness, more emotional connection, and the angrier you got, the more Malcolm would withdraw, feeling

quite overwhelmed. And, Malcolm, you were seeking contact with Rhonda in a sexual way, making
more demands for sex, while, Rhonda, you eventually withdrew.

Rhonda: It became too much. At first, I'd go through the motions.
It never seemed to be enough. Like a chore. Nothing
really in it for me. No touch, just all about him.

Therapist: So you both felt pressured. Rhonda, you performed,
but sex became a disconnected place for you. You
were both trying to connect and feel loved but in different ways and in different places.

The solution to Malcolm and Rhonda's growing disconnection, at least for an attachment-oriented emotionally focused
therapist, is to de-escalate these negative cycles and structure
more secure bonding interactions in all domains of the relationship. The therapeutic goal in Stage 2 is to create new levels of emotional safety and connection. Emotional safety then
fosters more positive and integrated sexual experiences. This
enables partners to risk expressing softer emotions and unmet
attachment needs, including sexual longings and desires.

Stage 2 of EFT: New Cycles of Emotional–Sexual Engagement and the "Sexual Softening Event"

In Stage 2 of EFT, the focus is on helping couples reengage
positive cycles of openness and emotional responsiveness.
During withdrawer reengagement and blamer softening change
events, partners take risks to confide attachment needs and
fears and to reach for and respond to each other. The therapist
also eventually encourages the couple to confide and risk in
the same manner in the area of physical closeness and sexuality. Through sexual softening change events, more emotionally engaged partners can then begin to disclose sexual fears
and needs directly to each other.

During these therapeutic moments, the EFT therapist
actively encourages the integration of attachment, caregiving, and sexuality. One partner's needs for loving touch and
dialogue as part of foreplay and another partner's desire to
be held after sex may be discussed. The therapist uses these
experiences to help couples express the attachment significance of these requests. For example, as a male partner with
premature ejaculation feels his partner's increased emotional
accessibility and responsiveness, his fears associated with

sexual arousal are calmed. He is better able to turn his attention safely outward without becoming overly stimulated by the emotional and sexual arousal levels in his body. His ability to regulate his arousal levels also increases as he is no longer confronted with an imminent fear of rejection or abandonment. Emotional safety provides a platform from which this partner may access and regulate his arousal levels in a context in which his partner no longer represents a source of potential emotional danger to him.

As emotional safety increases, partners risk asserting their attachment and sexual need and, further, begin to share the erotic wishes previously buried under shame, anger, and despair. The therapist guides partners to formulate and share these erotic cues, blocks to surrendering to sensation and sexual longings, and begins to offer the couple the possibility of a sexual relationship founded on a more secure emotional connection. This attachment-oriented model of sexuality encourages erotic exploration and play and sees good sex as a safe adventure in which erotic excitement arises from open moment-to-moment engagement with a safe and accessible partner.

The EFT therapist often provides information to normalize responses and support the couple's efforts to begin to extend their safe emotional engagement and exploration into their sexual relationship. For example, Stan is reassured to find out that in a 40-minute lovemaking session, many men will lose their erection for a few moments. Increased levels of attachment security and relationship satisfaction open up new possibilities for sexual interactions based on higher levels of emotional and sexual attunement. Once couples feel more securely connected, many partners are able to turn toward and explore blocks that occur in their sexual dance and move forward to more integrated and mutually reciprocal sexual relationships. Partners can then risk asking for the sex that they want and are also less threatened by the other's sexual desires and requests.

As part of the process of therapy, the EFT therapist may provide experiential exercises to allow a couple to explore physical intimacy gradually. In some cases where partners are asked not to attempt intercourse (because it is a predictable occasion of failure and distress), they are supported to reestablish a sense of physical comfort and intimacy gradually by touching, hugging, and synchronous breathing exercises (i.e., holding each other and being aware of synchronizing their breaths).

After a sense of emotional safety is reestablished, additional steps are added and each partner's reactions are explored in therapy. For example, Sue had withdrawn sexually and begun to turn away from Phil's gestures of affection because these moments often became demands for intercourse. Intercourse was put aside for a short period and Phil was first encouraged to give clear signals concerning his desire for affection and to ascertain Sue's openness and interest in a way that made her feel safe. After the preceding exercises had helped to reestablish a sense of safety, small steps were introduced to set up a corrective emotional experience of sexual contact.

During these exercises, the EFT therapist encourages partners to remain aware of any emotional cues that emerge. Partners reconnect to their own bodily cues so that they can process any emotional residue and attachment distress triggered by physical contact and closeness. Partners are requested to explore their inner emotional and sexual reactions to these exercises and discuss these in session.

Exercises at home progress in a sequential fashion. At first, partners may be asked to engage in nongenital touching and holding while fully clothed. As safety increases, partners are encouraged to begin to express their fears and make small steps to respond to these concerns. Eventually, as the couple experiences greater levels of comfort, sexual touching is reintroduced and, once more, the emotional experiences and sexual cues associated with these behaviors are explored in session. Partners gradually progress to sharing further longings for more touch, erotic foreplay, and, eventually, sexual and erotic wishes, dreams, and fantasies. Sexuality becomes a place that is emotionally and physically safe.

Sexual Softening Events
An in-session sexual "softening" occurs as fears and needs are expressed, the emotional safety in the relationship is increased, and physical intimacy is restored. Within this context, partners gain a more positive sense of self and other and the confidence required to assert their attachment and sexual wants and needs in the sexual realm of the relationship. During a moment-by-moment processing of couple partners' sexual experiences, partners are asked to be aware of times when their perception of and attention to internal cues are driven by attachment fears of abandonment and rejection, and to share these vulnerabilities with the other.

At home, partners are asked to explore their sexual experience and the sense of connection that sexual intimacy can bring as they become more sexually attuned into one another. Couples may identify blocks to this attunement, which the therapist then helps the couple explore in session. For example, Jim began to recognize how he often focused strictly on the pleasurable sensations of sex, excluding any awareness of his partner. In session, however, he became more and more aware of the emotional comfort provided by Alice in their lovemaking. He grew in his awareness of the implicit intimacy in the way Alice responded to his sexual moves and how he accommodated to her sexual gestures. Sexual attunement, through emotional and physical synchrony, integrates eroticism and bonding. Schore (2003) integrates emotion and physicality when he observes that "regulation theory suggests that attachment is, in essence, the right brain regulation of biological synchronicity between organisms" (p. 41). Good sex is really about the attuned coordination of physical responses and emotional cues.

Couples are encouraged to create these moments of physical and emotional connectedness, to share their own separate sexual desires, and to deal with attachment fears that may emerge as a result of the other's sexual responses. Partners are now able to co-construct a mutually enjoyable sexual adventure, which includes the possibility of sharing and engaging in each other's erotic wishes and desires in an emotionally safe context. Accessibility and responsiveness to erotic and emotional cues in the sexual realm create a sexual safe haven that fosters the integration of attachment, sexuality, and caregiving and more secure bonding.

A Moment of Sexual Softening

Jill and Danny, a couple in their late 30s, have endured several long-standing sexual issues that have worsened over time and now pose a threat to their marital relationship. They present with arousal issues and low sexual desire. Initially, Jill pursued Danny for sexual contact and, as time passed, Danny's waning sexual interest precipitated high levels of anger in Jill. In her anger she became more demanding during sexual contact and, at times, would be quite hurt and resentful when Danny lost his erection. Danny recalls enjoying sex initially, but eventually becoming bored and disinterested with sex when he no longer had the pleasurable sensations he used to feel.

Therapist: So, for you, Jill, underneath that anger was a really deep sense of hurt, not knowing whether you were significant to Danny. You weren't sure of that, right? When he'd shut down, you'd fly into angry demands for comfort through sexual contact. Can you talk about that hurt now?

Jill: I didn't think Danny was interested in me. He was so shut down. Not there for me. I needed something.

Therapist: And then during sex, when Danny would lose his erection, that became difficult for you.

Jill: It would be the straw that broke the camel's back.

Therapist: What feelings did that stir inside you?

Jill: I felt worthless. Hopeless.

Therapist: Afraid of whether you mattered to him as he withdrew emotionally and then sexually. You felt hopeless that he'd ever reach back for you. You couldn't find him anymore in the relationship, is that it?

Jill: I didn't know if I mattered. He left the relationship in so many ways. During sex, he wasn't there either. No affection. No connection in sex.

Therapist: You feared that somehow he was no longer anywhere to be found.

Jill: It was scary. It made me feel so hopeless. He didn't want or need me.

Therapist: And for you, Danny, somehow her growing sense of anger and her demands for more contact, more affection, more sexual contact became overwhelming, a place of pressure. Somehow you felt pressured to please her, perform for her, and eventually sex became a place of fear, a place of routine. There was nothing left in it for you.

Danny: I felt like I wasn't okay anywhere anymore. And her anger around sex was too much for me. It was always the same thing.

Therapist: You didn't realize that underneath her anger, there were these deep fears, and as she became angrier, you became overwhelmed by your own fears of rejection and eventually withdrew from sex. You began to perform in sex, giving her what she wanted, but eventually sex became a place that was disconnected and not pleasurable. And so you disconnected. You withdrew. She felt your withdrawal and became increasingly hopeless.

Danny: I was scared. I couldn't do anything right.

Therapist: You feared she would reject you and that you were inadequate and were failing. It was difficult to stay aroused, difficult to connect to what was pleasurable for you, and feel close to her at all. Could you turn to her now and let her know about these fears?

Danny (turning to Jill): I didn't think I was okay anywhere. I was so scared. More and more scared that you would leave if I didn't give you what you wanted sexually. I felt so much pressure. You always seemed to think my erection was so important and that was too much for me. I need to know that you want me and we can "do" this together. So I'm not on trial. I want so much to be lovers with you. I want to be close. I need your help to come close again. (Jill reaches over and strokes his hand.)

Stage 3 of EFT: Consolidation and Building on Couple Eroticism

In Stage 3 of EFT, partners can solve pragmatic problems such as lifestyle issues that may preclude time for lovemaking. They can create a joint story of their relationship problems and recovery that includes the sexual aspect of their bond and acts as a prototype for the future. For example, as their attachment fears subside and needs for safe connection are met, Danny and Jill are able to focus on their internal emotional and sexual states during sex. In the context of safety, they are able to engage in a manner in which both partners gain greater sexual satisfaction. Satisfying sexual encounters now strengthen the couple's bond and a more secure bond continues to build more erotic and more satisfying sex. As part of the last consolidation stage of an attachment-oriented couple therapy, partners formulate a story of their relationship distress and repair. Thus, couples are also encouraged to create their own coherent story of their sexual relationship, including their own model of "good sex," how problems are triggered, and how they are now able to deal with them.

ISSUES FOR SUPERVISION AND TRAINING

EFT therapists practicing couples and sex therapy need to educate themselves about the organic, physiological, and medical health issues that impact the human sexual system. Acquiring basic education about the human sexual system (e.g., male and female sexual physiology and functioning) helps the therapist educate clients about areas where their knowledge is lacking or misinformed. Clients will have expectations about their own and partners' sexual arousal, desire levels, and orgasms based on social and cultural scripts about normative sexual performances. Clients may also be lacking the language to describe their genitalia, sexual responses, and needs.

Therapists must also be sufficiently nonjudgmental so as to create safety for clients to explore their sexual experiences and biases. For example, clients will use a wide range of language to talk about sexual contact, including "lovemaking," "sex," and "fucking" and other expressions. Therapists must be able to accept the clients' language and use it to reflect the deeper emotional and sexual meanings associated with the clients' experiences. We suggest that EFT therapists who are uncomfortable with particular aspects of sexuality should refrain from dealing with couples with these sexual issues and refer couples to a colleague who can integrate a focus on sexuality, attachment, and ongoing patterns of affect regulation.

CONCLUSION

Fulfilling sexual interactions contributes to increased relationship satisfaction and stability among couples, whereas sexual dysfunction often leads to conflict, emotional distance, and disengagement. From our perspective, insecure attachment undermines sexual satisfaction and diminishes a couple's capacity to resolve important sexual differences and problems. Partners co-construct a bond that meets their attachment, caregiving, and sexual needs; however, sometimes, they struggle in an effort to integrate these needs into their relationship.

Helping couples create emotional safety and attunement is an essential first step in restoring physical and sexual intimacy. Within this context, partners can access their internal experience and risk asserting wants and needs in all domains of the relationship. As McCarthy and McCarthy (2003) conclude, "Sex works best when each spouse is open and receptive" (p. 32). This openness is evident in a partner's accessibility and responsiveness to his or her emotional and sexual needs and those of the partner.

We suggest that the compartmentalization of sexuality as separate from relationship issues and emotional life is always a mistake. Now that we have a comprehensive theory of adult love, we can help partners integrate these different elements into a stable, loving bond where each of these elements can enrich the other. The best recipe for sexual health and happiness is the creation of a safe, loving, emotional bond where physical intimacy is integrated with a sense of nurturing emotional connection.

REFERENCES

Bancroft, J. (1999). Central inhibition of sexual response in the male: A theoretical perspective. *Neuroscience and Biobehavioral Reviews, 23,* 763–784.

Bartels, A., & Zeki, S. (2004). The neural correlates of maternal and romantic love. *Neuroimage, 21,* 1155–1166.

Basson, R. (2000). The female sexual response: A different model. *Journal of Sex and Marital Therapy, 26,* 51–65.

Basson, R. (2007). Sexual desire/arousal disorders in women. In S. Leiblum (Ed.), *Principles and practice of sex therapy* (4th ed.; pp. 25–53). New York, NY: Guilford Press.

Birnbaum, G. E. (2007). Attachment orientations, sexual functioning and relationship satisfaction in a community sample of women. *Journal of Social and Personal Relationships, 24,* 21–35.

Birnbaum, G. E., Reis, H. T., Mikulincer, M., Gillath, O., & Orpaz, A. (2006). When sex is more than just sex: Attachment orientations, sexual experiences and relationship quality. *Journal of Personality and Social Psychology, 91,* 929–943.

Bogaert, A. F., & Sadava, S. (2002). Adult attachment and sexual behavior. *Personal Relationships, 9,* 191–204.

Bowlby, J. (1969). *Attachment and loss: Vol 1: Attachment.* New York, NY: Basic Books.

Brassard, A., Shaver, P. R., & Lussier, Y. (2007). Attachment, sexual experience and sexual pressure in romantic relationships: A dyadic approach. *Personal Relationships, 14,* 475–494.

Carter, S. (1998). Neuroendocrine perspectives on social attachment and love. *Psychoneuroendocrinology, 23,* 779–818.

Davis, D., Shaver, P. R., & Vernon, M. L. (2004). Attachment style and subjective motivations for sex. *Personality and Social Psychology Bulletin, 30,* 1076–1090.

Davis, D., Shaver, P. R., Widaman, K. F., Vernon, M., Follette, W. C., & Beitz, K. (2006). "I can't get no satisfaction": Insecure attachment, inhibited sexual communication, and sexual dissatisfaction. *Personal Relationships, 13,* 465–483.

Diamond, D., & Blatt, S. (2007). Introduction. In D. Diamond, S. Blatt, & J. Lichtenberg (Eds.), *Attachment and sexuality* (pp. 1–26). New York, NY: Analytic Press.

Feeney, J. A., Peterson, C., Gallois, C., & Terry, D. J. (2000). Attachment style and predictors of sexual attitudes and behaviors in late adolescence. *Psychology and Health, 14,* 1105–1122.

Gillath, O., & Schachner, D. A. (2006). How do sexuality and attachment interrelate? Goals, motives and strategies. In M. Mikulincer & G. Goodman (Eds.), *The dynamics of romantic love: Attachment, caregiving and sex* (pp. 337–355). New York, NY: Guilford Press.

Hazan, C., & Zeifman, D. (1994). *Sex and the psychological tether. Advances in personal relationships* (Vol. 5; pp. 151–177). London, England: Jessica Kingsley Publishers.

Hazan, C., Zeifman, D., & Middleton, K. (1994). Adult romantic attachment, affection and sex. Paper presented at the 7th International Conference on Personal Relationships, Groningen, the Netherlands, July 1994.

Heiman, J. (2007). Orgasmic disorders in women. In S. Leiblum (Ed.), *Principles and practice of sex therapy* (4th ed.; pp. 84–123). New York, NY: Guilford Press.

Johnson, S. M. (2008). *Hold me tight. Seven conversations for a lifetime of love.* New York, NY: Little Brown.

Johnson, S. M. (2009). Attachment and emotionally focused couple therapy: Perfect partners. In J. Obegi & E. Berant (Eds.), *Clinical applications of adult attachment* (pp. 410–433). New York, NY: Guilford Press.

Johnson, S. M., & Zuccarini, D. (in press). Integrating sex and attachment in emotionally focused couple therapy. *Journal of Marital and Family Therapy.*

Leiblum, S. R. (2007). *Principles and practice of sex therapy* (4th ed.). New York, NY: Guilford Press.

Masters, W., & Johnson, V. (1970). *Human sexual inadequacy.* Boston, MA: Little Brown.

McCarthy, B., & McCarthy, E. (2003). *Rekindling desire.* New York, NY: Brunner Routledge.

Metz, M. E., & McCarthy, B. W. (2004). *Coping with erectile dysfunction.* Oakland, CA: New Harbinger.

Mikulincer, M., & Shaver, P. (2007). *Attachment in adulthood: Structure, dynamics and change.* New York, NY: Guilford Press.

Schachner, D. A., & Shaver, P. R. (2004). Attachment dimensions and motives for sex. *Personal Relationships, 11,* 179–195.

Schnarch, D. M. (1997). *Passionate marriage: Sex love and intimacy in emotionally committed relationships.* New York, NY: W. W. Norton.

Schore, A. N. (2003). *Affect regulation and the repair of the self.* New York, NY: W. W. Norton.

Shafer, A. B. (2001). The big five and sexuality trait terms as predictors of relationships and sex. *Journal of Research in Personality, 35,* 313–338.

Smallbone, S. W., & Dadds, E. (2000). Attachment and coercive sexual behavior. *Sexual Abuse: Journal of Research and Treatment, 12,* 3–15.

Stephan, C. W., & Bachman, G. F. (1999). What's sex got to do with it? Attachment, love schemas and sexuality. *Personal Relationships, 6,* 111–123.

Stern, D. (2004). *The present moment in psychotherapy and everyday life.* New York, NY: W. W. Norton.

Ten

Rebuilding Bonds After the Traumatic Impact of Infidelity

JUDY A. MAKINEN AND LORIE EDIGER

INTRODUCTION

Cindy was in a state of shock and disbelief. But the evidence that she had discovered on John's computer was disturbingly conclusive. Raunchy e-mails from one of his lovers, the exchange of sexually explicit photographs, accessing pornographic Web sites and video chat rooms were some of the activities that had taken up so much of his time. How foolish she now felt. Despite her loneliness and frustration at his long hours at "work," she was supportive of his business pursuits. At times, she was acutely aware of his emotional distance but attributed it to work stress. How could she have been so stupid? After 15 years of marriage, how dare he? The sudden realization of months of deceit ripped through her like a sword.

Stories of infidelity are not new; they date back to antiquity. Although many people, cultures, and countries have different views on what constitutes infidelity, for many the effects are devastating. In Western culture, contemporary marital relationships are monogamous and generally viewed as sacrosanct. Nevertheless, it is not just the breach in the moral agreement of sexual exclusivity between partners that is destructive; it is also the loss of trust, deceit, and betrayal of shared values on which the relationship is built that is disorienting. Clearly, what makes infidelity so incredibly painful is that it involves someone deliberately using deception to violate established expectations or boundaries within the primary relationship.

This chapter endeavors to define infidelity, address the complexity regarding its prevalence, and elucidate its impact on both partners and the relationship. A clinical case is presented to demonstrate the efficacy of emotionally focused therapy (EFT) for couples wanting to recover from infidelity and its aftermath.

THE SHIFTING DEFINITION OF INFIDELITY

Adultery, cheating, sexual affairs, affairs of the heart, extra-dyadic relations, virtual affairs, and cybersex are only some of the terms that fall under the rubric of infidelity. There are a myriad of terms and definitions of infidelity in the research literature (Blow & Hartnett, 2005a). To complicate matters, what constitutes an act of infidelity varies across cultures, the type of relationship, and even between partners. For example, one person may not be threatened when his or her partner confides in a friend of the opposite sex. For another partner, a husband's innocuous glance at a bikini-clad woman on the beach may be intolerable.

Even in open relationships, where sexual involvement outside the primary relationship is deemed acceptable, infidelity may arise if a partner forms an emotional bond with another person. Despite the inconsistent definitions and different meanings for this construct, the literature describes three main types of infidelity that the majority of couples in therapy view as a betrayal: physical or sexual infidelity, emotional infidelity, and cyberinfidelity, which may or may not include pornography.

Physical infidelity refers to sexual intimacy with someone other than the partner to whom one is committed. Extradyadic sex can be a single occurrence, philandering, or a long-term relationship. In any case, sex outside the primary relationship is often viewed by the injured spouse as a "betrayal of fundamental trust," and it often involves a great deal of deception (Christensen & Jacobson, 2000, p. 285). Physical/sexual infidelity is the prototypical relationship betrayal. However, even though sexual intimacy most often occurs in affairs, this kind of intimacy is not a necessary component of perceived infidelity.

Emotional infidelity, or affairs of the heart, involves an emotional investment with a person outside the primary relationship that leads to channeling resources such as affection, time, and attention to that person (Glass, 2003). Although the line between platonic friendships and romantic love may be confusing, meeting secretly with a coworker, for example, and sharing intimate feelings and secrets with the new partner rather than with one's spouse is most often damaging to the primary relationship. In spite of the fact that sexual urges may have been suppressed to maintain the illusion that this competing relationship was merely a friendship, this does not, in and of itself, provide solace to an injured spouse.

With the widespread public use of the Internet, the way people access information and communicate with each other has been transformed dramatically. The Internet provides a completely new medium for sexual activity with unique dynamics and repercussions. Cyberinfidelity or online sexual activity occurs when one partner in a committed relationship uses the computer to violate promises or vows in a way that ultimately undermines the stability of the couple relationship (Maheu & Subotnik, 2001; Subotnik, 2007). This typically includes "sharing images, purchasing materials, downloading erotica, sexually explicit discussions, and searching for sexual partners" (Dew, Brubaker, & Hays, 2006, p. 196).

Whether perceived or real, infidelity poses a threat to the primary relationship (Johnson, 2005). The different types of infidelity and the multitude of meanings assigned to it clearly present a challenge to clinicians working with couples as well as to researchers studying this phenomenon.

PREVALENCE RATES

Infidelity occurs at an alarmingly high rate and is the most frequently cited grounds of divorce (Atkins, Baucom, & Jacobson, 2001; Gottman, 2004; Shackelford, Buss, & Bennett, 2002). Approximately 67% of couples will divorce before their 40th wedding anniversary (Gottman & Silver, 1999) and couple therapists report that 30–65% of couples in therapy have been unfaithful (Atkins et al., 2001; O'Leary, 2005).

One of the first studies on human sexual behavior found that 26% of married women and 50% of married men reported having had an affair during their married lives (Kinsey, Pomeroy, Martin, & Gebhard, 1953/1998). More recent figures from a large representative sample in the United States showed much lower rates, with 15% of women and 25% of men having had extramarital sex (Lauman, Gagnon, Michael, & Michaels, 1994). Accurate statistics, however, are difficult to obtain because of serious methodological limitations (Atkins et al., 2001; Blow & Hartnett, 2005a). Prevalence rates tend to measure extramarital sexual activity and, for the most part, the literature does not delineate the different types of infidelity (Blow & Hartnett, 2005b).

According to Glass (2003), emotional infidelity tends to be more common than sexual infidelity but is just as damaging to the primary relationship. She found that 25% of women and 44% of men reported having an affair where they had a strong emotional connection that was beyond friendship. Similarly, Snyder, Baucom, and Gordon (2007) found that 25% of women and 45% of men engaged in emotional infidelity but without sexual involvement. Blow and Hartnett (2005a) emphasized that "former President Bill Clinton's now infamous remark, 'I did not have sexual relations with that woman,' offers a particularly poignant illustration" of how people deny being unfaithful because it did not involve sexual intercourse (p. 186).

The prevalence of online sexual activity is more difficult to ascertain. Currently, there are over 1.9 billion Internet users worldwide, of which 266 million are from North America (Internet World Stats, 2010). It has been estimated that 31%, or approximately 70 million people, in North America visit sites with sexual content ranging from obtaining sexual health-related information to reading sexually explicit material to interactive cybersex (Goldberg et al., 2008; Hertlein & Webster, 2008). Online sexual activity is alluring because it is accessible, affordable, and anonymous (Cooper, Putman, Planchon, & Boies, 1999); also, it offers an emotional escape (Young, Griffin-Shelley, Cooper, O'Mara, & Buchanan, 2000). Even though Internet statistics have not been reported, the aforementioned draw and the ease with which people can meet others online may increase the prevalence of infidelity (Subotnik, 2007).

THE REPERCUSSIONS OF INFIDELITY

By definition, infidelity is shrouded in deceit and secrecy, which ostensibly causes irreparable damage to the relationship. Johnson (2005) views affairs through the lens of attachment theory, which offers a sound theoretical framework of adult romantic relationships. According to attachment theory, human beings are hardwired to form and maintain powerful emotional bonds (Shaver & Hazan, 1993). Practically every aspect of human experience is strongly influenced by the quality of these bonds.

A secure bond where partners mutually derive and provide closeness, comfort, and protection increases their ability to tolerate and cope with day-to-day stress and navigate through some difficult life experiences (e.g., loss, illness, etc.) and transitions (e.g., birth of a child, changing job, retirement). In essence, a felt sense of security in intimate relationships, which is about mutual emotional accessibility and responsiveness, creates resilience in the face of fear and helplessness and the ability to regulate powerful emotions. Threats to the security of the attachment bond activate powerful primary emotions, such as panic and sadness, and amplify the need for contact and comfort.

But when the security of the attachment bond is threatened by an attachment figure, as in the case of an unfaithful partner, this can be extremely destabilizing for the injured partner. Johnson (2005) points out that if the offending partner's involvement was minimal and he or she takes responsibility and expresses remorse, the threat may be lessened by comforting contact and reassurance. However, if the threat is perceived as more serious or if the relationship has not been a safe haven before the infidelity occurred, the injured partner may hyperactivate attachment anxieties and protests or try to deactivate needs and fears. This results in attacking behaviors or numbing out and defensive avoidance. Both these coping strategies often exacerbate personal hurt and distance between partners.

Attachment theory is also a "theory of trauma" (Atkinson, 1997, p. 3). People are particularly vulnerable and have difficulty regulating their affect when they do not have physical or emotional support. Disturbances in affect are central to all descriptions of traumatic stress (Stone, 1996). When a relationship has "absorbed a direct hit" as a result of infidelity (Bercaw & Bercaw, 2010, p. 33), the repercussions are interpersonally traumatic (Johnson, 2002; Snyder et al., 2007). The discovery of infidelity is like "a bomb, tearing through the fabric of the relationship like shrapnel through unprotected flesh" (Bercaw & Bercaw, 2010, p. 32).

Consequently, the injured partner may exhibit symptoms characteristic of posttraumatic stress disorder (PTSD). Disturbing memories, vivid images, and sensations puncture an injured partner's concentration and sleep. When the partner is awake, excessive rumination and hypervigilence are all consuming. Avoidance and numbing, which are both natural and self-protective strategies against the bombardment of intrusive symptoms, interfere with ongoing emotional engagement and attunement between partners.

Couples dealing with trauma inflicted by their partner tend to express more intense negative affect than typical distressed couples. These situations, where the attachment figure is both the source of and the possible solution to emotional pain, are inherently difficult for the injured partner to orient to and to tolerate and consequently lead to a fundamental disorganization of the attachment system (Johnson & Williams-Keeler, 1998). Traumatizing abandonments or relationship betrayals can be viewed as attachment injuries (Johnson, Makinen, & Millikin, 2001). An attachment injury is defined as an actual or perceived abandonment, a betrayal, or breach in trust during times of extreme vulnerability or intense need for support expected of attachment figures (Johnson et al., 2001; Makinen & Johnson, 2006).

By definition, infidelity would qualify as a particular type of attachment injury. Emotional and/or physical involvement with another often means fewer resources (e.g., time, affection, attention, etc.) for the spouse. In retrospect, the injured partner becomes acutely aware of all the times when the spouse was not accessible and responsive to his or her needs. These injuries define the relationship as insecure and are most difficult to manage.

However, the perceived attachment significance that is at the heart of the injury is key here, rather than the specific events that occurred. The shock of deceit, loss of trust, and alienation—not to mention knowing that one's partner put one at risk of possibly contracting sexually transmitted diseases—are traumatic (Hertlein, Wetchler, & Piercy, 2005). Rage, shame, powerlessness, victimization, and abandonment set in motion a variety of reactions including, but not limited to, acute anxiety, depression, suicidal ideation, and even violence (Gordon, Baucom, & Snyder, 2008). When the unfaithful spouse denies or minimizes his or her extradyadic involvement and/or fails to respond in a reassuring and reparative way, it only compounds the injury.

Similarly, when the injured spouse cannot accept reassurance, it becomes difficult to move forward. Therefore, the couple becomes stuck in a vicious cycle of negative emotions and ways of interacting (e.g., attack–defend, pursue–distance), which ultimately undermines their ability to heal their relationship (Halchuk, Makinen, & Johnson, 2010). Failed attempts to move beyond and repair the bond between partners only deepen both partners' despair and alienation. Seemingly small or innocuous incidents related to the initial injury also tend to evoke powerful negative emotional responses (Makinen & Johnson, 2006).

EFFECTIVE TREATMENT FOR INFIDELITY

Undoubtedly, infidelity is one of the most complex relational problems to treat and the most difficult from which to recover (Gottman, 2004). Both the trauma and the forgiveness literature have attempted to address particular kinds of betrayals or relationship traumas that make the resolution process difficult to achieve. For example, some suggest that when dealing with a traditional affair, it is important for the couple to construct a shared narrative about the affair that explains how and why the affair came to be (Allen & Atkins, 2005).

Baucom, Gordon, Snyder, Atkins, and Christensen (2006) concur that injured partners need to have a clear sense of why the affair occurred; otherwise, they cannot trust their partners not to hurt them again. They suggest an integrative approach by blending cognitive behavioral and insight-oriented strategies to facilitate the forgiveness process. Although this three-stage model of forgiveness has some empirical support with moderate treatment gains, the main criticisms are that the stages are not clearly articulated, key emotions are not processed, and there is no opportunity to address long-standing relationship issues beyond the forgiveness intervention (MacIntosh, Hall, & Johnson, 2007).

Emotionally focused therapy (Johnson, 2004) is a short-term, structured approach to changing patterns of relational negativity and the associated emotional responses often seen in distressed couples, with the goal of creating a secure attachment between partners. EFT has been effective in treating relationship distress that is complicated by other issues such as chronic illness, depression, and posttraumatic stress disorder (Furrow & Bradley, Chapter 1, this volume; Johnson, 2002; Johnson & Makinen, 2003). It is currently one of the best empirically supported treatments for distressed couples and has demonstrated clinical effectiveness with recovery rates between 70 and 73% and significant improvements in 86% of distressed couples (Baucom, Shoham, Mueser, Daiuto, & Stickle, 1998; Johnson, Hunsley, Greenberg, & Schindler, 1999). Furthermore, follow-up research shows that these changes are stable and couples continue to show improvements in marital functioning over time (Cloutier, Manion, Gordon-Walker, & Johnson, 2002).

EFT interventions and change processes are grounded in a clear theoretical foundation arising from a synthesis of the humanistic-experiential and systemic perspectives. Together, these two perspectives allow the therapist to focus on key emotions and on present interactional patterns. Given that EFT is also embedded in attachment theory—now considered the most cogent theory of adult love—the focus is on creating a safe haven so that partners can provide the appropriate comfort and caring responses. Secure romantic attachments correlate to positive aspects of relationship functioning, including high levels of trust, commitment, interdependence, and higher dyadic satisfaction (Mikulincer, 1998).

The process of change in EFT is delineated into three stages:

- De-escalation of the negative cycle
- Restructuring the emotional bond (including withdrawer reengagement and blamer softening events)
- Consolidation

Each of these stages has specific steps with the goal of expanding constricted emotional responses that prime the negative interactions that undermine relationship repair (e.g., hostility, resentment) and accessing underlying softer emotions (e.g., loneliness) and the expression of vulnerability to create new patterns of positive interaction. De-escalation in couples dealing with infidelity is achieved when both partners can see and identify the pernicious cycle (e.g., attack–defend) and are able to place the infidelity into the context of this cycle. Negative cycles and the lack of safe emotional engagement set the stage for infidelity and prevent healing interactions once the affair is revealed. Couples dealing with infidelity express emotions that are more volatile and the cycle is more extreme than what is seen in a typical distressed couple.

In Stage 1 of EFT, the goal is to place infidelity in the context of the negative cycle, where the injured partner venomously attacks and the unfaithful partner deflects, defends, and withdraws, and frame the cycle as the enemy. This creates some safety to begin exploring attachment fears, grief, hurt, shame, and attachment significance, which leads to interactions that are more positive.

However, once couples enter Stage 2 of EFT, the unresolved relationship trauma and the lack of trust block risk taking and prevent key positive shifts in interactions. The attachment injury of the affair creates an impasse in therapy, which typically emerges when the therapist attempts to reengage the withdrawn partner. At this point, the injured partner reexperiences the traumatic injury and intense vulnerability as he or she is invited to risk deeper levels of engagement with the now more accessible other. This usually results in an explicit or implicit refusal to risk further hurt and risk placing the self once again in the unfaithful partner's hands.

To address these impasses, Johnson et al. (2001) developed an attachment injury resolution model that delineates key steps in processing and resolving traumatic emotions associated with betrayal and abandonment in a manner that leads to forgiveness as well as reconciliation. This model has been successfully empirically validated (Makinen & Johnson, 2006) and the gains in dyadic adjustment and forgiveness remained stable at 3-year follow-up (Halchuk et al., 2010).

The steps and interventions in this model are the same for distressed couples that have experienced infidelity as for those who are recovering from other forms of attachment injuries, such as perceived abandonment after a miscarriage or serious medical diagnoses. The key steps identified in the resolution of attachment injuries when addressing infidelity or other forms of emotional wounds that emerge in the second stage of EFT and block the progress of therapy are as follows:

1. The injured partner begins to describe the incident in which he or she felt betrayed, abandoned, and helpless and experienced a violation of trust that damaged his or her belief in the relationship as a secure bond. The incident is now compellingly alive and present rather than a calm recollection. The partner often tries to discount, deny, or minimize the incident and the injured partner's pain and moves to a defensive stance.

2. With the therapist's help, the injured spouse stays in touch with the injury and begins explicitly to articulate its impact and attachment significance. Newly formulated emotions frequently emerge at this point. Anger often evolves into vivid, clear expressions of hurt, helplessness, fear, and shame. The connection of the injury to the present negative cycles in the relationship becomes clear. For example, a spouse says, "I feel so wounded. I just verbally smack him to show him that he can't just wipe out my hurt. This has

changed everything; I'm not sure of anything anymore. How can I let him close? I can't, even when he
says he is sorry."

3. The partner, supported by the therapist, begins to hear
and understand the significance of the wounding event
and to understand it in attachment terms as a reflection
of his or her importance to the injured partner, rather
than as a reflection of his or her personal inadequacies
or "crimes." This partner is then guided to acknowledge the injured partner's pain and suffering and elab-
orate on how the wounding event evolved for him or
her, so that his or her actions become clear and understandable to the injured partner.

4. The injured partner then tentatively moves toward a
more integrated and complete articulation of the injury.
A core moment of pain and wounding where loss and
despair flooded this partner is often pinpointed. With
the help of the therapist, the negative shift in cognitions
about the self, the partner, and the viability of secure
connection and the tsunami of emotions and body sensations and coping strategies are made into a coherent
and organized narrative. This encapsulates the loss
surrounding the injury and specific attachment fears
and longings. This partner, supported by the therapist,
allows the other to witness his or her vulnerability.

5. The other spouse now becomes more emotionally
engaged and acknowledges responsibility for his or her
part in the attachment injury or infidelity and is able
to express empathy, regret, and/or remorse in a direct,
congruent, and emotionally engaged manner. The level
of emotional engagement is key in an effective apology.
Such an apology must come from the heart in a way
that communicates directly to the wounded partner
that the speaker feels his or her pain and owns the
actions that caused this pain.

6. Supported by the therapist, the injured spouse then
risks asking for the comfort and caring from the partner that were unavailable at the time of the injurious
event, the discovery of the infidelity, or the couple's
previous discussions of the infidelity or injury.

7. The other spouse responds in a caring manner that
acts as an antidote to the traumatic experience of
the attachment injury. The partners are then able to
construct together a new narrative of the injury. This

narrative is ordered and includes, for the injured partner, a clear and acceptable sense of how the other came
to respond in a defensive manner or became involved
with another person and how this crisis in their relationship is able to be resolved.

Once the attachment injury is resolved, the therapist can
more effectively foster the growth of trust and other responses
that continue to nurture positive cycles of bonding and connection. The couple can then complete change events, such as
a softening, where the more blaming spouse can confide his or
her attachment needs and the other can respond. This process
defines the relationship as a safe haven, fostering the resolution of other difficulties and entry into the final consolidation
stage of therapy.

A CLINICAL CASE DESCRIPTION AND TRANSCRIPT

The following case illustrates the practical application of the
attachment injury resolution model. John (37) and Cindy (35)
were self-referred for couple therapy after Cindy discovered
John was unfaithful. They have been married for 15 years and
have three children between the ages of 6 and 10 years. Cindy
is a hairdresser and has worked part-time ever since the birth
of their second child. John is a successful partner in a large
law firm.

According to Cindy, she never feels like a priority because
John devotes most of his time to building his law practice. She
has been disappointed for years about his limited involvement in her life and the lives of their children, stating, "He
always makes promises but never keeps them." Although she
claims that she has learned not to count on him, she still gets
furious at him for promising things he does not deliver and
vehemently expresses her frustration with him when this happens. Sexual intimacy has also begun to wane. Because she
was jealous about the amount of time John was spending on
his laptop in the evenings, Cindy investigated one day when
he stepped out of the house. She was horrified to discover his
online sexual activities.

John's perspective is quite different. He acknowledged putting a lot of energy into work in the early years of their marriage. He was always driven to succeed and was constantly
terrified of failing. He would come home after a long, stressful day longing for rest and reassurance, only to be met with

angry tirades from Cindy about how irresponsible he was for
not calling to let her know he would be late. Feeling like a
failure in his relationship, he focused more on work. To escape
from work and relationship stress, John turned to the pornography that he purchased when away on business.

About a year before, he had purchased a laptop and for the
first time discovered Internet pornography. He found pop-up
ads that he became curious about, thinking that "just looking" would not do any harm. Eventually he learned about chat
rooms, some of them for married people like him wishing for
a little extra action. He had "met" several women this way,
shared sexual fantasies, and had cybersex with them. It had
been easy to rationalize these activities because he had never
met any of these women in person, and no one else would ever
know about it, or so he thought. When he had seen how hurt
and upset Cindy was over her discoveries on his computer, he
had discontinued these activities. But Cindy did not believe
he had stopped because he was "as distant as ever."

Cindy and John's pattern of interaction is pursue–withdraw,
with Cindy exhibiting angry, outraged, pursuing behavior and
John making a few vain attempts at defending himself before
lapsing into detached silence. On the dyadic adjustment scale,
they fell into the moderately distressed range (85), with Cindy
more distressed (79) than John (91). Both partners expressed a
strong commitment to repairing their relationship.

During the initial sessions, the therapist created a solid
alliance with John and Cindy through empathic attunement,
reflection, validation, and reframing. Part of this process
involved validation of Cindy's feelings of betrayal. The negative interactive cycle was identified and delineated. By the
end of the fifth session, they had de-escalated (Stage 1). John
and Cindy were beginning to identify the negative cycle as the
problem and they were beginning to explore underlying emotions, thus creating more safety to begin the attachment injury
resolution process.

The following transcript is from the sixth joint session. They
had just returned from a weekend at the lake. This session represents the beginning of Step 5 for John, which is the beginning of deepening emotion toward withdrawer reengagement.

Therapist: So how was your weekend?
Cindy: We have been doing so much better and I have been
feeling closer but the weekend was horrible, just horrible. We were going to the lake to spend some time

together and maybe sort out some of this stuff. First off, I was the one who had to do all of the arranging, laundry, and food preparation and bring the kids to the babysitter. John didn't even get home from work till 10:00 the night before and spent 5 minutes throwing some of his things in a bag.

Therapist: So it was frustrating; you did everything by yourself and felt alone, yes?

Cindy: Yeah, but that's not the worst part! When we are at the lake, we took a stroll along the beach and I was feeling a little closer and then suddenly I notice John's eyes wandering to the women in skimpy swimsuits. I just couldn't help but think about all of his pornography and the fact that he would actually "do it" with someone else online. I was *furious!*

Therapist: So seeing John's eyes wander at the beach touched on that wound of John's indiscretions. You were flooded with emotions and felt such fury. It's like you're not even there, like you don't matter to him.

Cindy: Yes, that's exactly it. So I kept all this inside because I didn't want to lose it right there in public, and when we get back to our room he tries to kiss me, and just like a powder keg, I exploded! I don't even remember what I said, but I let him have it.

Therapist: So when you saw John looking at other women and then try to kiss you, that was the spark that lit that powder keg inside you, and you just exploded. It reminded you of the times he had desired the other women online, and that perhaps he didn't really desire you. (Cindy nods and cries.)

John (defensively crossing his arms): I wasn't looking at women and I just wanted to kiss my wife. What's so terrible about that?

Therapist (to John): I realize this is hard for you to hear, John, but, if it's okay, I'd like to just stay with Cindy's feelings for a few more moments. (Therapist turns to Cindy.) You were furious with John, but also, underneath, you were cut to the quick by the thought that he doesn't love and care about you—that he's only interested in what you can offer sexually. Am I getting this?

Cindy (weeping): Yes, and it's always been that way...it's like he never really loved me, and his affairs with these other women are proof enough. (John lets out a loud, exasperated sigh.)

Therapist (leaning forward, using a soft, slow voice): So it feels like John has never loved you, never really cared about you, and that's what hurts; it hurts so much… that you're not important to him. It hurts, and it leaves you feeling so alone.

Cindy (still crying): Yes, that's exactly it.

Therapist: And then what happens is that you keep that terrible hurt inside until you are alone with John, and then it just takes a little spark, like John trying to kiss you, to ignite that pain, and it explodes as fury. But, really, what is happening inside you is this terrible hurt that is all about not being wanted, being left alone. (Therapist turns to John.) And then, what happens for you John? What happened for you when Cindy exploded?

John: Well, it's nothing new; it happens a lot at home too. What can I do? She isn't reasonable at times like that; there's nothing I can say that she would listen to.

Therapist: So what did you do?

John: I left. I just walked out because talking wasn't going to help. At that point, she had made up her mind that I was a rat, and there was no sense staying around to get stomped on.

Therapist: I see. So there was nothing you could say that would make a difference and if you stayed it might be dangerous for you in some way, so you left.

John: Well, I don't know if I thought it out quite that way in the moment. It was just a reaction—sort of like self-protection.

Cindy: As if I could hurt you if I tried!

Therapist: Cindy, I realize that it's really hard to hear John right now, but I think this is important. (Therapist turns to John.) So you felt at that moment like a rat about to be stomped, like here comes the boot—I'd better get out of here? And just a moment before you were trying to give Cindy a kiss; that must have been kind of a surprise for you when she exploded like that. What was that like for you?

John: Well, yeah, it did catch me off guard, I guess. I was a little scared about kissing her anyway because it's been so long, and I guess, now that I think about it, I was pretty nervous about that, so when she started going off at me, I just—I don't know—I just got out of there as fast as I could.

Therapist: So there you were taking this enormous risk, making yourself vulnerable, and you were really scared, scared of failure, scared of rejection.

John: Yeah, that's pretty accurate.

Therapist: And then, suddenly the worst of your fears comes true: You get stomped, like a rat, right out of the blue. And then—help me understand this next part—were you overwhelmed? Afraid? What was going on inside you right before you turned and left?

John: Maybe a little of both—for sure scared; I was scared. I know it sounds stupid, but that's what I was feeling; it's what I often feel when she gets so mad at me.

Therapist: So this is a familiar feeling, this fear? As you talk about it, I can see you tensing up right now, like you may have to run for your life at any moment. It's like Cindy has the power to crush you, to wound you deeply, and that terrifies you, so you run. Is that it?

John (tense body, clenched fists): Yes, that's accurate.

Therapist (leaning forward, speaking softly, slowly): What's happening for you right now, John, as you sit here, talking about this? I see your fists clench and your body go tense. What's happening right now inside of you?

John: Well, I *am* really tense. I guess this affects me a lot. The pornography helped relieve stress; I just felt like a failure in my marriage.

Therapist (voice soft, slow): What Cindy thinks about you is really important to you. You are terrified that she will reject you, that she will stomp on you and wound you deeply. That would be devastating for you, so you tense up, ready to run, but really behind the tension, you are scared, terrified.

John: Yes, I am really scared of what Cindy thinks about me.

Therapist: Could you tell Cindy that right now? Turn to her and say, "What you think about me is really important to me."

John (turns to Cindy, speaking in a somewhat shaky voice): What you think about me really matters to me.

Cindy: Well, it sure doesn't feel that way; it feels like you don't care what I think about anything.

Therapist: So this is a new experience for you, Cindy, to see
this part of John that cares deeply about what you
think and is terrified of failing you. It makes sense
that this would feel strange because the pattern that
has gripped your relationship coerces John into hiding these feelings and running away to protect himself from rejection.

In this excerpt, the therapist supported both partners and
created enough safety for Cindy to describe the traumatic
impact of John's online indiscretions. This was not a calm
recounting of events; Cindy was furious and she felt like a fool
for trusting him. Feeling threatened that he would be "stomped
on," John minimized and defended his position.

In Step 2 of the attachment injury resolution model, John and
Cindy articulated the impact of the infidelity and its attachment
significance. With the help of the therapist, Cindy was able to
access emotions underneath her fury, such as loneliness and fear
that she did not matter to John. Similarly, John acknowledged
feeling scared and afraid of being a failure in his marriage.

In Step 3, John was more emotionally engaged and able to
acknowledge that he devoted most of his time to work at the
expense of his family and that he understood Cindy's disappointment, anger, and loneliness. Although he felt quite competent at work, he admitted to feeling like a failure on the home
front. John elaborated on how pornography and his serendipi-
tous online sexual activity became an outlet for his stress
and loneliness: "Somehow in my mind it was okay; I never
intended to betray or hurt Cindy."

In Step 4, Cindy moved to a more precise articulation of
the betrayal and the rush of emotions surrounding the attachment trauma:

> How dare you! [Her eyes well up.] After all the years of me sup-
> porting you, how could you be so callous and turn to cyber-
> mates to feel better? [Tears are streaming down her face.] I feel so
> small and insignificant—like I never mattered to you. You have
> jeopardized everything we have: our marriage, our children,
> and our future. You have trampled on my heart. I am crushed.

With the therapist's help, John remained silent but stayed
engaged and listened to Cindy.

In Step 5, rather than minimize, rationalize, and defend his
position, John took full responsibility for his actions:

[His head is down and he speaks in a low voice.] I am such a foolish man and feel so ashamed for what I have done. [He looks up at Cindy.] I have hurt you and there is no excuse for my behavior. I do not want to throw away our marriage. There is no other; you are my priority. I'm not sure I'm worthy of forgiveness, but help me please...How can I make you feel safe again?

In Step 6, with the therapist's support, Cindy slowly moved from "I don't know what will make me feel safe; I guess I need time" to asserting her needs in a way that John could hear and respond to (e.g., "I want to be your confidant—the person you come to when you need support. I want to spend time with you—to laugh again, to hold me when I'm sad, and reassure me when I'm scared").

In Step 7, putting his hand on Cindy's knee, John said, "I want that for us...to be there for each other."

Cindy and John eventually were able to express and hear those needs in each other. Although John was fairly quick to express his deep care for Cindy and his fear of her rejection (withdrawer engagement), it took several sessions for Cindy to take this in and to soften toward him (blamer softening). This was consistent with the loss of trust given John's online sexual activity.

Rebuilding trust is one of the biggest challenges when working with a couple that has experienced the attachment trauma of infidelity. It is usually very difficult for the injured partner to trust that the spouse cares about and desires him or her. It has been suggested that rather than directly focusing on trust building, a better strategy for therapy is to focus on building emotional intimacy (Pittman & Wagers, 2005). This is precisely what the EFT therapist accomplished for John and Cindy. Although lack of trust can be a barrier to intimacy, identifying and expressing attachment longings eventually moved John and Cindy toward greater accessibility, responsiveness, and intimacy and helped Cindy to believe that John really cared for her. From there, trust evolved naturally.

By the end of therapy (17 sessions), Cindy was able to express her desire for closeness without anger, and John was able to hear that expression and respond to it without feeling rejected or criticized. This new and more positive pattern of relating and communicating their attachment needs and feelings for one another created closeness they had previously experienced in their marriage.

At times, John found this new dance a little uncomfortable, but Cindy's affirmation and encouragement motivated him to stay present. John began spending less time at work and did not bring work home in the evenings. He said this was partly because he was committed to working on their marriage and spending time with his family, and partly because he was finding home to be an increasingly pleasant and supportive place to be. Although Cindy was occasionally struck by the fear that John's thoughts were on some online sexual fantasy rather than with her in the moment, John was able to help alleviate this fear by talking to her out loud when they made love. These fears became progressively less obtrusive for Cindy over time.

CONCLUSION

An experienced EFT therapist is particularly skilled in addressing raw emotions, understanding relationship traumas, and slowly choreographing risk taking and the growth of trust between partners. A bonded relationship is the natural healing arena for emotional wounds, even when these wounds have been inflicted by the attachment figure in this relationship. In these cases, the therapist helps the wounded client deal with the dilemma that the other partner is the source of pain and fear and also the longed-for haven of comfort and healing reassurance. Empathic responsiveness, the effective owning of hurtful actions, and engaged reassuring emotional connection are key elements in the much needed assistance one partner can offer to a wounded other.

Essentially, EFT goals and interventions are the same when used with typical distressed couples as they are for couples presenting with more complex issues such as infidelity. However, in the latter couples, in Stage 1, there are more extreme responses of panic and anger with which to deal and the initial injury, as well as how the couple has failed to heal it, must be framed within the couple's negative interactional cycle. In Stage 2 of EFT, once the more withdrawn partner has become more available and the wounded partner is asked to risk deeper engagement, the therapist guides both into the systematic steps of the forgiveness of injury process where the abandonment, rejection, and separation distress associated with the affair can be healed. Partners can then, as in the general EFT process, share fears and ask for needs to be met, resulting in reconciliation and a more secure bond.

REFERENCES

Allen, E. S., & Atkins, D. C. (2005). The multidimensional and developmental nature of infidelity: Practical applications. *Journal of Clinical Psychology, 61,* 1371–1382.

Atkins, D. D., Baucom, D. H., & Jacobson, N. S. (2001). Understanding infidelity: Correlates in a national random sample. *Journal of Family Psychology, 15,* 735–749.

Atkinson, L. (1997). Attachment and psychopathology: From laboratory to clinic. In L. Atkinson & K. J. Zucker (Eds.), *Attachment and psychopathology* (pp. 3–16). New York, NY: Guilford Press.

Baucom, D., Shoham, V., Mueser, K., Daiuto, A., & Stickle, T. (1998). Empirically supported couple and family interventions for marital distress and adult mental health problems. *Journal of Consulting and Clinical Psychology, 66,* 53–88.

Baucom, D. H., Gordon, K. C., Snyder, D. K., Atkins, D. C., & Christensen, A. (2006). Treating affair couples: Clinical considerations and initial findings. *Journal of Cognitive Psychotherapy: An International Quarterly, 20,* 375–392.

Bercaw, B., & Bercaw, G. (2010). Finding healthy sexuality in recovering relationships. *Family Therapy Magazine, 9*(1), 32–37.

Blow, A. J., & Hartnett, K. (2005a). Infidelity in committed relationships I: A methodological review. *Journal of Marital and Family Therapy, 31,* 183–216.

Blow, A. J., & Hartnett, K. (2005b). Infidelity in committed relationships I: A substantive review. *Journal of Marital and Family Therapy, 31,* 217–233.

Christensen, A., & Jacobson, N. S. (2000). *Reconcilable differences.* New York, NY: Guilford Press.

Cloutier, P. F., Manion, I. G., Gordon-Walker, J., & Johnson, S. M. (2002). Emotionally focused interventions for couples with chronically ill children: A 2-year follow-up. *Journal of Marital and Family Therapy, 28,* 391–399.

Cooper, A., Putman, D. E., Planchon, L. A., & Boies, S. C. (1999). Online sexual compulsivity: Getting tangled in the net. *Sexual Addiction and Compulsivity, 6,* 79–104.

Dew, B., Brubaker, M., & Hays, D. (2006). From the altar to the Internet: Married men and their online sexual behavior. *Sexual Addiction and Compulsivity, 13,* 195–207.

Glass, S. (2003). *Not just friends: Protect your relationship from infidelity and heal the trauma of betrayal.* New York, NY: Simon & Schuster.

Goldberg, P. D., Peterson, B. D., Rosen, K. H., & Sara, M. L. (2008). Cybersex: The impact of a contemporary problem on the practices of marriage and family therapists. *Journal of Marital and Family Therapy, 34,* 469–480.

Gordon, K. C., Baucom, D. H., & Snyder, D. K. (2008). Optimal strategies in couple therapy: Treating couples dealing with the trauma of infidelity. *Journal of Contemporary Psychotherapy, 38,* 151–160.

Gottman, J. M., & Silver, N. (1999). *The seven principles for making marriage work.* New York, NY: Three Rivers Press.

Gottman, J. S. (2004). Extramarital affairs: The pearl in the oyster. In J. S. Gottman (Ed.), *The marriage clinic casebook* (pp. 47–68). New York, NY: W. W. Norton & Company.

Halchuk, R., Makinen, J., & Johnson, S. (2010). Resolving attachment injuries in couples: A 3-year follow-up study. *Journal of Couple and Relationship Therapy, 9,* 31–47.

Hertlein, K. M., & Webster, M. (2008). Technology, relationships, and problems: A research synthesis. *Journal of Marital and Family Therapy, 34,* 445–460.

Hertlein, K. M., Wetchler, J. L., & Piercy, F. P. (2005). Infidelity: An overview. In F. P. Piercy, K. M. Hertlein, & J. L. Wetchler (Eds.), *Handbook of the clinical treatment of infidelity* (pp. 5–16). New York, NY: Haworth Press.

Internet World Stats. (2010, June 30). World internet usage and population statistics. Retrieved December 2, 2010 from http://www.internetworldstats.com/stats.htm

Johnson, S. M. (2002). *Emotionally focused couple therapy with trauma survivors: Strengthening attachment bonds.* New York, NY: Guilford Press.

Johnson, S. M. (2004). *The practice of emotionally focused marital therapy: Creating connections* (2nd ed.). New York, NY: Brunner/Mazel.

Johnson, S. M. (2005). Broken bonds: An emotionally focused approach to infidelity. *Journal of Couple and Relationship Therapy, 4*(2/3), 17–29.

Johnson, S. M., Hunsley, J., Greenberg, L. S., & Schindler, D. (1999). Emotionally focused couples therapy: Status and challenges. *Clinical Psychology: Science and Practice, 6,* 67–79.

Johnson, S. M., & Makinen, J. A. (2003). Posttraumatic stress. In D. K. Snyder & M. A. Whisman (Eds.), *Treating difficult couples* (pp. 208–329). New York, NY: Guilford Press.

Johnson, S. M., Makinen, J. A., & Millikin, J. W. (2001). Attachment injuries in couple relationships: A new perspective in impasses in couples therapy. *Journal of Marital and Family Therapy, 27,* 145–155.

Johnson, S. M., & Williams-Keeler, L. (1998). Creating healing relationships for couples dealing with trauma: The use of emotionally focused couples therapy. *Journal of Marital and Family Therapy, 24,* 25–40.

Kinsey, A. C., Pomeroy, W. B., Martin, C. E., & Gebhard, P. H. (1953/1998). *Sexual behavior in the human female.* Bloomington, IN: Indiana University Press.

Lauman, E. O., Gagnon, J. H., Michael, R. T., & Michaels, S. (1994). *The social organization of sexuality.* Chicago, IL: University of Chicago Press.

MacIntosh, H. B., Hall, J., & Johnson, S. M. (2007). Forgive and forget: A comparison of emotionally focused and cognitive-behavioral models of forgiveness and intervention in the context of couple infidelity. In P. R. Peluso (Ed.), *Infidelity: A practitioner's guide to working with couples in crisis* (pp. 127–147). New York, NY: Routledge.

Maheu, M. M., & Subotnik, R. B. (2001). *Infidelity on the Internet: Virtual relationship and real betrayal.* Naperville, IL: Sourcebooks.

Makinen, J. A., & Johnson, S. (2006). Resolving attachment injuries in couples using EFT: Steps toward forgiveness and reconciliation. *Journal of Consulting and Clinical Psychology, 74,* 1055–1064.

Mikulincer, M. (1998). Attachment working models and the sense of trust: An exploration of interaction goals and affect regulation. *Journal of Personality and Social Psychology, 74,* 1209–1224.

O'Leary, K. D. (2005). Commentary on intrapersonal, interpersonal, and contextual factors in extramarital involvement. *Clinical Psychology: Science and Practice, 12,* 131–133.

Pittman, F. S., & Wagers, T. P. (2005). Teaching fidelity. *Journal of Clinical Psychology: In Session, 61,* 1407–1419.

Shackelford, T. K., Buss, D. M., & Bennett, K. (2002). Forgiveness or breakup: Sex differences in responses to a partner's infidelity. *Cognition and Emotion, 16,* 299–307.

Shaver, P., & Hazan, C. (1993). Adult romantic attachment: Theory and evidence. In D. Perlman & W. Jones (Eds.), *Advances in personal relationships* (Vol. 4; pp. 29–70). Philadelphia, PA: Jessica Kingsley.

Snyder, D. K., Baucom, D. H., & Gordon, K. C. (2007). *Getting past the affair: A program to help you cope, heal, and move on together or apart.* New York, NY: Guilford Press.

Stone, A. (1996). Trauma and affect. In D. Nathanson (Ed.), *Knowing and feeling* (pp. 288–302). New York, NY: Norton.

Subotnik, R. (2007). Cyber-infidelity. In P. R. Peluso (Ed.), *Infidelity: A practitioner's guide to working with couples in crisis* (pp. 169–190). New York, NY: Routledge.

Young, K. S., Griffin-Shelley, E., Cooper, A., O'Mara, J., & Buchanan, J. (2000). Online infidelity: A new dimension in couple relationships with implications for evaluation and treatment. *Sexual Addiction and Compulsivity, 7,* 59–74.

III

Specific Treatment Populations and Emotionally Focused Couple Therapy

Eleven

Emotionally Focused Therapy for Remarried Couples
Making New Connections and Facing Competing Attachments

JAMES L. FURROW AND GAIL PALMER

INTRODUCTION

Remarriage offers couples the promise of a second chance at love and connection, often following the loss of a previous relationship through death or divorce. Couples are seldom prepared for the unique challenges and opportunities faced in forming a marriage that commonly includes one and sometimes two existing families. For some partners, the earned wisdom of past relationships and the hope for a revived vision of a new family are realized in their remarriage. For others, these hopes fail to materialize amid the complexity of competing interests and emotional loyalties that can overwhelm the resources most needed in a new developing family.

At the center of this unfolding drama is the remarried couple, who may find themselves caught between their hopes for a bright future together, the pressures of balancing competing interests, and the ghosts of relationships past. This chapter explores the use of EFT with remarried couples and examines ways in which the EFT therapist can help couples build bonds in the midst of existing family commitments.

REMARRIED COUPLES

Estimates of the rates of remarriage in the United States vary based on the ways in which families are counted. As many as 1 in 10 children under the age of 18 is living with a biological parent and a step- or adoptive parent. Typical estimates suggest that stepfamilies are 11% of households in America, while others using more inclusive criteria report rates closer to one in six households (Stewart, 2007). The most common stepfamily household is headed by a biological mother, her child or children, and a stepfather.

Stepfamilies, and stepmothers in particular, have long been stigmatized by negative labels and assumptions about remarried families. These families are not seen on equal footing with first marriages, but rather have been portrayed as abnormal compared to nondivorced households that are considered more normal (Ganong & Coleman, 2004). The effect of this negative cultural bias can create a self-fulfilling prophecy particularly when remarried relationships fall into distress. Family researchers and therapists continue to challenge these stereotypes and the need for a professional and public appreciation of the unique roles and challenges faced by these more complex family systems (Ahrons & Rodgers, 1987; Walsh, 2003).

Most American stepfamilies are preceded by a divorce. Remarried couples face a slightly greater risk for divorce (5–10%), particularly when either partner enters remarriage with a child from a previous marriage (Bramlett & Mosher, 2001, 2002). While the increased risk is small, the demands of blending existing families is significant because both children and adults must adjust to new relationships within the stepfamily and accommodate new and existing relationships outside the household (Bumpass & Lu, 2000).

The process of stepfamily development requires time as newly remarried couples strengthen their bond and stepchildren and stepparents develop relationships that they did not choose. The development of a common identity as a new family requires attention to the unique experiences and needs of children, parents, and couples in the context of this developing family (Papernow, 1993). A remarried couple's ability to remain responsive and accessible to each other is critical for retaining a more emotionally stable and securely connected relationship in the midst of competing emotional demands.

COMMON ISSUES FACING REMARRIED COUPLES

Couples entering stepfamily life together must navigate a number of challenges in the development of a strong bond. These include managing their personal experience of unrealistic or underinformed expectations, facing parenting challenges while supporting stepparent and stepchild relationships, and addressing internal fears and strains in managing the transition to a new family reality. For a detailed literature review of these and similar challenges facing remarried couples, see Falke and Larson (2007). In this chapter we review four primary challenges: (1) unrealistic and unmet expectations, (2) partnering and parenting, (3) unresolved loss and loyalty struggles, and (4) children in stepfamilies.

Unrealistic and Unmet Expectations

Remarried couples often see their new family life as a second chance at marriage. These couples commonly adopt various myths about stepfamily life, including the assumption that all couples' relationships are the same and their remarriage will be like a first marriage (Visher & Visher, 1988). Even though it is obvious to all that there are different people involved in the remarried couple's life, the psychological expectation is that one can start over and have marriage on its original terms. As a result, these couples fail to anticipate the unique ways in which remarriage is different from a first-time marriage.

Remarried couples in general tend to have couple relationships that are less cohesive than a first marriage (Coleman, Ganong, & Fine, 2000). If either adult is also a parent, the couple may find that parents have a stronger emotional tie to their children than to their remarried spouse (Anderson & White, 1986). Parents can presume the hope of an "instant love" between a child and a stepparent, but often the subtle pressure and expectation of this "love" threatens the safety of a stepparent and stepchild's relationship (Bray & Kelly, 1998). The pain of these unmet expectations can also lead to an emerging distance in the couple's relationship as secretly they hold on to hopes that their life together will be less fraught with disappointment.

Shifts in emotional ties defining biological and step-relationships require time (Papernow, 1993) and families often come to appreciate the uniqueness of the relationships, though they are often different from what was expected. While these

relationships do not always fit partners' expectations, a couple
can find new ways to value these unique relationships. Doug,
a father in a blended family composed of two children from
his wife Sara and one son from his first marriage, described
how he has come to reconcile his experience of stepfamily life
as unique:

> It's part of becoming, you know; our family is melded into a
> new family. But it's a very distinctive and different concept of
> being a family. Because Sara and I know that there's a family
> within our family and that's my wife, Sara, Lee, and Cindy. And
> sometimes that's like there's a heart connection; there's a birth
> connection between those three. And we need to respect that.
> And then my son Dave and I, we have that. So sometimes it's
> okay if we play on that a little bit. But then we also know that
> we have chosen to get together, to merge these three groups.

Partnering and Parenting

Couples with children from a previous marriage find their
own marital adjustment tied to their children's adjustment to
stepfamily life. Bray and Kelly (1998) conclude that within an
intact original family, a couple's relationship typically has a
significant influence on a child's adjustment and on how the
couple parent together. For stepfamilies, the direction of this
influence seems to flow in the opposite direction. The effect
of children on the quality of a remarried couple's relationship
is more often than not compelling and negative, and the critical relationship determining this influence is the stepchild–
stepparent relationship (Falke & Larson, 2007).

Parenting issues for couples in stepfamilies involve both
issues of trust (inclusion) and issues of control (power). For
example, a stepfather may assume responsibility for disciplining a child (power) without having established a basic level
of shared trust or mutual interest (inclusion). Doherty and
Colangelo (1984) concluded that actions of power and control
flow first from inclusion and, without this as a base, conflict
will erupt as the parent's influence is based almost solely on
positional power without an earned basis of trust. Parental
discipline poses a challenge to stepparenting relationships,
particularly when parental demands are imposed on relationships that have yet to develop a felt sense of mutual respect
and security. Postdivorce parenting requires that adults rene-
gotiate both issues of influence and expectations for closeness
with children at a time of family transition (Emery & Dillon,

1994). The same is true in remarriage, where parents and step-parents must continue to find ways to honor their family differences while at the same time working together to nurture a deeper sense of belonging (Papernow, 1993).

Remarried partners are easily divided by parenting issues. The biological ties of parent and child relationships are often more compelling than those of step-relations and often carry more influence in the family than a couple's developing bond. Fine and Kurdek (1995) found that stepparents were more likely to attribute marital problems to stemming from the relational issues in stepparenting rather than parenting issues with biological children. The spillover of negative stepparent–stepchild relationships can easily undermine the stability of a couple's relationship as parenting issues are charged by parental guilt and loyalty to children.

Delaying stepparent involvement in parental discipline may prove helpful for many couples in reducing the escalation of loyalty conflicts between stepparents and stepchildren because stepparents are encouraged to "earn" their influence in the lives of stepchildren (Visher, Visher, & Pasley, 2003). A biological parent's support of her child's relationship to a nonresidential biological parent is also a factor commonly associated with better adjustments for children and the remarried family as a whole (Buunk & Massaers, 1999; Knox & Zusman, 2001).

Parenting tasks alone place demands on remarried couples. Parent role strain is common in family households that are reorganizing following periods of single parenting. Couples may assume that partners will adopt specific responsibilities based on past patterns of relating. Role ambiguity for the stepparent is a significant source of frustration for remarried couples as partners struggle to find a place in the family and to identify what is expected of them (Falke & Larson, 2007). Parenting tasks are complicated when parents and stepparents must consolidate the demands of raising children across varied developmental stages, all at the same time. These different needs and challenges may demand that parents respond equally to the instrumental needs of a toddler and the socio-emotional needs of an adolescent.

This developmental "mash up" strains parents caught between the child-centric needs of a preschooler while managing more flexible boundaries with the egocentric expectations of a young adult. The couple's ability to recognize and attend to their own relationship needs is challenged by the complex demands of integrating children's varying developmental demands and available resources all at once. Equally, the diversity of partners' parenting experiences can bring greater family resilience and resourcefulness when remarried parents are able to work together from the secure base of their relationship.

Unresolved Loss and Loyalty Struggles

Couples and children in stepfamilies must make sense of being in relationships where being a family embodies both past and present experience. In the early stages of stepfamily development, a child may cling to a strong loyalty to "the family we used to be." While understanding the child's attachment to the past, the parent is torn by the emotional commitments she has made to "move on" together as a new family. In turn, her remarried partner may experience his spouse's struggle between the past and present as a sign of ambivalence about the remarriage.

The emotional tensions enacted in the everyday life of the family can create reactive patterns of insecurity for couples and families alike. These patterns can be triggered as stepfamilies negotiate the varying interests and needs of a two-family or binuclear system (Ahrons & Rodgers, 1987). These tensions may lie dormant in families until particular nodal events (e.g., weddings, graduations, funerals) highlight the tensions between the family that was and the family that is.

Postdivorce parenting poses unique challenges to remarried couples. The continued presence of and contact with a former partner can prompt insecurity for remarried partners, particularly when their own relationship is under duress. The process of emotional detachment from a former partner takes time, and physical distance often is limited, particularly when the former couple shares joint custody of their biological children. A conflictual divorce may reinforce patterns of defensiveness that continue to pervade postdivorce parenting.

In turn, the persisting distress between divorced partners may draw in a new partner, who responds with sympathy for their spouse, and may lead to a growing frustration over the negative effects of a relationship over which they have no influence (Ahrons & Rodgers, 1987; Johnston & Campbell, 1988). Finally, financial obligations to a former partner and children from a previous marriage may create resentment for remarried spouses, particularly when the loss of this income has a perceived or demonstrable impact on the remarried couple's resources (Knox & Zusman, 2001).

The psychological presence of a former partner can be equally difficult for remarried couples. Knox and Zusman (2001) reported that as many as one in three remarried wives described their husbands as still emotionally attached to a former spouse. Others found that a majority of remarried men expressed regret over divorcing their first wife within the first years of their remarriage (Reibstein, 1998). Unresolved losses present an enduring obstacle, particularly for partners who experienced rejection in their previous marriage. Feelings of insecurity and a sense of failure from the previous relationship often color a partner's emotional availability to his or her remarried spouse (Pacey, 2005). Similarly, biological parents may confront guilt over their children's unresolved losses, which are attributed to the parents' divorce.

Children in Stepfamilies

Generally, children in stepfamilies are more likely to confront challenges in social, emotional, and academic functioning compared to children of similar age in nondivorced nuclear families (Hetherington, 1999). John and Emily Visher (1996) summarized children's challenges in a stepfamily as a struggle with "loss, loyalty, and a lack of control" (p. 150). Stepchildren in many stepfamilies face reduced contact with their noncustodial biological parent. This loss of contact may be complicated by the boundary ambiguity defining many postdivorce parent–child relationships. Braver and O'Connell (1998) suggest that divorce leaves many noncustodial parents feeling "parentally disenfranchised" or of little practical or psychological consequence to their children. Stepchildren uniquely experience the resulting physical and emotional distance as a loss, which in a developing stepfamily may go unacknowledged by the other biological parent. These losses fuel loyalty struggles as children seek to find a place to belong.

Adolescents face unique challenges in stepfamilies. Youth can find themselves caught between two households, while at the same time seeking to establish a level of individuation from and intimacy with their biological parents (Bray & Harvey, 1995). Remarriage increases the loyalty binds for youth as family pressures youth to emotionally invest in the blended family. Similarly, adolescents may experience greater expectations to accept the influence of stepparents in relationships in which they have little or no emotional investment. An adolescent's anger or acting-out behavior may escalate tensions for the remarried couple. Partners divide on parental issues as stepparents either engage or withdraw from a parent–child conflict and biological parents feel caught between the needs of the child and the expectations of their partner. Loyalty issues are particularly problematic when the remarriage follows infidelity involving the biological parent and the stepparent. In this case, the child's loss and loyalty conflicts are directly linked with a parental breach of trust (Pam & Pearson, 1998).

Parenting and stepparenting demands compete for the emotional energy that remarried partners seek to invest in their marriage. The unspoken irony for families working through these transitions is that parents and children alike feel a loss of influence and control over attaining what they need and what they want most. The experiences of stepchildren and stepparents are not the same as those in the family that shares biological and emotional ties (Papernow, 1993). Adolescents in particular are sensitive to the loss of their perceived influence in the family. A youth's struggle to gain acceptance on his or her own terms often parallels the struggle of a stepparent to fit in.

The risk for remarried couples is that parenting conflicts can create a divide between partners over their attempts to resolve tensions in the family as a whole. For example, when a stepfather seeks to reign in the acting-out behavior of his stepson as a favor to his wife, he becomes confused by her frustration and criticism that his actions are overly harsh and ineffective. The stepfather becomes discouraged that his attempts to help are not appreciated and he withdraws from her criticism. She is confused and angered by his withdrawal when she mistakes his coping response as a further effort to control the situation. The stepfamily bonds and their relationship feel more fragile as a result.

ATTACHMENT AND REMARRIED COUPLES

Attachment and Loss

An understanding of loss is essential in conceptualizing the relational patterns and attachment-related dynamics of a remarried family. Stepfamilies have been described as being "born of loss" (Visher et al., 2003) to indicate the pervasive role that this emotional theme plays in the formation of a stepfamily. Parents and children experience loss differently and, when loss goes unacknowledged, loyalty conflicts emerge. Newly remarried couples may find it difficult or threatening to attend to a child's experience of loss in the transition to a new family life. For the couple, remarriage represents the beginning of a new life together. But for a child, this change marks the end of hopes for reunification or, for some, the loss of a favored status in their parent's life. These losses organize the family's experience as children externalize their grief through acting out or internalize their pain in more anxious and depressive ways and parents must make choices of how to respond to the resulting distress. Couples can mistake the loyalty conflicts as power struggles rather than signs of the unspoken losses that organize this new chapter in a family's unfolding story (Doherty, 1999).

In their remarriage, Susan and Matt found themselves locked in struggles with their adolescent children. These challenges escalated over time as angry outbursts, substance use, and parasuicidal behaviors marked the significant pain of each child involved. Both Matt and Susan grew distant as each parent defended his or her biological child and complained about the increasingly unreasonable behavior of the stepson or stepdaughter. Parents grew weary and as partners they began to feel alienated from each other, particularly when they were with the children. The family became locked in their struggles to manage extreme behaviors and to limit the damage done by escalating conflicts. A vicious pattern driven by parental control, personal shame, and the family's unspoken fears took over the family.

For many couples, the losses of remarriage reflect the losses children experience as a result of a family estrangement in which they were not directly involved. Younger children may internalize a degree of ownership for this loss, assuming a hidden responsibility for the demise of their parents' former marriage. A divorced parent experiences this loss directly. The residual effects of the divorce on parenting relationships and on couple relationships in remarriage are influenced by the nature of the dissolution and the perceived choice the adult had in determining the matter (Pam & Pearson, 1998). Physical separations can be experienced as traumatic moments for divorcing couples and the psychological impact of these losses may continue to organize a partner's experience of felt security in a future remarriage, including greater sensitivity to any signs of a disconnection in this new relationship (Guttmann, 1993). A therapist's ability to explore and understand the dimensions of loss that extend into remarriage is crucial in terms of making sense of the patterns of distress more common to remarried couples.

John Bowlby (1973) recognized that the losses experienced through estrangement are distinctly different from those experienced in death. In estrangement, the continued presence of an attachment figure complicates the process of mourning this loss. Further, this experience of loss may include vacillations in levels of affection in these relationships, which foster conflicting impressions of emotional sentiment and intention (Hazan & Shaver, 1992). The resolution of these losses typically requires an extended period of time before emotional detachment can occur (Feeney & Monin, 2008). Bowlby's observations are helpful in understanding the challenges facing stepfamilies where a remarriage has followed a recent divorce. The changes experienced in more rapid marital transitions often increase the relational distress experienced between parents and children and, as a result, this distress can come between remarried partners.

Competing attachments are the chief challenge facing remarried families. The remarried couple must find ways to balance the need to strengthen their marital relationship without foregoing the emotional needs of their children. In the beginning stages of stepfamily life, balancing these attachment-related needs takes place in a context where the most vulnerable bond (couple) receives the most attention and the most powerful bonds (parental) may be taken for granted. Ironically, spouses, parents, and children all tend to question their own place and belonging in a family that is powered more by hopes and aspirations than the experience of an enduring emotional bond.

A reduction in a biological parent's accessibility and responsiveness fosters insecurity and secondary emotional responses in children with both biological parents and stepparents. Frustrated that their bids for attachment remain unacknowledged or dismissed, children respond in predictable patterns of protest and despair. Typical adjustment issues faced by children from divorced families reflect attachment-related distress, where the loss of parental support fosters patterns of insecurity and corresponding attempts to reengage parental figures. A child's access to parental attachment figures is essential to supporting the efforts of a child to make space for a new adult in her or his family. Children need to stay attached to their biological parents and also to make room for a parent's new relationship with another adult.

Conflicts emerge between couples when parenting tension and role expectations heighten patterns of emotional withdrawal and critical demands. For example, Steve expresses frustration about his stepdaughter Gwen's insolence and his wife Julie's laissez-faire response. Steve's critical concern, which has become an expected refrain, leaves Julie cool and indifferent to his demands that she address Gwen's increasingly rebellious streak. Gwen responds to Steve's complaints by threatening to move in with her biological father, who "still cares about me." Julie feels caught in reassuring Steve about his place in the family and the fear she has that, in doing so, she will push Gwen farther away. Julie is holding on to the hope that when Gwen moves on to college in a couple of years, she and Steve can have a less complicated life together. Steve is losing his patience in a family where he feels obligated to provide support and increasingly unwanted. All this is heightened when Julie confides in Gwen's father about her fears and concerns related to their daughter's growing defiance, for which Steve feels that he is increasingly to blame.

EFT AND INTERVENING WITH REMARRIED COUPLES

The overlapping impact of competing attachments typically results in the EFT therapist beginning with family treatment. Emotionally focused family therapy (EFFT) follows a progression and emphasis similar to that of its more established sister, EFCT (emotionally focused couple therapy). The therapist works with family members to access underlying emotions and attachment needs, thoughtfully reframing a family's issues in terms of these unspoken fears and needs. The sessions also promote the acceptance of other family members' experiences and create opportunities for the sharing of attachment needs (Palmer & Efron, 2007).

The therapist identifies problematic patterns in dyads and triads in a process with multiple family members. Session work then includes the therapist working exclusively in dyads around these patterns rather than with the family as a whole. This is particularly important because blended families tend to confuse attachment-related issues between biological parents and children (Furrow & Palmer, 2007). The therapist focuses a parent's attention and fosters a positive response to her children's primary emotions and emerging attachment needs.

The EFFT therapist helps family members clarify potential competing attachments by working within specific dyads (e.g., biological parent and child, remarried couple) separately.

The goal of EFFT with remarried families is to help all members deal with the transition, including grieving the "old" family and engaging loving bonds in the new family. The process assumes that a parent has a responsibility to initiate an accessible and responsive position with his or her child. In EFCT this responsibility is regarded as shared or reciprocal, but in EFFT the therapist is working to help the parent "reach toward" her child's vulnerability as an offer of support.

Similar to the priority given in couples therapy to engaging a more withdrawn partner first, in EFFT it is necessary for the therapist to engage the parent before engaging a child in sharing attachment-related needs and wants. A parent's secondary responses and underlying emotions are processed first to assure that the parent is more available and responsive to a child's underlying emotion. As parents become more responsive to their child's needs, new patterns of security emerge for the family. In the final phase of therapy, the therapist focuses on strengthening the various ways family members can emotionally invest in the remarried family. Over time, the family makes new ways both practically and emotionally to foster a shared sense of being family.

EFT AND THE REMARRIED COUPLE

Treatment of remarried couples in EFCT follows a three-stage model of change. First, in Stage 1, the therapist clarifies the boundary between former spouses and the current family/relationship. Issues related to disputed custody arrangements and similar conflicts with a former partner are referred outside treatment to family mediation. Negotiation of these issues is not part of couple therapy. This enables the therapist to remain focused on process of the remarried couple's relationship, where patterns of competing attachments typically color the distress the remarried pair experience.

Themes of rejection and abandonment are common for children of divorced parents and also common among stepparents. In the early stages of a developing stepfamily, stepparents are the "outsiders" both historically and emotionally (Papernow, 1993). Other patterns involve a responsible but ineffective parent who may vacillate between placating his or her child and recruiting the past or new partner to provide parental support. These parents struggle with guilt over the impact of a previous divorce on the child and hope to appease the child

Table 11.1 Common Descriptions of Underlying Emotional Experience

Biological Parent	Child	Stepparent
Guilt–shame	Abandoned–alone	Rejected
Alone–overwhelmed	Afraid	Inadequate
Afraid of failure	Inadequate	Afraid to fail
Invisible	Not important	Excluded
Not important	Judged–criticized	Afraid–scared
Desperate	Excluded	Judged–criticized

and the present partner at the same time. Many of the underlying emotions experienced by parents, children, or stepparents may be shared in session as individuals confide these often unacknowledged experiences (Table 11.1). The therapist reframes the couple's stuck pattern that has overtaken their best efforts to support the building of this new family and partnership. The underlying experience of each partner is validated, including efforts to make a difference in the midst of this family's transition.

CASE EXAMPLE

Mark and Jenny, a couple in their 30s, sought family therapy for problems they were having with Mark's daughter, Olivia, age 6. The couple had been married for over a year and Olivia lived with them on a half-time basis. Mark and his first wife, Sharon, had been married for 6 years prior to adopting Olivia, who was a toddler at the time. It was shortly after the adoption that Mark and Sharon divorced. Mark had been sharing the custody of Olivia with Sharon for a period of 2 years before meeting Jenny and the couple dated for a year before marrying. Jenny's marriage to Mark was her first and she had been living alone prior to their wedding.

Mark and Jenny were seen together at the initial intake session, where Jenny defined the "family problem" as Olivia's "pathological and destructive behavior." For Jenny, "Olivia's behaviors are rude and her manners are intolerable. She completely ignores me when I speak to her and she completely avoids me in the house." Jenny's intensity increased as she continued to share her concerns about Olivia's inconsistent grooming habits and poor table manners. By contrast, Mark responded in a staid and calm manner:

> I really don't see her quite this way. Yes, Olivia does have issues with her manners and she is rude to Jenny, but this is from her mother Sharon, my ex—not from what is happening in our home. Besides, Olivia is 6 years old and has gone through a number of adjustments this past year. So I think we just need to give her some time.

Mark expressed appreciation for Jenny's recent support of Olivia during her evaluation and treatment for a learning disorder. The therapist shifted the focus to the couple's relationship after determining that Olivia's behavioral problems were minor and her learning difficulties were being addressed.

Mark and Jenny summarized the troubling arguments they have when trying to talk about their differing perceptions of Olivia. The therapist tracked their accounts, focusing on each person's reaction while seeking to elicit each partner's emotional experience. In frustration, Jenny shared her growing resentment of Olivia's dismissive behavior and her anger at Mark's lack of concern for her feelings. Mark expressed his concerns for Olivia and her adjustment to the new family arrangement, side-stepping Jenny's complaints. Jenny saw this as Mark "taking sides" and experienced this as his withdrawal from her. Over time, silence had grown between this couple as they became more reluctant to speak these concerns at home. Sadly, the silence became unbearable for both of them, especially when Olivia was out of the home.

Their typical pattern followed a predictable spiral of escalation. As Mark withdrew, Jenny's criticisms of Olivia heightened. Mark responded by focusing more on Olivia. Tearfully, Jenny recounted a recent argument that ended with Mark's tersely suggesting to Jenny that she "grow up" while turning and walking off with Olivia "with great kindness and gentleness." Mark showed very little response to Jenny's tears as he concluded with resignation, "I am so exhausted. I am trying to do it all and it just never seems good enough." The therapist guided their attention away from the issue of Olivia's behavior problems and increased attention to the negative pattern that had come to define their relationship.

Common to the early stages of stepfamily development, their pattern was consistent with the insider/outsider positions that typically define the unique experiences of being a biological parent versus being a stepparent. Jenny felt like she was left out of Mark and Olivia's tight bond. Mark felt stranded in a "no-win" situation, caught between his wife, who wanted his allegiance, and his daughter, who needed his support. The couple was caught in a struggle of competing attachments.

As treatment unfolded, the therapist helped to clarify the cycle (Step 2) and elicit each partner's underlying emotions and the attachment needs that were getting lost in the distance produced by their problematic pattern. Jen and Mark began to experience more hope as their pattern came into focus and the therapist drew attention to the couple's strengths: the deep love they shared for each other and the ways in which they had worked as a team to secure treatment for Olivia's learning difficulties. In light of these strengths, it was the negative impact of the cycle that threatened their ability to work as a team and undermined their efforts to support each other. The couple welcomed the therapist's shift in focus. Talking together, the couple began to see the need to strengthen their bond as the goal, rather than trying to "fix" Olivia or blame each other.

Following individual sessions with both partners, the therapist had a better understanding of their different attachment histories and their unique experience of the negative pattern that left them in despair. The security of the therapist's alliance enabled the couple to explore the frustrations, disappointments, and hurt that had developed between them. Both Mark and Jenny expressed a reluctance to really look at their relationship because of their fears about losing their young and vulnerable marriage. Mark had already "failed" in one marriage and Jen had waited a long time before finding Mark. Both owned a sense of embarrassment at having to seek help for a marriage less than a year old. Ironically, the couple's focus on Olivia allowed them to avoid looking at the one resource that would help Olivia the most: a strong and secure marriage.

The therapist helped the couple explore and process the emotional histories they each brought to the relationship. As they recognized the distance and distress resulting from their pattern and the resource their relationship could provide to Olivia, Mark and Jen began to explore how things had become so distant between them. In reviewing their attachment histories, Jen began to appreciate how her parent's efforts to promote her self-reliance in the face of the chronic illnesses she faced as a child had made her successful professionally, but also more likely to rely on herself rather than others, including Mark. Mark recalled a close relationship with his mother, but felt distant from a father whom he hardly knew, one who never gave him the support that he needed. In his first marriage, Mark was the caretaker for a wife he did not feel he could count on in any significant way. In contrast, Jen was the first woman he felt he could rely on emotionally, although he did not know how to access her support.

As therapy continued, the couple was better able to recognize the pattern of pursuit and withdraw that developed as their emotions and needs went unspoken and unacknowledged. Mark identified his tendency to retreat from Jen, often pulling away through a mix of criticism and dismissal of Jen's feelings. His retreat was complicated by his need to care for Olivia and the guilt he felt around failing her as a father. Rather than just turning away from Jen, he would often turn toward Olivia. If Jenny upped the ante by complaining further about Olivia, Mark's frustration would lead him to close off from Jenny, effectively shutting her out. In turn, Jen saw that her attacks and lashing out at Mark occurred when she felt the painful isolation of his withdrawal. This cycle left Mark feeling defeated. He felt he was working hard to please Jen and shared how he felt unable to meet her needs, particularly when he seemed hopelessly caught "in the middle" between Jenny and Olivia.

The following transcript illustrates the therapist delineating the couple's pattern and evoking each partner's underlying emotional experience:

Therapist: So, Mark, when you say that you feel in the middle with Jen and Olivia, I am wondering what that's like for you.

Mark: Frustrating. I find that I am the mediator, caught between both sides, and if I say something Jen doesn't like, I get swatted down. If I ignore Olivia, I feel guilty. I have a lot on my plate with all of Olivia's needs, but there are just all these barriers—it's just too difficult to communicate.

Therapist: And when you feel swatted down, when you are working hard to please Jen, you want both of the people you love to be happy. And then no matter how hard you try, Jen isn't happy. That must be hard. (Therapist reframes Mark's actions in an attachment context.)

Mark: It's discouraging. It's like I just don't have the tools and it's better if I just stay quiet. (He turns away and looks down.)

Therapist: This is where you shut down—yes? Where you shut her out? It is just too painful to stay here. (Mark sighs, remaining silent.) What is happening for you right now, as we talk about this? You just sighed. It feels like there is a lot in that sigh. (The evocative question draws on the emotion in the room.)

Mark (eyes welling, flushed face): It makes me feel sad. I need Jen. I count on her.

Therapist: Jen is very important to you. It saddens you when you can't reach her. I am wondering if she knows this about you. (Therapist is accessing and processing underlying emotion in the context of the relationship.)

Mark: I don't know; she should know.

Therapist: I am wondering if you can tell her about the sadness. Can you tell her here right now? (Therapist directs an enactment for Mark to share his underlying experience.)

Mark (turns and looks at Jen): You are everything to me. I wish you knew that. It's hard for me sometimes. I get scared and sad.

As Mark accessed his underlying emotion, Jen experienced him differently and saw that he was not dismissing her or choosing his daughter over her. Predictably, the dialogue opened up a space for the couple where Mark was able to talk more directly to Jen about his needs. Mark shared how hard it was for him to ask for what he needed and how often he felt that he needed to "hunker down" and handle everything on his own. He believed that issues with Olivia were essentially "his problem." Jen responded that when she was not included, she felt helpless, powerless, and not important to Mark.

These times were very hard for Jen because she wanted nothing more than to support him, especially when she could see him struggling. Mark was moved by her words and he began to take steps to reengage Jen by letting her know how much he needed her help and support. He wanted her to know they were both on the "same team." He shared that, in those times, he just needed her acceptance and tolerance and it was helpful for her to "stay out" of trying to fix Olivia. What he needed, instead, was for her to put those things aside and come and stand beside him.

This was a risk for Mark. He feared Jen's disapproval, and asking directly for his needs to be met meant he had to be vulnerable. The therapist reframed Mark's request in attachment terms, using Mark's words about being a team and working to strengthen the bond they shared as means to clarify Mark's attachment bid to Jen. While owning his primary role as Olivia's father, Mark also expressed some specific ways Jen could make a difference for Olivia. This included helping him with the more "feminine" aspects of Olivia's life.

Jen expressed relief around knowing specifically how Mark needed her. She also felt appreciation for having her own special role in the family. Jen began to feel like she mattered to Mark as a partner, and she could see how they could better work at parenting Olivia as a team. Mark began to see Jen as an ally and began to seek her out for help and support. He recalled a time when he asked Jen to help Olivia get ready for a special occasion, saying, "There was no way I could have got those barrettes right." Both smiled as they recounted Olivia's delight in having Jen's input and "good hair"!

Mark's willingness to trust Jen and share his need for her and his need to support his daughter foreshadowed Jen's willingness to share the attachment fears and longings that were triggered for her in the couple's struggles. Jen fought to find her place in "this family" she was joining. When issues with Olivia were a concern, she would try to help Mark "fix" Olivia in hopes of securing a place alongside him. When Mark would withdraw and exclude her, Jen would either withdraw or redouble her efforts to make a difference. This became a desperate place for Jen. For her, there was no "real honeymoon" and no place to be a couple. Instead she was always a part of a family of three. This was a loss she felt deeply. When Mark focused on Olivia, Jen felt all the more rejected and alone, like she had been "jilted" or "put off." When she needed him, Mark turned to the other female in his life.

In Session 10, the therapist retraced the steps of accessing and deepening the attachment emotions and longing with Jen. This touched the hurt that often left her feeling insecure with Mark. This "terrible loneliness" would leave Jen feeling that she "was doing something wrong" and she would cringe in the face of the rejection that seemed so evident in Mark's withdrawal. Mark, now more reengaged, responded by offering words of reassurance. He wanted Jen to be able to turn to him so that he could support and take care of her. Following what felt like an invitation from Mark, the therapist turned to Jen, encouraging her to reach out for Mark's support, particularly on issues related to Olivia.

Jen: I need you to know where I am coming from and not see me as the mean and wicked stepmom. I love Olivia. She is a part of you, but there are times I just don't like her. I need to be able to talk to you about that, without you just shutting down or walling me out.

Therapist: What's that like, Mark, for you to hear this from Jen?

Mark: What am I supposed to do then when there is a conflict with Olivia? I need to protect her.

Therapist: Before you go there, Mark, can you stay here? I am wondering, right now, what it is like to hear Jen say this to you right now.

Mark: Well, actually, it makes me feel closer to her. To hear her say she loves Olivia, that makes me feel closer to her and maybe we can work out how to deal with issues with Olivia together.

While taking steps of increasing vulnerability, Jen held back from her deeper, more vulnerable attachment need. There was still more work ahead; however, the couple found greater security in the relationship as they took risks with each other. By Session 12, Jen reported, "Mark makes me feel good most of the time." Note in the following excerpt how the therapist now follows Jen's experience to return to the opportunity she has to reach for Mark in a new way.

Therapist: So I am wondering what it is like for you now. You both are saying things are pretty good and, Jen, you said that the two of you are better now, I am wondering how that is feeling for you?

Jen: Well we do have things moving pretty smoothly but I still feel nervous. I have my doubts.

Therapist: It's hard really to hold onto this. It sounds like part of you feels pretty good, but there is another part: where the doubt comes up, where you wonder whether this is something you can really hold on to. "Are we really a solid couple?" (Therapist prompts attachment-related fear.)

Jen: Yes, I mean what happens if there is another crisis with Olivia? It's so hard if we cannot agree and then I don't see the light at the end of the tunnel.

Therapist: Then it gets dark. If you can't find a way to connect, you have lost him somehow and that sounds scary.

Jen: It's like echoes of the past. It's going to be challenging all over again.

Therapist: These echoes, these doubts—these are the things that are scary?

Jen: I am not sure. I think it will depend on how well Olivia does.

Therapist: That must be scary not to know, not to be certain. "Can I really trust you? Will you be there for me? Or will I lose you?" (Therapist offers evocative question with heightening.)

Jen: I have always been alone.

Therapist: Yes, fighting your own battles, struggling all alone. That's what you are used to. To even imagine there is someone just for you, to be there for you—that seems almost unreal...unnatural somehow. (This empathic conjecture is drawing her to the leading edge of her experience.)

Jen: You got it (starts to cry).

Therapist: Yes, that hurts. It's so scary even to imagine that Mark is there. That you are that special to him and that he would want to be there, just for you. Does Mark know how scared you get sometimes? (Therapist is heightening her underlying fear in an attachment context.)

Jen: I am not sure. Do you?

Mark: You don't talk to me about this...

Therapist: Is this something you would like to hear about?

Mark: Yes. That is what I am here for. I want to know.

Therapist: What would that be like to share a bit of this? Is this something you can let him know? (Therapist is setting up the enactment.)

Jen (shakes her head): I am not that scared.

Therapist: This is too hard, to turn to Mark right now, that is too hard. It feels like you need to be careful. (Therapist is heightening attachment-related affect.)

Jen: I am just not sure. I really don't know.

Therapist: It's hard to know. "If I turn, what will happen?" This seems risky somehow.

Jen: I am not sure if he will be there. Can he really be there?

Therapist: Those are the doubts. That is what echoes. Will he be there? I am so scared that he won't. We've come so far and I am afraid we will lose it all. This is too hard to say to him? (Therapist is processing Jen's fears of reaching to Mark with her vulnerability.)

Jen: It is scary.
Therapist: Yes, this is hard; can you tell him what you need?
Jen (raising her face to him): I need to know you are there for me.

Jen acknowledged her need for Mark from a new position of greater vulnerability. Inside, she questioned whether she really belonged and if she really mattered to him. Her challenge was to let Mark into her fear and to seek the comfort she had been longing to know. Her risk to reach out to Mark led to a shift in how she approached him with her needs and fears. Together, the couple began to find new ways to strengthen the security of their relationship. As a couple, Jen and Mark grew in their confidence to confide in each other and as a family the couple's strengthened bond became a resource to Olivia. Jen saw Olivia as a valued part of their life together rather than an obstacle to what she needed most in her marriage.

Olivia in turn was more expressive and supportive of Jen as well. Mark acknowledged the sense of hope he experienced when they acted as a family working together as one. He expressed specific appreciation for the partnership he felt with Jen. The couple developed a code word for describing their new cycle called "PVR": patience, validation, and recognition. By Session 14, Mark and Jen described their relationship as a sanctuary and a resource they both could rely on and they felt confident about moving forward together in the future as a couple and as parent and stepparent to Olivia.

CONCLUSION

For many couples, the hopes found in remarriage are tested by the changes and challenges of stepfamily adjustment. Remarried couples may find themselves in patterns of insecurity where the competing attachments of biological and step relationships impact each partner's availability and responsiveness. The EFT therapist helps couples access the emotional experience underlying these patterns, and the EFT process fosters new opportunities for couples to reengage and respond to the attachment bids made by both children and spouses in these developing families. A therapist's work with these emotional ties strengthens the relationship of the couple and creates a new resource for both parents and children.

REFERENCES

Ahrons, C., & Rodgers, R. (1987). *Divorced families: Meeting the challenge of divorce and remarriage.* New York, NY: Norton.

Anderson, J. Z., & White, G. D. (1986). An empirical investigation of interaction and relationship patterns in functional and dysfunctional nuclear and step families. *Family Process, 25,* 407–422.

Bowlby, J. (1973). *Attachment and loss: Vol. 2. Separation: Anxiety and anger.* New York, NY: Basic Books.

Bramlett, M. D., & Mosher, W. D. (2001). First marriage, dissolution, divorce, and remarriage: United States (advanced data from vital and health statistics no. 323). Hyattsville, MD: National Center for Health Statistics.

Bramlett, M. D., & Mosher, W. D. (2002). Cohabitation, marriage, divorce, and remarriage in the United States (vital and health statistics, series 223, no. 22). Hyattsville, MD: National Center for Health Statistics.

Braver, S. L., & O'Connell, D. (1998). *Divorced dads: Shattering the myths.* New York, NY: Tarcher/Putman.

Bray, J. H., & Harvey, D. (1995). Adolescents in stepfamilies: Developmental and family interventions. *Psychotherapy, 32,* 122–130.

Bray, J. H., & Kelly, J. (1998). *Stepfamilies: Love, marriage, and parenting in the first decade.* New York, NY: Broadway Books.

Bumpass, L. L., & Lu, H. H. (2000). Trends in cohabitation and implications for children's family contexts in the United States. *Population Studies, 54,* 29–41.

Buunk, B. P., & Massaers, W. (1999). The nature of the relationship between remarried individuals and former spouses and its impact on marital satisfaction. *Journal of Family Psychology, 13,* 165–174.

Coleman, M., Ganong, L. H., & Fine, M. A. (2000). Reinvestigating remarriage: Another decade of progress. *Journal of Marriage and the Family, 62,* 1288–1307.

Doherty, W. J. (1999). Divided loyalties: The challenges of stepfamily life. *Family Therapy Networker, 54,* 32–38.

Doherty, W. J., & Colangelo, N. (1984). The family FIRO model: A modest proposal for organizing family treatment. *Journal of Marital and Family Therapy, 10,* 19–29.

Emery, R. E., & Dillon, P. (1994). Conceptualizing the divorce process: Renegotiating boundaries of intimacy and power in the divorced family system. *Family Relations, 43,* 374–379.

Falke, S. I., & Larson, J. H. (2007). Premarital predictors of remarital quality: Implications for clinicians. *Contemporary Family Therapy, 29,* 9–23.

Feeney, B. C., & Monin, J. K. (2008). An attachment-theoretical perspective on divorce. In J. Cassidy and P. R. Shaver (Eds.), *Handbook of attachment,* 2nd ed. (pp. 934–957). New York, NY: Guilford Press.

Fine, M. A., & Kurdek, L. A. (1995). Relation between marital quality and stepparent–child relationship quality for parents and stepparents in stepfamilies. *Journal of Family Psychology, 9,* 216–233.

Furrow, J. L., & Palmer, G. (2007). EFFT and blended families: Building bonds from the inside out. *Journal of Systemic Therapies, 26,* 44–58.

Ganong, L. H., & Coleman, M. (2004). *Stepfamily relationships: Development, dynamics, and intervention.* New York, NY: Kluwer.

Guttmann, J. (1993). *Divorce in psychosocial perspective: Theory and research.* Hillsdale, NJ: Lawrence Erlbaum Associates.

Hazan, C., & Shaver, P. R. (1992). Broken attachments: Relationship loss from the perspective of attachment theory. In T. L. Orbuch (Ed.), *Close relationship loss: Theoretical approaches.* New York, NY: Springer.

Hetherington, E. M. (1999). Family functioning and the adjustment of adolescent siblings in diverse family types. In E. M. Hetherington, S. H. Henderson, & D. Reisss (Eds.), *Adolescent siblings in stepfamilies. Monographs of the Society for Research in Child Development* (pp. 1–25). Ann Arbor, MI: Society for Research in Child Development.

Johnston, J. R., & Campbell, L. E. (1988). *Impasses of divorce: The dynamics and resolution of family conflict.* New York, NY: Simon & Schuster.

Knox, D., & Zusman, M. E. (2001). Marrying a man without baggage: Implications for second wives. *Journal of Divorce and Remarriage, 35,* 67–79.

Pacey, S. (2005). Step change: The interplay of sexual and parenting problems when couples form stepfamilies. *Sexual and Relationship Therapy, 20,* 359–369.

Palmer, G., & Efron, D. (2007). Emotionally focused family therapy: Developing the model. *Journal of Systemic Therapies, 26,* 1724.

Pam, A., & Pearson, J. (1998). *Splitting up: Enmeshment and estrangement in the process of divorce.* New York, NY: Guilford Press.

Papernow, P. L. (1993). *Becoming a stepfamily: Patterns of development in remarried families.* San Francisco, CA: Jossey–Bass.

Reibstein, J. (1998). Attachment, pain and detachment for the adults of divorce. *Sexual and Marital Therapy, 13,* 351–360.

Stewart, S. D. (2007). *Brave new stepfamilies: Diverse paths toward stepfamily living.* Thousand Oaks, CA: Sage.

Visher, J. S., & Visher, E. (1988). *Old loyalties, new ties: Therapeutic strategies with stepfamilies.* New York, NY: Brunner/Mazel.

Visher, J. S., & Visher, E. (1996). *Therapy with stepfamilies.* New York, NY: Brunner/Mazel.

Visher, J. S., Visher, E., & Pasley, K. (2003). Remarriage families and stepparenting. In F. Walsh (Ed.), *Normal family processes* (3rd ed.; pp. 153–175). New York, NY: Guilford Press.

Walsh, F. (2003). Changing families in a changing world: Reconstructing family normality. In F. Walsh (Ed.), *Normal family processes: Growing diversity and complexity* (3rd ed.; pp. 3–26). New York, NY: Guilford Press.

Twelve

Emotionally Focused Therapy With Culturally Diverse Couples

TING LIU AND ANDREA WITTENBORN

INTRODUCTION

Couple therapists are often surprised and challenged by the contrast between their clients' and their own assumptions regarding intimate relationships. Cultural backgrounds and ethnic differences often present unique challenges to and opportunities for therapists in maintaining a working alliance with couples where these differences become prominent. Consider the following example of one therapist's experience:

> Shelley is a couple therapist with an active private practice. She recently began providing treatment to Julie and An-Ping, who want to address the increasing conflict they have been experiencing after 14 years of marriage. An-Ping is a 54-year-old Asian man who runs a successful family business with his wife. He described himself as dominant, self-disciplined, and traditional. Julie reported that she was tired of feeling unimportant with no power at home. Julie is a 42-year-old Caucasian woman who was in an abusive relationship prior to marrying An-Ping.
>
> In the first session, Julie complained that she could not even buy a pair of haircutting scissors without her husband's permission. An-Ping defended himself by commenting that he has always tried hard to fulfill his duties as a husband and he does not understand why Julie is not more appreciative of his efforts. After trying to help An-Ping understand the importance of showing affection to Julie with little success, Shelley became more and more frustrated with An-Ping's condescending tone and his lack of empathy toward his wife. Shelley eventually asked

An-Ping if he would be willing to change some of his gender-stereotypical behaviors in order to save his marriage. An-Ping looked at Julie and said firmly and coldly, "If changing me is the only way to keep you, then no, I am not going to change." He then quietly stood up and walked out of the therapy room. Julie was devastated and was ready to give up on their relationship.

A therapist's frustration or misunderstanding when working with clients holding different cultural expectations can produce unfavorable results, as demonstrated in the preceding case example in which the therapist and male client held differing beliefs regarding gender roles. An inability to attune to these differences appropriately also undermines the therapeutic alliance, which may compound the risk of negative client outcomes. Therapists face many challenges when working with clients from diverse backgrounds and need to be aware and respectful of clients' cultural heritages.

Some may wonder if emotionally focused therapy (EFT) is appropriate for working with culturally diverse clients, especially those from a culture that discourages emotional expression or appears to "undervalue" the marital bond. In this chapter, we will discuss literature that outlines the value of using EFT with diverse couples, such as research on the universality of basic attachment needs and how, while attachment processes are similar, emotional signaling behaviors vary. The chapter will then provide guiding principles and practices for working sensitively with culturally diverse couples using EFT. The treatment guidelines, including opportunities for improving outcomes and strengthening the working alliance, will be illustrated in a case study.

IS EFT MULTICULTURALLY APPROPRIATE?

Clinical Competence and Cultural Diversity

Literature on multicultural training in therapy largely focuses on increasing therapists' cultural competence in working with ethnic clients (African Americans, American Indians, Asian Americans, and Hispanics and Latinos) currently living in or immigrating to the United States (Sue, Arredondo, & McDavis, 1992). The curriculum of multicultural training typically includes three stages (Pedersen, 1988; Sue et al., 1992). The first stage focuses on the dimension of beliefs or attitudes that helps trainees develop awareness of their own attitudes, opinions, assumptions, biases, and stereotypes about other cultures, and how their values and biases may obstruct their multicultural work. The second stage focuses on the dimension of knowledge in which trainees develop a good understanding of their own culture and minority cultures. The third stage focuses on the dimension of skills in which specific clinical techniques and strategies needed for culturally competent work with ethnic clients are taught.

In Stage 3 of multicultural training, EFT therapists must learn how to tailor the interventions they are delivering to the specific cultural or ethnic populations they are treating. Using an EFT intervention as an example, having a therapist touch, lean forward, or move closer to the client is suggested when heightening the client's emotional experience. These nonverbal behaviors were proven to predict better client outcome (Hall, Harrigan, & Rosenthal, 1995), mainly because they indicate support and closeness in Western society. However, the same nonverbal behaviors may be seen as invasive, inappropriate, or threatening to clients with firm boundaries regarding maintaining physical distance, particularly between opposite genders.

A therapist's ability to become aware of and respect clients' divergent levels of comfort regarding physical closeness and distance is a reflection of Stages 1 and 2 training. Stage 3 training would enable clinicians to determine appropriate strategies toward the same goal of heightening emotional experience while simultaneously being sensitive to clients' differing beliefs. For example, when working with a client who values physical distance in professional settings, a culturally competent therapist might rely less on physical touch or closeness and more on softening her or his voice.

To work in the presence of these cultural differences, such as divergent beliefs about physical space and emotional expression, more appropriately in therapy, recommendations in the multicultural counseling literature often suggest taking an approach that is just the opposite of what an EFT therapist is trained to do. For example, Sue and Sue (1999) provide suggestions taken from the counseling literature when working with Chinese American clients. They suggest that the therapist should refrain from asking too many personal questions during the early phase of treatment, should focus on the presenting problem determined by the client, and should focus on resolving the presenting problem in order to treat clients in a minimum number of sessions.

Based on these recommendations, one might wonder whether EFT is a relevant approach for working with clients from culturally diverse (or, more specifically, Chinese) backgrounds. For example, the differences between the aforementioned suggestions (Sue & Sue, 1999) and EFT theories and interventions are apparent, including the following:

- EFT therapists focus on many "personal issues," such as the client's attachment history and needs, as well as the interactional cycles in which couples engage.
- EFT therapists explore emotional experiences that some cultural groups who tend to be overtly reserved in emotional and affective expression may find difficult to express.
- EFT therapists see the presenting problem determined by clients as a result of their destructive patterns of interaction as they try to fulfill their attachment needs for longing and connection.
- Instead of focusing on resolving clients' specific presenting problem, the primary goal of EFT is to reestablish connection between partners because EFT therapists believe that partners will resolve their presenting problems once the emotional bond is securely established.
- Because EFT is experience based as opposed to skill based, EFT therapists view their role as process consultants instead of teaching techniques or giving expert advice, which some cultures may expect from therapists.

However, while typical multicultural recommendations and EFT interventions may appear to conflict, the EFT theoretical underpinnings of attachment theory and understanding of the importance of emotion are applicable across cultures, lending validity to the cross-cultural relevance of the approach.

Attachment Needs Are Universal

Attachment theory, the theoretical foundation of EFT, is based in part on evolutionary theory, and research supports its validity across cultures. Attachment behaviors and processes have been observed in many cultures in both Western and non-Western (e.g., Africa, China, Indonesia, Israel, and Japan) communities, as well as in primates and other species (see van IJzendoorn & Sagi-Schwartz, 2008, for a review). In fact, attachment scholars have been interested in whether attachment processes, as conceptualized by Western theorists, occurred in divergent cultures since early in the development of the theory, when Mary Ainsworth (1967) first began describing patterns of attachment in her Uganda study.

While, as clinicians, we need to be sensitive to varying displays of secure-base behavior, we can be confident in our goal of increasing security in attachment relationships across cultures. Research demonstrates that attachment security is not just a Western preference, but rather is normative (van IJzendoorn & Bakermans-Kranenburg, 1996; van IJzendoorn & Sagi-Schwartz, 2008) and preferred among diverse cultures (Posada et al., 1995). Using the Attachment Q-Sort, a validated measure of attachment consisting of 90 cards describing attachment behaviors, researchers asked mothers from divergent cultures to sort the cards to describe the "ideal" child (Posada et al., 1995). Mothers from China, Columbia, Germany, Israel, Japan, and the United States all described the ideal child as one with a secure attachment (as conceptualized by expert coders from each of these cultures). In a meta-analysis, attachment security was also found to be normative across cultures in adulthood, as assessed by the well-established Adult Attachment Interview (van IJzendoorn & Bakersman-Kranenburg, 1996).

While the concept of attachment security extends to differing cultures, the expression of attachment behaviors differs (van IJzendoorn & Sagi-Schwartz, 2008). Consider, for example, differences between North American infants and Gusii (of Kenya) infants. In a well-established research procedure for measuring patterns of attachment, the "strange situation," infants experience separations from and reunions with their caregivers. While secure North American infants would likely anticipate a hug upon reuniting with their parents, Gusii infants, who are accustomed to being greeted with handshakes from their caregivers, expected to engage in shaking the hand of their caregiver during reunions (Kermoian & Leiderman, 1986). Insecure Gusii infants either avoided the adult or reached for a handshake and then pulled away as the adult approached, which is conceptually similar to insecure North American infant responses.

While Gusii infants displayed attachment behaviors differently, the distribution of patterns of attachment was similar to distributions found in Western cultures. Therefore, while the secure-base phenomenon still existed and was conceptually similar to Bowlby's original ideas, and patterns of attachment were similarly distributed, the behaviors observed in attachment processes among Gusii infants were different from those in Western cultures.

The study of Gusii infants has important implications for clinical work with diverse couples and reminds clinicians to be sensitive to how culturally diverse partners display secure-base behavior and attachment needs. In other words, the attachment needs of feeling loved, accepted, and secure are universal, whereas the specific expressions of love and attachment behaviors vary. In couple partnerships, we might witness this cultural display difference as ranging from secure-base behavior that displays "more intimate" signs of affection such as holding one another in session to more reserved acts of support. Returning to our opening case as an example, An-Ping is likely to display his secure-base-seeking and caregiving responses differently than the therapist, and perhaps his wife, might expect.

Cultural Influences on Emotional Expression

Previous research supports the idea that judgments of facial expressions generally result in universal consensus (Ekman, 1972; Ekman et al., 1987). Ekman and his colleagues showed over 3,000 pictures of facial expressions of six emotions to participants across five cultures. Participants achieved accuracy rates of between 80 and 90%. Later, Ekman and Friesen (1971) went to Papua, New Guinea, to study people of the Fore, who had not been exposed to Western media or Western culture. Fore participants also achieved accuracy rates between 80 and 90% in identifying the six emotions in the photos.

While people's outward emotional expression appears similar across cultures, studies show that cultures may differ in their display rules. Display rules are culturally constructed rules for the management and modification of emotional expression, including how and to whom it is appropriate to express different emotions. The expression of emotions appears to hold greater intrapersonal meaning in individualistic as opposed to collectivistic cultures (Matsumoto et al., 2008). Research shows that individualism is related to higher levels of emotional expressivity. However, collectivistic cultures, placing more value on the group, may limit emotional expressivity, believing personal feelings to be less important than interpersonal dynamics and having concerns that such expression may serve as a threat to the larger group.

Research found differences in emotion elicitation, regulation, symbolic representation, and social sharing for people from different cultural backgrounds. For example, ethnographic studies suggested that greater emphasis was placed on emotional moderation and control in Chinese culture than in mainstream European American culture (Potter, 1988;

Russell & Yik, 1996; Sue & Sue, 1999). Song (1985) administered the Minnesota Multiphasic Personality Inventory to Chinese participants and found they were "more emotionally reserved, introverted, fond of tranquility, and habituated to self-restraints compared to Westerners" (p. 53).

The Rogerian theoretical underpinnings of EFT assert unconditional acceptance and empathy, which enable EFT therapists to "decode" different ways of expressing adult love and to enter the client's emotional world. EFT therapists can show genuine curiosity while spontaneously validating clients' emotional experience, such as "There must have been good reasons for you to show no emotional reaction outwardly when he described how unimportant you were in his life; can you help me understand?" EFT therapists can also identify nonverbal cues to help clients access their emotions—for example, "I notice when he defended his viewpoint, you tightened your lip and did not say a word. I am wondering if you were holding back for some reason. Is that right?"

GUIDING PRINCIPLES FOR DEALING WITH CULTURAL DIFFERENCES IN EFT

In this section, we provide three guiding principles for working with cultural differences in EFT, as well as brief case scenarios and intervention examples for each principle.

Principle 1: Identify the Meanings and Functions Associated With the Expression of Emotions and Attachment Behavior

In couple relationships, especially in a conflictual situation when emotional intensity is high, people may exhibit certain emotional expressions that seem bizarre on the surface. Therapists should observe and work to understand differences around emotion elicitation, regulation, symbolic representation, and social sharing, as well as how this relates to clients' attachment histories and behaviors. This allows clients to explore the meanings and intentions behind their actions and, as a result, can promote mutual understanding and empathy within their partnerships. The EFT therapist serves as a process consultant and a collaborator to help clients unpack their emotional experiences and the roles they play in their relationships. Stage 1 interventions can be used to create secure alliances with each partner and help clients access their unmet attachment needs and underlying feelings. In addition, EFT therapists must

Closely monitor their own biases and assumptions.

Maintain a collaborative and empathic stance.

Explore and learn about the culturally constructed rules of display and functions of client's expression of emotions and attachment needs.

Explicitly highlight any negative impact the display rules have on a couple's relationship.

Example: Ravi is a 45-year-old Indian man who always wears a smile on his face, even when his wife is weeping or screaming at him. He has been confronted by both his wife and a former therapist about his "inappropriate expression" and "heartlessness."

In this scenario, the therapist should help both partners identify the function(s) of Ravi's smile and how it feeds into the couple's interactional cycle. From an EFT point of view, Ravi may be using his smile to (a) mask his feelings of anxiety, helplessness, or embarrassment; (b) self-regulate his emotional arousal elicited in the disagreement; (c) placate and soothe his wife's intense response; or (d) distance himself for self-protection purposes. Instead of quickly assuming that Ravi is uncaring and/or has poor social skills, the therapist can use EFT interventions to reconstruct the meaning of his emotional expression to promote understanding.

Empathic reflection: I understand that you have been criticized many times about your smile. I can see how difficult it is for you to be accused of being heartless and cold. It seems to frustrate you.

Empathic conjecture: I am wondering, and please correct me if I am wrong, if there is something about your smile that you haven't been able to explain to others, that if by smiling you are able to remain calm. Is that right?

Reframing: So your smiling is not intended to deny or ignore your wife's pain. Instead, you smile to soothe your own anxiety when you become aware of her disappointment and hurt. You smile to keep the situation contained and keep it from becoming overwhelming so that you can better respond to her concerns. This is probably a strategy you developed long ago.

Principle 2: Consider the Socially Constructed Meanings of Emotion

Some emotions are associated with strongly negative meanings in different cultures. In collective cultures in which the individual needs to yield to group needs, clients, particularly females, may find it difficult to access needs and emotions that may be associated with "selfishness" or disrespect to people with more power. Using guilt as an example to understand the different meanings of emotions, research on Americans suggests that guilt implies "wrong" (Wharton, 1990), whereas Chinese discriminate the concept of guilt by the subjective source of wrongdoing to three types (law violation, not living to a personally defined responsibility, and moral transgression) (Bedford, 2004). Moreover, there are more than 130 words for guilt in the Chinese language. As such, it appears that the Chinese may experience many different shadings of guilt.

In turn, therapists must be aware that clients' emotions may be elicited for reasons that are different from their own. EFT therapists can use their own curiosity and empathic reflection skills to ensure they understand clients' experiences correctly. Therapists should be careful not to invalidate clients' own perceived emotional experiences and their causes. Instead of aiming to correct the "wrong perception" of emotions, the therapist can unpack clients' emotional experiences to understand how these experiences have contributed to the dysfunctional cycle in their partnership.

Therapists should monitor their interpretations of or assumptions about clients' emotional reactions. For example, a Chinese man's admitted guilt may not indicate his confession of wrongdoing. In turn, the significance of clients' emotions can be easily misinterpreted, perhaps leading the therapist in such an example erroneously to assume the client is admitting an offense; thus, therapists should be cautious to explore the meaning that clients apply to their emotional expression rather than operating from their own assumptions.

Finally, in our second guiding principle, we suggest that EFT therapists (1) be sensitive to the differences in the meanings of emotions cross culturally, (2) validate clients' unique perceptions and experiences of emotions, and (3) regularly check with clients to make sure their experiences are accurately understood.

Example: Jia-Min entered therapy with her husband of 14 years, Wei-Hao. Jia-Min had found several text messages sent from her husband's cell phone to a female coworker of his. Wei-Hao admitted to having had an emotional affair with this coworker, but denied any sexual involvement. Wei-Hao also expressed feeling extremely guilty for hurting his wife. Jia-Min denied any distrust of her husband because she believed a good wife should trust her husband unconditionally.

In this scenario, Wei-Hao's guilt was associated with hurting Jia-Min. The therapist could further explore his experience of feeling guilty by asking questions such as "Help me understand here. What happened to you when you experienced this intense feeling of guilt? What made you feel guilty? What did you do when you felt this way? How did she respond?" In terms of Jia-Min, it would be important to explore her beliefs about "trust" and a wife's role.

> *Empathic reflection and tracking:* You want to be able to trust him and it is difficult for you to do that after what happened. It is like there are two parts of you: You think, as a wife, you should trust and appreciate him, and you feel guilty for not trusting him. But the other part of you says, "Don't forgive him too easily; don't be a fool again." You don't like to be jealous and overreactive, but you are torn and confused. If he is the husband you have known for years, why would he intentionally do things to hurt you? But if he is not the person you thought he was, what does that make you?
>
> *Heightening:* You don't want to be deceived and hurt again. Underneath your anger and jealousy, I also hear a lot of pain in your voice. You believed him when he told you he was not the kind of guy who could express love and affection verbally and overtly. You trusted him and you accepted who he was. You have never pushed him to say affectionate and sweet words to you—only to learn that he is capable of doing it, just not to you.

Principle 3: Find Words and Metaphors to Which Clients Can Relate—Borrow Clients' Words and Slice Their Experiences Thinner

In EFT, clients' words and metaphors are commonly used to heighten emotion. Similarly, the usage of images or metaphors about universal experiences is highly recommended when working with diverse clients. The goal is to avoid different interpretations due to cultural differences. For example, walking on fire, hugging a porcupine, suffocating, drowning, and tiptoeing can all be easily understood cross culturally. Animal-related metaphors should be applied with caution and may require a better understanding of the animal's cultural meaning. For instance, dragons represent the emperor and power in Asia; mice, snakes, and foxes are associated with sneakiness, dishonesty, and evil intention; and crows are associated with bad luck or death.

> *Example:* Jorge is a 40-year-old Mexican man. He was referred to couples therapy by a psychiatrist who used to treat his wife, Anna. Anna has made three unsuccessful suicide attempts in the past and continues to feel depressed and suicidal. Jorge denied any indication of vulnerable feelings, such as helplessness, fear, sadness, or shame.

To help Jorge access his underlying, more vulnerable emotions, the therapist could try to reduce the intensity of the emotion-laden words chosen to reflect his emotional experience, which, in EFT, is called "slicing it thinner." For example, the therapist could start with "scared" and gradually reduce the intensity from "afraid" to "anxious" to "worried," or, finally, to "a little concerned," which might more accurately reflect Jorge's internal experience. The therapist could then use "a little concerned" as an opportunity to begin Jorge's journey of accessing his vulnerability. In terms of the usage of metaphor, a commonly used metaphor such as "white knight" might not represent Jorge's expressed need of protecting his wife, whereas the metaphor "guardian angel" might be a better fit.

Note here that emotional words, images, and metaphors are all tools to help clients access their underlying vulnerable feelings. The goal here is not to help clients learn language to "label" their emotional experiences. Rather, the use of appropriate images and metaphors can help clients access their vulnerable states without becoming defensive or avoidant.

CASE EXAMPLE

After consulting with her supervisor, Shelley, the therapist in the opening case example, invited An-Ping and Julie back to therapy. To repair the damaged alliance with An-Ping, Shelley

first apologized for making him feel blamed or like he had
been given an ultimatum. Shelley then asked An-Ping for a
second chance to better understand him. An-Ping was hesitant. She asked him if he had experienced similar situations
in the past and if he was interested in learning why he might
receive such responses. She also reflected on An-Ping's experience of being underappreciated and treated unfairly in such
situations. An-Ping recalled having had similar experiences
with others in the past and reluctantly agreed to come back for
"one last session."

The therapist faced three culture-related challenges when
working with this couple. First, she needed to be aware that
she and the couple, the husband in particular, may have differing views on the importance of overtly showing love and affection. Second, she should discern her own gender-related values
and beliefs when dealing with power differential between the
spouses. Third, the therapist needed to find ways to empathize
genuinely with An-Ping even when he talked in a condescending and patronizing tone to both his wife and the therapist.
(Therapists should be reminded here that displaying empathy
in this situation can be done without supporting the client's
condescending tone.) The tasks the therapist needed to complete
during the following several sessions included reestablishing
a strong therapeutic alliance with both partners, identifying
attachment positions and the interactional cycle, and identifying underlying primary emotions and attachment needs.

Julie told the therapist that she had packed her belongings
and had been ready to walk out the door after the last session.
She had also told several of their friends and family members
about leaving An-Ping and said, "Everyone told me I should
have done it a long time ago." However, Julie reported that she
did not believe An-Ping was a bad person and believed that it
was silly to get divorced over such "trivial" things.

Case History

An-Ping and Julie had been married for 14 years and had no
children. An-Ping had been married once before. His first wife
had left him for another man who was "more human." Julie
and An-Ping met when she began working for him. An-Ping
was impressed by her sense of responsibility, competency,
and respect for his cultural tradition. Julie had just ended an
abusive relationship and was attracted to him by his stability and even temper. After they got married, they each managed

a different branch of the company and lived separately for the first 9 years of their marriage. They began living together 5 years prior to entering therapy, when Julie was promoted to a higher position. As they spent more time together, their conflict escalated.

Julie described herself as shy, conflict avoidant, and passive. For most of their marriage, Julie said that she had tried not to say anything when her needs were unmet because she did not like to deal with An-Ping's angry attacks and defensive retaliations. Julie reported that she had started to communicate with An-Ping approximately 4 years ago about her feelings and needs when she realized how unhappy she was about her life, but all the attempts to communicate had failed miserably. At this time, she resorted to her previous strategies of withholding her concerns. An-Ping said that he did not understand Julie at all. He experienced Julie as whiny and unappreciative, whereas his view of himself was of a hardworking and logical person. An-Ping said that he had always treated Julie as his equal and expected her to push back when he pushed too hard. He reported no interest in playing mindreading games with Julie and was frustrated by how she held back from communicating with him.

After two sessions, Shelly started to formulate the couple's attachment positions and interactional pattern. The therapist used a recent fight over a pair of scissors to help this couple understand the dysfunctional cycle in which they are stuck.

Session 3

Julie: We got into another fight over something trivial. I had a pair of scissors that I used to cut my hair. They were expensive and I had to place a special order. I knew he was going to disapprove of this purchase, so I hid the scissors from him. When I came home that night and saw him using my expensive scissors to clean the drain I freaked out, but calmly asked him, "Are they my scissors?" And he immediately got upset because he thought I was questioning his authority. He became argumentative and defensive.

Therapist: So for you, Julie, even though you were upset, you felt you had little chance of being heard and valued, so you thought you would approach him calmly, essentially keeping your concern silent. (Therapist turns to An-Ping.) But for you, your priority was to fix the drain. You did not pay attention to the tool you used, and you were surprised by her reaction. Is that right?

An-Ping: Right. The drain was clogged by hair, her long hair. I found a pair of scissors in the drawer that could fix it. A pair of scissors is a pair of scissors. When she challenged me about the scissors, what had upset me was not about my authority being threatened. What had upset me was the fact that she cared about scissors more than a clogged drain. I was picking up after her mess, her hair. I did not expect her to appreciate me, but at least not criticize me for a stupid pair of scissors.

Therapist: You found her concern confusing.

An-Ping: No, I actually felt sorry for her. She grew up poor, so even a pair of scissors was so valuable to her that she could not see the bigger picture. (Julie turns away, looking sad and defeated.)

Therapist: So this was another example of how you fought about small things. (She turns to An-Ping.) You were upset, because you really do not understand why Julie was so mad at you when you were only trying to take care of your property. When you tried to put yourself in her shoes and make sense of her reaction (turning to Julie), his comments made you feel put down and criticized. And you were frustrated that he just did not get it. It didn't matter how many times you tried to communicate with him, to explain to him, he didn't get it.

Julie: Not only that, he did not want to listen at all. He did not want to hear what I had to say. (She assumes a mocking tone.) "That is just a pair of scissors, why would you care so much! It's your hair in the drain."

An-Ping: Do you remember what we had discussed? I told you that I would clean the scissors after I was done, and it was just hair. The hair won't hurt your scissors. Scissors are made of metal, you know.

Therapist: So you were trying to reassure Julie that you would not damage the scissors and would return the scissors to her the way you found them.

Julie: He said he was just trying to explain himself, but his voice was so loud and he was so angry with me. His tone and words did not sound caring at all.

Therapist: Other than feeling frustrated, you also felt hurt and criticized.

Julie: Yes, it was like he was telling me I am stupid and pitiful to care about my scissors. We had an almost identical fight about magazines. When he needed some paper to put under his cereal bowl, he just ripped my *Cosmopolitan* magazine that I hadn't read. When I confronted him for not using his *National Geographic,* he said he used a junk magazine with no value to keep. Sometimes I feel that he is not in his right mind and there is no use to continue a conversation.

Therapist: So did you just stay silent to make peace or would you ask him to resume the conversation later after you both calmed down?

An-Ping: In 14 years of marriage, you have never told me to calm down and come back to talk about it later. We just argue and then drop it. You overreact to everything. It is really stupid to react like this over some junk magazines.

Therapist: So let me make sure I understand what usually happens at home. Julie, you usually just drop it to try to stop it from escalating. You don't talk to him about your anger, frustration, and pain. Over time, these seemingly trivial incidents then build up, and you both become upset very quickly. What I am hearing from you is that you two have different values and different priorities, which is not uncommon in most couples. The sad thing is that when you try to explain yourself to one another, hoping to help your partner understand you, all the other person hears is anger and criticism. (Therapist speaks to An-Ping.) Even when Julie tried to speak very carefully, using a tentative and polite tone, you picked up on her anger when she asked, "Is that my magazine?"

An-Ping: Yeah. She spoke very calmly today, but she is usually critical and angry at home.

Therapist: You experience Julie as critical and angry, and you immediately become defensive. Instead of asking her what had upset her, you jumped into attack mode by saying, "Why are you so upset over stupid scissors or junk magazines?" But (to Julie) that's not your experience at all. You don't experience yourself as critical

and angry. In fact, you have tried to control your tone
and tip-toe around him for fear of his attack.

Julie (starts crying): I have tried so hard to stay calm because
his verbal attack is so vicious. I am afraid of what he
may say.

Therapist: It is quite upsetting to hear that, after all your effort,
he still experiences you as critical and angry.

Julie: I end up becoming the mature and self-restrained one.
I have to bite my tongue all the time.

Therapist (to An-Ping): So, you feel misunderstood and underappreciated that at times, even when you mean well,
Julie can take it the wrong way. When you unintentionally hurt Julie's feelings, you want to reassure
her, but your defensive tone comes out and makes it
seem like you're putting her down or attacking her.
Then, when Julie appears angrier and more hurt by
your explanation, you become frustrated and helpless, and you explode out of anger because you feel
really stuck. (Therapist turns to Julie.) But you experience him as stubborn and dominant. You don't think
he cares about what you have to say and he appears
angry from the beginning. He says some pretty hurtful and demeaning things that make you feel stupid
and small. So you become silent, move away, and
hope things will smooth over. You tell yourself that
such trivial things are not worth feeling attacked like
this and feeling hurt so badly. (She turns to An-Ping.)
When she moves away, while part of you is still frustrated, part of you is relieved. Relieved that you don't
have to argue anymore and you can move on. But
the more you both withdraw, the more issues are left
unresolved, and the more sensitive and distant you
become and the more distant and alone you feel in
the relationship. Does this sound right?

Between Sessions 3 and 7, the therapist focused on helping An-Ping and Julie recognize the cultural impact on their
differences by (1) identifying the culturally constructed
meanings and functions of their emotional experiences, (2)
developing empathy and acceptance of one another, and (3)
reconstructing new interactional patterns that promote connection. The couple was able to begin accessing their underlying feelings and attachment needs. An-Ping was slowly able to
hear Julie without getting angrily defensive. Julie was able to

stay engaged in the conversation and share her feelings with An-Ping. Their destructive cycle had been de-escalated.

In the eighth session, Julie brought up another incident in which An-Ping brought used furniture home from their office after she had asked to buy a new chair for the den. Julie was able to talk to An-Ping about feeling discounted. Julie told An-Ping how she felt incompetent, small, and unlovable (withdrawer reengagement). An-Ping, without becoming defensive, apologized for making a false assumption about Julie's wishes and agreed that Julie should make the decision about whether to buy a new chair. An-Ping was able to respond in a more empathic and supportive manner. The interaction pattern between the couple started to shift. The following segment presents a softening moment for An-Ping when he was able to talk to Julie about the pressure to be her superhero and never ask for anything from anyone.

Julie: I understand you tried to help, but I want to be part of this process. I do not need you to take things over and do it on your own all the time. I want a partnership. (An-Ping is silent for a while.)

Therapist: What's happening for you, An-Ping? You look sad and you became quiet.

An-Ping: I just realized that I have never asked anything from anyone before in my whole life. I am the oldest son in my family, and it is my responsibility to take care of my younger siblings. When I took over the family business, it became my responsibility to take care of the business and my elderly parents. People count on me, you know.

Therapist: This is new to you, that someone asks to share responsibility with you.

An-Ping: But I don't need her help. I don't need to share responsibility with anyone. I can do it all by myself. I can take care of her, give her what she wants, and keep her happy. Isn't that enough?

Therapist: So what you are saying is that you are used to taking care of everything, and sharing responsibility seems unnecessary to you because you are capable of doing it all by yourself. I also hear something else: that—and correct me if I am wrong—sharing responsibility or asking for help indicates incompetence or failure, as if you fail to fulfill your role as a husband, a son, and an older brother. Is that right?

An-Ping: Yes, I have never even asked her or my first wife to cook, to iron clothes, to do laundry for me. I don't pay much attention to my own feelings or needs. It would be selfish.

Therapist: You never ask anything from anyone because you think you should be able to do everything by yourself. It would be a sign of weakness for you to ask people to do things for you.

An-Ping: Yes, it is weak. It would mean that I'm incompetent.

Therapist: So when you feel tired and confused, you can never picture yourself asking Julie to help you, because it is weak and makes you feel too vulnerable.

An-Ping: Yes, I usually don't think about my feelings. I focus on how to problem solve and just do it. I don't want to burden her with my problems.

Therapist: So even when you are tired and helpless, you still fight the battle alone. You can never imagine yourself turning to Julie and asking for her support.

An-Ping: No, I can't.

Therapist: Can you tell her that you can never imagine asking for her help because it makes you feel too vulnerable, so you stay distant instead? You would rather be alone than show her any weakness.

An-Ping (to Julie): I can't image asking for your help. I can't image you would want to be married to someone who is weak and incompetent. I want to be strong and dependable. I want to take care of you.

Julie: I want you to take care of me, but I also want a chance to take care of you too. That's why we got married, to take care of each other. I want a husband, not a superhero.

In this case example, several cultural issues were identified and addressed. First, in terms of gender issues, An-Ping seemed dominant, condescending, and self-absorbed when dealing with Julie's different opinions. The therapist addressed this issue by increasing An-Ping's empathy toward his wife, helping him understand the negative impact of his demeanor on their marriage, and empowering Julie to find her voice in the marriage. Second, the cultural differences between partners were evident with regard to "help seeking." For example, An-Ping considered reaching out to Julie as selfish and incompetent, whereas Julie had never felt needed by him.

The steps the therapist took to help the couple process their interactional cycle in the context of their cultural differences included (1) unpacking and validating how their emotional experience and display rules were constructed culturally, (2) developing mutual empathy between partners, (3) identifying the negative impact of some cultural beliefs on their marriage, and (4) reconstructing a new interactional cycle that promoted connections. As a result, Julie and An-Ping continued to express themselves at the level of their more vulnerable emotions. Over the course of treatment, Julie became more engaged in the relationship, in part, by expressing her needs more assertively. At the same time, An-Ping continued to respond less defensively and was more responsive to his wife's needs.

In summary, each of us will unintentionally make insensitive missteps during the course of treatment with clients who are from cultures or ethnic heritages different from our own. However, as this case example demonstrates, such missteps that cause damage in therapeutic alliance can be repaired. When working with culturally diverse couples, EFT therapists should monitor the therapeutic process closely to tune in to clients and avoid misunderstandings or misinterpretations of a client's emotional experience.

TRAINING/SUPERVISION

As previously discussed, attachment needs are universal, but culturally competent EFT therapists must be aware of and sensitive to how their clients display these needs, as well as how they provide secure-base support to partners. However, this can be a difficult feat at times. As clinical supervisors, we have witnessed clinicians interpret attachment behaviors related to preoccupation or avoidance as normative for particular cultural groups. At the same time, we have also witnessed clinicians interpret more overtly reserved, "less intimate" methods of secure-base behavior as evidence of attachment avoidance or more overt, "intimate" methods as attachment preoccupation. We recommend that EFT therapists take the time to tune in sensitively to secure-base use and support behaviors, as well as underlying attachment needs, when intervening and be cautious of ascribing inaccurate meanings based on personal biases to the ways in which these needs are displayed.

Regarding emotional experiencing, EFT therapists can attune to clients' language instead of labeling their experiences for them. Indeed, regardless of clients' cultural backgrounds, EFT therapists are always encouraged to do this. For example, when working with overtly reserved clients, clinicians can borrow clients' language, such as "getting along better" or "less conflict," instead of using "more love, affection, and intimacy," which may better connect to their internal experience.

However, even the most culturally competent therapists will inevitably respond in ways that sometimes traverse clients' areas of sensitivity. Such situations can be repaired by acknowledging this and responding sensitively. In these instances, seeking support through supervision or peer consultation may be necessary (Christiansen et al., 2009). Clinical supervisors and peers are removed from the emotional intensity experienced in the therapeutic relationship, allowing them to consider the evidence anew and provide recommendations for intervention.

CONCLUSION

In sum, prior research supports attachment as a universal phenomenon, lending cross-cultural validity to EFT. As clinicians who strive toward culturally competent practice, EFT therapists can accept that, while clients might display their attachment needs differently, they have universal needs for safety and love. While the EFT model appears valuable for clients of various cultures and ethnic heritages, EFT therapists should follow some principles that provide sensitive care, such as identifying the meanings and functions associated with the expression of emotions, considering the socially constructed meanings of expressed emotions, and using language and metaphors that reflect clients' inner experiences.

In order to do this effectively, therapists should be aware of their own cultural backgrounds and biases, learn about the culture of the couples they are treating, and recognize the impact cultural differences may have on their own relationships with clients, as well as within the relationships of the couples they treat. However, as demonstrated in the case example, missteps can easily occur. Remaining aware of and having the humility to address such difficulties has the potential to repair the therapeutic relationship and create the strong therapeutic alliance needed to use EFT interventions successfully.

REFERENCES

Ainsworth, M. (1967). *Infancy in Uganda: Infant care and the growth of love.* Baltimore, MD: Johns Hopkins University Press.

Bedford, O. (2004). The individual experience of guilt and shame in Chinese culture. *Culture and Psychology, 10,* 29–52.

Christiansen, A., Thomas, V., Lowe, W., Kafescioglu, N., Karakurt, G., Smith, W., & Wittenborn, A. (2009). Multicultural supervision: Lessons learned about an ongoing struggle. *Journal of Marital and Family Therapy, 36,* 284–295.

Ekman, P. & Friesen, W. V. (1971). Constants across cultures in the face and emotion. *Journal of Personality and Social Psychology, 17,* 124–129.

Ekman, P. (1972). Universals and cultural differences in facial expressions of emotion. In J. Cole (Ed.), *Nebraska Symposium on Motivation, 1971* (pp. 207–283). Lincoln: University of Nebraska Press.

Ekman, P., Friesen, W. V., O'Sullivan, M., Chan, A., Diacoyanni-Tarlatzis, Heider, K., Krause, R., LeCompte, W. A., Pitcarn, T., Ricci-Bitti, P. E., Scherer, K., Tomita, M., & Tzavaras, A. (1987). Universals and cultural differences in the judgments of facial expressions of emotion. *Journal of Personality and Social Psychology, 53,* 712–717.

Hall, J., Harrigan, J., & Rosenthal, R. (1995). Nonverbal behavior in clinician–patient interaction. *Applied and Preventive Psychology, 4,* 21–37.

Kermoian, R., & Leiderman, P. H. (1986). Infant attachment to mother and child caretaker in an East African community. *International Journal of Behavioral Development, 9,* 455–469.

Matsumoto, D. et al. (2008). Mapping expressive differences around the world: The relationship between emotional display rules and individualism versus collectivism. *Journal of Cross-Cultural Psychology, 39,* 55–74.

Pedersen, P. (1988). *A handbook for developing multicultural awareness.* Alexandria, VA: American Association for Developing Multicultural Awareness.

Posada, G., Gao, Y., Wu, F., Posado, R., Tascon, M., Schoelmerich, A., et al. (1995). The secure-base phenomenon across cultures: Children's behavior, mothers' preferences, and experts' concepts. In B. E. Vaughn, G. Posada, & K. Kondo-Ikemura (Eds.), Caregiving, cultural, and cognitive perspectives on secure-base behavior and working models: New growing points of attachment theory and research. *Monographs of the Society for Research in Child Development, 60,* 27–48.

Russell, J., & Yik, M. (1996). Emotion among the Chinese. In M. Bond (Ed.), *The handbook of Chinese psychology* (pp. 166–188). Hong Kong: Oxford University Press.

Song, W. (1985). The test anxiety and characteristic trait in Chinese college students. *Chinese Mental Health Journal, 4,* 3–22.

Sue, D., Arredondo, P., & McDavis, R. (1992). Multicultural competencies/standards: A pressing need. *Journal of Counseling and Development, 70,* 477–486.

Sue, D. W., & Sue, W. (1999). Counseling Asian Americans. In *Counseling the culturally different: Theory and practice* (3rd ed.; pp. 255–271). New York, NY: John Wiley & Sons.

van IJzendoorn, M. H., & Bakermans-Kranenburg, M. J. (1996). Attachment representations in mothers, fathers, adolescents, and clinical groups: A meta-analytic search for normative data. *Journal of Consulting and Clinical Psychology, 64,* 8–21.

van IJzendoorn, M. H., & Sagi-Schwartz, A. (2008). Cross-cultural patterns of attachment: Universal and contextual dimensions. In J. Cassidy & P. R. Shaver (Eds.), *Handbook of attachment: Theory, research, and clinical applications* (2nd ed.; pp. 880–905). New York, NY: Guilford Press.

Wharton, B. (1990). The hidden face of shame: The shadow, shame and separation. *Journal of Analytical Psychology, 35,* 279–299.

Thirteen

Emotionally Focused Therapy for Gay and Lesbian Couples
Strong Identities, Strong Bonds

DINO ZUCCARINI AND LEIGH KAROS

INTRODUCTION

Attachment longings lie deep within all of us regardless of race, ethnicity, gender, and sexual orientation. Whether in a same-sex or heterosexual couple, the yearning, searching, and reaching for an emotionally accessible and responsive partner to assuage distress is a lifelong endeavor. Sensitive responding to attachment-related emotions and needs defines the self and other in a positive manner. Inaccessibility evokes attachment fears, redefines the self and other in negative terms, and evokes self-protective strategies, anxious preoccupation, or emotional avoidance. For example, Jane desperately pursues Mary for contact comfort and reassurances in a lesbian relationship in similar fashion that Tom pursues Margaret in a heterosexual relationship. Protective strategies are similar in same-sex and heterosexual relationships (Ridge & Feeney, 1998) with insecurity associated with diminished relational commitment (Kurdek, 2002) and satisfaction (Elizur & Mintzer, 2003).

For the past 25 years, emotionally focused therapy (EFT) has been employed with diverse couples, including same-sex couples. As with heterosexual couples, EFT views attachment insecurity and recurring separation distress as the primary

317

source of conflict and unhappiness in same-sex couples and promotes more secure bonding by facilitating a partner's emotional accessibility and responsiveness to attachment-related emotions and needs (Johnson, 2002). Most gay and lesbian (GL) individuals, however, will face inordinate levels of sexual identity-related stress (SIS). They will experience internal and external threats as they form their sexual identities, integrate this identity with other personal and social identities, and strive to live authentically in a heterosexual culture.

This chronic state of SIS can impede positive sexual identity development and disrupt same-sex bonding. The purpose of this chapter is to explicate an EFT model for same-sex couples to address the impact of SIS on positive identity development and GL attachment bonds. This chapter expands upon previous efforts to extend EFT to work with GL couples (Josephson, 2003).

POSITIVE GL SEXUAL IDENTITY AND SAME-SEX BONDING: AN ATTACHMENT PERSPECTIVE

Positive sexual identity development is facilitated in secure attachment contexts and supportive social contexts. From an attachment perspective, GL individuals' attachment systems are chronically activated as they face SIS in a heterosexist world (Mohr, 1999). As such, they are particularly in need of a secure attachment bond. Greater emotional support by attachment figures is necessary to develop a positive GL identity. Research affirms that secure attachment may facilitate the safe exploration of identity that promotes the greater likelihood of positive GL identity development and secure same-sex relationships (Elizur & Mintzer, 2001; Jellison & McConnel, 2003; Mohr, 1999, 2003). Many gays and lesbians, however, will be deprived of a crucial sense of connection, positive mirroring, and social validation while forming their identities. Research suggests that individuals who develop a negative GL identity and internalized homophobia are more likely to be insecurely attached (e.g., avoidant, anxious, or fearful avoidant) (Mohr, 2003).

From our perspective, contextual support influences whether one develops a positive sense of sexual identity, which is a key factor in the ability to create secure GL attachment bonds. Heterosexual identity development mostly occurs in supportive attachment and social contexts. Emotional support, guidance, and positive mirroring from attachment figures, peers, and the outside world while developing sexual identity provide many heterosexuals with a sense of being lovable, worthy of care, and desirable on the basis of sexual interests. Others are also deemed trustworthy as a result of their support and positive mirroring of the sexual self. Facilitative social contexts provide the necessary positive mirroring and emotional safety to explore and gain a sense of confidence in one's sexual identity and capacity to form relationships with others in the world on the basis of this identity.

GL sexual identity development, however, is mostly contextually unsupported. We contend that the foremost difference one must consider in working with GL couples is the devastating impact that an overwhelmingly heterosexist world has on GL identity development and how such a milieu imposes chronic stress on the lives of GLs. Identity development most often occurs in attachment contexts that provide minimal emotional support and guidance, and in social environments that are potentially hostile to homosexuality.

Sexual identity development, which is crucial for survival and necessary for secure pair bonding, is obstructed for GLs within this context. The identity-development process involves translating inner realities, sexual interests, and attachment needs for same-sex others into a coherent sense of identity that will link the sexual self to others for the purpose of forming social ties and attachment bonds. Within a heterosexist culture, GL sexual identity development and the growth of a general positive model of self are disrupted with serious consequences for same-sex pair bonding and the psychological and physiological regulation benefits of secure attachment bonds (Cassidy & Shaver, 2008).

Most GLs will face inordinate levels of SIS as they strive to form their identities as gay and lesbian individuals, integrate these identities with other personal and social identities, and live authentically on the basis of their GL identity. In a heterosexist culture attachment figures, peers, and social communities often respond negatively to one's emerging and newly formed GL identity. During moments in which chronic SIS activates the attachment system there will be an increased need for emotional support from others, but GL individuals will often experience abandonment and rejection instead. These emotional experiences and attachment distress related to GL identity development will negatively influence the view of self and other and diminish the likelihood of forming strong social ties and attachment bonds with a partner. Confidence in exploring and integrating same-sex sexual interests and attachment needs in the context of same-sex relationships is diminished when abandonment and rejection have occurred on the basis of sexual self-definition.

Emotional residues and attachment distress related to identity development experiences block open emotional engagement with others, including same-sex partners in GL attachment bonds. Self-protective strategies employed to deal with difficult emotional experiences related to SIS, such as anxious preoccupation or emotional avoidance, will impede same-sex bonding. GL partners are also less likely to risk seeking support to assuage SIS in their same-sex relationships. A negative sense of sexual identity is perpetuated when lingering negative emotional residues and views of self and other associated with SIS cannot be processed and resolved.

In some circumstances negative emotional experiences and attachment fears related to a GL identity block the acceptance of sexual orientation and seriously undermine any kind of safe emotional engagement in GL relationships. Self-protective strategies adopted to manage emotional distress related to SIS also diminish GL partners' capacities to assuage each other's distressing emotional experiences in a heterosexual world.

EFT therapists assess and attune to the emotional realities and self-protective strategies adopted to manage negative emotional residues related to a GL identity that may then block authenticity and engagement in close same-sex relationships. Understanding the attachment significance of GL identity-related experiences and the impact of these experiences on same-sex attachment is critical. Creating a secure base in session to explore negative emotional experiences and attachment distress related to SIS can restore relationships as a potential safe haven. Partners are then supported to risk reaching for emotional care, comfort, and support previously unavailable all the while forming their identities, integrating their GL identity with other personal and social identities, and experiencing chronic stress in a heterosexist world.

This type of engagement provides GLs with a corrective emotional experience of sharing attachment-related emotions and needs associated with SIS. Negative models of self and other associated with the sexual self can then be revised and greater self-acceptance promoted. Same-sex sexual interests and attachment needs for others can then be integrated within the context of a same-sex bond. This process promotes stronger identities and stronger bonds.

SOURCES OF IDENTITY-RELATED STRESS

Sexual Identity Formation: The Trauma of Coming Out

Coming out can be a traumatic experience. Upon initial awareness and acknowledgment of same-sex desires, one grapples with intense negative feelings and emotions, such as confusion, shame, guilt, disgust, fears of rejection and abandonment, and grief at anticipated loss of family, friends, and heterosexual ideals. For GL individuals threats of harm from others and feelings of helplessness in terms of resolving their circumstances contribute to a sense of their relationships and the world around them as unpredictable. Many individuals will fear others' responses and refrain from self-disclosure (D'Augelli, 1991). Fears of rejection and abandonment will block them from reaching for an attachment figure precisely at moments of greatest need for protection and care.

Attachment security may influence the coming-out experience. In secure attachment contexts, coming out to parents often occurs earlier than in insecure contexts (Mohr, 2003). However, in most cases there will be a protracted period of isolation, aloneness, and emotional distress. Secure attachment can also be undermined in circumstances when attachment figures hold antihomosexual sentiments (Mohr, 2003). In insecure attachment contexts, anticipated threats of rejection and abandonment, often on the basis of same-sex desires, evolve into a negative sense of self and of others.

Upon disclosure of a GL sexual identity, rejecting responses may be traumatic. The intensity of these responses may range from expressions of disappointment, sadness, anger, hurt, and rage to verbal/physical aggression including violence. Older gays and lesbians may recall harsher interpersonal and social responses upon coming out than younger GLs. However, a significant percentage of gay and lesbian adolescents still continue to experience outright rejection and verbal and physical assaults from family and members of their community (D'Augelli, Scott, & Pilkington, 1998; Hershberger & D'Augelli, 1995) while having less access to interpersonal supports (Safren & Heimberg, 1999; Tharinger & Wells, 2000). Heightened sensitivities to rejection and abandonment in relationships on the basis of a GL identity are often the emotional legacy of these coming-out experiences. Emotional residues may influence the GLs' attachment experiences with a partner.

To survive, some GLs also internalize negative messages about homosexuality as a means to gain approval or to avoid rejection by others. Internalized homonegativity involves the internalization of dominant heterosexist values and a view of homosexuality as inferior. These internalized views may include hostility, fear, and shame directed at one's self and other gay and lesbian people. These affective responses often interfere with awareness of primary attachment needs and longings sensitivity to the needs of significant others. A core sense of shame, fears about the adequacy of the self, and guilt about having failed parental and social expectations will impede a GL individual's capacity for emotional closeness in same-sex relationships. For example, Martha's fears of getting too close to April are related to a deep sense of defectiveness in relation to her lesbian identity and the harsh, rejecting responses she experienced upon revealing her same-sex interests to others.

During adolescence, a crucial formative period for sexual identity, GL youth are more vulnerable to experiencing a deepening sense of shame, fear, and isolation. A lack of access to romantic partners, hostility toward homosexuality, bullying, and emotional and financial dependency on disapproving parents may all interfere with the coming-out process and with seeking out same-sex romantic relationships. Fears of verbal and physical abuse and rejection compel many GL's to continue hiding their orientation in both high school and beyond (D'Augelli & Hershberger, 1993). Opportunities to explore same-sex interests and learn how to create connection on the basis of these interests may be lost. Instead, rejection from family and peers reinforce avoidance and anxiety, further diminish the likelihood of disclosure (Elizur & Mintzer, 2001).

Many GLs opt to disconnect from the painful emotional realities of rejection and forego needs for same-sex connection by adopting a survival strategy of invisibility. With deactivation of the attachment system they try to bury same-sex desires and attachment needs while engaging in dutiful performances aimed at "passing" as heterosexual. Attempting to appear as heterosexual has dire consequences on same-sex relationship quality (Berger, 1990). For some this strategy will prevail for a lifetime and block the possibility of integrating

same-sex sexual interests and attachment needs in close relationships by shrouding proximity to same-sex partners in
fear, shame, and guilt. For example, Sam often has difficulties relaxing after his day at work. He withdraws to manage
his stress from passing as heterosexual at work. Sam has fears
about turning to Don to talk about his emotional experiences
at work because he feels he cannot comfortably talk to anyone
about his identity-related struggles.

Some GL adolescents may risk relationships to claim an
authentic self, but most will wait to enter into same-sex relationships until after they have left the family home. For many,
these initial relationships will be fraught with a sense of danger and shrouded in secrecy and awkwardness, and they are
as emotionally intense as first-time romantic love in young
heterosexual couples. Too often GLs must attempt to meet the
milestones of romantic and sexual identity development in
isolation rather than in the context of supportive others who
can provide guidance, validation, and social reference points
that normalize the discovery of their emerging sexual selves.

Identity Integration: Blending a GL Identity With Personal and Social Identities

A heterosexist world wreaks emotional havoc on individuals
with same-sex interests when striving to weave a newly formed
GL sexual identity with preexisting personal and social identities. Weaving sexual identity with preexisting personal social
identities triggers fears of painful rejection and abandonment.
In this chapter we explore the threats faced by GLs when integrating their newly formed GL identity with other personal
(e.g., son, daughter) and social (e.g., gender, race, ethnicity)
identities.

Integrating a GL Identity in Families of Origin

In secure attachment contexts GLs may be embraced as a
gay son or lesbian daughter. However, in insecure contexts
compromised by antihomosexual sentiments, difficult sac-
rifices are made to maintain a family identity and minimize
attachment distress. GL individuals will adopt different
self-protective strategies within their families of origin with
dire consequences to self-acceptance and same-sex bonding.

First, GLs anticipating harsh rejection may employ an
avoidant coping strategy. They thwart anticipated and real

experiences of painful rejection by subverting their sexual identities within their families of origin. They maintain attachment on the basis of remaining dutiful and obligated to parents, while same-sex needs and relationships often remain unacknowledged or minimally tolerated. This strategy may involve obligatory family visits during the holiday seasons to the dismay of an unacknowledged relationship partner.

Second, by adopting an anxious coping strategy, some GLs may relentlessly express their anger, hurt, and feelings of betrayal about the lack of acceptance of their sexual orientation and unequal treatment of their same-sex relationships while remaining preoccupied by subsequent fears of abandonment. Threats in families of momentary separation and abandonment on the basis of sexual orientation can heighten anxiety in same-sex relationships. Ongoing family rejection may ultimately lead to full withdrawal from any emotional connection with one's family of origin and thereby have negative implications for models of self and other in close relationships.

Attachment distress on the basis of sexual identity in families of origin may spill over into GL couple relationships. Some GLs prioritize wants and needs of families of origin over those of relationship partners. For example, they may choose to prioritize demands to attend family gatherings (e.g., holidays, weddings) and override the needs of their partner. Partner inaccessibility and unresponsiveness as a result of a sense of duty and preoccupation with family relationships can become a source of conflict.

Julio is critical and angry with Brad based on his unavailability during important holidays. Brad fears rejection from his parents and is not ready to face these fears by confronting his parents about his desires to have his partner present during holiday festivities. Instead Brad withdraws from Julio to manage his distress and their conflict. Partners such as Brad who seek out emotional distance from their significant other as a strategy to manage attachment allegiance conflicts between family of origin and same-sex relationships. Relationship partners may be initially compassionate about these circumstances, but over time they may disrupt the same-sex attachment bond. Attachment injuries may also be experienced when dutifulness or preoccupation with one's family of origin results in abandonment of a partner during moments when this partner's attachment need is acute.

Integrating Sexual Identity With Other Social Identities

Gender

In childhood and adolescence, many GLs will be defensively preoccupied with integrating their sexual and gender identities. In a heterosexist culture several myths exist about the association between gender and sexual orientation. A masculine male is assumed to be heterosexual, while a more effeminate male is suspected of being gay. A more feminine female is assumed to be heterosexual, whereas a more masculine female is possibly presumed to be a lesbian. Effeminate men and masculine women, regardless of sexual orientation, often experience discrimination and verbal and physical aggression for possibly being homosexual.

GLs are particularly sensitive to these circumstances and experience significant distress as they try to reconcile their sexual orientation with societal gender expectations. Fears of rejection and a sense of inadequacy may ensue when there is gender nonconformity. Research affirms that gender nonconformity involves greater rejection by both peers and family (Landolt, Bartholomew, Saffrey, Oram, & Perlman, 2004). Gender nonconformity heightens the threat or actual experiences of rejection, and exacerbates self-protective strategies to manage the distress associated with gender nonconformity and a GL sexual identity.

To manage fears of rejection based on gender and sexuality, some GLs may compulsively subscribe to gender performances of traditional masculinity or femininity. They may either rigidly adopt gender prescriptions consistent with their biological sex or compulsively celebrate their gender nonconformity. Preoccupation with integrating gender and sexual identity may come at the cost of emotional authenticity and thus undermine emotional closeness in same-sex relationships.

Ethnicity, Race, Religion, and Geography

Integrating ethnic, cultural, racial, and rural identities with a GL identity may further exacerbate attachment distress in one's family of origin and sociocultural communities. GLs in liberal, urban jurisdictions that have not faced identity integration challenges may more readily work through the trauma of coming out and revise negative models of self and other. Identity allegiance issues, however, can stall positive identity development by creating emotionally laden conflicts about how to integrate sexual identity with other social identities. Some GLs will give primacy to their racial, ethnic, or religious identity group over their sexual identity (Greene, 1997; Hyeouk & Adkins, 2009).

Identifying as GL in conservative, ethnic, racial, and religious communities or rural jurisdictions may involve isolation from an entire social community. The overlay of heterosexist imperatives within many social communities imposes difficult decisions about social definition on gays and lesbians, forcing them to prioritize their allegiances to their sexual identity or to their cultural, ethnic, and racial identities (Greene, 1994). The process of facing such a dilemma often leaves emotional wounds that can compromise a GL's ability to be open and responsive in close same-sex relationships.

Feelings of anger, hopelessness, despair, guilt, shame and attachment distress are heightened as GLs strive to reconcile biologically hardwired sexual and attachment needs for same-sex others with various identities. In an avoidant strategy, fears of rejection lead some individuals to minimize or dismissively exclude sexual and/or attachment-related emotion and needs for same-sex partners and to place greater importance on other social identity membership to maintain attachments and community ties. Primary attachment to family and social ties to other communities may undermine the formation and maintenance of same-sex attachment bonds.

A heightened sense of danger in these contexts may promote living in isolation, remaining "in the closet," foregoing cohabitation, and maintaining emotional and/or physical distance in same-sex relationships. Partner availability, accessibility, and responsiveness are affected by GLs' efforts to manage fears of exclusion from families and social communities. Others will align themselves with their sexual identity, either by choice or because of rejection, and may subsequently experience further minority stress, isolation, and social marginalization in the predominantly white GL communities in North America.

Sexual Identity Development in the Gay and Lesbian Community and Same-Sex Bonding

Defining sexual identity within the context of the gay and lesbian community may present further challenges to same-sex pair bonding. A myriad of gay and lesbian identities coexist within the GL community and provide a plethora of choices for constructing one's reality as a GL individual or as relationship partner. The majority of lesbians and somewhat fewer gays will seek out a same-sex partner to establish a stable, satisfying, and enduring emotional bond that mirrors traditional heterosexual pair bonds, including a preference for monogamy.

Once in committed relationships, these GL pairs do not differ from heterosexual couples in terms of attachment security (Roisman, Clausell, Holland, Fortuna, & Elieff, 2008). In these cases, inner realities of same-sex sexual interests and attachment needs are integrated into the fabric of their GL identities facilitating secure same-sex bonding. For some, however, anticipation or actual experiences of rejection during sexual identity development will render such bonds highly insecure or altogether impossible to forge. Others will have difficulties integrating sexuality with dependency needs as a result of these experiences.

Relatively more GLs opt for nontraditional relationship structures compared to heterosexual couples. A significant number of gay men will engage in satisfying nonmonogamy (Kurdek, 1995; LaSala, 2004; Peplau & Fingerhut, 2007). For the majority of gay men in open relationships, sexual contact with others often precludes emotional involvement with these other partners (Shernoff, 1995). Rules of sexual engagement will be established to protect from potential emotional and physical risks.

On the other hand, fewer gay men than lesbians have ventured into the world of polyamory, a relationship form in which couple partners may seek out both sexual fulfillment and emotional engagement with others. By virtue of the greater complexity of these relationship structures, polyamory may present a significant threat to same-sex bonds as partners struggle to define relationship boundaries that satisfy attachment needs for emotional safety and security. When sensitive, reliable, and attuned responding—particularly during moments of heightened attachment distress and fear—is not present, open relationships can become a great source of insecurity.

Chronic Stress in a Heterosexist World

Living authentically as an openly GL individual in a same-sex relationship is a chronic source of minority stress. GLs are mindful of their second-class status and that their sexual identity, along with their feelings of love and desire, are open for public debate and judgment. The external threats that accompany heterosexism are pervasive and do not cease, with serious consequences to same-sex bonding. Chronic activation of the attachment system in a heterosexist cultural context amplifies attachment needs for same-sex partners (Mohr, 2008).

Attachment anxiety proliferates in same-sex relationships in the aftermath of a partner experiencing violence related to sexual orientation (Mohr & Fassinger, 2007). For some gays and lesbians, attachment system hypoactivation involves an over-regulation of emotional and attachment distress that becomes expressed in emotional withdrawal. The necessity of coping with the rejection experiences associated with coming out and living openly as a gay or lesbian individual with one's family and community is a life-long process expecially in the face of heterosexism. Secure attachment, however, can buffer GLs against the negative emotional experiences associated with chronic SIS.

A heterosexist cultural context constitutes a constant and chronic source of stress wrought with threats of rejection, regardless of previous experience. It colors the perception of physical and emotional safety in any transaction involving openly identifying one's sexual identity. Some couples will attempt to constrict their entire lives to the safety of the gay and lesbian community on the basis of their discomfort with and fear of the outside world. Considerable pressure can also be placed on the relationship to buffer high levels of emotional distress based on increasing isolation and anticipated or real external threats. For example, one partner may disclose sexual identity at work, while the other does not due to fears of discrimination. When one partner has come out and the other has not, the disparity creates pressure on individual partners and their relationships as they strive to manage distress related to "staying in" or "coming out" of the closet.

Partners may struggle in terms of where to draw a line regarding when and to whom to disclose their identities. Attachment anxiety or avoidance may be reinforced as strategies to manage internal distress related to circumstances of rejection or differences in partners' sexual identity disclosure. Anxiety may be related to overestimates of the degree of threat involved in coming out or environmental threats, while avoidance may be related to underestimates of the reality of the danger involved (Mohr, 2008). Others will accurately perceive the perils of heterosexism and, on the basis of their assessment of risk, constrict authenticity. Differences in the degree to which partners are out to their families, social communities, employers, and colleagues can be a serious source of conflict in gay and lesbian relationships.

AN EFT MODEL FOR GAYS AND LESBIANS

Case Conceptualization: The Same, yet Different

In its clinical application EFT targets emotional responses to restructure rigid, negative interaction cycles—such as pursue–withdraw interactions—that block safe emotional engagement and contribute to attachment insecurity. EFT with GL couples is implemented as usual, but with special consideration and sensitivity directed toward how GLs and their relationships are subject to unique sources of SIS that have implications for the regulation of emotion and emerging views of self and other. The therapist must assess whether SIS in a heterosexist world is actively impeding positive gay identity development and the process of secure bonding. The conceptualization of couple distress must then be broadened to address the impact of heterosexism on each partner's sense of self and GL identity and the expression of attachment needs.

Treatment may require an exploration of the unprocessed emotional history and attachment distress including traumatic experiences related to SIS and current environmental stressors. The regulation strategies adopted to manage emotional and attachment distress in a heterosexist world will often shape a partner's position in the couple's negative cycle (i.e., an anxiously attached partner's critical, angry, pursuit and/or an avoidantly attached partner's withdrawal). Typical patterns of couple distress may also be colored by emotional processes and a history of insecurity prompted by the rejection and bias of heterosexism.

Secondary reactive emotional responding and negative traumatic experiences in heterosexist contexts often make it difficult for GL partners to process primary fears and attachment-related emotions. These experiences and the self-protective strategies adopted to survive external threats are systematically unpacked to support partners in understanding the emotional and attachment implications of growing up as a GL. Partner inaccessibility, for example, can be reframed as a consequence of numbing in order to survive in a heterosexist world. Accessibility and responsiveness between GL partners, including emotional support concerning past and current SIS, creates emotional closeness and strengthens the couple relationship. Facing the ongoing stress of living in a hetero-sexist world together also then strengthens the bond between partners.

Stage 1: Assessment of the Impact of Heterosexist Culture and Cycle De-Escalation

Assessment

The initial assessment session evolves as usual with the objectives of identifying core emotional issues and mapping out the cycle and rigid interaction patterns underlying conflicts. Individual partner assessments may require an additional time or a second session, depending on issues related to sexual identity formation, integration experiences, and current life stressors related to sexual identity. Specifically, two broader questions should be integrated into these individual sessions:

- What are the emotional residues and self-protective strategies that have been evoked in coming out and surviving in current life contexts?
- What is the impact of these experiences on sense of self and emotional engagement in close relationships?

The therapist must attune to the presence of secondary reactive emotional responses related to SIS and current life stressors. GL clients, however, will vary widely in terms of their coming-out experiences; current environmental stressors related to age, ethnicity, race, cultural background, and geography, as well as relationship and attachment history.

Through this assessment, the EFT therapist ascertains whether SIS is impeding emotional engagement with a partner, as well as the extent to which each partner is able to make the same-sex relationship a priority. Referrals for individual therapy may be warranted when clients are experiencing extreme negative emotional reactions or use rigid self-protective strategies to manage ongoing SIS that interfere with bonding with a same-sex partner. For example, a partner with internalized homophobia may have difficulties surrendering to more vulnerable emotions in the context of a close relationship because closeness brings the client into a place of deep discomfort with his or her own sexual orientation.

In some cases, individuals may need to explore the risks of prioritizing their same-sex relationship, which may, for example, involve coming out to others as a gay or lesbian person. The EFT therapist needs to refrain from suggesting, however, that clients come out or directly address chronic environmental stressors associated with being GL without a full evaluation of the real threats to the client's emotional and physical safety as well as readiness to address these issues. In some cases, referrals to therapists who specialize in gay and lesbian identity development issues or gay and lesbian community resources may be useful to support positive identity development.

The Cycle

The therapist integrates an understanding of the emotional regulation strategies employed by GL clients to protect themselves in a heterosexist world. These strategies inform the conceptualization of each partner's position in the couple dance. Numbing and reactive anger associated with becoming and being a GL person texture a partner's ability to trust and sense of entitlement to care and exacerbate anxious preoccupation or emotional avoidance. The internalization of homonegativity to avoid painful rejection or gain approval by heterosexual others and traumatic experiences upon coming out can also result in the extreme ambivalence and dysregulation of fearful avoidant attachment. These emotional responses are placed within the context of the cycle and construed as fueling each partner's position in the negative cycle that typically defines the couple's emotional disconnection.

The therapist reflects and validates these secondary responses as reactions to nonsupportive attachment figures and social contexts in a heterosexist culture and normalizes the self-protective strategies adopted to survive anticipated or actual rejection and abandonment. Reflection and validation of these emotional realities will facilitate a safe therapeutic milieu and promote processing of these emotional experiences. Secondary reactive responses and associated negative models of self are also understood and reframed in the context of the couple's negative cycle.

Partner responses are also reframed to elucidate underlying attachment vulnerabilities related to sexual identity development. The attachment implications of these experiences are explored and contextualized as contributing to fears of accessing, expressing, and responding to more vulnerable attachment-related emotions in same-sex relationships. By the end of Stage 1, partners gain awareness of how each partner's position in the cycle has been influenced by the unprocessed emotional residues and self-protective strategies evoked to manage emotional and attachment distress while forming and synthesizing gay identities and surviving chronic stress.

Stage 1 of EFT With Daniel and Robert

The following transcript segment represents a key moment in EFT with Daniel and Robert, a gay male couple in their early 30s who have been together for 4 years. The couple present with typical pursue–withdraw dynamics fueled by lingering negative feelings and emotions pertaining to their struggles with being gay. Robert's difficulties gaining acknowledgment and acceptance within his family of origin of his gay identity and same-sex relationship has resulted in many relationship conflicts. For example, Robert has historically spent Christmas holidays with his family of origin, much to Daniel's dismay.

The therapist reflects and validates Robert's emotional experiences and his efforts to protect himself from the overwhelming distress he experiences in his family, who refuse to accept his homosexuality and his same-sex relationship. These emotional experiences and strategies are linked to Robert's current position in the cycle as a withdrawer. His underlying fear of rejection is accessed and understood in the context of painful rejection that has undermined optimal sexual identity development. Robert has become increasingly withdrawn as his sense of hopelessness and fear of rejection by both his family and Daniel grow. He has been unable to reach out to Daniel to assuage his distress and thus is becoming increasingly fearful of eventually being rejected by Daniel. He is between two worlds and safe in neither of these worlds.

Therapist: Becoming a gay man has been so hard for you, Robert. It has come with so many threats from the outside world from the beginning. The costs continue to be great, especially the lack of acceptance of your relationship and sexuality on the part of your family. It seems like there has been so much hurt, pain, and rejection when it comes to your being a gay man and your way of dealing with this has been to withdraw. You fear losing your relationship with your parents and now you fear losing your relationship with Daniel, so you withdraw.

Robert: I get all stuck—stuck in fear. I'm not really sure where to go. I have to manage these tugs and pulls. It feels hopeless.

Therapist: So you withdraw and you are left all alone with difficult feelings again—like when you first came out, fearing rejection from your parents. And now, still, these same feelings emerge as you try to convince your family to accept your gay identity and same-sex relationship. Then, as you withdraw to deal with these feelings, your partner feels threatened. He demands that you make him the priority and you feel stuck, so you withdraw even more, overwhelmed by fear.

Robert: Yes. It's frightening because I'm afraid of being rejected on all sides. No matter where I turn.

Stage 2: New Cycles of Emotional Engagement

In Stage 2, the preceding struggles and strategies, which reduce a partner's emotional accessibility and constrict emotional responses in same-sex relationships, are further explored and placed within the context of the cycle. The EFT therapist reflects these emotional realities and validates the emotional risk and need to self-protect as a result of the anticipated or past loss. A lesbian partner's reactive anger at perceived lack of closeness with her partner may be exacerbated by her rejection by work colleagues or the larger community. She may also be experiencing feelings of failure or guilt for not having adhered to heterosexist cultural ideals.

Fears of inadequacy and rejection increase sensitivity to abandonment by the partner and fuel reactive blaming or numbing withdrawal. A gay male may be frozen by the overwhelming grief of multiple losses of friends and former partners to AIDS and thus be unable to risk emotional closeness in his current relationship. A lesbian woman may have learned to block her own self-expression and needs in order to avoid others' threatening responses.

Withdrawer Reengagement

Withdrawer reengagement occurs when the withdrawn partner is invited to consider the possibilities of ending his or her emotional isolation by sharing attachment fears and needs. This process is the same as in heterosexual couples, but also integrates negative emotion experiences and traumatic abuses associated with being a GL person in a heterosexist world.

Interaction patterns are restructured to facilitate new cycles of open emotional engagement, attunement, and responsiveness whereby the more withdrawn partner accesses and expresses attachment-related emotions and needs for nurturance and protection to sooth key moments of threat in the relationship and ongoing SIS. A pursuer's accessibility and responsiveness allows for the safe emotional engagement that was previously often unthinkable in close relationships with others because of issues related to GL identity development.

Blamer Softening

During blamer softening, the ability to risk expressing more vulnerable attachment emotions and needs occurs. Attachment fears are often extreme in GL partners for all the reasons summarized before. Momentary relapses into critical, relentless pursuing may also result from heightened needs for attention and soothing that arise from past and current injuries related to SIS. For example, fears of discrimination on the basis of sexual orientation at work or fears of abandonment by family members on the basis of being gay or lesbian may suddenly heighten needs for contact comfort and attention from one's partner. An HIV-positive individual's increasing sense of social marginalization and fears of discrimination may also initiate panic and desperate efforts to restore contact with the significant other.

In therapy, a withdrawn partner's emotional reengagement creates emotional safety for the previously blaming partner, who can then risk asserting needs and longings for attention, care, and support. In some cases, attachment injuries occur as a result of a partner's emotional inaccessibility, which is experienced as abandonment during key moments of heightened need for care particularly when related to sexual identity development issues discussed in this chapter.

The softening process also creates a more secure bond that is a healing arena for gay partners. Mutual accessibility and responsiveness to the emotional distress arising from a heterosexist world defines the relationship as a safe haven. Isolation is diminished and partners are able to buffer each other from stress and the emotional residues of their experiences of heterosexism. Same-sex sexual desire and attachment longings can now be integrated into the context of same-sex pair bonds. An integrated identity arises from and is essential to secure same-sex attachment relationships. Partners are then better able to attune to each other's emotional realities within their intimate relationship and learn to deal with SIS in a manner that promotes a deeper emotional connection.

Stage 2 of EFT With Gabriela and Maxine

Gabriela and Maxine, partners for 6 years, reside together in a socially and politically conservative jurisdiction that does not support legalization of gay and lesbian marriages or adoption rights. They present with a negative cycle of pursue–withdraw. Gabriela is a 28-year-old woman from a very strict, religious, Italian family. She anticipates serious harm—including possible verbal and physical aggression, broken family ties, and community isolation—in the event that her sexual orientation becomes public knowledge. Fearing abandonment and rejection by her family and ethnic community, she has become increasingly vigilant about Maxine's availability to her.

In surviving heterosexist contexts, Maxine, a 39-year-old woman, has often opted for a strategy of invisibility in her efforts to adapt in a homophobic family context and now in her workplace as a senior lawyer for a large, conservative legal firm. She has not come out at work, but has experienced threats in the form of derogatory jokes and overhearing vicious gossip about her sexuality. She fears that she will not be promoted as a result. At times, she fears for her physical safety in her neighborhood because she was previously the victim of aggression on the basis of her nonfeminine appearance. Maxine has always valued her self-reliance and has opted to avoid processing emotional and attachment distress or current stressors resulting from her current heterosexist context. In addition, she feels overwhelmed by Gabriela's high demands for attention. Within these fears and demands, she has become increasingly withdrawn to manage her distress and is unable to access Gabriela for emotional support.

In this segment, the therapist ties the couple's pursue–withdraw cycle to SIS. Both women feel isolated, helpless, and fearful, yet are unable to access each other for emotional comfort. The therapist makes links between heterosexism, Gabriela's negative view of self, and her attachment fears Gabriela is supported to reach out to Maxine for comfort and support from a more authentic and vulnerable place.

Therapist: So for you, Gabriela, first learning you were a lesbian came with a lot of distress, a sense that somehow you might be defective and unlovable for your longings and desires—so much so that you fear that you may even be abandoned by family members and your community.

Gabriela: I was raised to see it as wrong, that lesbians and gays die old, alone, and unhappy, and can't have families. Growing up, my parents would say they would kill one of us if we were one of those. It's a disgrace in my culture.

Therapist: So it never seemed possible to you that you could be a lesbian and still be lovable and okay. Instead, you feared harm and threats of abandonment by others. So, for you, fears of abandonment have gone hand in hand with your lesbian identity. You get really frightened and a bit helpless about what to do.

Gabriela: I'm afraid that no one will love me, can love me, for who I am.

Therapist: And a heterosexist world has taught you that you are unlovable as a lesbian and this comes with threats that you will be abandoned. That's when your fears overtake you and you desperately pursue Maxine. So when Maxine does not respond to you when you call out her name, that's when you get angry; you ring the alarm bells as loudly as you can, right? You get that desperate feeling that you're going to die alone. You are alone and the world is against you. That must be so frightening for you.

Gabriela: I can barely breathe then.

Therapist: So you reach for Maxine; you get angry, not sure if she will be there, but angry to get her attention and contact at any cost. But it's also hard to reach out to Maxine, when you feel like it's not okay, that you're unlovable as a lesbian. Does that fit?

Gabriela: Yes. She's all I have. I need her. It's hard though. She's so independent—always working. I don't feel okay with me because I'm scared, but her love makes me feel okay.

Therapist: It's been hard for you to feel okay as a lesbian and maybe we need to look at ways in which we can help you feel better about yourself here, to find ways of moving you toward more comfort with yourself in the world. It's a journey. Maybe Maxine can help, yes? Can you risk turning to her now, to let her know what's been going on inside, and how she might comfort you in your isolation, when you get scared that

> you're unlovable and will be abandoned by others in
> the outside world and even perhaps by her?

Maxine's increased responsiveness to Gabriela's new coherent and compelling pleas for support restore the couple partnership as a safe haven and offer a secure base from which to go
out into the world, including further developing their lesbian
identities. Through therapy, Gabriela has decided to be more
emotionally distant toward her family and seek out friends'
support to develop a more positive lesbian identity. She is now
able to turn to Maxine with the fears, grief, and loss related to
her identity integration and the loss of connection to her family and cultural community. Maxine is also able to reach for
Gabriela's comfort to assuage emotional distress related to her
workplace and, with Gabriela's support decides to confront
homophobic attitudes at work. Emotional engagement around
SIS enhances emotional connection in the relationship and
offers a sense of protection, comfort, and support against the
dangers of the outside world.

While Gabriela and Maxine were able to create a sense of connectedness, in some cases, a partner may continue to maintain
allegiance to preexisting personal, social, or cultural identities
that preclude increased emotional availability and engagement
in the relationship. Some individuals may not be able to make
the same-sex partner a priority. In these circumstances, the
attachment implications of such circumstances must be expli-
cated by the therapist, and difficult decisions must be made by
both partners about the future of the relationship.

Stage 3: Reconsolidation and Facilitating Positive Sexual Identity Development

In Stage 3, partners explore together ways to resolve varying
identity issues or chronic threats related to sexual orientation.
For example, they may opt to establish relationship boundaries to protect their same-sex attachment bond; this may
include placing limits on their engagement with nonsupportive members of their families of origin and social communities. In another scenario, a partner may decide, based on his or
her emotional readiness, that it is time to come out to family
members as a means of prioritizing the same-sex relationship.
An isolated couple may decide to engage with the gay and lesbian community.

External threats in a heterosexist system, however, may continue to impede partner accessibility when SIS becomes emotionally overwhelming. These identity-related stresses must be explored thoroughly and the emotional impact of these issues on attachment security explored openly. Partners can often then find creative solutions. For example, couple partners may decide to text message each other when at work to reduce fears of discrimination in homophobic work contexts.

SUPERVISION AND TRAINING ISSUES: COMBATING THE IMPACT OF HETEROSEXISM

Awareness of how a heterosexist system pervades the contexts of GLs' lives and affects their ongoing sense of personhood, as well as same-sex attachment bonds, is crucial for EFT supervisors and trainees working with same-sex couples. Acquiring knowledge about these issues, as well as the social, political, and legal circumstances of GLs within the therapist's jurisdiction, promotes a stronger working alliance with these couples and facilitates the therapist's empathy for emotional experiences related to SIS. GL clients also benefit from the positive affirmation of their sexual orientation and their efforts to create same-sex love connections in a world that obfuscates same-sex bonding.

Therapists who do not hold positive views of homosexuality or who disapprove of gay and lesbian social, political, and legal equality, including same-sex marriage rights, are often compromised in their ability to affirm and support their clients as they struggle to live openly and authentically in their same-sex relationships. Therapists who hold heterosexist views that go unchecked run the risk of retraumatizing gays and lesbians by minimizing past and current painful emotional realities and thus exacerbating the emotional injuries sustained. The opportunity for a corrective emotional experience with the therapist is then lost.

Genuineness, positive regard, and attunement to the chronic emotional and attachment distress related to SIS and affirmation of same-sex relationships are all essential components of a strong working alliance with this population. GLs will vary in terms of their comfort with their sexual identity, their integration in gay and lesbian communities, and their personal journeys of healing from the wounds inflicted in nonsupportive attachment and social contexts. Therapists must also be prepared to address their own heterosexism, internalized homonegativity, and negative emotional reactions in order to support their clients adequately.

Providing education and affirming GLs' sexual orientations and efforts to create same-sex bonds may also be pivotal in supporting self-acceptance of a client's sexual orientation. When a client exhibits significant discomfort with his sexual identity, a referral for individual therapy may be warranted to support positive identity development.

CONCLUSION

EFT therapists working with gays and lesbians can readily apply EFT as usual for some gay and lesbian couples. In many cases, however, the trauma of coming out, forming and integrating sexual identity within the fabric of one's personal and social worlds, and the chronic environmental stressors in a heterosexist world wreak emotional havoc in the lives of GLs often impeding emotional closeness and intimacy in same-sex relationships. Attempting to live authentically and loving same-sex partners on the margins of society leave emotional residues in the lives of GLs and increase the need for safe haven relationships while also making these relationships more difficult. Heterosexism leaves an indelible mark on gays and the emotional regulation strategies employed to manage the negative emotional experiences associated with SIS often interfere with GLs' ability to create secure same-sex pair bonds.

The EFT model for GLs put forward in this chapter links GL individuals' experiences in a heterosexist world to secondary emotional responses and associated negative views of self and other that block intimate and authentic emotional engagement. These fears impede the processing of vulnerable, primary attachment-related emotions in close, same-sex relationships. Open emotional engagement allows for ongoing coherent identity development and the integration of sexual and attachment needs in the context of same-sex pair bonds. Partner accessibility and responsiveness to vulnerable emotions related to SIS strengthen identities and promote more secure bonding in GL relationships. Secure attachment is a universal need for all couples. The EFT therapist is committed to making this the norm for all partners.

REFERENCES

Berger, R. M. (1990). Passing: Impact on the quality of same-sex couple relationships. *Social Work, 35,* 328–332.

Cassidy, J., & Shaver, P. R. (2008). *Handbook of attachment: Theory, research, and clinical applications book.* New York, NY: Guilford Press.

D'Augelli, A. R. (1991). Gay men in college: Identity processes and adaptations. *Journal of College Student Development, 32,* 140–146.

D'Augelli, A. R., & Hershberger, S. L. (1993). Lesbian, gay, and bisexual youth in community settings: Personal challenges and mental health problems. *American Journal of Community Psychology, 21,* 421–448.

D'Augelli, A. R., Scott, L. H., & Pilkington, N. W. (1998). Lesbian, gay, and bisexual youth and their families: Disclosure of sexual orientation and its consequences. *American Journal of Orthopsychiatry, 68,* 361–371.

Elizur, Y., & Mintzer, A. (2001). A framework for the formation of gay male identity: Processes associated with adult attachment style and support from family and friends. *Archives of Sexual Behavior, 30*(2), 143–167.

Elizur, Y., & Mintzer, A. (2003). Gay males' intimate relationship quality: The roles of attachment security, gay identity, social support, and income. *Personal Relationships, 10,* 411–435.

Greene, B. (1994). Ethnic minority lesbians and gay men: Mental health treatment issues. *Journal of Consulting and Clinical Psychology, 62,* 243–251.

Greene, B. (1997). Lesbian women of color: Triple jeopardy. In L. Comas-Diaz & B. Greene (Eds.), *Women of color: Integrating ethnic and gender identities in psychotherapy* (pp. 389–427). New York, NY: Guilford Press.

Hershberger, S. L., & D'Augelli, A. R. (1995). The impact of victimization on the mental health and suicidality of lesbian, gay, and bisexual youths. *Developmental Psychology, 31,* 65–74.

Hyeouk, C. H., & Adkins, C. (2009). A model of Asian and Pacific Islander sexual minority acculturation. *Journal of LGBT Youth, 6,* 155–173.

Jellison, W. A., & McConnel, A. R. (2003). The mediating effects of attitudes toward homosexuality between secure attachment and disclosure outcomes among gay men. *Journal of Homosexuality, 46,* 159–177.

Johnson, S. M. (2002). *Emotionally focused couple therapy with trauma survivors: Strengthening attachment bonds.* New York, NY: Guildford Press.

Josephson, G. J. (2003). Using an attachment-based intervention with same-sex couples. In S. M. Johnson & V. E. Whiffen (Eds.), *Attachment processes in couple and family therapy* (pp. 300–320). New York, NY: Guilford Press.

Kurdek, L. A. (1995). Lesbian and gay couples. In A. R. D'Augelli & C. J. Patterson (Eds.), *Lesbian, gay, and bisexual identities over the lifespan: Psychological perspectives* (pp. 243–261). New York, NY: Oxford University Press.

Kurdek, L. A. (2002). On being insecure about the assessment of attachment styles. *Journal of Social and Personal Relationships, 19,* 803–826.

Landolt, M. A., Bartholomew, K., Saffrey, C., Oram, D., & Perlman, D. (2004). Gender nonconformity, childhood rejection, and adult attachment: A study of gay men. *Archives of Sexual Behavior, 33,* 117–128.

LaSala, M. C. (2004). Extradyadic sex and gay male couples: Comparing monogamous and nonmonogamous relationships. *Families in Society: Journal of Contemporary Human Services, 85,* 405–412.

Mohr, J. J. (1999). Same-sex romantic attachment. In J. Cassidy & P. R. Shaver (Eds.), *Handbook of attachment: Theory, research, and clinical applications* (pp. 378–394). New York, NY: Guilford Press.

Mohr, J. J. (2003). Self-acceptance and self-disclosure of sexual orientation in lesbian, gay, and bisexual adults: An attachment perspective. *Journal of Counseling Psychology, 50*(4), 482–495.

Mohr, J. J. (2008). Same-sex romantic attachment. In J. Cassidy & P. R. Shaver (Eds.), *Handbook of attachment theory and research* (2nd ed.; pp. 482–502). New York, NY: Guilford Press.

Mohr, J. J., & Fassinger, R. E. (2007). Attachment in same-sex couples: Basic processes and minority stress effects. In J. J. Mohr (chair), *Attachment and caregiving in same-sex romantic relationships.* Symposium conducted at the meeting of the American Psychological Association, San Francisco, CA.

Peplau, L. A., & Fingerhut, A. W. (2007). The close relationships of lesbians and gay men. *Annual Review of Psychology, 58,* 10.1–10.20.

Ridge, S. R., & Feeney, J. A. (1998). Relationship history and relationship attitudes in gay males and lesbians: Attachment style and gender differences. *Australian and New Zealand Journal of Psychiatry, 32,* 848–859.

Roisman, G. I., Clausell, E., Holland, A., Fortuna, K., & Elieff, C. (2008). Adult romantic relationships as contexts of human development: A multimethod comparison of same-sex couples with opposite-sex dating, engaged, and married dyads. *Developmental Psychology, 44,* 91–101.

Safren, S. A., & Heimberg, R. G. (1999). Depression, hopelessness, suicidality, and related factors in sexual minority and heterosexual adolescents. *Journal of Consulting and Clinical Psychology, 67,* 859–866.

Shernoff, M. (1995). Male couples and their relationship styles. *Journal of Gay & Lesbian Social Services, 2*(2), 43–58.

Tharinger, D., & Wells, G. (2000). An attachment perspective on the developmental challenges of gay and lesbian adolescents: The need for continuity of caregiving from family and schools. *School Psychology Review, 29,* 158–172.

Fourteen

Spirituality and Emotionally Focused Couple Therapy
Exploring Common Ground

JAMES L. FURROW, SUSAN M. JOHNSON,
BRENT BRADLEY, AND JOHN AMODEO

INTRODUCTION

Couples in distress often face painful struggles that raise searching questions about one's faith in love, commitment, and another person. These struggles may prompt existential questions as one is challenged by various choices and uncertainties about what is of ultimate importance or value. Many of the couples facing issues like those covered in this book turn to faith and spirituality as a source of purpose and hope. Increasingly, spirituality is recognized as a source of resilience for couples and families (e.g., Anderson & Worthen, 1997; Walsh, 2008).

Couple and family therapists are exploring ways to incorporate spiritual practices like mindfulness (Gehart & McCollum, 2007) and prayer (Beach, Fincham, Hurt, McNair, & Stanley, 2008) into their practices. Recent attention has been given to transformative factors that promote resilience and flourishing among couples. These factors include areas common to religious practice, including forgiveness, sacrificial commitment, and prayer (Fincham, Stanley, & Beach, 2007). Researchers and practitioners are increasingly looking to spirituality and faith as a resource for couples and families seeking healing and growth.

In this chapter we explore the common ground of spirituality, religiousness, and EFT practice. First, Susan Johnson and

John Amodeo explore the use of EFT with Buddhist thought and practice. They illustrate how EFT's emphasis on interdependence and connection fits well within the rich traditions of Buddhism and practices of mindfulness. Then James Furrow and Brent Bradley illustrate EFT with a highly religious Christian couple. This presentation examines a practical approach to working with deeply held religious values, philosophies, and life perspectives. They explore how a couple's religious background provides an essential context for informing in-session experience. Finally, key themes are presented that highlight ways in which an EFT therapist may work from a genuine position of understanding and appreciation for the spirituality and religious perspectives of their couples.

EFT AND THE BUDDHIST PERSPECTIVE: AN EASY CONNECTION

> Buddhism is an "immanent" approach to spirituality, suggesting that what we seek is happening right in front of our noses within the experience of day to day living. The thirst is...to embrace each moment wholeheartedly. In contrast, a "transcendental" approach is a "trickle-down" methodology, in which repeated experiences of mystical union (closeness to God) gradually make our daily experience more complete. (Germer, 2005, p. 23)

> Buddhist teachings are not a religion, they are a science of mind. (Dalai Lama)

At first glance, it may appear that Buddhism and EFT are resoundingly antagonistic. EFT draws upon research suggesting that distress and conflict are generated by our inability to create strong and reliable intimate attachments. Buddhism, on the other hand, is often understood to be a path of nonattachment. Desires and longings are often seen as the source of suffering. Can we reconcile these seemingly contradictory paths into one that converges and complements both? Can EFT practitioners work with Buddhist-orientated clients in a way that is consistent with their clients' worldview? Are there ways in which Buddhist practice might even be parallel to the practice of EFT?

In fact, there are many points of convergence here. In both perspectives, experience is preeminent. The Dalai Lama insists that one should not accept any principle without first verifying it in one's own experience (reason is considered to be the second resource and scripture the last). Both the EFT therapist and the Buddhist value direct evidence and thus value science.

Traditionally, Buddhism has focused on suffering—on the worldly ills of sickness, old age, and death—and offered an eightfold path to alleviate human misery. If the Buddha were alive today, where the divorce rate is high and the disappointments of romantic love have been seared into many people's hearts, he might have added relationships to this list of afflictions. Modern Buddhists, such as the Dalai Lama, also stress the key existential significance of human connection by stating that while human beings can live without religion or meditation, they cannot live without "human affection."

There are points of apparent divergence. The Buddha's first Noble Truth is that life is marked by *dukkha,* which has been translated as suffering, dissatisfaction, imperfection, or angst. His second Noble Truth is that this pervasive unease is caused by *tanha,* which means "thirst." Many authors have equated tanha with desire but "craving" appears to be a more accurate translation. Buddhist writer and psychiatrist Mark Epstein (2005) explains that tanha "connotes what we might also call clinging, the attempt to hold on to an ungraspable experience, not the desire for happiness or completion" (p. 10). Differentiating desire from craving and clinging has important implications. Clinical experience suggests that interpreting the cause of suffering as desire can turn people against themselves, thereby prolonging suffering. Psychologist and Buddhist teacher Tara Brach (2003) stresses the importance of working with our desires rather than eliminating them:

> The Buddha never intended to make desire itself the problem. When he said craving causes suffering, he was referring not to our natural inclination as living beings to have wants and needs, but to our habit of clinging to experience that must, by nature, pass away. (p. 129)

Clients who believe that liberation means eliminating desire often feel shame around their genetically wired longing for human connection. Rather than welcoming the felt experience around their longings, they may judge themselves for the hurt and fear that may arise from the frustrated longing to love and be loved. Such clients may need gentle coaxing to recognize that longing is hardwired into us and that we suffer less as we learn to accept our desires and feelings rather than judge them. Such clients may recognize that their attempt to eliminate longings for secure connection only leads to their indirect expression, which generates confusion for their partner and frustration for themselves. The Buddhist tanha can be seen as synonymous with the Western concept of anxious, insecure attachment (Kuar Sahdra, Shaver, & Warren Brown, 2010), which is addressed in EFT.

The Buddha's teaching is known as the "middle way." This is a path that lies somewhere between the strict asceticism that the preenlightened Buddha tried and rejected and the path of self-indulgence. The middle way is neither to try to extinguish desires and longings nor to get lost in them. This balanced path parallels the conceptualization of health in secure attachment; security is a state where longings are accepted without obsessive and desperate clinging or numbed denial. EFT offers a path to more secure connection where we can work skillfully with our longings and associated feelings so that we minimize the suffering associated with them and maximize the possibility of intrapsychic balance and rich connections with others.

Buddhists are encouraged to take refuge in the "Three Jewels": the Buddha (the awakened mind and heart), the *dharma* (the teachings or the truth), and the *sangha* (the spiritual community). Taking refuge in the sangha has implications that are especially compatible with the goals of EFT. The Buddhist monk Thich Nhat Hanh (2008) suggests that a couple can be a "refuge for each other" and that the key problem in relationships is reactive anger and fear, which EFT addresses. Embracing interdependence (a key tenet of Buddhism) and building supportive relationships and community can be facilitated by the specific practices central to EFT.

IMPLEMENTING EFT WITH BUDDHIST COUPLES

Commentators note that experiential interventions, especially those that work with the "felt sense" of a problem, are "strikingly similar" to the Buddhist practice of mindfulness (Germer, 2005). There are specific ways in which Buddhist practice fits and complements a humanistic experiential and systemic therapy such as EFT. Buddhist and EFT practitioners seem to see key human problems and the path toward healthy functioning in similar terms. The most obvious connection is that both give priority to the cultivation of deepening levels of *awareness.* Both have as a goal that as human beings we should be more fully alive and awake in our lives (as a word, "buddha" means "to awaken"). Both see health and growth as dependent on the ability to be fully engaged in the *present moment*—entering the stream of ongoing experience.

A Buddhist teacher and an EFT therapist both aspire to help others recognize when they are on automatic pilot and be able to relate to and engage with their experience in a different way. Both approaches help others attend to the process of experiencing as it occurs and become more aware of their active part in how this process unfolds. Both promote the awareness of how we *actively construct* mental models, our reality, and thus our relationships with others. In both, growth involves *accepting experience with open curiosity* as it occurs rather than restricting, disowning, or distancing by becoming absorbed in cognitive categorization. The EFT therapist is "mindful" in the Buddhist sense in that he or she directs focused attention to the active creation of present experience with open receptivity and acceptance and attempts to help clients do the same.

Both EFT and Buddhism value *emotional regulation.* As the Buddhist writer Jack Kornfield (1993) notes, "It is the feeling level that controls most of our inner life" (p. 107). Both direct attention to the human tendency to become flooded and carried away by strong emotions in a way that perpetuates dysfunctional patterns and suffering. Both offer ways to liberate us from the need to numb ourselves and limit our engagement in the present moment. A Buddhist might talk of establishing equanimity while an EFT therapist might talk of ordering difficult experience and being able to hold a "working distance" from emotional experience. Both Buddhism and a humanistic therapy such as EFT address the emotional impact of existential realities rather than pragmatic problem solving per se, encouraging clients or students to deal actively with Yalom's (1980) existential givens and the anxiety they create. These givens are death, isolation, freedom, and meaninglessness. Both advocate a focus on dealing with emotion so that it does not distort or narrow the flow of our moment-to-moment experience.

In terms of relationships, EFT and Buddhist teachings give priority to acceptance, *compassion,* and openness to others. Empathic acceptance and responsiveness are the scaffold on which EFT is built. This focus derives from the humanistic stance of Carl Rogers, the father of experiential therapy, as well as from an attachment view of relationships. In this view, empathic responsiveness builds a safe haven that minimizes fear and offers a secure base that maximizes full engagement with the world and exploratory learning. In a similar vein, the Dalai Lama teaches monks to yell "mother" when they feel afraid (Begley, 2007). He teaches them, in effect, to use and prime the attachment system in a way that has the potential to calm the nervous system and promote more conscious choice in terms of response. Research suggests that attachment security appears to increase altruism and compassion for others (Mikulincer, Shaver, Gillath, & Nitzberg, 2005).

Buddhism espouses the interdependence of all sentient beings. This stance echoes attachment theory, which focuses on the compelling connection between attachment figures and how this felt sense of connection with others shapes our physiological functioning, ongoing sense of self, emotional reality, and ways of cognitively framing our world. This Buddhist perspective also fits with the systemic orientation of attachment and of EFT that views individuals in terms of the feedback loops they create with other beings and that then shape their inner and outer realities.

We are suggesting, then, that experiential therapy models and Buddhist viewpoint and methods of practice are not only highly compatible but also in fact parallel in many significant ways, specifically regarding a focus on increased engagement with the present process of experiencing. The father of the experiential approach, Carl Rogers (1961), offered an image of a fully functioning person as one who is open to experience and to both difficult and positive emotions, able to tune in to and trust the self and others (labeled "organismic trusting"), more able to live existentially in the moment without rigid defenses, and experientially free to choose from different alternatives. This might also be a description of a secure person in terms of attachment. More securely attached people respond with lower physiological reactivity to ego-threatening stimuli (Diamond, Hicks, & Otter Henderson, 2006). It might also be a description of a good Buddhist.

The main way that the Buddhist perspective appears to be currently influencing the field of psychotherapy is through the increasing use of forms of mindfulness as part of therapy. This chapter will now focus on mindfulness and how it links with the EFT model. The term "mindfulness" can be used in many different ways—as a trait, as a skill or technique to reduce stress or distress, as a way of being, and as a spiritual practice. The word is an English translation of the Pali word "sati" and connotes awareness and attention (Germer, 2005, p. 5). It is used here in this chapter to connote moment-by-moment awareness and attentional focus. Mental judgments of experience are considered to block our ability to see experience as it is, so there is also a focus on the acceptance of experience.

EFT AS BUDDHISM IN PRACTICE: BRINGING AWARENESS/MINDFULNESS TO RELATIONSHIPS

In Buddhism there are essentially two forms of meditation (Goleman, 1996): concentration (*samatha*) meditation, where perhaps a focus on a sound, an image, or the breath calms the mind, and insight (*vipassana,* meaning "clear seeing") meditation, which is often commonly referred to as mindfulness practice. The latter can be described as "coming to grips with who we are" and "settling into our current experience...in an alert and openhearted way" (Germer, 2005, p.16). According to Buddhism, we reduce suffering and move toward liberation by practicing the "four foundations of mindfulness." These are mindfulness of the body, feelings, consciousness, and mental objects. The mindfulness of mental objects also includes what we normally call "feelings" or emotions.

Thus, Buddhism and EFT concur concerning the centrality of bringing awareness to the full range of our primary experience. Jon Kabat-Zinn (1994), known for his mindfulness-based stress reduction (MBRS) programs, defines mindfulness as "paying attention in a particular way, on purpose, in the present moment, and nonjudgmentally." (p. 4) The practice of mindfulness, called the heart of Buddhist meditation, is then simply a way of attending to one's experience and inquiring deeply into oneself and one's reality.

Using the preceding definition, it is clear that although experiential therapies such as EFT or Gendlin's Focusing (1981) do not usually see themselves as teaching "mindfulness," it is implicit in the practice of these therapies. For example, in focusing and EFT, clients are gently invited to notice their authentic, primary experience rather than get lost in the secondary emotions and reactions that generate suffering, especially when these are dumped on their unsuspecting partner. Bringing "mindful" awareness to our experience enables us to uncover and distil emotions that we might normally circumvent. These newly arising emotions then open up new ways to see and respond to our own experience and to our partner. Writing about Buddhist practice, Kornfield (1993) could also be writing about the process of EFT when he states, "When we let ourselves become vulnerable, new things can be born in us...and most remarkably that which we have sought is often just there, buried under the problem and the weakness itself" (p. 79).

An EFT therapist intent on expanding present awareness will first take a nonjudgmental stance to each client's experience to induce a calm focus on experience and model acceptance of this experience. He or she will then direct each client's focus to the moment-by-moment process of experiencing, asking, "What is happening as you see your partner turn away from you?" The experienced EFT therapist, like an experienced meditator, knows how to shift the focus gently from mental chatter about content issues that occupy our minds and enables clients to attend to the current edge of awareness, or the flow of experience, until some deeper or more primary sense emerges.

This process parallels suggestions made by Buddhist teachers (Thich Nhat Hanh, 2008) that difficult feelings are best embraced in the same way a parent comforts her child, offering reassurance and an enduring concern. In this process, body sensations, cues from the environment, meaning connections, and a desire to move in tune with these elements all come together into a new integration of experience. This step-by-step attending to and unpacking of the elements in emotionally loaded experiences is well outlined in the EFT literature (Johnson, 2004).

Buddhist practice also specifically invites exploring thoughts, feelings, and body sensations with friendly curiosity. In EFT, this is a process of discovery and at one stroke elucidates a specific, compelling, felt sense and also the way in which an individual can pay attention and listen into his or her experience to create this clear felt sense. The client has a meta-awareness that he or she is shaping and revising his or her reality. For example, John says to his wife in a couple session:

> I spend so much of my time sitting in this anger for you. Telling myself that this relationship is hopeless and it's your fault. But right now, I am getting that I am not that angry. All my ranting is just my way of pushing away my fear. I can feel that fear now in the center of my chest. It tells me that you are unreachable and that I am alone. And it already feels better just to tell you this and not fight it anymore.

As in mindfulness practice, EFT focuses on the present and on process. The person is seen as a process with an infinite capacity for change and growth rather then a static product. Ricard points out that "Buddhism defines a person as a constantly changing dynamic stream" (Begley, 2007, p. 13). The Buddhist concept of impermanence reflects a view of all things as constantly in a *process* of transformation. The self is a "collection of cells, molecules and atoms...in constant flux" (Fulton & Siegel, 2005, p. 40). A key aspect of secure attachment is that models of self and other are not rigid or static but rather are constantly able to be revised to match with new experience. Thich Nhat Hanh (2008) comments that the Buddha taught that "the seeds of beauty and goodness can always be found in each of us."

Carl Rogers and John Bowlby would have agreed completely. The way to positive transformation, however, is not to strive toward a set goal in a top-down manner, but rather to immerse oneself in the bottom-up process of experiencing, which allows more fluidity, presence, and intimacy in the dance with one's companions. As stated in the Tao Te Ching (Johanson & Kurtz, 1991), "A good traveler has no fixed plans and is not intent upon arriving." (p. 27) The EFT therapist repeatedly returns to the here and now and to the process of clarifying and shaping inner experience and interactional dance. A focus on present process is always an open door (rather than the dead end offered by rehearsed thoughts and remembered or habitual moves and stories).

For example, John engages in a long story that "proves" how inaccessible his wife Maria is and that this is "the reality." He concludes that she will always be this way and there is no point in talking about this or coming to therapy anymore. The EFT therapist asks, "This is what you say to yourself at these times? That this is just a done deal and all you can do is to rant occasionally and then shut down and try not to care? She will never respond to you?" John agrees and adds that it is a waste of time talking about this. The therapist comments, "So you are giving up and grieving. You cannot keep trying; is that it?" He nods emphatically. "It's hopeless and there is nothing I can do," he says. The therapist stays with this helplessness and asks John to taste it, to put it into words, and then to tell his partner. As he does this, his experience changes to deep sadness. As he shares this with his wife, she is able to tune in to him and move to comfort him. He revises the way he sees her and interacts with her. She is also able to respond to him differently.

The EFT therapist, like an experienced meditator, maintains focus and trusts the process of unfolding experience and inter-action. In EFT, the point is not to "cure" or to "fix" problems; in fact, a focus on this is most often part of the problem. One partner is intent on fixing problems while the other is starved for this person simply to be emotionally present with him or her. The therapist attempts to be present with and accepting of each client's experience and to be open and accessible to different elements of this experience. The therapist remains grounded in the "here and now" and learns from clients just as clients learn from him or her. The therapist endeavors to be aware of any blocks to his or her ability to be present, focused, accepting, and engaged with clients and to be willing to struggle with this block.

The EFT therapist could also be considered as engaging in a Buddhist practice when she tunes clients in to how they construct their own and their partner's suffering in terms of the negative cycle of interactions that each creates and is vic-timized by. This process elucidates how avoiding or becoming immersed in emotional responses and set ways of perceiving one's partner simply re-creates the problem of emotional star-vation and isolation from moment to moment. Anxious grasp-ing that leads to criticism and control and avoiding that leads to stonewalling and distancing are the signs of insecure attach-ment and the royal route into relationship distress (Johnson, 2008). These signs of distress and insecure attachment paral-lel the grasping referred to as tanha in Buddhism.

It is easy to state the preceding parallels, but are we perhaps forgetting here that EFT is a couple intervention? The classic image of Buddhism is that of a meditator, apparently complete unto himself, communing with his own mind. How does this fit with a focus on close relationships? Specifically, how might the EFT therapist's shaping of new enactments be considered in the light of Buddhist thought and mindfulness?

In a classic EFT enactment, the heightening of awareness of core fears and needs moves partners into being able to reach for their partner in a more open, ordered, and coherent way. The clear, poignant, emotional signals that are then sent naturally elicit caring and compassion in the other partner and begin a positive cycle of responsiveness and increased emotional pres-ence. The bond that then develops provides a secure base for the continued personal and spiritual growth of both partners. More secure attachment seems to promote the very qualities that we associate with mindfulness practice (Siegel, 2007).

It is significant that, in 2006, while visiting Vancouver in Canada, the Dalai Lama said, "I am now 71 years old. I feel, still, deep in my mind, my first experience, my mother's care. I can still feel it. That immediately gives me inner peace, inner calmness" (Scott, 2006). This spiritual leader is obviously very comfortable with the Buddhist doctrines concerning interdependence and with an attachment relationship as a source of comfort, strength, and meaning. The Buddhist focus on heightened attunement to and engagement with self and the active creation of attuned compassionate interactions with others fits very well with the EFT focus on bonding enactments.

In Buddhist psychology, there are practices that deliberately cultivate the four "brahma viharas" (limitless qualities of the heart), including loving kindness, compassion, sympathetic joy, and equanimity (which includes allowing success or failure without attaching self-worth to such outcomes). These are viewed as complementing mindfulness and providing an antidote to negative states such as anger and hatred. These practices focus on attitude and intention (Morgan & Morgan, 2005). However, they are forms of meditation where, for example, one sits alone and evokes an image (perhaps of one's mother) and imagines feelings of gratitude. In EFT, interdependence is experienced directly and compassion is evoked and enacted in the moment with a partner. Secure attachment appears to impact all the qualities mentioned before. Equanimity, which implies a trust in oneself and others, would seem to be particularly dependent on positive attachment experiences with others. The resulting sense of worthiness and efficacy would then allow a "trust in the workability of all experience" (Morgan, 2005, p. 141). The links between attachment and mindfulness as a therapeutic process have also been addressed elsewhere in the literature (Wallin, 2007).

It is important to note that all of the preceding links depend on how Buddhism and terms such as mindfulness are used. Mindfulness can be used to stay away from emotion, as a mode of detachment that will numb vulnerability, or as a self-contained practice that may distance others. Some practitioners suggest that in meditation one is to be "neutral" to what is observed, although Germer (2005) explicitly states that "mindfulness is not detached witnessing. It is experiencing the mind and body more intimately" (p. 9). Buddhist meditation has been associated at times with an obsessive focus on the mind, with thinking about thoughts, or simplistically as a technique for enhancing tranquility. Taken in a reductionistic sense, Buddhist practices might also simply be seen as changing our attitude toward unpleasant experience or acknowledging that "what we resist persists" (Williams Teasdale, Segal, & Kabat-Zinn, 2007, p. 75).

Buddhist psychology and mindfulness as a practice can, of course, also give rise to interventions that are very different from EFT. For example, directly teaching mindfulness meditation is fast becoming an accepted technique in individual psychotherapy. Cognitive-behavorial interventions for problems such as depression actively teach mindfulness meditation (Williams Teasdale et al., 2007). Mindfulness, as described in Kabat-Zinn's mindfulness program for individual clients (1990), has also been taught as part of relationship enhancement intervention (Carson, Carson, Gil, & Baucom, 2004) with well-educated middle-class couples.

On a pragmatic level, when a therapist is dealing with clients who espouse Buddhism as an orientation, it is probably counterproductive to discuss the fine points of Buddhism. However, it is helpful to have some awareness of Buddhist principles and how they are consonant with the EFT perspective. For example, the Buddhist viewpoint suggests that suffering is created by clinging and aversion. We crave and cling to experiences that are pleasant and push away experiences that are threatening or unpleasant. Buddhist clients may be quick to recognize how we avoid unpleasant feelings due to our aversion to them. These clients are likely to be familiar with the notion that, in fact, we suffer less when we are mindful of the full range of our authentic experience, including feelings we might habitually push away because they are uncomfortable or unpleasant.

The therapist can also deepen an alliance with these clients by conveying an appreciation for the Buddhist path. Wording such as the following may be helpful if the therapist perceives that the client is using Buddhist principles to avoid or deny feelings and longings: "Well, I'm not an expert on Buddhism, but I understand that the Buddha talked about the middle way. I wonder if that means not pushing away our feelings and needs but finding a way to honor them and find skillful means [the Sanskrit word, 'upaya'] to work with them" or "I'm sure you know more about Buddhism than I do, but my understanding is that mindfulness of feelings is a part of Buddhist practice."

Many Buddhist-oriented clients also recognize that they are missing something and are receptive to new ways of seeing things that complement their spiritual path. They may recognize that close relationships are a prime arena for spiritual practice because the conflicts that arise interpersonally often reflect the stuck places or discord within themselves.

EFT AND THE HIGHLY RELIGIOUS COUPLE: A FAITH-SENSITIVE APPROACH

Couples vary in the degree to which religious or spiritual beliefs and practices shape their understanding of love and marriage. Various religious traditions prescribe distinct ideals and expectations about the essential purpose of marriage and guidance for its practice. In light of the breadth of religious traditions and varied couple practices, we focus on one type of couple: the highly religious couple from a Christian tradition. This section describes how EFT works with couples in which faith and its role in marriage are of utmost importance.

Religiousness and Relationships

The pithy adage that "a couple who prays together stays together" is arguably an oversimplification of the relationship of religion and marriage. Still, there is ample research documenting the positive association between religiousness and positive marital outcomes. Studies have shown a positive relationship between religiousness and higher levels of marital satisfaction and lower rates of separation and divorce (Mahoney et al., 1999). Religious factors have also been identified as "protective factors" reducing the risk of infidelity (Atkins & Kessel, 2008) and divorce (Booth, Johnson, Branaman, & Sicca, 1995; Clydesdale, 1997).

These positive effects, while generally robust, cannot always be assumed (Baucom, 2001). For example, some religious individuals report higher levels of commitment to marriages that are themselves less rewarding or have high rates of conflict (Mahoney et al., 1999). A couple's commitment to marriage may or may not be a good indicator of the quality of that relationship, particularly for religious couples. Butler and Harper (1994) identified a number ways religious couples reactively triangulate God into rigid devitalizing patterns in their relationship. A partner may overspiritualize differences in their relationship by taking the moral high ground and using that spiritually one-up position to coerce the other partner and even the therapist (Rotz, Russell, & Wright, 1993). It is little wonder that many therapists keep their distance from religious topics and issues with couples, often seeing these issues as fraught with risk of value imposition or advancing a view that religion is simply a taboo topic (Prest & Keller, 1993).

Two Perspectives

In this section we examine two issues that are relevant in working with highly religious couples. The examples included are couples from a protestant Christian background. These examples illustrate how an EFT therapist may interact with a couple whose religious values prominently shape how they experience their relationship. We also explore how therapists can effectively work with these couples' attachment to God as a relevant source of intimate security.

Sanctification

Highly religious couples typically use religious or spiritual language to describe the significance of their relationship. In studies of the effects of religion on marriage, this tendency to attach spiritual importance to marriage has been called "sanctification of marriage" (Mahoney et al., 1999). Sanctification is most clearly seen among couples who make a divine or sacred attribution to the character and significance of their relationship (Pargament & Mahoney, 2005). A couple might describe their relationship as a "gift of God" or express an intention to strive for a "Christ-centered" relationship. Both illustrate the ways in which couples look toward a transcendent reality for deeper meaning in the adult intimate loving bond they share.

Sanctification is understood as having a more immediate effect on couples lives because it is likely to be expressed in how a couple makes sense of their relationship (e.g., shared beliefs and values) and how they experience life together (e.g., common practices). More importantly, couples often invest more energy in prioritizing their relationship as they seek to preserve and protect that which is seen as sacred. These couples experience and express emotions as part of their spiritual lives. They integrate their love, adoration, gratitude, and humanity through a spirituality lens. A husband, for example, sees his wife's listening and sympathetic ear as ultimately being a reflection of godliness in her. He simultaneously is grateful to and for her, but also to God.

Sanctification provides a more proximal means for understanding the effects of religiousness on marriage. In turn, therapists can better understand the spiritual investment couples have made and the importance attributed to those commitments as acts of faith. These commitments often hold deep meaning for couples seeking to embody a type of love that reflects a worldview centered in God's love and faithfulness. These couples may look to God as a resource to strengthen their relationship. Through acts of religious devotion, these couples seek to live more faithfully to God and to one another. Pargament and Mahoney (2005) consider sanctification a source of strength and significant vulnerability. Distress or loss of this relationship is more likely to have significant impact because the relationship itself means more as a result of sanctification.

In the Christian tradition, marriage is understood as a gift from God. Christian couples make promises or vows of unqualified commitment in marriage. Marriage represents more than a social contract. Instead, the couple pledges marriage as a covenant with God and each other. A covenantal commitment assumes an exclusive and permanent union reflecting a pledge of faithfulness in light of the very faithfulness of God (Atkinson, 1979). More than a religious rule, covenant provides an ethical vision for relationships and an expression of God's grace and love personally and communally. For example, theologian Karl Barth (1961) considered the practice of making and keeping covenants essential to what it means to be human (i.e., created in the image of God).

Sanctification in these terms assumes that marriage has meaning given by God. A couple's devotion to one another is both horizontal (toward one another) and vertical (unto God). The essence of covenant assumes a dependence on another in which both partners' essential being and belonging take place in the context of a relationship with God (Bruggemann, 1979). God's faithfulness provides a model and means for fulfilling a sanctified understanding and way of being in marriage. For Christians, a covenantal promise is based on a faithful promise from God and one made to another.

CASE EXAMPLE

The following case example illustrates an EFT therapist (third author) working with a Christian couple in which sanctification figures prominently in their relationship. Both partners share a strong commitment to their faith and its role in their relationship. This excerpt is from Stage 2, in which the therapist is facilitating a softening event. (Note: T = therapist; F = female; M = male.)

T: You guys are doing so much better. I am really proud of you. It's obvious that you really care a lot for each other, and for your relationship. It's very nice to see.

M: Absolutely. I firmly believe, no, I know, that God sent her to me. It's an answer to prayer (eyes tear up).

T: Yes, this means a lot to you. I see you are tearing up as you say this. (M nods as more tears flow and he drops his head down. F moves closer to him and strokes his back, then rests her head on his.)

M: I am just SO thankful for her. I really am. And yet I still get angry and say things that hurt her, and then I go away and feel so terrible. You know, here I am and I am sure God brought her to me. And yet I throw it in her face, and God's face, too, because I treat her badly.

T: I hear you; you get caught in this pattern. This pattern happens and you end up saying things that hurt her, and you feel awful. Awful because you are hurting her and awful because God brought her to you.

M: Yeah, it really does. How can I stop this?

T: Tell me, what happens inside when you get caught in this trap? When you guys fight, and you aren't feeling connected, and then you come out and attack her more deeply—what's going on inside then? (Silence. M takes a deep breath.)

T (softly and slowly): Yes, and you take a deep breath now. What's happening inside? Are you going to that place...that place that happens when you guys get into a fight and it suddenly moves to a deeper level? Are you feeling that now?

M: Yeah, I am feeling it now.

T (softly): Can you let us into that place now? What's happening inside?

M (5-second silence): My heart hurts. It feels just like it did when I was growing up. I feel alone...and I feel like a failure. Despite all that's happened to me, I still find a way to screw it up. (M's pain points to his negative "view of self" and he responds by blaming himself. He is also experiencing a profound loneliness, but it is difficult for him to access pain at this level. It is important that the therapist reflect both his pain and shaming response. The therapist uses an empathic conjecture to help delineate these co-informing experiences.)

T: Yes...You go to a place that you are very familiar with. This is a place of great loneliness, right? (M nods in agreement.) As a child, at the end of the day, you often felt very lonely. You prayed for God to send someone to you, someone safe, someone that would understand you and love you, and someone who would stick with you. Am I understanding? (M nods.) And yet there is this other part. And this part tells you that you are not good enough to deserve this, right? (M nods.) This part accuses you. It says, "You are deficient. You are not good enough. You don't deserve her."

T: Can you tell me more about that part?

M: That part condemns me. I know that God loves me, but this part comes in and really lays it to me as soon as I do something that God does not approve of. I know that I am not supposed to attack her out of my anger. I know that. And when I do that, this part really makes this clear.

T: This part accuses you. Convicts you as guilty. It says, "No way you deserve her."

M: Yep. I "know" that God has forgiven me and loves me. In my head I know that. And I believe that. But still, when we disconnect and I am alone after that, I don't at all feel forgiven, or worthy. I just feel like the worst sinner.

T: Help me out. This part says, "You are unworthy...unlovable even...You don't deserve her. She will eventually see the 'real you' and leave." Is that close?

M: No, no, that's it. That is exactly it. (The husband's sense of shame is experienced as a relational failure and a spiritual struggle. The therapist reflects his self-critical responses and appeals to his fear of rejection. The husband's internal struggle to love and be loved highlights the ways he feels disconnected from her and from God. The therapist seeks to heighten his felt sense of rejection.)

T: Can you feel this accuser part right now?

M: Oh yeah. I "believe" that you won't leave me. (He looks at his partner.) But when this part accuses me, I do get really scared that you might eventually leave me if I don't stop getting so angry with you. It's awful. (He cries again.)

F: I won't leave you. I love you. My commitment is to you, in the eyes of God.

T: Right. (to F) When you see this part, you want to comfort and reassure him, right? (Therapist reflects the process. She is offering him reassurance using a common language of their faith.)

F: Yes. Very much so. He can be too hard on himself. (She puts her hand on his leg.)

T (to M): Can you feel her touch now? (He nods yes.) (T is heightening his awareness of his wife's responsiveness.)

M: Yes. But when she reassures me, it makes that part go away. But when we fight and disconnect, I go straight back to feeling alone...and afraid that she's had enough... that she sees me as weak and a failure spiritually.

T: When you guys disconnect, you easily go to a place that you know all too well. A part that accuses you, says, "You are not worthy of her. She will leave you in due time." This part has been with you since childhood. Now, in this relationship, when you guys fight and emotionally disconnect, you go to this part and it scares the heck out of you. (M nods yes; his head falls downward.)

T: Can you, right now, can you now turn to her and let her into this place? She's here for you right now. She wants you to let her in and to let her fight this accusing part with you; (to F) is that fair?

F: Yes! (She looks at him.) I would love to help you fight this, if you would only let me in. I've seen it, honey. I feel it too when you go there.

T (to M): She wants to join you in this battle. Can you turn to her now and let her in on how scared you get? How filthy you feel spiritually, and how it's just so lonely and painful for you? Can you begin now to let her in by sharing what this is like for you? (Therapist heightens the shame in the context of his faith.)

M turns to F. There is a 15-second silence.

F: You can trust me. I can take it. I will be fine. Please let me in...Let me help you please.

M (to F): When we fight and then emotionally disconnect, I get so afraid that maybe we won't be able to reconnect. A part of me blames me and takes me to places that

I hate to go. I am so afraid right now to tell you this. (looks down to the floor)

T (to M): It's great what you're doing right now. You're really risking. It takes a lot of love to risk like this—especially with her. She means the MOST to you. (Therapist provides support framing his bid for her support as an expression of his connection to her.)

M (head still down, looking at floor): Absolutely.

T (to F): What's it like right now for you inside? What is happening now as he risks inviting you into this place, this place of such loneliness and fear—fear that if you see him you might leave him?

F: It makes me love him so much. It makes me that much more grateful to God for bringing us together. I mean, what he sees as weak and fearful—when I see that part I love him even more. I feel incredibly sad for him, yes, but I also feel so much love for him. I just want to squeeze him so tightly to me when I see this place in him. (Her response illustrates a sense of purpose that their faith gives to their relationship. Sharing her experience as an expression of her faith also speaks to his fears spiritually.)

T: Wow. That's awesome. Could you say this directly to him now please? My guess is he's afraid right now that you feel just the opposite. Would you please turn and share this with him directly? (The wife turns and reassures him similarly to what she previously stated. The couple embraces and the therapist remains quiet as the wife holds him, and strokes his hair, and wipes tears from his eyes.)

T (approximately 3 minutes later): Guys, I can't help but wonder what Jesus thinks about you two right now. You know he's here in this, and he sees you. What would he say if we could hear him right now? (Therapist frames the connection couple is making within a spiritual framework. This validates both the reaching for each other and the connection they share, which is both relational and spiritual.)

F: He'd be very happy for us. He'd be pleased that we are doing this because he brought us together and he wants us to be "one." He wants us to be intimate, and to share everything, and to serve each other. He's smiling.

M: Yeah, this is what He wants for us. When I share this with her, and she loves me anyway, man, this just sets me up so well to serve Him. When I know she is here for me no matter what, I am freed to really go and help and serve others. It makes me so much better as a youth pastor.

T: When you guys find each other in these "sacred" places, you know this is what God wants for you. (They both nod and smile.) (Therapist reframes the risks taken together and their felt intimacy as having a spiritual purpose.) Wow, what's this like for each of you right now?

F: It's awesome. When he lets me in like this, I feel so much love toward him. I can feel it all in my body. When he needs me like this I feel so incredibly special. I KNOW this is what God wants for us.

M: Yeah, this is special. I feel loved in the deepest ways. Both from her and from God. This is the kind of husband God wants me to be, too, I am sure of it. And I am so thankful for her. If I can just move away from anger, and let her into my fears and loneliness instead, that would be awesome.

T: Like you just did here today?

M: Yes.

As this process of his risking emotionally with her is repeated in future sessions, the husband becomes clearer about his attachment needs and is able to ask for them to be held by her with clear and specific language, such as "I get so lonely when this happens. I desperately need you to comfort and reassure me that I am your love, and that you still see me in your eyes as a man of God." Their experience and faith together connect to a transcending purpose or ideal in their relationship. The therapist works with the sanctified understanding of their relationship as a resource. The couple's struggle and pain are validated as a reflection of their distress when their relationship is threatened (Pargament & Mahoney, 2005).

ATTACHMENT TO GOD

Abide with me; fast falls the eventide;
The darkness deepens; Lord with me abide.
When other helpers fail and comforts flee,
Help of the helpless, O abide with me.

H. F. Lyte (1847/1941; no. 552)

God may be experienced as an attachment-like figure for highly religious couples, particularly those affiliating in monotheistic religious traditions. Bowlby (1969) described childhood attachment figures as being "stronger and wiser." He also recognized that while dependence on these figures is essential in childhood, this dependence is of common importance across the life span and is often most evident as a natural response to distress (loss, pain, or need). Studies in the psychology of religion provide broad support for conceptualizing the development of religiousness in the context of attachment dynamics (Granqvist & Kirkpatrick, 2008). Religious themes relating to God as a caring and loving parental figure provide a context for how one might experience God as an attachment-like figure.

Others have stressed that a relationship with God may be experienced more directly, with God representing the ultimate attachment figure—one that ultimately provides a safe haven and secure base (Miner, 2007; Noller, 1992). Individuals draw near to God seeking safety in times of difficulty, often through corporate and private religious practice (e.g., prayer, worship). Faith in God provides a secure base in facing unknown circumstances that call for a "step of faith." These steps may include partners' taking new steps to risk vulnerability in working through their relationship distress. Couples sharing a common faith in God may seek solace and comfort from God in the midst of marital distress.

The emergence of an attachment to God can be understood based on two developmental different pathways (Granqvist & Kirkpatrick, 2008). One approach follows a compensation model for explaining how a history of inconsistent and nonresponsive parenting creates a psychological condition in which individuals seek an attachment-like relationship to God. This attachment to God compensates for the lack of a sufficient attachment in childhood. Research findings demonstrate that those experiencing greater benefits from an attachment with God are more likely to report insensitive mothers (Kirkpatrick & Shaver, 1992).

The compensation model has been criticized as a deficit-based approach to religion (Noller, 1992) and as limited in its conceptualization by emphasizing God's transcendence at the exclusion of God's immanence or presence (Miner, 2007). More recent developments counter this concern by emphasizing the ways in which an attachment to God may provide a basis for earned security (Granqvist, Mikulincer, & Shaver, 2010).

The second pathway for developing an attachment to God emphasizes the correspondence of a person's experience of previous attachment relations and experience of God (Granqvist et al., 2010). This explanation assumes that there is continuity in a person's view of self and other (internal working model) and his or her relationships over time, including God. For example, when a person has a more anxious or fearful attachment style, one might expect that the person in times of distress would seek reassurance and comfort from God in anxious ways. For example, one partner describes her frustration at feeling God's absence in a time of significant need. She feels ashamed and reasons that either she lacks faith or is displeasing in God's sight. With further reflection, she identifies similar experiences with her father, whom she felt kept her at an emotional distance.

This pathway places more emphasis on more immediate social influences, where parental relations can provide a basis of support or a reason for felt insecurity. For example, research studies have shown that a parent's faith and practice are more likely to correspond to his or her children's religiousness in the context of a relationship characterized by security (Granqvist & Kirkpatrick, 2008).

For EFT therapists, understanding a partner's relationship to God provides unique insight into core attachment dynamics in their relations. Generally, therapists have expressed limited interest in the place of God in treating couples. In contrast Butler and Harper (1994) recognized the ways that many religious couples conceive of God as a dynamic participant in their life together. God plays a significant role in many couples' experience of marriage (Griffith, 1986).

Following these pathways of religious development, an EFT therapist may shape specific practices to assess the role of attachment to God and its importance in a couple's relationship. From a correspondence perspective, therapists may include questions about partners' views of God while gathering an attachment history. Therapists might assess a withdrawn partner's childhood memories and include a focus on God. In the following example, an EFT therapist explores a husband's attachment history. Charlie is a pastor who is struggling with depression and distress in his marriage.

Therapist: When you were young, say 8 or 10, who did you turn to for support when you were troubled or needed comfort?

Charlie: My parents were going through a divorce at that time and I was on my own most of the time. I didn't see my father much and my mom was busy trying to meet our needs.

Therapist: What would you do when something was bothering you?

Charlie: I guess most days I would just listen to music. Classic rock, mostly. I would get lost in the loud music and it took my mind off things.

Therapist: Sounds like you were all alone at those times, just trying to make the pain go away. Sounds like a lonely place. Where was God in all of this?

Charlie: Well, my family stopped going to church around the time of the divorce. I didn't miss much because God was more an idea than a person to me. My mom had a strong faith and that is how she got through the tough days.

Therapist: But you…you were alone?

Charlie: Yeah, I just tried to go on. My faith came later in my life.

Therapist: And so now, what is it like when you are struggling, you are feeling all alone in your marriage, at work, and in your faith?

Charlie: That's hard. Sometimes I see God differently. He is a part of my life, but sometimes that is more a belief than something I really know or feel. (He pauses, looking at the floor.) I guess I have been neglecting that area of my life. I need to pray more or something.

As the therapist explores Charlie's attachment history, the focus is on a possible link between his attachment history and experience of God. The therapist also asked about his relationship with God and his experience in the present. In session, Charlie begins to access the shame he experiences in his relationship with God, an experience also common in his distant relationship with his wife.

The EFT therapist may also draw upon a client's attachment to God as a resource. In the following dialog, the therapist is following the compensation model and exploring how faith can provide a secure base for exploring new steps of vulnerability and trust. The therapist appeals to the partner's relationship to God as a source of stability and ultimate safety. It is important to note that the therapist is building upon the client's description of her experience of God as an attachment figure, rather than introducing God as a possible attachment figure. The therapist is working from the client's experience. In the following example, Sarah describes how her faith got her through the loss of her mother—a time when her husband remained distant neglecting her when she needed him most.

Sarah: God was my rock. I cried. I prayed. I felt so alone. I knew Jeff had pressure at work and the kids needed things, but no one saw how devastating this was for me. I had a hole in my heart and no one seemed to care. I felt like God knew.

Therapist: You felt like no one saw this hole that had opened in your heart. The loss of your mother left you feeling empty. Heartbroken and devastated. (Therapist speaks softly.)

Sarah (tearing up): Yes, it was. I mean I appreciate all Jeff did to keep things going, but he was so busy and I just faded into the background. So I would be up late at night crying. The house was quiet and I was praying, crying, and reading my Bible. Psalm 23 became so real to me. I was walking in the shadow of death.

Therapist: I see tears come to your eyes as you recall how devastating this loss was. And you can see how Jeff was trying but missing you. And somehow you found some comfort in your faith. God knew your pain. You felt safe, you could turn to him?

Sarah: I kind of felt like all I had was God. I lost my mom. My husband was gone on business. All I could do was pray.

Therapist: And when you prayed, what was that like? What did you tell God?

Sarah (pausing, searching to find words): I cried. I hurt in ways like I did not know were possible. It was my mom. It was Jeff. My heart broke. I sobbed. I figured that God knew what I was going through. I felt so alone.

Therapist: The tears still come. God heard your tears. Did Jeff know what this time was like for you? Does he know how much you needed him too?

The therapist reflects and validates the support Sarah found in her faith. For religious clients, honoring their attachment to God opens additional resources to exploring their experience and needs in their relationship together. Therapists can heighten the importance of Sarah's attachment relationship to God as a present support rather than framing this attachment as a potential substitute (Noller, 1992). The therapist does not pose God as a replacement or substitute for Jeff or a competing attachment. Instead, the therapist heightens the comfort Sarah found in her faith. Her prayers provided an authentic expression of pain and a base to begin to explore sharing vulnerably with Jeff. Private prayer is analogous to proximity seeking in times of distress (Kirkpatrick, 2005). These prayers are often a point of connection to core attachment affective states. Processing these prayers gives the therapist access to emotions most relevant in Sarah's relationship with Jeff.

Later, while processing Sarah's injury, the therapist may reframe the safety Sarah has found in her relationship with God as a resource for taking new steps of vulnerability with Jeff. Sarah's felt assurance and acceptance by God can provide an experiential base of support for facing the fears she has in trusting Jeff again. She acknowledged that she forgave Jeff, but she could not really trust him as she once had. When working through this attachment injury, the therapist returned to the strength and comfort Sarah found in God as a base for risking vulnerability with Jeff again, and her response to Jeff's reassurance of his commitment and concern for her. After taking this risk with Jeff, she acknowledged that her forgiveness felt different this time. It was "from the heart."

WORKING WITH HIGHLY RELIGIOUS CLIENTS

EFT provides a unique resource for therapists working with highly religious clients. Often religious couples are devoted to the religious ideals of a sanctified marriage, which frequently holds significant symbolic and personal meaning. Relational distress may leave these couples at increasing risk of a form of marital disaffection (Kayser, 1993) in which their commitment to marriage fails to inform any vibrancy in their everyday lives together. The attachment focus and process experiential approach of EFT offers religious couples an opportunity to deeply explore, understand, and engage in the devotion and promise they hold in marriage itself.

An EFT therapist does not need to be religious to work with a highly religious couple. It is important, however, that the therapist is able to understand and appreciate the degree to which religious devotion is often an expression of affection or devotion. As such it can be quite powerful to help couples access a "felt sense of God" in their individual and shared experience. Couples who possess a strong sense of sanctification in their marriage are likely to find it difficult not to express themselves without bringing God into the discussion of their relationship. These moments offer therapists key opportunities to deepen a couple's felt experience through acknowledging and honoring what a couple holds as sacred. Attachment language and concepts provide a means for these couples to share more intimately about their joys and struggles of being known and loved.

CONCLUSION

As a collaborative and empathic approach EFT allows for spiritual beliefs or desires to be honored and integrated in therapy. Pargament (2007) suggested ways to incorporate a spiritual dimension actively into therapy by helping clients explore questions such as "What do I strive for in my life?" and "What do I hold sacred?" These type of questions can fluidly be incorporated into a humanistic experiential therapy, such as EFT, that includes an existential dimension. Exploring these connections often enhances a couple's intimacy and commitment at a profound level.

The authors of this chapter believe that key spiritual traditions of Christianity and Buddhism, while very different, can nevertheless be consonant with this approach. EFT provides therapists with resources that may help couples who are more in touch with the meaning of their relationship than meaningful experiences of love. Our approach in this chapter is not to argue for a Buddhist or Christian version of EFT but rather to explore common ground that therapists may find in working with couples who understand their most significant relationships in the context of faith and spirituality.

William James (1911/1924) suggests that "compared to what we ought to be, we are only half awake." Spiritual traditions often exhort us to a deeper engagement with meaning in our lives. For many couples these traditions provide a way to know more essentially the vitality of love and life. EFT offers direction to engage couples in their quest for a more meaning-filled connection. Therapist awareness of spiritual traditions provides an important resource in helping couples embrace the significance of the attachments they seek.

REFERENCES

Anderson, D. A., & Worthen, D. (1997). Exploring a fourth dimension: Spirituality as a resource for the couple therapist. *Journal of Marital and Family Therapy, 23,* 3–12.

Atkins, D. C., & Kessel, D. E. (2008). Religiousness and infidelity: Attendance, but not faith and prayer, predict marital fidelity. *Journal of Marriage and Family, 70,* 407–418.

Atkinson, D. (1979). *To have and to hold: The marriage covenant and the discipline of divorce.* Grand Rapids, MI: Eerdmans.

Barth, K. (1961). *Church dogmatics, 3/4.* Oxford, England: T. & T. Clark.

Baucom, D. H. (2001). Religion and the science of relationships: Is a happy marriage possible? *Journal of Family Psychology, 15,* 652–656.

Beach, S. R. H., Fincham, F. D., Hurt, T. R., McNair, L. M., & Stanley, S. M. (2008). Prayer and marital intervention: A conceptual framework. *Journal of Social and Clinical Psychology, 27,* 641–669.

Begley, S. (2007). *Train your mind: Change your brain.* New York, NY: Ballantine Books.

Booth, A., Johnson, D. R., Branaman, A., & Sicca, A. (1995). Belief and behavior: Does religion matter in today's marriage? *Journal of Marriage and the Family, 57,* 661–671.

Bowlby, J. (1969). *Attachment and loss: Vol. 1. Attachment.* New York, NY: Basic Books.

Brach, T. (2003). *Radical acceptance.* New York, NY: Bantam Books.

Bruggemann, W. (1979). Covenanting as human vocation: A discussion of the relation of Bible and pastoral care. *Interpretation: A Journal of Bible and Theology, 33,* 115–129.

Butler, M. H., & Harper, J. M. (1994). The divine triangle: God in the marital system of religious couples, *Family Process, 33,* 277–286.

Carson, J. W., Carson, K. M., Gil, K., & Baucom, D. H. (2004). Mindfulness-based relationship enhancement. *Behavior Therapy, 35,* 471–494.

Clydesdale, T. T. (1997). Family behaviors among early U.S. baby boomers: Exploring the effects of religion and income change, 1965–1982. *Social Forces, 76,* 605–635.

Diamond, L. M., Hicks, A. M., & Otter Henderson, K., (2006). Physiological evidence of repressive coping among attachment avoidant adults. *Journal of Social and Personal Relationships, 23,* 205–229.

Epstein, M. (2005). *Open to desire.* New York, NY: Gotham Books.

Fincham, F. D., Stanley, S., & Beach, S. R. H. (2007). Transformative processes in marriage: An analysis of emerging trends. *Journal of Marriage and Family, 69,* 275–292.

Fulton, P. R., & Siegel, R. D. (2005). Buddhist and Western philosophy. In C. Germer, R. Siegel, & P. Fulton (Eds.), *Mindfulness and psychotherapy* (pp. 28–51). New York, NY: Guilford Press.

Gehart, D., & McCollum, E. (2007). Engaging suffering: Towards a mindful revisioning of family therapy practice. *Journal of Marital and Family Therapy, 33,* 214–226.

Gendlin, E. (1981). *Focusing.* New York, NY: Bantam Books.

Germer, C. (2005). Mindfulness.What is it? What does it matter? In C. Germer, R. Siegel, & P. Fulton (Eds.), *Mindfulness and psychotherapy* (pp. 3–27). New York, NY: Guilford Press.

Goleman, D. (1996). *The meditative mind.* New York, NY: Tarcher.

Granqvist, P., & Kirkpatrick, L. A. (2008). Attachment and religious representations and behavior. In J. Cassidy & P. R. Shaver (Eds.), *Handbook of attachment: Theory, research, and clinical applications* (2nd ed.; pp. 906–933). New York, NY: Guilford Press.

Granqvist, P., Mikulincer, M., & Shaver, P. R. (2010). Religion as attachment: Normative processes and individual differences. *Personality and Social Psychology Review, 14,* 49–59.

Griffith, J. L. (1986). Employing the God–family relationship in therapy with religious families. *Family Process, 25,* 609–618.

Hanh, T. N. (2008). Growing together. *Shambhala Sun.*

James, W. (1911, republished in 1924). *Memories and studies.* New York, NY: Longmans.

Johanson, G., & Kurtz, R. (1991). *Grace unfolding: Psychotherapy in the spirit of the Tao-te-ching.* New York, NY: Bell Tower.

Johnson, S. M. (2004). *The practice of emotionally focused couple therapy: Creating connection.* New York, NY: Brunner Routledge.

Johnson, S. M. (2008). *Hold me tight: Seven conversations for a lifetime of love.* New York, NY: Little Brown.

Kabat-Zinn, J. (1990). *Full catastrophe living: Using the wisdom of your body and mind to face stress, pain, and illness.* New York: Delacorte.

Kabat-Zinn, J. (1994). *"Wherever you go there you are." Mindfulness meditation in everyday life.* New York, NY: Hyperion.

Kayser, K. (1993). *When love dies: The process of marital disaffection.* New York, NY: Guilford Press.

Kirkpatrick, L. A. (2005). *Attachment, evolution, and the psychology of religion.* New York, NY: Guilford Press.

Kirkpatrick, L. A., & Shaver, P. R. (1992). An attachment: Theoretical approach to romantic love and religious belief. *Personality and Social Psychology Bulletin, 18,* 266–275.

Kornfield, J. (1993). *A path with heart.* New York, NY: Bantam.

Kuar Sahdra, B., Shaver, P. R., & Warren Brown, K. (2010). A scale to measure nonattachment: A Buddhist complement to Western research on attachment and adaptive functioning. *Journal of Personality Assessment, 92,* 116–127.

Mahoney, A., Pargament, K. I., Jewell, T., Swank, A. B., Scott, E., Emery, E., & Rye, M. (1999). Marriage and the spiritual realm: The role of proximal and distal religious constructs in marital functioning. *Journal of Family Psychology, 12,* 321–338.

Mikulincer, M., Shaver P., Gillath, O., & Nitzberg, R. A. (2005). Attachment, caregiving and altruism: Boosting attachment security increases compassion and helping. *Journal of Personality and Social Psychology, 89,* 817–839.

Miner, M. H. (2007). Back to the basics in attachment to God: Revisiting theory in light of theology. *Journal of Psychology and Theology, 35,* 112–122.

Morgan, S. (2005). Depression: Turning toward life. In C. Germer, R. D. Siegel, & P. Fulton (Eds.), *Mindfulness and psychotherapy* (pp. 130–151). New York, NY: W. W. Norton.

Morgan, W. D., & Morgan, S. T. (2005). Cultivating attention and empathy. In C. Germer, R. D. Siegel, & P. Fulton (Eds.), *Mindfulness and psychotherapy* (pp. 73–90). New York, NY: W. W. Norton.

Noller, P. (1992). Religion conceptualized as an attachment process: Another deficiency approach to the psychology of religion? *International Journal for the Psychology of Religion, 2,* 29–36.

Pargament, K. I. (2007). *Spiritually integrated psychotherapy.* New York, NY: Guilford Press.

Pargament, K. I., & Mahoney, A. (2005). Sacred matters: Sanctification as a vital topic for the psychology of religion. *International Journal for the Psychology of Religion, 15,* 179–198.

Prest, L., & Keller, J. (1993). Spirituality and family therapy: Spiritual beliefs, myths, and metaphors. *Journal of Marital and Family Therapy, 19,* 137–148.

Rogers, C. (1961). *On becoming a person: A therapist's view of psychotherapy.* Boston, MA: Houghton Mifflin.

Rotz, E., Russell, C. S., & Wright, D. (1993). The therapist who is perceived as "spiritually correct": Strategies for avoiding collusion with the "spiritually one-up" spouse. *Journal of Marital and Family Therapy, 19,* 369–376.

Scott, M. (2006). "Bonding the key, Dali Lama says." *Vancouver Sun,* September 8, 2006.

Siegel, D. (2007). *Reflection and attunement in the cultivation of well-being.* New York, NY: W. W. Norton.

Wallin, D. J. (2007). *Attachment in psychotherapy.* New York, NY: Guilford Press.

Walsh, F. (2008). *Spiritual resources in family therapy* (2nd ed.). New York, NY: Guilford Press.

Williams Teasdale, M., Segal, J., & Kabat-Zinn, J. (2007). *The mindful way through depression.* New York, NY: Guilford Press.

Yalom, I. D. (1980). *Existential psychotherapy.* New York, NY: Basic Books.

Fifteen

Lessons Learned
Expanding the Practice of Emotionally Focused Therapy for Couples

JAMES L. FURROW, BRENT BRADLEY,
AND SUSAN M. JOHNSON

INTRODUCTION

Practitioners and researchers continue to expand the scope and relevance of EFT to couple therapy. Grounded in a humanistic tradition, the practice of EFT represents a discovery-oriented tradition steeped in experiential learning that values the inherent strengths and resources that individuals possess. The cases summarized in this volume illustrate the ongoing lessons learned by therapists working with the everyday challenges found among their couples. This chapter reviews key themes and interventions that comprise the innovative practices explored in this casebook. Several common themes are explored in this review. These include the EFT therapist's work with complex cycles, adult attachment and caregiving, and an unchanging focus, even in the face of diverse couples and problems, on attachment affect, therapeutic process, and the present moment.

WORKING WITH COMPLEX CYCLES

EFT therapists help distressed couples experience and recognize in session the cyclical patterns of negative affect dominating their relationships. For couples coping with the impact of

disease, psychological disorders, or specific, complex relationship challenges, these cycles can prove especially challenging
for the couple and therapist alike. These patterns of distress
directly impact a couple's ability to deal with the personal and
relational demands that physical and psychological disorders
often bring. In turn, these disorders often become part of the
couple's pattern, influencing the reactive strategies of pursuit
and distance that define their distress.

This recursive, two-way effect complicates the therapist's
attempts to deescalate destructive patterns because these disorders and problems become intertwined with the couple's
cycle. They trigger reactive responses and hinder coping
resources. In the worst-case scenario, attachment anxiety and
relationship distress exacerbate other problems and coping
issues, and these factors then perpetuate relationship distress.

Paul and Sheri, for example, presented with a complex cycle.
They sought couple therapy to address the ongoing conflict
faced when discussing possibly beginning a family. Paul had
been diagnosed with a major affective disorder, which he managed with individual therapy and antidepressant medication.
He was susceptible to periods of relapse when he took himself off his medication. In these depressive episodes, he would
retreat from social contact and neglect his business responsibilities. They would experience extended periods of financial
distress as a result. Sheri feared how they would manage if she
reduced her work responsibilities to care for their child and
they had to rely primarily on his income. Their arguments led
to extended periods of distress dominated by Sheri's anxious
attempts to help Paul manage his depression and Paul's withdrawal in shame. He feared the responsibilities of fatherhood,
including being the primary financial provider, and worried
that once Sheri realized this, she would leave him for someone
who could provide better. Sheri felt particularly stuck because
this pattern would often result in a return of Paul's depressive
symptoms and a more profound ambivalence about her ability
to express her needs in the relationship.

This example illustrates how a psychological disorder can
challenge a couple's ability to cope with the impact of a disorder and organize complex multilayered conflicts around the
disorder. Patterns of distress can evolve in ways that result
in cycles organized around mutual withdrawal. In the initial
presentation, for example, Sheri was in a withdrawn position. She had retreated from her previous efforts to stabilize

Paul's depression and their marriage and had taken up a more distant and detached emotional stance in their relationship. Similarly, Paul's introverted withdrawal took on a new dimension as a result of the deep sense of shame triggered by his depression and what he believed was Sheri's exasperation with his failures. Treating this couple's distress requires treating the depression and the conflict associated with its effects (Chapter 4). Similar patterns emerge for couples where a partner is struggling with the effects of posttraumatic stress disorder (PTSD) (Chapter 7), sexual disorders (Chapter 9), or an addiction (Chapter 8).

Complex cycles are also common for couples facing the debilitating effects of physical illness. Steill and Gailey (Chapter 5) illustrate poignantly the impact of a partner's loss of language functioning and the disruptive influence of this disability on the couple's established patterns of emotional responsiveness and accessibility. Aphasia's impact on verbal communication unbalances a couple's ability to remain emotionally connected in a time of profound personal vulnerability.

Naaman and colleagues (Chapter 6) describe the powerful impact of life-threatening illness and its organizing influence on patterns of attachment and caregiving. Fears and anticipatory loss challenge each partner's most fundamental means for sustaining security at a time when both are faced with the potential loss of life. Cancer diagnosis, prognosis, and treatment can heighten fears and increase needs for support in ways that are different for each partner, thus increasing the likelihood of greater attachment insecurity. Extended periods of caregiving without respite can also deplete a partner's emotional resources, increasing the risk of mutual withdrawal. The couple's pattern is both symptom and cause of deteriorating sources of emotional support.

The EFT therapist may also encounter complex patterns among couples working through attachment injuries and competing attachments. Makinen and Ediger (Chapter 10) describe how a partner's infidelity can organize fixed patterns of defensiveness around specific "attachment injuries" (Makinen & Johnson, 2006). A couple's reactive cycle becomes more complex when an attachment injury takes precedence in shaping how an injured partner regulates the emotions that inform more surface-reactive patterns of pursuit and/or distance. The therapist must assist a couple in resolving these injuries prior to choreographing key change events in Stage 2 of EFT. Failure to attend to an attachment injury will typically result in a therapeutic impasse reflected in a partner's refusal to risk and reach for the other because issues of vulnerability and safety remain tied to a specific unresolved attachment injury.

Competing attachments may also take precedence in organizing a remarried couple's pattern of distress. Though not a breach of trust, parent, stepparent, and child loyalty conflicts in remarried families pose specific obstacles to the felt security of a remarried couple. Furrow and Palmer (Chapter 11) describe how these competing attachments pose unique challenges for couples. Their relationship is the most vulnerable bond in the remarried family. Reactive cycles are fueled by conflicting interests of partners, parents, and children as they seek to find security in relationships where conflicts around boundaries and intimacy abound (Emery & Dillon, 1994).

Assessment of these complex cycles is critical in the early stages of EFT. Therapist attention to the role of a disease, disorder, or relationship issue (e.g., attachment injuries, competing attachments) organizes how the therapist will approach cycle de-escalation. Successful treatment in these cases often involves additional treatment of these external influences through adjunctive treatments (e.g., individual therapy for depression), professional collaboration (e.g., enlisting a speech therapist to deal with aphasia in sessions), or psychoeducation (e.g., concerning trauma, remarried families) or adopting a specific approach to EFT treatment (e.g., attachment injury resolution). These complex cycles involve disentangling the effects of the disorder on the couple's typical pattern of distress while at the same time fostering a greater awareness of how the pattern itself shapes and impacts the couple's experience of these disorders or relational threats.

SECURE ATTACHMENT, RESILIENCE, AND CAREGIVING

A second theme evident in the casework presented in this volume highlights the EFT therapist's efforts to promote attachment security that provides couples with new resources that maximize resilience. As Johnson notes (Chapter 2), securely attached couples are better able to regulate their own emotional experience and maintain an emotional balance in their relationship. These couples are more open and empathic to the needs of their loved ones and also more readily receive the support and care of others.

Relationships of mutual accessibility and responsiveness result in a more positive and resilient sense of self. For Bradley (Chapter 3), the EFT therapist actively enhances this resilience through processing emotional experience in a way that promotes the integration of a person's experience of self and ways of connecting with the primary attachment figure. Secure attachment provides couples a haven of safety in times of trouble and a secure base that enables adults to be more resourceful by being more fully present and engaged with the world around them. Attachment security promotes resilience.

Attachment theory offers therapists a long awaited theory of adult intimacy and love. It provides an understanding of relational distress and a framework for relational growth. Mikulincer and Shaver (2007) suggest that attachment security sustains positive emotions, enabling couples to (as the field of positive psychology terms it) "broaden and build" their response to everyday experiences and challenges (Fredrickson, 2001). Individuals who maintain a felt sense of security (i.e., an individual experiences seeking support from others as an effective form of emotional regulation) are, as a result, more resilient and effective in responding to adversity. Attachment security provides a means to moderate the effects of distress and enable partners to remain engaged in more positive and adaptive emotional states (Mikulincer & Shaver, 2007).

Several authors in this volume powerfully illustrate how attachment security enables couples to respond more effectively to the challenges of disease or psychological disorder. A partner struggling under the daily demands of caregiving may assume a more withdrawn position in the couple's relationship as he or she copes with the dominating influence of illness on the partner and the loss of that partner's emotional availability. Similarly, the debilitating effects of depression and trauma impact a couple's ability to respond effectively to the singular demands of dealing with particular psychological symptoms. The diminished responsiveness of the psychologically affected partner increases relational distress as the caregiving responses of the nonaffected partner appear to lose their impact and both partners experience a growing despair and hopelessness.

Through EFT, the therapist accesses, accepts, and expands the couple's fears and vulnerabilities, enabling partners to work together more effectively against the devitalizing effects of psychological disorders. Restoring the vitality of an attachment bond unleashes new resources that make real differences in the challenges presented by psychological problems. A more secure bond promotes access to social support, compassion, and better overall health (Mikulincer & Shaver, 2009). EFT provides corrective emotional experiences (Johnson, 2009) that enable couples to find each other in sacred places and become much more resilient both relationally and individually.

In general, EFT therapists work to promote use of resources that couples already possess but are unable to access in the midst of overwhelming relational distress. In the final stage of EFT, "consolidation," the therapist promotes actions of investment into the security of their relationship. In *Hold Me Tight*, for example, Johnson (2008) illustrates several ways couples can promote and expand their new, safe connection.

Through attachment rituals and storytelling, partners are encouraged to foster a more resilient relationship through enhancing positive emotions (Fredrickson & Losada, 2006). Couples are encouraged to engage in a process of affirmation and validation that includes being more responsive to areas of strength and vulnerability. The process of changing behavioral patterns and internal working models begins and ends with accessing and expanding core affect states. As more secure emotional experiences are shared, couples find new resources associated with more positive views of self and other.

Resilient couples recognize the power of positive heart-to-heart emotional experience and its shaping role in how they experience themselves and their world (Johnson, 2009). EFT supports the creation of positive emotions such as joy, surprise, and love to create powerful, enthralling responses that act as antidotes to negative patterns and emotions, and as antecedents to secure bonding. These responses appear to inoculate couples against relapse into negative patterns and emotional starvation and offer them a sense of competence in being able to shape their mutual dance. Couples with such bonds are not only better able to regulate emotional distress but also more likely to express compassion and altruistic responses (Mikulincer & Shaver, 2009). Beyond a couple's beliefs and expectations, a felt sense of emotional connection and unity provides a bond of safety and security that enables creativity, hope, and hardiness in the face of life's adversity.

AN UNCHANGING FOCUS

Finally, amid the various innovations and examples set forth, there is an elegant simplicity to EFT. First, the steps in a couples dance are outlined. Couples in distress move in one of two directions when an attachment response is needed from an apparently unavailable partner. Partners respond by amplifying their signals for connection or they attempt to deactivate these signals or dampen them in some way. Both strategies lead the couple farther away from the effective dependency they seek. Second, emotions even at their most extreme, are seen as reflecting an exquisite inherent logic. This logic arises from a mammalian brain obsessed with cues of safety and danger and with the threat of isolation. Emotions and emotional signals shape predictable patterns of behavior, particularly in times of distress (e.g., anxious pursuit, avoidant withdrawal). The most primary needs, longings, and fears that define a close relationship are outlined, addressed, and used as part of the EFT therapy process.

Throughout this volume, therapists working with a diversity of presenting problems retain an unchanging focus on emotion. Bradley (Chapter 3) identifies a therapist's ability to access, process, and deeply engage couples in their attachment-related affect as essential to successful EFT treatment. Therapists working with emotion enable clients to access a range of emotions, including anger (mostly reactive), sadness, shame (associated with an apparently unlovable sense of the self), and, most predominantly in EFT, with different forms of attachment fear. This fear is triggered by threats of abandonment, rejection, and emotional isolation.

For Panksepp (1998), the salience of this fear is understood as a form of "primal panic" and is primed when there is a perceived disconnection from one's key attachment figure. The ways in which couples learn to respond to this panic inform how their attachment relationship evolves. Attachment is a behavioral system hardwired for our physical and emotional survival. The EFT therapist constantly maximizes the transforming power of core emotional experience in three specific ways: (1) working with attachment-related affect, (2) slowing the processes of experiencing and interaction, and (3) maintaining a present focus in the session.

Working With Attachment-Related Affect

EFT therapists use attachment theory as a guide for creating an empathic connection with their clients and between partners as a couple. The attachment perspective also helps therapists validate client experiences and shape the specific responses that build close relationships. For example, a therapist understands and validates Lisa's panic and disorganization when confronted with Tom's isolating withdrawal. Her best attempts to modulate her anxious despair when confronting Tom only increase this despair and the distance between them. Attachment theory helps to make sense of her desperation. Lisa's response is natural and expected in the face of her failed attempts to connect with Tom. The EFT therapist names and orders the anxieties that distort attachment signals to help clients awaken the longings that cue new efforts to reach, risk, and respond.

Restoring attachment security is a primary goal in EFT treatment. This requires increasing the responsiveness of each partner to the other's attachment needs and longings, which are often unspoken, hidden in their attachment fear. From this perspective, the EFT therapist reframes these patterns of distress in terms of the underlying emotion accessing the pain and fear partners confront when they are not able to reach their partner in a time of need. Then a therapist is able to guide a partner to reattune to his or her partner's attachment-related affect, making these adaptive signals clear and their mutual responses to distress more effective. Emotional attunement enables partners to become more responsive and available in the moment.

Slowing the Process

EFT therapists are often challenged when working with couples that have great difficulty accessing or regulating their emotional experience. This is particularly challenging when these reactive processes are informed by past traumatic experience, including threats to physical well-being (PTSD) or threats to the relationship (e.g., infidelity). Organic changes in the brain (e.g., aphasia) may also result in destructive emotional outbursts. Johnson and Faller (Chapter 7) find that therapists must be active in processing the emotional distress found among couples facing traumatic past experiences. The EFT therapist works with partners to ground their experience in session and assists clients in gaining a clear focus amid diffuse and ever-changing emotional experiences. The pace of therapy often slows to promote safety as the therapist takes more time to revisit cogent emotional experiences repeatedly while "slicing thinner" the steps taken in approaching these undefined and sometimes threatening emotional experiences (see Johnson, 2002).

Similar attention is given to going more slowly and promoting safety for couples facing the destabilizing threats that infidelity and attachment injuries prompt. Makinen and Ediger (Chapter 10) highlight the importance of a therapist's empathic engagement in helping wounded partners begin to risk with one who is both a source of pain and a source of potential comfort. Setbacks and relapses may also extend the length of treatment because the therapist must slow the process to maintain a strong alliance with partners who experience significant risks in the face of felt insecurity and past offenses.

The therapist's pace and repetition in emotional processing have implications at a neurological level. When confronted with a threat to well-being, neuroscience research indicates that the brain holds onto fear cues in order to promote survival (Porges, 2009). While it is hard to wipe out this neural wiring, it is possible to add to it. The EFT therapist must slow the therapy process to offer couples new ways to encode what may be experienced as a "hot" response. The therapist may calmly present, at least five or six times, to an anxious partner (while calming her, holding her "safe," and heightening the cues to this new way of seeing) that, when her partner turns his face away, it is fear and helplessness that she is seeing rather than indifference or rejection. EFT facilitates corrective emotional experiences through expanding well-honed fear-primed pathways with more adaptive responses. This expansion also involves the validation and acceptance of these fears rather than attempts to compartmentalize or negate them (Johnson, 2009).

Maintaining a Present Focus

The EFT therapist focuses on and trusts the process of unfolding experience and interaction. Recent attention emphasizes the role of mindfulness as a resource in regulating emotional experience. Germer (2005) noted in his work on mindfulness that experiential therapies have a striking similarity to mindfulness. For example, Carl Rogers considered the accurate reflection of experience a revelation and essential to personal growth. Experiential approaches encourage a direct, focused, nonjudgmental attention to the ongoing unfolding of present, moment-to-moment experience. In EFT and in mindfulness, the focus is on the present and the self as a process. The valuing of compassion associated with mindfulness finds an easy parallel in the safe acceptance offered by the EFT therapist (see Chapter 14). This acceptance allows for the optimal processing and integration of moment-to-moment experience and interaction.

The therapist's safe acceptance provides a base for exploring use of EFT with couples from diverse backgrounds. Liu and Wittenborn (Chapter 12) conclude that the EFT therapist must work from a position of observation and learning when working with couples in a multicultural context. The therapist actively promotes a relationship of mutual understanding through attention to unique cultural differences in emotional expression (e.g., elicitation, regulation, symbolism, and social interaction) as they occur in the present moment in a session. Similarly, the EFT therapist working with same-sex couples (Chapter 13) is responsive to the personal and social effects of heterosexism on their immediate experience of felt security as a gay or lesbian couple. A shared awareness of and responsiveness to these sociocultural influences enable the EFT therapist to support couples in recognizing how their present escalating patterns of insecurity may be directly shaped by the chronic stress and the unique demands of sustaining a same-sex relationship in a heterosexist culture.

Furrow and Bradley (Chapter 14) illustrate how accessing and processing emotional experience within the context of a couple's faith provide a resource for expanding and deepening each partner's responsiveness and accessibility in areas of spiritual significance. EFT therapists foster an experiential base for honoring and understanding the unique values and transcending experiences partners share and deepening spiritual connection at key moments.

Effective emotional regulation and the integration of emotional experience are essential to the maintenance of felt security in a couple's relationship (see Chapter 3). This regulation and reordering of key experiences occur as the experiences are being perceived and encoded in the brain—as they occur—rather than retrieved from the past or after the fact. It is the therapist's work both "within and in-between" that promotes an increased awareness for each person in the present moment. Johnson (Chapter 2) describes EFT as a "conversation about a conversation," in which the therapist fosters a moment-to-moment engagement of each partner's experience, helping each seek and find a sense of intrapersonal coherence and interpersonal connection.

The transforming power of EFT is based in a process of immersion in the "here and now" experience of couples focusing on the emotional experience that informs and results from a deeply held need for security in relationships of attachment significance. Promoting this awareness and focus on being present and responsive to present experience begins with the therapist. Johnson and Amodeo (Chapter 14) describe the work of EFT as a reciprocal process of learning that is informed by the therapist's willingness to attend, accept, and engage a client's experience as it is in the present moment.

CONCLUSION

Over the last 25 years, EFT therapists have learned that to make significant change in a couple's relationship we have to go to deep levels of attachment affect and be able to have an attuned, resonant, focused encounter. As Johnson contends, "If we can create this safe connection, any difference or problem is solvable. If we cannot, every difference and problem is an abyss" (plenary address, *Psychotherapy Networker,* March 2009). Over the years, as adult attachment theory and research have grown, EFT has become more and more of an attachment-based intervention. Indeed, at this point in time, EFT is the only approach to couple therapy that can claim that it is based on a systematic, coherent, and rigorously tested theory of adult love and bonding. It makes sense then that EFT will continue to grow as an attachment-oriented model.

It is the power of attachment affect that resides at the heart of EFT's theory of change. Therapeutic change is founded in accessing primary affect states within an attachment context. This is what drives success in EFT. To be effective, the therapist must learn to help partners find these core affective states and, once there, to join with them and to allow new meanings and attachment needs and wants to emerge more clearly into awareness. Talking about attachment with couples is not the point here. The EFT therapist is an emotional compass of sorts and must point couples to their core affective states and learn to relate together within them.

In ongoing research we are exploring how EFT can change the multilayered phenomena—affect regulation, cognitive models, interactional behaviors, and physiological responses to threat—that are human attachment. The hope of the EFT therapist is to be able to plug into the two most powerful motivators in the dance between partners: emotion and attachment longings. These forces, common to all, allow for an effective response to the unique problems and present challenges facing relationships today. The couples described in this book have all taught us something new and precious. They have also confirmed for us the power of the EFT model to make a difference and help couples build the safe haven relationships that we all long for.

REFERENCES

Emery, R. E., & Dillon, P. (1994). Conceptualizing the divorce process. *Family Relations, 43,* 374–379.

Fredrickson, B. L. (2001). The role of positive emotions in positive psychology: The broaden-build theory of positive emotions. *American Psychologist, 56,* 218–226.

Fredrickson, B. L., & Losada, M. (2005). Positive affect and the complex dynamics of human flourishing. *American Psychologist, 60,* 678–686.

Johnson, S. M. (2002). *Emotionally focused couple therapy with trauma survivors: Strengthening attachment bonds.* New York, NY: Guilford Press.

Johnson, S. M. (2008). *Hold me tight: Seven conversations for a lifetime of love.* New York, NY: Little Brown.

Johnson, S. M. (2009). Extravagant emotion. Understanding and transforming love relationships in emotionally focused therapy. In D. Fosha, D. Siegel, & M. Solomon (Eds.), *The healing power of emotion: Affective neuroscience, development, clinical practice* (pp. 257–279). New York, NY: W. W. Norton Press.

Johnson, S. M. (2009). The experience of connection: The science of love and loving. Plenary address at the Psytchotherapy Networker Symposium, Washington, D.C.

Makinen, J. A., & Johnson, S. (2006). Resolving attachment injuries in couples using EFT: Steps toward forgiveness and reconciliation. *Journal of Consulting and Clinical Psychology, 74,* 1055–1064.

Mikulincer, M., & Shaver, P. R. (2007). *Attachment in adulthood: Structure, dynamics, and change.* New York, NY: Guilford Press.

Mikulincer, M., & Shaver, P. R. (2009). An attachment and behavioral systems perspective on social support. *Journal of Social and Personal Relationships, 26,* 7–19.

Panksepp, J. (1998). *Affective neuroscience: The foundations of human and animal emotions.* New York, NY: Oxford University Press.

Porges, S. W. (2009). Reciprocal influences between body and brain in the perception and expression of affect: A polyvagal perspective. In D. Fosha, D. Siegel, & M. Solomon (Eds.), *The healing power of emotion: Affective neuroscience, development, clinical practice* (pp. 27–54). New York, NY: W. W. Norton.

Index

Exercise
  control mechanism, 156
  major depressive disorder, 90
Exercises, sexual issues, 239
Existential living, 35
Expanding, attachment affect, 77
Experiential emotion, 20–21
Expression, function identification, 301–302

F

Facilitating positive development, 337–338
FACT-B measure, 159
Faith, *see* Spirituality
Faith-sensitive approach, 355–357
Families of origin, integration, 323–324
Family buy-in, 118–119
Faux attachment, 200
Final sessions, depression, 107
Financial obligations, 276
First responders, *see* Posttraumatic stress disorder (PTSD)

G

Gay and lesbian couples
  assessment, 330–331
  attachment systems, 318–321
  blamer softening, 334
  case studies, 332–333, 335–337
  chronic stress, 327–329
  coming out trauma, 321–323
  conceptualization, 329–338
  cycle de-escalation, 331–332
  development in the community, 326–327
  emotional engagement, new cycles, 333–334
  emotionally focused therapy, 329–338
  ethnicity integration, 325–326
  facilitating positive development, 337–338
  families of origin, integration, 323–324
  gender integration, 325
  geography integration, 325–326
  heterosexism, combating, 338–339
  identity integration, 323–326
  identity related stress, sources, 321–329
  new cycles, emotional engagement, 333–334
  race integration, 325–326
  reconsolidation, 337–338
  religion integration, 325–326
  same-sex bonding, 326–327
  sexual identity development, 337–338
  sexual identity formation, 321–323
  social identities, integration, 325–326
  supervision and training, 338–339
  withdrawer reengagement, 333–334
Gender integration, 325
Gendlin's Focusing, 349
Geography integration, 325–326
Global aphasia, 115, *see also* Aphasia impairment
Goal, couple therapy as modality, 32–37
God, attachment to, 362–367, *see also* Spirituality
Gusii infants, 299

H

Healing, 178–179
Heightening, 304
Heterosexism, combating, 338–339